ADVANCES IN
THE BEHAVIORAL
MEASUREMENT OF CHILDREN

Volume 1 · 1984

ADVANCES IN THE BEHAVIORAL MEASUREMENT OF CHILDREN

A Research Annual

Editor: ROSLYN A. GLOW
Children's Motivation &
Learning Unit
The University of Adelaide

VOLUME 1 · 1984

 JAI PRESS INC.

Greenwich, Connecticut   *London, England*

CONTENTS

LIST OF CONTRIBUTORS

Thomas J. Boll

Department of Psychology
University of Alabama,
Birmingham

Stephen E. Breuning

Western Psychiatric Institute
and Clinic
University of Pittsburgh
School of Medicine

R. H. Day

Chairman, Department of Psychology
Monash University

David P. Farrington

Institute of Criminology
Cambridge University

Peter H. Glow

Department of Psychology
University of Adelaide

Roslyn A. Glow

Children's Motivation &
Learning Unit
Department of Psychology
University of Adelaide

Jacqueline Goodnow

Department of Psychology
Macquarie University

Alan Hayes

Fred and Eleanor Schonnel
Educational Research Center
University of Queensland

Anne E. Hogan

Mailman Center for Child
Development
University of Miami

Roland D. Maurio

Department of Psychiatry
and Behavioral Science
University of Washington
School of Medicine

B. E. McKenzie

Department of Psychology
La Trobe University

John Murry

Boys Town
Omaha, Nebraska

Peter C. Mundy

Mailman Center for Child
Development
University of Miami

Carol Parker

Department of Psychology
Western Michigan University

Alan D. Poling

Department of Psychology
Western Michigan University

Jeffrey M. Siebert

Mailman Center for Child
Development
University of Miami

Brenda D. Townes

Department of Psychiatry
and Behavioral Science
University of Washington
School of Medicine

Eric C. Trupin

Department of Psychiatry
and Behavioral Science
University of Washington
School of Medicine

Peter Paul Vitaliano

Department of Psychiatry
and Behavioral Science
University of Washington
School of Medicine

ABOUT THE SERIES

Historically, child psychology has been much influenced by the child welfare movement. Presently, two trends are apparent. The first is an interest in the study of child behavior and the process of development for its own sake. The second is an increasing awareness of the need for methodological rigor among child researchers with applied interests.

This series is designed to promote the cumulativeness of research effort in the study of child behavior. By placing methodological issues in the foreground it is hoped that the similarities of endeavours with theoretical and applied ends will be as apparent as their differences. In this series emphasis is given to presentation of a degree of detail with respect to both data and measurement procedures. This should allow independent assessment to be made of the adequacy of each methodological solution to the problem at hand and provide models and techniques for the solution of new problems in the future.

Roslyn A. Glow
Series Editor

ANALYZING STATES IN THE
BEHAVIOR OF MOTHER AND INFANT

Alan Hayes, Jacqueline Goodnow, and John Murray

ABSTRACT

Renewed interest in development in infancy has led to the exploration of new methods and techniques for the description and analysis of parent and infant behaviors. Two sets of methodological problems have been encountered. The first involves decisions about what to measure (i.e., which features of the mother and infant behavioral streams). The second raises issues of how to measure (i.e., which techniques of recording, coding, and analyzing selected behaviors). Both sets of problems reflect recent changes in theoretical conceptions of development in infancy as well as advances in the technology for operationalizing these new approaches. The major shift in theoretical conceptions involves the wider acceptance of the metaphor of the infant as an "active" contributor to developmental processes, with a consequent rise in the use of "dyadic" models of development and new emphasis on describing mother–infant behavior in the prelinguistic stage as "dialogic" or "conversational." Research within this paradigm has been facilitated by the availability of new technology and techniques enabling a variety of sequential analyses.

Advances in the Behavioral Measurement of Children, Volume 1, pages 1–27.

Such techniques are not without problems at the stages of observation, coding, and analysis of the behavioral records. The observational and coding stages present problems of what to observe and how the observation sessions will be organized, problems which have direct implications at the stage of analysis. Some of the central theoretical and methodological issues are illustrated with data from a study of the visual regard and vocalization of primiparous mothers and their infants (aged 1 to 6 months). Comparisons are also provided with the results of a selection of other studies of gaze and vocalization. On the basis of these discussions, suggestions are made for the further development of concepts, methods, and techniques for the study of the behavior of mothers and their infants.

I. INTRODUCTION

In the wake of an emphasis on infants as active contributors to mother–infant interactions, considerable research effort has been directed toward the question: What is the nature or the form of the interaction? Does it display the structure of a "conversation" or "dialogue," with partners taking turns, the behavior of one carefully synchronized with that of the other in a "reciprocal" or "mutually contingent" pattern? Or is this a deceptive appearance? If not completely true, when and in what way does the behavior of the dyad come closest to or depart most clearly from the structure of a dialogue?

Answering such questions has led to agreement that the dyad is the proper unit of analysis, and to a rise of interest in examining the frequency and duration of various dyadic states (e.g., the frequency of the two parties talking together, being silent together, or only one talking). It has also led to a rise of interest in measuring behavior over time, pinning down the sequence of behaviors and the probabilities of moving from one state to the next.

Section II in this paper describes how people have come to ask questions about the form or structure of interactions, and have come to use some particular ways of measuring changes in dyadic states. It then proceeds to the problem of what to measure, by way of indicating variables that could account for contradictions in current data (and, accordingly, varying interpretations of mother–infant exchanges). These variables include the age of the infant, the specific behavior being sampled (e.g., vocalization vs. facial gaze), the task in which mother and infant are engaged (e.g., "free interaction" vs. a set task), and the way in which behavior is sampled over time (e.g., interval coding, time sampling, or continuous observation). This section points to the need for a study that uses variations in task and age of infant, and includes two behaviors often studied separately and thought to be different in the extent to which they contain a dialogic pattern (vocalization and visual gaze). It also points to the need for data based on continuous observation, a technique not previously used in studies of contingencies and transitional probabilities, but essential if we are to be sure that we have an accurate picture of the duration of any state and of the sequence of states.

Such decisions about what to measure, however, bring with them the demand to solve a number of more specific "how to measure" problems. These are to be found in many studies of interactions. They demand solution, however, when one moves into continuous observation, a technique that presents in marked form problems of recording, coding, reducing, and analyzing data. Section III describes how these problems can be solved, in part by the use of new computer and hardware programs.

Section IV deals with a recurrent difficulty in the interpretation of data on interactions, namely, the difficulty of comparing data drawn from different slices or intervals of time. The section suggests a way of coping with this difficulty, allowing one to ask how far data on continuous observation confirms the picture of interactions drawn from observations of short segments of time.

The final section (V) points to some difficulties that still remain in the analysis of interactions, difficulties that may require the solution again of particular design and measurement problems. To anticipate somewhat, the area has come to restrict the range of behaviors that are studied, even though advances in measurement now allow more diversity. The area also has yet to come to terms with differences between mother and infant in their capacities to remember events over time, and investigators face an apparent contradiction between methods that stress the microanalysis of overt events and concepts that stress the importance of the "subjective meanings" that mothers at least give to their own behaviors and the behaviors they observe.

II. CLARIFYING MEASUREMENT NEEDS

The rise of interest in dyadic states may be viewed as accompanying a shift from viewing infants as passively shaped to viewing them as active and intrinsically social. The link between concept and method is well expressed by Schaffer (1971): "Infants are not empty vessels . . . they are active partners in even the earliest social encounters—and a much finer analysis is therefore required—an analysis that will take into consideration not only the stimulation offered by the mother but also the infant's own characteristics and what these, in turn, evoke in maternal responsiveness" (pp. 174–175). With this approach to infants, and with a stress on bidirectional influences provoked especially by Bell (1968), the study of mother–infant behaviors has rapidly moved to a point expressed succinctly by Cairns (1977): "The dyad has become the preferred unit of analysis, not the responses of individuals taken separately. Even when dyadic language is not employed, writers today are sensitive to mutual contingencies within relationships" (p. 2).

The nature of such "mutual contingencies," however, is a far-from-settled issue and, over time, has been described in different terms. For Rheingold

(1966), for instance, the essence of the interaction lay in reinforcement. The "infant, by his appearance and behavior, modifies the behavior of other social objects. He not only evokes responses from them but maintains and shapes their responses by reinforcing some and not others" (p. 12). For Papousek and Papousek (1977), patterns of relationship were less simple: behavior needed to be regarded as both a response to a partner's immediately preceding behavior and a stimulus for the partner's subsequent behavior. Such intertwining is often expressed in the current literature in the form of describing prelinguistic exchanges between mothers and infants as "conversational" in nature. The exchanges appear to exhibit "turn-taking" in both verbal and nonverbal behaviors (e.g., Brazelton, Koslowski, & Main, 1974; Freedle & Lewis, 1977; Newson & Newson, 1975; Schaffer, 1979; Snow, 1977; Trevarthen, 1977). The precise ordering of the responses of mother and infant gives many interactions the appearance of "well practiced games" (Bell, 1971). Not only does the interaction give the appearance of a dialogue, but the mother regards the infant's acts as meaningful and intentional communicative gestures (Newson, 1974). Theoretically, the point has been made that "we can think of dialogue as a necessary context for language acquisition as well as other kinds of learning, and we would be inclined to pursue any phenomenon in early infancy which bears a resemblance to dialogue" (Kaye, 1977, p. 94).

How far, however, are the behaviors of mother and infant linked together? Newson and Newson (1975), for example, consider that "the infant's action sequences are temporally organized so that they can mesh—with a high degree of precision—with similar patterns of action produced by his human caretaker" (p. 440). More moderately, Schaffer (1979) speaks of "pseudo-dialogues," and Bateson (1975) of "proto-conversations," while Stern, Jaffe, Beebe, and Bennett (1975) regard both mother and infant as often violating the rules of conversational dialogue, and Snow (1977) describes the mothers of infants as consistently attempting "to maintain conversation with a conversationally inadequate partner" (p. 13).

To choose among such possibilities, investigators have turned to the analysis of dyadic states, combining the states of both mother and infant and asking about the frequencies and durations of various states and the probabilities of transition from one state to another. Table 1 displays a set of four dyadic states: two in which both parties display similar behavior (e.g., both silent or both talking), and two in which one partner is active while the other is not.

The frequency and duration of various states, together with the transitional probabilities, then become the basis for inferring the nature of the interaction or, more specifically, for drawing conclusions about the extent to which a "dialogue" or "reciprocity" occurs.

A high incidence of vocal alternation, for instance, has been regarded as evidence of "conversational" structure. In contrast, the presence of mother and infant talking together has been used as evidence against a complete "conversa-

Table 1. Definition of Dyadic States Derived from the Combination of Mother and Infant Binary States

State	Mother's State[1]	
	Infant OFF (Silent or Not Looking)	ON (Vocalizing or Looking)
OFF (Silent or Not Looking) ON (Vocalizing or Looking)	A. Quiescent State (QS) C. Infant State (IS)	B. Mother State (MS) D. Coacting State (CS)

Note:
[1] The state names are after Bakeman & Brown (1977).

tional'' structure. In analyzing a mother's interactions with 3-month-old twins, for example, Stern et al. (1975) found a greater than chance occurrence of *both* vocal alternation and coaction patterns. Such results, they argue, suggest that conversational rules are being violated. The coacting pattern in particular—with both parties talking—may have a special purpose, occurring throughout life in times of arousal and serving ''more as a bonding function than as an exchange of information'' (Stern, 1977, p. 25).

Clearly, there is far from complete agreement about the nature of mother–infant interaction. The lack of agreement and the lack of clarity, we propose, are related to problems of measurement and design. More specifically, the differences among studies could be due to variations in:

- The age of the infant
- The specific behavior being sampled
- The specific task in which mother and infant are engaged
- The time intervals chosen for sample behavior

The age of the infant. An intuitively appealing hypothesis occurs in the area of vocal interaction: With increasing age the dyad develops a more closely alternating structure. This suggestion is consistent with the finding by Schaffer, Collis, and Parsons (1977) that by the end of the first year relatively few overlapping vocalizations occur. It also fits with Snow's (1977) report that from 3 months on the structure of the interaction is slowly but consistently coming to be regulated in a manner more like adult conversation, although the onus for carrying the conversation remains with the mother until well into the second and third years of the infant's life. These several reports point to the need for sampling at least a range in age (1 to 6 months in the study to be reported).

The specific behavior being sampled. Most of the stress in this paper so far has been on vocalization behaviors. Of equal interest in research has been the nature of interactions involving facial gaze. Do the two behaviors display dialoguelike patterns to an equal degree? Bakeman and Brown (1977), for instance, have suggested that facial gaze may fit a dialogue description less well than vocalization does. The frequency of the mother's gaze at the infant, they suggest, "obscures the behavioral dialogue" (p. 197). As long as a study includes only the one behavior, however—vocalization or visual gaze—we are not able to compare the two. The study to be reported accordingly covers both.

The task engaging mother and infant. One way of determining whether behaviors are contingent upon one another is to analyze dyadic states and transitional probabilities, starting from the assumption that a particular mathematical model (e.g., a Markov chain model) can be applied to the relationships observed. For a more experimental approach, we might compare results in one situation with those in one where we alter dramatically the input of one party, namely, the mother. If the infant's behavior still shows the same features, the argument for reciprocity would be weakened.

A baseline situation is provided by the kind of "free interaction" instruction used by Trevarthen (1977), for example, "Have a chat with your baby, just as if you were at home." In a comparison situation, mothers may be asked to move their heads from side to side or to move their hands together and apart, using behaviors for which there are reports of early imitation (Maratos, 1973). The study to be reported uses both "free interaction" and "directed modeling."

Observation times. How much of the stream of behavior should one sample? If not all, then in what segments? What is the effect of choosing various segments? These questions are part of what Wright (1960) has called the problem of "continuum coverage." To cope with it, several techniques have been proposed.

One technique is the use of *interval coding:* The observer selects an interval for observation (e.g., 10 sec) and then makes a judgment as to whether or not particular behavior has occurred *within* that interval. This is the technique used, for example, by Lewis and Freedle (1973) and by Bakeman and Brown (1977), adopting, respectively, intervals of 10 and 5 sec. One difficulty with this technique is that the choice of intervals reflects predominantly issues of convenience and the constraints of available technology. "The use of these periods (10 sec) is arbitrary and was determined on the basis of ease of recording—as well as obtaining a small time unit" (Lewis & Freedle, 1973, p. 137); "a 5 sec interval more accurately reflects the precision of the total observation system including the human observers" (Bakeman & Brown, 1977, p. 197). The intervals chosen may not reflect the durations of behaviors, especially when the behaviors involved are likely to vary in duration (e.g., longer periods of silence than activity). In addition, while interval coding may enable one to describe the overall incidence of states or behaviors, it seems far from optimal when one wishes to develop an accurate picture of transitions from state to state.

A different technique is the use of *point coding.* This requires the coder to check behavior at specified points in time, with these separated by a predetermined time interval. In Stern's (1974) study, for example, the coder noted the state of the dyad every 600 msec. (Continuous records of facial gaze were available, but the coding was at every 600 msec.) This is a common approach in studies of interaction but it is not without its problems, especially when transitional probabilities are involved. Suppose, for example, that some states are of much longer duration than 600 msec. These states are likely to yield a picture of a very high probability of staying in a particular state. A low probability of staying is more likely to occur when there is a closer match between the duration of a state and the sampling time. In other words, the values of the probabilities of staying in any state can be increased or decreased by reducing or enlarging the interval between points, and the probability of the infant being coded as staying in the same state from one point to another may say more about the choice of sampling time than about the transitional probability structure as it occurred in reality.

Continuous coding does capture the precise transitional structure. In the study described in Section III, a coder follows a single behavior for a single subject on videotapes observed in real time, and keeps a continuous record of that behavior as "on" or "off." That procedure presents its own problems. It demands, for instance, a coder for each actor (in the present case, one for the infant and one for the mother). It also demands that we find feasible ways of reducing the data into summary form. These demands are relatively formidable, especially if two behaviors are to be covered (gaze and vocalization). They certainly help account for continuous observation being avoided as a measurement technique. Ways of overcoming these problems, however, can be found. They are described in Section III.

Overall, a survey of the current research on interaction brings out the need to measure in a way that allows continuous observation and solves the problems it presents; that allows one to sort out the effects of task, task-setting, and age of infant; and that in general moves toward as direct a test as possible of contingencies between the actions of mother and infant. An approach toward these problems of measurement, and a description of the results generated, is given in the study described in Section III.

III. A SPECIFIC STUDY: METHODS AND RESULTS

Setting, Subjects, and Procedures

Setting

An early problem in measuring interactions is the choice of setting or locale, guided by the hope of finding one where observation will least disturb the "normal" functioning of the dyad. The home is not necessarily the best solution.

It presents logistical problems if one wishes to videotape. And it becomes an unfamiliar "laboratory" when an unfamiliar researcher and/or obtrusive equipment are introduced (Schaffer, 1977). An infant health care center, providing mainly "checkup" services for "well" babies, provided a solution. It minimized the intrusiveness and inconvenience to the mother, reduced the logistical problems, and provided an environment acceptably familiar to the participants. In addition, the cooperation of the Centre made it possible for the clinic staff to explain the project to the mother in the course of her regular visit to the Centre. This arrangement made the project a part of the routine of the clinic.

Subjects

Twenty-four English-speaking primiparous mothers and their healthy full-term infants were involved. Dyads were selected according to the following broad criteria: (a) that the mother was willing to participate after the purpose of the study ("to obtain recorded segments of infants with their mothers") had been explained to her; (b) that the functioning of the dyad was not, in the opinion of the clinic sister, currently affected to any significant degree by medical, psychological, or social problems; and (c) that the infant was sufficiently alert to allow filming of the dyadic interaction. The selected group included infants covering a wide postnatal age range, from 4 to 30 weeks, with a mean age of 15.4 weeks and standard deviation of 6.9.

Recording Methods

Sessions were conducted in a large, well-lit room. All sessions were videotaped on a Sony ½-in. (12.5 mm) reel-to-reel videotape recorder, using a tripod-mounted CASY video camera (VR 621) and concealed Sony onmidirectional microphone. A freestanding cloth screen (1200 mm wide × 1210 mm high) concealed the investigator and the video recorder from the mother and infant. While concealed, the investigator could observe the proceedings on a video monitor (Sanyo 300 mm) coupled to the recording equipment.

The observational arrangements were similar to those used by Trevarthen (1977). The mother and infant sat facing each other. In the present study the infant sat in a molded plastic infant seat (Frazer, NY8/3) atop a 760-mm-high table. The seating arrangement put the faces of mother and infant on approximately the same level. To minimize the mother's awareness of being filmed, a 1000 mm × 1000 mm mirror, positioned to the right of the infant, enabled filming of both faces in juxtaposition using the single video camera. The camera was approximately 3 m from the infant's face, and focused over the mother's left shoulder. This arrangement enabled the collection of videotaped records of sufficient quality to allow the detailed analysis of dyadic gaze and vocalization. Postsession interviews confirmed the success of this filming arrangement in minimizing the mother's awareness of being filmed.

General Procedures

The clinic sister brought each mother and infant to the observation room and introduced them to the investigator. The general details of the study were reiterated, and the mother was thanked for her willingness to take part. The investigator then recorded the infant's name, birth date, and sex. The mother was asked to place her child in the infant seat and fasten the safety harness. She was then asked to sit in front of her infant.

Each dyad was observed in two situations: Free Interaction and Directed Modeling. In the Free Interaction Situation the mother was given the following instruction (based on the procedure of Trevarthen, 1977): "I'd like you to have a chat with your baby, just as if you were at home. Try to be as natural as you can. I'll tell you when to begin." A 3-min segment of interaction was then recorded. If the baby became upset, recording was interrupted and recommenced only after the infant had been settled. This resulted in slight variations in the total duration of the Free Interaction Situation.

In the Directed Modeling Situation, the investigator demonstrated to the mother a set of six models (derived from Maratos, 1973). The set consisted of tongue protrusion, silently and with the sound "mmm"; mouth opening, silently and with the sound "aaa"; rhythmic side-to-side head movement; and rhythmically moving the hands together and apart. Each model was to be presented four times in succession. The mother was asked to perform each model "slowly and deliberately, and as far as possible when your infant is attending to you." Any uncertainties were clarified and the mother's attention was drawn to the card in front of her, which listed the models. The investigator cued the mother to commence and ceased recording 10 sec after the sequence of modeled behaviors had been completed. The duration of the Directed Modeling Situation therefore varied according to the time the mother took to complete the set of models.

Each mother was then questioned concerning her awareness of being filmed, shown a small segment of the recording, thanked for her cooperation, and escorted from the room.

Coding and Data Analysis

Developing the Coding System

The whole point of continuous observation is to obtain as complete a record as possible of salient single behaviors such as facial gaze and vocalization. This is more easily said than done. It required, in practice, the development of an event recorder which preserved both the sequence and duration of a single behavior. This consisted of a tone generator coupled to a UHER 4200 reel-to-reel stereo tape recorder. With it, we could proceed to tackling the problems of simplifying coding and obtaining a summary of behaviors.

Two coders viewed the videotapes in real time. They produced separate records of the mother's and infant's behavior by marking either the left or right channel of the stereo tape with a tone (1 kHz) whenever the particular behavior occurred. For a behavior such as facial gaze, an audiotape was produced that had the mother's behavior on the left channel, coded in terms of the presence and absence of the tone (corresponding to the events of "looking at" and "looking away from" her infant's face). The binary record for the infant's behavior was simultaneously coded on the right channel of the audiotape by the second coder. A major advantage of the system is that each coder has only to decide between two states, "on" or "off," for a single behavior and for the individual being observed.

After the videotape record has been coded, the audiotape recorder was interfaced with a Data General Nova 2 minicomputer, which produced a dyadic state summary. This summary gives a description of the dyad in terms of the four mutually exclusive states that result from the combination of the mother and infant binary records (Table I).

Initially the computer produced a punched paper tape listing of the sequence of dyadic states and their durations (in msec.). From this record a number of summary measures can be derived (see Table 3, in the *Results* section, below). These include the number of exits from each state (the number of exits is equivalent to the frequency of the state ± 1), the mean duration of stays, and the total time spent in each state (expressed in seconds and as a percentage of the total time). In addition a state transitional probability matrix is produced, which summarizes the dynamics of the sequence of dyadic states by listing the probabilities of movements from each dyadic state to the other three states over the coded period. (The BASIC programs for producing dyadic state records and summary measures are available from the first author. The assistance of Len Glue in developing the coding system is most gratefully acknowledged.)

Coder Reliability

The degree of interobserver reliability is a function of the accuracy of the coder's decisions as to the binary state of the behavior of the individual being observed and the length of time that the individual is in this state. Making these decisions correctly depends not only on the observers' levels of vigilance but also on the degree of match between their definitions of what constitutes the presence or absence of the behavior being coded.

Facial gaze was judged from the orientation of the eyes and the face in relation to the face of the dyadic partner. As Argyle and Cook (1976, p. 56) conclude, there is sufficient evidence from psychophysical experiments to indicate that at a distance of 3 m "face directed gaze can be clearly distinguished." Vocalization was coded in terms of the utterances by mother and infant. In the case of the mother an utterance was defined as a word string expressing a single idea and bounded by a pause of at least 1 sec. The pause was judged by the observer and, as coding was in real time, the measured duration of each utterance possibly overestimated the actual length of the utterance slightly. This was, however, regarded as a reasonably consistent error. In practice, utterances were quite easily identifiable, as other researchers have also reported (Bateson, 1975; Snow, 1977).

The two behaviors presented quite different coding problems. For the coding of facial gaze the problem was correctly identifying the behavior; for vocalization the major problem was in judging the duration of the behavior. In general, however, the coders seem to have managed these difficulties and produced sufficiently reliable results.

To assess interobserver reliability a 25% sample of the dyadic records was recoded with the coders reversing their roles. The observer who had coded the mother in the original coding of the data now coded the infant's behavior, while the other coder now observed the mother's behavior. As before, a punched paper tape of the dyadic states and their durations was produced from the audiotape records for the recorded data.

The original records and the recoded records could now be compared using the minicomputer. The Nova was programmed to assess the match between the original and recoded records in terms of the amount of overlap between the two. (The BASIC program for overlap calculation is available from the first author.) Separate overlap percentages were computed for the mother and infant binary processes. The data produced included a measure of the total overlap, which is the amount of time the recoded record was in agreement with the original record, expressed as a percentage of the total duration of the original record. Overlap percentages for the "on" and the "off" states of the mother and infant binary records were also produced. The mother's "on" overlap, for example, represented the total time that the "on" state for the recoded record was in agreement with the original record. This was expressed as a percentage of the total time that the mother was coded as in the "on" state in the original record.

The "on," "off," and total overlap percentages for the facial gaze and vocalization records are given in Table 2. For facial gaze the mean total overlaps for mother and infant were 88% and 80%, respectively, while for vocalization they were 74.08% and 94.42%, respectively. These are sufficiently high to suggest acceptable interobserver reliability.

A further check on reliability can be gained by calculating correlation coefficients for each of the state measures across the two sets of records, and for the transitional probabilities. With a few exceptions (concentrated around states that were infrequent and of short duration), the correlation coefficients were highly significant, indicating reliability.

Data Analysis

Facial gaze and vocalization data were analyzed separately. For each data set the dyadic summaries were grouped according to the situation and the age and sex of the infant. The infant age factor was dichotomously defined (younger and

Table 2.   Mean On, Off and Total Overlap Percentages
for the Original and Recoded Records of a Twenty Five
Percent Sample of the Dyads

	Mean overlap percentage		
	On	*Off*	*Total*
		Facial gaze	
Infants	68.17	77.83	80.08
Mothers	91.58	57.67	88.00
		Vocalization	
Infants	34.83	96.25	94.42
Mothers	60.75	76.50	74.08

older) by splitting the sample of dyads at the median infant age (16 weeks). Each of the summary measures was analyzed as a $2 \times 2 \times 2$ (Situation $\times$ Age $\times$ Sex) nonorthogonal analysis of variance. The need for a nonorthogonal model arose because some dyads did not produce data for every dyadic state. If a state does not occur in a particular dyad it can be legitimately included as a zero in the analyses of state exits and percentage occurrence, but not in the mean duration and transitional probability analyses. A mean duration of zero seconds is meaningless, as is a transitional probability matrix with a row total of zero.

Zero entries presented another measurement problem to be solved. A program had to be written that differentiated the components of the analysis in which zero represented missing data from those which constituted legitimate zero scores. (The assistance of Richard Wilson and Tony Elliott is gratefully acknowledged.) Once this program had been developed each summary component for facial gaze and vocalization could be analyzed using the one program, despite the variable degree of nonorthogonality in the data. The results of these analyses are detailed in the following section.

Results

Given a solution to a number of measurement problems, we are now in a position to answer the main substantive questions:

- Do facial gaze and vocalization show similar features?
- Do they show the features of a dialogue in which each partner is closely tuned to the other?

Broadly speaking, the results show some differences between the two behaviors. As one example, the effect of age is more marked on gaze behavior than on vocalization. In addition, the transitional probabilities from one state to another are often different. Both behaviors, however, show the same general departure from any finely tuned dialogue—the interaction is quite asymmetrical. The contributions of mother and infant are by no means equivalent: The mother spends a much higher proportion of her time looking at and vocalizing to the infant than the infant does towards the mother. In addition, the changes in task (from Free Interaction to Directed Modeling) alter the mother's behavior but not the infant's, again suggesting a lack of close tuning to one another.

The detailed results are presented in Table 3 (data for each state summary measure), Tables 4 and 5 (age and sex effects for gaze and vocalization, respectively), and Tables 6 and 7 (transitional probabilities for gaze and vocalization). The comments below deal first with the measures of states (Tables 3, 4, and 5), treating gaze first and then vocalization. For each behavior, results are noted first for Free Interaction and then for Directed Modeling.

Gaze: Percentage of Occurrence (Table 3, A)

The percentage of occurrence for mother and infant in Free Interaction provides the most global summary of the activity of the dyad. The salient feature is the general asymmetry of the amounts of time spent in facial gaze by mother and infant. The mothers spent an average of 92.96% of the interaction time looking at the infant's face. In contrast, infants looked at the mother's face for only 37.79% of the interaction.

Similar figures occur in the Directed Modeling situation (81.70% for mothers, 46.9% for infants). The difference between the two situations was significant only for mothers [$F(1,40) = 24.05$, $p < .001$].

Gaze: Percentage of Time in Each State (Table 3, B)

In Free Interaction, the state with the highest frequency was mother-alone acting (MS). This state accounted for 56.83% of the interaction time. Coacting (CS) was the next highest occurrence (36.17%). The low incidence of neither party looking at the other (QS, 5.29%) might well be expected. The low incidence of the infant looking at the mother without her also looking at the infant, however (IS, 1.58%), is less expected, and striking.

Similar figures were obtained for the two most frequent states in the Directed Modeling situation (mother-alone; 44.37%; mother and infant gazing at each other, 37.54%). The frequency of occasions when neither is looking at the other, however, is slightly higher in Directed Modeling than in Free Interaction (9.29% vs. 1.58%)—a significant difference reflecting the mother's modeling activity. The percentages for this state (QS) are nonetheless still low.

Gaze: Mean Numbers of Exits and of State Durations (Table 3, D & E)

The durations of stay in each state correspond with the number of exits. The mother-alone state (MS) has the longest mean duration (6.36 sec) and the highest

Table 3. Aspects of Facial Gaze and Vocalization in Two Situations: Free
Interaction (FI) and Directed Modeling (DM)

The aspects are:

A. Total occurrence (percentage) for mother and infant.
B. Mean percentage of time in each state (QS, IS, MS, CS).
C. Mean total time (sec) in each state (QS, IS, MS, CS).
D. Mean number of exits from each state (QS, IS, MS, CS).
E. Mean duration (sec) of stay in each state (QS, IS, MS, CS).

Aspect	Facial Gaze			Vocalization		
	FI	DM	F (1, 40)	FI	DM	F (1, 40)
A. Mother	92.96	81.70	24.05***	40.92	16.41	55.31***
Infant	37.79	46.79	1.04	6.00	8.79	1.31
B. QS	5.29	8.92	3.32	55.33	76.41	33.95***
IS	1.58	9.29	16.65***	3.75	7.16	3.12
MS	56.83	44.37	2.52	38.62	14.79	54.81***
CS	36.17	37.54	0.03	2.25	1.46	1.47
C. QS	9.51	16.38	4.31*	98.38	138.86	12.73***
IS	3.01	14.86	18.20***	7.08	13.64	3.03
MS	103.48	90.81	0.47	49.54	27.94	37.73***
CS	66.41	63.99	0.03	4.04	3.07	0.52
D QS	9.12	10.58	0.55	91.25	54.29	17.83***
IS	3.79	9.46	7.81**	19.04	27.71	1.50
MS	18.58	17.24	0.29	86.58	34.00	46.98***
CS	13.92	16.83	1.56	15.37	7.96	4.70*
E. QS	0.91	1.44	7.26[1]*	1.19	3.72	25.40***
IS	0.79	1.62	14.06[2]***	0.32	0.44	4.63[1]*
MS	6.36	4.82	1.41	0.80	0.93	2.18
CS	4.60	3.94	0.75	0.25	0.35	3.91[3]

Notes:
[1]$df = 1, 39$
[2]$df = 1, 29$
[3]$df = 1, 34$
  *$p < .05$
 **$p < .01$
***$p < .001$

number of exits (18.58). The coacting state (CS) is the next in order (mean
duration, 4.60 sec; mean number of exits, 13.92). The duration of the infant
gazing alone at the mother (IS) is extremely brief (.79 sec), as are also moments
of neither looking at the other (QS, .91 sec).

With Directed Modeling, the only significant change from the Free Interaction
data occurs with the infant-only gazing (IS). The mean duration of this state has

increased significantly (from .79 to 1.62 sec, $p < .001$), probably reflecting the change in the mother's involvement in tasks and her somewhat diminished gazing at the infant.

Gaze: Age and Sex Effects

There are no main effects for the sex of infant factor, and no significant two- or three-factor interactions. Main effects for age of infant occur on three of the measures shown in Table 3: total time in quiescent state (QS), number of exits from the QS, and number of exits from the MS. On all three measures, dyads with older infants displayed the higher scores. The results for significant effects are shown in Table 4.

Vocalization: Percentage of Occurrence (Table 3, A)

The asymmetry of the contributions of mothers and infants is again striking. The average percentage of occurrence for mothers is 40.92%; for infants, 6.00%. The degree of asymmetry is less, but still present, in Directed Modeling, with the change occurring in the mother's behavior rather than the infant's. Clearly the change in situation affects the one party but not the other.

Vocalization: Percentage of Time in Each State (Table 3, B)

The most striking feature is the high incidence of occasions when both parties are silent (55.33% in Free Interaction, 76.41% in Directed Modeling). Most of the vocalizations are by the mother alone (38.62% and 14.79% in the two task situations), and occasions when both are talking are rare (2.25% and 1.46%). Furthermore, it is again only the mother's amount of talking that shows a significant difference between the two task situations. The infant's behavior is not affected by the change in task or by the changes in the mother's behavior—an

Table 4. Components of Facial Gaze Analysis Showing Significant Age Main Effects

	Means		
Component	*Younger*	*Older*	*F* (1, 40)
Exits from QS	7.38	12.34	6.41**
Duration of QS (sec)	9.57	16.32	4.15*
Exits from MS	14.25	21.62	9.36**

Notes:
 *$p < .05$
 **$p < .025$
 ***$p < .005$

effect that hardly speaks for any fine responsiveness to the mother's vocalizations.

Vocalization: Number of Exits and Mean State Durations (Table 3, D & E)

The frequency of exits again shows considerable variation from one state to another. In both task situations, the state showing the longest durations and the largest number of exits is the state of mutual silence (QS). The scores, however, are significantly different between the two task situations. With Directed Modeling, the mean duration of stay in the QS increases markedly (from 1.19 to 3.72 sec). The number of exits from the QS also changes (from 91.25 to 54.29), and the mean number of exits from the mother-alone state (MS) also shows a marked and significant decline (from 86.58 to 34.00, $p < .001$). These changes in duration and exits, it should be noted, occur against a background of no significant difference in the total time spent in the two task situations.

Vocalization: Age and Sex Effects

Several significant interactions may be noted, all suggesting that older females and younger males are more active than their counterparts (younger females and older males). Significant effects appear on two measures: the percentage of time spent in the infant-alone speaking (IS), and in the mean duration of the IS. These are supported by trends toward significance for the percentage of time spent in

Table 5. Mean Values for Vocalization Summary Measures that Produced Significant Interactions (Age × Situation or Age × Gender)

	Variable		
		Infant Age Group	
	Situation or		
Measure	*Infant Gender*	*Younger*	*Older*
p IS → QS	Free Interaction	.66	.81
	Modelling	.94	.92
p IS → CS	Free Interaction	.32	.17
	Modelling	.06	.07
p CS → MS	Female	.79	.42
	Male	.68	.64
IS: Mean duration	Female	.29	.52
(in sec.)	Male	.37	.34
IS: Percentage	Female	2.30	7.40
time	Male	7.36	4.43
Infant Vocalization	Female	3.60	9.00
Percentage	Male	9.64	6.71
QS: No. of exits	Female	58.70	79.30
	Male	83.00	67.93

infant vocalization ($p < .10$), and in the number of exits from the QS ($p < .10$). The detailed results are shown in Table 5.

Transitional Probabilities: Gaze (Table 6)

Table 6 presents the mean probabilities of transitions from state to state. The table starts with results from the present study in the two task situations (Free Interaction and Directed Modeling). It includes also results from work by Stern (1974) and by Bakeman and Brown (1977). Comparing these latter results with those of the present study—especially with the Free Interaction data—allows one to ask directly about the effect of various techniques for observing interaction. The question of comparability is the focus of Section IV. For the moment, we shall restrict attention to a comparison of the two task situations in the present study.

In Free Interaction, the most salient features are the high probability of the mother initiating activity following a quiescent state (p QS–MS = .95) and the high probability of the infant breaking up the coacting state, leaving the mother looking at the infant (p CS–MS = .84; p CS–IS = .16). Also high is the

Table 6. Mean State Transitional Probabilities for Facial Gaze in the Free Interaction (a) and Directed Modeling (b) Situations, Combined with the Probabilities Adapted from Figure 4 of Stern (1974, p. 205) and Bakeman and Brown (1977, p. 200). The Values Obtained after Proportionally Distributing the Probabilities of Remaining in Each State ("Adjusted") are Shown in Italics.

Cell of Matrix	FI	DM	Stern (1974)[1] Original	Stern (1974)[1] Adjusted	Bakeman & Brown (1977)[2] Original	Bakeman & Brown (1977)[2] Adjusted
QS → IS	.04	.23	.02	*.08*	.06	*.28*
QS → MS	.95	.77	.28	*.92*	.14	*.72*
QS → QS	—	—	.90	—	.78	—
IS → QS	.20	.35	.37	*.42*	.14	*.43*
IS → CS	.80	.64	.52	*.58*	.18	*.57*
IS → IS	—	—	.11	—	.68	—
MS → QS	.39	.34	.02	*.16*	.16	*.64*
MS → CS	.61	.65	.08	*.84*	.09	*.36*
MS → MS	—	—	.90	—	.74	—
CS → IS	.16	.40	.01	*.07*	.16	*.43*
CS → MS	.84	.55	.10	*.93*	.20	*.57*
CS → CS	—	—	.89	—	.59	—

Notes:
[1]Sampling time = .6 sec
[2]Sampling time = 5 sec

probability of the mother joining the infant in mutual facial gaze (p IS–CS = .80). The probability of the infant moving to join the mother in mutual gaze is not as high (p MS–CS = .61). All in all, the mother appears to play the sustaining role.

A change in task to Directed Modeling alters some of the probability values but does not change the overall pattern. The probability of the mother maintaining her gaze after a period of mutual gaze (p CS–MS) has dropped from .84 to .60, and the drop is significant: F (1,40) = 12.23; p < .005. The related probability of moving from mutual gaze to the infant alone gazing at the mother is also significantly higher than in Free Interaction: p CS–IS is .40 as against the earlier .16; F (1,40) = 12.35, p < .005. Not significantly altered, however, is the asymmetrical contribution of mother and infant. The infant still terminates the mutual gaze more often than the mother does (p CS–MS = .60 vs. p CS–IS = .40). And the mother still initiates the transition from a quiescent, nongaze state far more often than the infant does (p QS–MS = .77 vs. p QS–IS = .23).

Transitional Probabilities (Vocalization, Table 7)

The results are presented in Table 7, covering again the two task situations in the present study and the results from studies by other investigators using different observation techniques and allowing a comparison of results across studies (again discussed in Section IV).

The pattern of transitions shows some interesting similarities and differences from the facial gaze data. The mother appears to be again the more likely initiator (p QS–MS = .85). The probabilities of movement from either a mother or an infant vocalization to a mutual vocalization, however, are low (p MS–CS = .10 and p IS–CS = .25). Interestingly, the probability of the mother joining her infant in vocalization (S–CS) is more than double that of the infant joining the mother (MS–CS). Transitions from the mutual vocalization state (CS) have a higher probability of being to a mother vocalization state (p CS–MS = .64) than to an infant vocalization state (p CS–IS = .32). In further contrast to the facial gaze data, the probabilities of movement to the QS are high in the vocalization analyses, while for facial gaze the opposite applies. There is a high mean probability of the dyad returning to the QS after either a mother-alone (p MS–QS = .88), or an infant-alone state (p IS–QS = .73).

With a shift in task to Directed Modeling, four of the eight main transitions (i.e., excluding the improbable transitions) show significant changes from those observed in Free Interaction. The most salient pair of changes occurs for the transitions from the QS. There is still a high probability of the mother vocalizing first after a period of silence (p QS–MS = .59). However, the probability has decreased significantly from that in the Free Interaction Situation [F (1,40) = 22.95; p < .001]. In contrast, the probability of the infant initiating activity from

Table 7. Mean State Transitional Probabilities for Vocalization in the Free Interaction (a) and Directed Modeling (b) Situations, Combined with the Probabilities Adapted from Freedle and Lewis (1977) and Anderson, Vietze, and Dokecki (1977). The Values Obtained after Proportionally Distributing the Probabilities of Remaining in Each State ("Adjusted") are Shown in Italics.

Cell of Matrix	FI	DM	Freedle & Lewis[1] (1977)		Anderson, Vietze & Dokecki[2] (1977)	
			Original	*Adjusted*	*Original*	*Adjusted*
QS → IS	.15	.42	.09	*.30*	.01	*.20*
QS → MS	.85	.59	.21	*.70*	—	*.80*
QS → CS	.01	.00[3]	.07	—	—	—
QS → QS	—	—	.57	—	—	—
IS → QS	.73	.93	.42	*.92*	.12	*.65*
IS → CS	.25	.06	.04	*.08*	.07	*.35*
IS → MS	.02	.01	.15	—	—	—
IS → IS	—	—	.39	—	—	—
MS → QS	.88	.83	.25	*.65*	.04	*.70*
MS → CS	.10	.15	.14	*.35*	.02	*.30*
MS → IS	.01	.01	.05	—	—	—
MS → MS	—	—	.57	—	—	—
CS → IS	.32	.34	.03	*.15*	.03	*.20*
CS → MS	.64	.65	.15	*.85*	.10	*.80*
CS → QS	.04	.01	.14	—	—	—
CS → CS	—	—	.63	—	—	—

Notes:

[1]Table 4 of Freedle and Lewis (1977) presents the probabilities expressed as percentages. However, in the text they are expressed as proportions. To facilitate comparison the probabilities are presented as proportions. Only the data for the infant seat situation are presented here. Freedle and Lewis included two additional vocalization states, mother vocalizing to another person (e.g. the observer) and infant vocalizing while the mother vocalized to another person. The values of these have not been included.

[2]Estimates from Figures 1 and 2 of Anderson et al. (1977).

[3]Actual value .002

the silent state has increased significantly [p QS–IS = .415; F (1,40) = 23.47; p < .001]. Together, these changes result in a reduced level of asymmetry.

The probabilities of transition from the IS have also changed significantly, with a decrease in the probability of transitions from IS to CS and a complementary increase in the probability of movement from IS to QS. Transitions from the MS, however, are quite stable and suggest that there has been no significant change in the infants' pattern of responding to mother-alone vocalizations. In effect, the mother's activity may vary, but the transitions from state to state show a relatively unchanged pattern for the infant: a picture that does not argue for finely tuned responsiveness on both sides.

IV. COMPARING RESULTS ACROSS STUDIES

The data in the present study came from the technique of continuous observation, a technique selected to avoid the possible artifacts of data based on sampling only sections of behavior (interval or point sampling). How far are results comparable to earlier studies? And what indications are there that particular earlier techniques may have altered the dyadic states observed and the probabilities of transition from one state to another?

Such questions of comparability may be explored at two levels. We may ask first whether the general quality of mother–infant interaction is similar across studies. And we may ask whether there is equivalence in the specific probabilities of being in or exiting from a particular state.

The quality of interaction in facial gaze.   The Free Interaction data provide the best basis for comparison. Within this, the most salient feature is the fact that for over half of the time the mother continues to look at the infant even though the infant is looking away from her. An infant gazing at the mother without a reciprocal gaze by the mother is a rare event. Further, when such behavior does occur, the duration is short.

The level of asymmetry in the contributions of mother and infant is reasonably consistent with the results of several other studies. On average, infants in Stern's (1974) study spent 49% of the session in facial gaze. Peery and Stern (1975) report that mothers looked at their infants for 70% of a play session, about twice the time of their infants. Further, the mean duration of each look by the mother was, on average, four times longer than her infant's. In Bakeman and Brown's (1977) study, the mothers looked at their infant's face for 88.40% of the observation time. Similarly, Schaffer et al. (1977) report that mothers spent an average of 90% of the session watching their infant. Overall, the mother emerges as persistent in maintaining gaze despite a much less responsive partner. In Fogel's (1977) terms, the mother provides a stable frame for her infant's fluctuating behavior.

Comparing probabilities.   Two studies in particular have reported transitional probabilities for dyadic states: one by Stern (1974), and one by Bakeman and Brown (1977).

In Stern's (1974) study, the state of the dyad was checked every 600 msec. With such a technique, the exact values of the probabilities of staying in any state can be increased or decreased by reducing or enlarging the sampling interval. In effect, we cannot make an uncorrected comparison of values across studies.

We could ignore the exact values and compare the relative magnitudes of transitions. It is also possible to *rescale* the probabilities of transitions from a state (i.e., omitting the probability of remaining in the same state). This gives a matrix comparable to the transitional probability matrix gained from continuous observation. The rescaling is achieved by dividing each of the probabilities of transition from a particular state by the sum of the probabilities for each of the transitions from that state. For example, in Table 4 the transition values derived from Stern (1974) show that the probability of transition from QS to IS is .023, and from QS to MS is .281. The sum of these two probabilities is .304. Dividing each transitional probability by the scaling factor .304 gives the rescaled values of .076 and .924 (values shown in parentheses).

The similarities between the patterns of asymmetry in both studies are immediately apparent. Three of the four pairs of transitions reported by Stern show the same pattern of asymmetry observed in the Free Interaction Situation of the present study (although the degree of asymmetry of transitions to the CS is more marked in Stern's data). The pair of transitions to the QS is the exception to the pattern of probabilities obtained in the present study. In Stern's study there is a higher probability of moving from IS to QS than to CS. Despite this difference, the dynamic pattern of the dyadic facial gaze states is essentially quite similar to that reported by Stern.

It is also possible to compare the pattern of transitional probabilities for facial gaze in the present study with results reported by Bakeman and Brown (1977) for "dialogic behavior." Under this term, they grouped "all behaviors on the part of the infant or mother which could be responsive to the other or to which the other could respond" (p. 197). Facial gaze was excluded from this set, on the grounds that the steadiness of the mother's gaze "obscures the behavioral dialogue" (p. 197).

Bakeman and Brown (1977) used a 5 sec interval coding technique, with behavior recorded if it occurred anywhere within that interval. For all these differences from the present study, however, the pattern of results (once again excluding the probabilities of remaining in the same state and rescaling) bears a striking similarity to the data in the present study (Table 4). For dialogic behavior the mother has a higher probability of returning to the MS (rather than the IS) following a mutual dialogic state (CS). As was the case for facial gaze, there is a higher probability of the CS than the QS following an infant-alone dialogic state (IS). And finally, following an MS, there is a higher probability of the dyad moving to the QS than to the CS.

These similarities seem to indicate that an asymmetry similar to that of the facial gaze component also characterizes other aspects of the dyadic interaction, aspects which Bakeman and Brown (1977) considered a priori to be more dialogic in structure than facial gaze.

The quality of interaction in vocalization. In comparison with gaze behavior, studies of vocalization yield far less agreement on the general quality of interaction, with descriptions ranging from "conversations" (Newson, 1974), "well-practiced games" (Bell, 1971), and "turn-taking" (Trevarthen, 1977) to "proto-conversations" (Bateson, 1975) and "pseudo-dialogues" (Schaffer, 1979). In general, the results of the present study do not lend support to the notion of both partners showing marked responsiveness and reciprocity. The contributions of mother and infant are far from equivalent. A clearer picture of comparability, however, emerges from looking at studies that have specifically reported transitional probabilities.

Comparing probabilities. Several studies have examined the transitional probability structure of vocalization states in mother–infant dyads. Stern et al. (1975) have reported the differences between pairs of probabilities relating to the initiation and termination of vocalization by mother and infant. The four-state transitional probability matrix is not reported, however, and so the results are difficult to compare with those from the present study. Complete sets and transitional probability matrices have been presented by Lewis and his co-workers (Freedle & Lewis, 1977; Lewis & Freedle, 1973; Lewis & Lee-Painter, 1974). The most extensive study to date by this group is presented in Freedle and Lewis (1977).

Table 6 presents the transitional probabilities reported by Freedle and Lewis for vocal interactions in a situation similar to that of the present study, with rescaled values again shown in parentheses. Some interesting similarities emerge when the patterns of state transitional probabilities are examined (once again, for purposes of comparison, the probabilities of remaining in the same state are disregarded). As in the present study, the mother emerges as the more likely to vocalize following a period of silence. There is also a higher probability of returning to a mother-alone state, rather than to an infant-alone state, following a period of coacting vocalization. However, in contrast to the results of the present study, the probabilities of transitions to the coacting vocalization state reported by Freedle and Lewis (1977) are higher from the mother-alone state than from the infant-alone state. As in the results of the present study, Freedle and Lewis (1977) report a higher probability of moving to the quiescent state than to the coacting state following either a mother-alone or an infant-alone vocalization. It is also of interest that the improbable transitions (from CS–QS, QS–CS, MS–IS, and IS–MS) are higher in the Freedle and Lewis (1977) data for both situations, than the results for the Free Interaction situation of the present study. The increased probability of these transitions, together with the very low probabilities of remaining in the infant-alone state, may arise from the long (10 sec) coding interval used by Freedle and Lewis. For a behavior like vocalization an interval of this coarseness may lead to results which poorly represent the actual distribution of vocalization states in time.

Anderson, Vietze, and Dokecki (1977) have also examined dyadic vocalization by using a four-state, first-order transitional probability matrix. Their data derive from a study of mothers and 3-month-old infants observed in the home. Although a 1-sec interval sampling procedure was used, Anderson et al. (1977) do not report the probabilities of remaining in the same state. Instead they report the pairs of probabilities that relate to maternal and infant onset and offset of vocalization, which correspond to the eight main transitions examined in the present study. Inspection of Table 7 indicates a similar pattern of asymmetry to that obtained in the present study (although once again the actual probabilities reported are much smaller, because of the use of an interval sampling procedure). Briefly summarized, there are higher probabilities of the mother vocalizing following a period of silence (QS), and of joining her infant in mutual vocalization (CS) following an infant-alone vocalization (IS). One difference between the Anderson et al. (1977) results and those of the present study is the higher probability of silence after an infant-alone vocalization than after a mother-alone vocalization. The difference may stem from the use of the 1 sec interval sampling procedure. Anderson et al. (1977) recognize the problems of adopting such a procedure: "It was not possible to differentiate those instances in which a vocal onset by one dyad member during an interval in which the other was already vocalizing represented simultaneous or rapid (less than 1 sec) alternation of vocal response" (p. 1679).

A similar problem may arise in instances where vocalizations and pauses occur within a 1 sec interval. This may in part explain the difference between the Anderson et al. (1977) results and those in the present study. Apart from this difference, the pattern of probabilities shows a similar asymmetry to that found in the present study. Interestingly, the overall vocal contributions of mothers and infants in the Anderson et al. (1977) study are also asymmetrical, with mothers spending an average of 56.40% of the situation talking, while infants vocalized for only 13.70% of the time.

Apart from the exceptions noted above, the asymmetrical pattern of transitional probabilities found in the present study is consistent with the patterns found by Freedle and Lewis (1977) and Anderson et al. (1977), despite the fact that the actual probabilities vary as a function of the sampling interval chosen. In addition, comparison with the transitional probabilities reported by Lewis and Freedle (1977) and Anderson et al. (1977) clearly demonstrates the impact of sampling interval size upon the magnitude of the transitional probabilities.

V. PROBLEMS OF THE FUTURE

We can clearly solve a number of measurement problems in the study of interactions, moving us further toward answering questions about the nature of relationships between two parties in an exchange. For mothers and infants, and for the behaviors of gaze and vocalization, for instance, we can now say that the evidence from continuous observation techniques points toward a far-from-equal pattern of contributions. Overall, the mother spends a much higher proportion of her time looking at, and talking to, the infant, than the infant displays in exchange. Moreover, the infant's level and pattern of activity shows a relative stability in the face of a change in what the mother is doing. Qualitatively, the mother appears in both behaviors to be supplying a "stable frame" for the infant's behavior (Fogel, 1977). More graphically, if we focus on talk alone, the mother appears to be consistently attempting "to maintain conversation with a conversationally inadequate partner," using repetitions, questions, and "sequences in which the mother takes both parts" (Snow, 1977, p. 13).

Some unsolved problems still remain. One concerns the degree of contingency between the actions or states of one partner and those of the other. We can observe the frequency of various states and the transitional probabilities for various states, and make inferences about dependencies in the relationship. But these temporal or sequential figures do not allow a direct test of dependency or reciprocity. Techniques of analysis directed toward allowing less inferential statements have been proposed in several studies (e.g., Anderson et al., 1977; Stern, 1974; Thomas & Martin, 1976), but as these studies recognize, difficulties still remain.

More broadly, we should look forward to the exploration of behaviors other than gaze and vocalization. We are now at a point where the quantification of observational data has been made a great deal easier by the development of computer-based, electronic data-coding devices (cf. Celhoffer, Boukydis, Minde, & Muir, 1977; Dawkins, 1971; Fitzpatrick, 1977; Stephenson & Roberts, 1977; Torgerson, 1977; and White, 1971).

In theory, the technology and analytic procedures are available to permit attention to extensive sets of behaviors. In practice, researchers have tended to microanalyze a restricted set of features of mother–infant interaction. In particular, emphasis has been placed upon the salient visual, vocal, and tactile aspects of behavior such as looking, holding, laughing, crying, and touching. The choice has in part been motivated by a concern for identifying variables that are "easily observable," in Rosenthal's (1973) sense of requiring minimal interpretation. In part, also, the motivation has been historical. Looking, vocalizing, and holding were identified in early studies of mother–infant interaction as high-incidence behaviors (Moss, 1967). They are also behaviors that both mother and infant display in early infancy. Nonetheless, they are not the only behaviors that mothers and infants exhibit.

For either the standard behaviors or a new set, we might in the future begin to ask more broadly about the functions of behaviors. It may not be sufficient to describe interactions between mothers and infants as "conversational" in structure. Among adults, for example, a behavior such as gaze serves a wide range of communicative functions. These involve the collection of information, the signaling of intent to communicate, the establishment and recognition of relationships (Argyle & Dean, 1965), the provision of feedback, the achievement of "affiliative balance" (Argyle, Lalljee, & Cook, 1968), and the regulation of conversational speech (Argyle et al., 1968; Kendon, 1967). Such functions may not be limited to adults. One specific suggestion in this direction comes from Stern (1977, p. 25), proposing that mutual gaze provides a "magic moment" for mother and infant and serves the function of bonding.

One final problem for the future lies in the need to resolve a difference between current concepts and current methods. There is, at present, a rising interest in asking about the meanings or interpretations given to behaviors, in addition to observing the behaviors themselves. Theory increasingly uses terms such as "intersubjectivity" (Newson, 1974, 1977; Newson & Newson, 1975; Trevarthen, 1977), "shared meanings" (Newson, 1974), or "joint reference" (Newson, 1977). Sameroff and Harris (1979, p. 363) speak of parents' "interpretive schemes," while Parke (1978) notes that "in our enthusiasm to give the infant proper recognition as a contributor to the interactive process, the assumptions have been simplified concerning the partner's capacities . . . by treating them as coacting equals" (p. 76). The adult's capacity for both memory and interpretation are, in fact, clearly not the same as the infant's.

The microanalysis of overt behaviors, however, does not address the problem of "meanings" or "interpretations," shared or held singly. It represents in large part a philosophic position expressed by Blurton-Jones and Woodson (1979): "We are not concerned . . . with the way people think about their behavior; we are interested in the way in which it can be observed that they behave" (p. 99). Such an opposition between two lines of interest seems unnecessary. It should be possible both to explore the intentions or meanings that parties to an exchange attribute to each other's behavior (and to their own), *and* to link such ideas to the analysis of overt behaviors: in effect, not throwing the infant out with the bathwater. Just how such a link can be made, however, is a major and a challenging measurement problem.

ACKNOWLEDGMENTS

We are happy to acknowledge our debt to several people: to Sisters Wells, Novotny, Babb, and Hopkins of the Wollongong Baby Health Centre for enthusiastic cooperation; to E. Venturato, L. Cheng, and G. Cuthbertson for expert assistance with audiovisual equipment; to B. Chisholm for thoughtful help in designing and building the infant seat; to J. O'Brien and D. Cairns for valuable assistance in computing; to J. Hayes for many hours of tedious coding; and—a most particular debt—to L. Glue and T. Elliott for their major role in solving computing and electronic problems that seemed at times insoluble. The work reported is part of a PhD thesis carried out at Macquarie University by the first author, with advice from John Murray and Jacqueline Goodnow. Requests for reprints should be sent to the first author: Dr. A. Hayes, Schonell Education Research Centre, University of Queensland, 4067.

REFERENCES

Anderson, B. J., Vietze, P., & Dokecki, R. R. Reciprocity in vocal interactions of mothers and infants. *Child Development*, 1977, *48*, 1676–1681.

Argyle, M., & Cook, M. *Gaze and mutual gaze*. London: Cambridge University Press, 1976.

Argyle, M., & Dean, J. Eye contact, distance and affiliation. *Sociometry*, 1965, *28*, 289–304.

Argyle, M., Lalljee, M., & Cook, M. The effects of visibility on interaction in a dyad. *Human Relations*, 1968, *21*, 3–17.

Bakeman, R., & Brown, J. V. Behavioral dialogues: An approach to the assessment of mother–infant interaction. *Child Development*, 1977, *48*, 195–203.

Bateson, M. C. Mother–infant exchanges: The epigenesis of conversational interaction. *Annals of the New York Academy of Sciences*, 1975, *263*, 101–113.

Bell, R. Q. A reinterpretation of the direction of effects in studies of socialization. *Psychological Review*, 1968, *75*, 81–95.

Bell, R. Q. Stimulus control of parent or caretaker behavior by offspring. *Developmental Psychology*, 1971, *4*, 63–72.

Blurton-Jones, N., & Woodson, R. H. Describing behavior: The ethologists' perspective. In M. E. Lamb, S. J. Suomi, & G. R. Stephenson (Eds.), *Social interaction analysis: Methodological issues*. Madison, Wisc.: The University of Wisconsin Press, 1979.

Brazelton, T. B., Koslowski, B., & Main, M. The origins of reciprocity: The early mother–infant interaction. In M. Lewis and L. A. Rosenblum (Eds.), *The effect of the infant on its caregiver*. New York: Wiley-Interscience, 1974.

Cairns, R. B. Beyond social attachment: The dynamics of interactional development. In T. Alloway, P. Pliner, & L. Krames (Eds.), *Attachment behavior*. New York: Plenum Press, 1977.

Celhoffer, L., Boukydis, C., Minde, K., & Muir, E. The DCR-II event recorder: A portable high-speed digital cassette system with direct computer access. *Behavior Research Methods and Instrumentation*, 1977, *9*, 442–446.

Cohen, L. Attention-getting and attention-holding processes of infant visual preferences. *Child Development*, 1972, *43*, 869–879.

Dawkins, R. A cheap method of recording behavioural events, for direct computer-access. *Behaviour*, 1971, *40*, 162–173.

Fitzpatrick, L. J. Automated data collection for observed events. *Behavior Research Methods and Instrumentation*, 1977, *9*, 447–451.

Fogel, A. Temporal organization in mother–infant face-to-face interaction. In H. R. Schaffer (Ed.), *Studies in mother-infant interaction*. London: Academic Press, 1977.

Freedle, R., & Lewis, M. Prelinguistic conversations. In M. Lewis, & L. Rosenblum (Eds.), *Interaction, conversation and the development of language*. New York: John Wiley & Sons, 1977.

Hays, W. L. *Statistics*. New York: Holt, Rinehart and Winston, 1963.

Kaye, K. Toward the origin of dialogue. In H. R. Schaffer (Ed.), *Studies in mother-infant interaction*. London: Academic Press, 1977.

Kendon, A. Some functions of gaze-direction in social interaction. *Acta Psychologica*, 1967, *26*, 22–63.

Lewis, M., & Freedle, R. Mother infant dyad. The cradle of meaning. In P. Pliner, L. Krames, & T. Alloway (Eds.), *Communication and affect: Language and thought*. New York: Academic Press, 1973.

Lewis, M., & Lee-Painter, S. An interactional approach to the mother–infant dyad. In M. Lewis, & L. Rosenblum (Eds.), *The effect of the infant on its caregiver*. New York: John Wiley & Sons, 1974.

Maratos, O. *The origin and development of imitation in the first six months of life*. Paper presented at the Annual Meeting of the British Psychological Society, Liverpool, April, 1973.

Moss, H. A. Sex, age, and state as determinants of mother–infant interaction. *Merrill-Palmer Quarterly*, 1967, *13*, 19–36.

Newson, J. Towards a theory of infant understanding. *Bulletin of the British Psychological Society*, 1974, *27*, 251–257.

Newson, J. An intersubjective approach to the systematic description of mother–infant interaction. In H. R. Schaffer (Ed.), *Studies in mother–infant interaction*. London: Academic Press, 1977.

Newson, J., & Newson, E. Intersubjectivity and the transmission of culture: On the social origins of symbolic functioning. *Bulletin of the British Psychological Society*, 1975, *28*, 437–446.

Papousek, H., & Papousek, M. Mothering and the cognitive head-start: Psychobiological considerations. In H. R. Schaffer (Ed.), *Studies in mother–infant interaction*. London: Academic Press, 1977.

Parke, R. D. Parent–infant interaction: Progress, paradigms, and problems. In G. P. Sackett (Ed.), *Observing behavior. Vol. 1: Theory and applications in mental retardation*. Baltimore: University Park Press, 1978.

Peery, J. C., & Stern, D. N. Mother–infant gazing during play, bottle feeding, and spoon feeding. *Journal of Psychology*, 1975, *91*, 207–213.

Rheingold, H. L. The development of social behavior in the human infant. In H. W. Stevenson (Ed.), Concept of development. *Monographs of the Society for Research in Child Development*, 1966, *31*, No. 5 (Serial No. 107), 1–17.

Rosenthal, M. K. The study of infant-environmental interaction: Some comments on trends and methodologies. *Journal of Child Psychology and Psychiatry*, 1973, *14*, 301–317.

Sameroff, A. J., & Harris, A. E. Dialectical approaches to early thought and language. In M. Bornstein, & W. Kessen (Eds.), *Psychological development from infancy: Image to intention*. Hillsdale, N.J.: Lawrence Erlbaum Associates, 1979.

Schaffer, H. R. Cognitive structure and early social behaviour. In H. R. Schaffer (Eds.), *The origins of human social relations*. London: Academic Press, 1971.

Schaffer, H. R. Early interactive development. In H. R. Schaffer (Ed.), *Studies in mother–infant interaction*. London: Academic Press, 1977.

Schaffer, H. R. Acquiring the concept of dialogue. In M. H. Bornstein, & W. Kessen (Eds.), *Psychological development from infancy: Image to intention*. Hillsdale, N.J.: Lawrence Erlbaum Associates, 1979.

Schaffer, H. R., Collis, G. M., & Parsons, G. Vocal interchange and visual regard in verbal and preverbal children. In H. R. Schaffer (Ed.), *Studies in mother–infant interaction*. London: Academic Press, 1977.

Snow, C. E. The development of conversation between mothers and babies. *Journal of Child Language*, 1977, *4*, 1–22.

Stephenson, G. R., & Roberts, T. W. The SSR System 7: A general encoding system with computerized transcription. *Behavior Research Methods and Instrumentation*, 1977, *9*, 434–441.

Stern, D. N. Mother and infant at play: The dyadic interaction involving facial, vocal, and gaze behaviors. In M. Lewis, & L. A. Rosenblum (Eds.), *The effect of the infant on its caregiver*. New York: John Wiley & Sons, 1974.

Stern, D. N. *The first relationship: Infant and mother*. London: Fontana/Open Books, 1977.

Stern, D. N., Jaffe, J., Beebe, B., & Bennett, S. L. Vocalizing in unison and in alternation: Two modes of communication within the mother–infant dyad. *Annals of the New York Academy of Science*, 1975, *263*, 89–100.

Thomas, E. A. C., & Martin, J. A. Analyses of parent–infant interaction. *Psychological Review*, 1976, *83*, 141–156.

Torgerson, L. Datamyte 900. *Behavior Research Methods and Instrumentation*, 1977, *9*, 405–406.

Trevarthen, C. Descriptive analyses of infant communicative behaviour. In H. F. Schaffer (Ed.), *Studies in mother–infant interaction*. London: Academic Press, 1977.

White, R. E. C. WRATS: A computer compatible system for automatically recording and transcribing behavioural data. *Behaviour*, 1971, *40*, 135–161.

Wright, H. F. Observational child study. In P. H. Mussen (Ed.), *Handbook of research methods in child development*. New York: John Wiley & Sons, 1960.

Yarrow, L. J., Rubenstein, J. L., & Pedersen, F. A. *Infant and environment: Early cognitive and motivational development*. New York: John Wiley & Sons, 1975.

LOCALIZATION OF FIXED OBJECTS AND EVENTS FOLLOWING OBSERVER MOVEMENT:

THE DEVELOPMENT OF POSITION CONSTANCY IN INFANCY

B. E. McKenzie and R. H. Day

ABSTRACT

Position constancy refers to the ability of individuals to localize fixed objects in space as their own positions change. The findings of earlier experiments on visual and manual search converge in suggesting that young infants are limited initially to a subject-centered spatial system in which objects are localized solely in relation to the self. In a series of experiments we show that several factors influence young infants' localization of a target when their own position, but not that of the target, changes. These include the type of training used, the availability of local and distal

Advances in the Behavioral Measurement of Children, Volume 1, pages 29–54.
ISBN: 0-89232-282-9

referents in the testing environment, and the degree of change in observer position. Earlier conclusions reflect not so much the infant's ability to coordinate notions of where objects are in space, but limitations on the effective measurement of this ability. Given the appropriate conditions of testing, it is clear that infants as young as 6 months of age are able to locate objects relative to other objects and possibly in terms of their mutual relation to the observer. Infants perceive this relation earlier for stimulus arrays in the frontal field within a space encompassing their own range of active movements. Conclusions concerning coding for spatial position have been shown to be dependent on the manner of measurement of this behavior.

I. INTRODUCTION

The spatial representation of objects or events by preschool or school age children may be investigated by a variety of methods. Children have been required, for instance, to indicate, on a map of a familiar environment, the position of selected targets, or to select which of an array of figures best represents an object rotated 180° about its vertical axis. They may be made to walk along a route during which an object is mislaid at a recognized point and asked to conduct a search for the missing object. But the child who cannot talk, walk, or draw poses a special problem for those concerned with the early development of spatial concepts. Our aim here is to evaluate some of the methods that have been used to study spatial representation in the first 18 months of human infancy. We shall be concerned with children's ability to localize fixed objects or events in space following changes in their position relative to them. While several recent reviews (Bremner, in press; Gratch, 1975) have been focused mainly on problems of spatial localization following transformation in object position, the central problem in this chapter is the perceived stability of object position over transformations in observer position, i.e., position constancy.

In most situations, adults experience little difficulty in noting the position of an object relative to other objects and to themselves, monitoring the direction and extent of their own movements, and integrating this information to locate the object from a new point in space. They are said to have used a system of objective spatial coordinates with themselves included as one of the items within the system. Imagine entering an unknown town with unnamed streets. You wish to find the police station. You discover that it is situated midway between the sea front on your left and a prominent cathedral on your right. When you next visit the town, entering at a point opposite to that of the first occasion, the police station may be readily found providing that you note the position of the landmarks relative to yourself, keep track of your own movements, and update the landmark positions relative to yourself by keeping the cathedral on your left and the sea front on your right. Imagine, however, that you enter the town at night and no landmarks are visible. You are then obliged to use a self-referent system in which knowledge of your own position is defined in terms of the direction and extent of the movements you have made (e.g., turn right, go straight ahead, turn left). Young infants are thought to be limited to the use of such self-referent systems, with the location of objects or events defined only in relation to some subjective framework. The developmental problem of how this subjective or self-referent system becomes transformed into an objective or allocentric system has been the central issue of several studies.

In reviewing empirical work bearing on this problem, we became aware of the sensitivity of infants to variation in the kind of spatial information provided. We will argue that, from an early age, a variety of systems of spatial representation is available and that the current view that young infants can use only an egocentric spatial reference system is more a reflection of methods of assessment than of the young child's repertoire of reference systems. We wish to emphasize the intimate dependence of performance on the type and the richness of spatial information that is available. The major developmental problem is not the transformation of a self-referent into an objective reference system, but rather the specification of the conditions that promote the use of one or several different systems.

Since a prerequisite for an understanding of object position is that objects should be perceived as possessing surfaces and boundaries distinct from those of their surroundings and of other adjacent or occluding objects, we shall briefly review the question of object perception and the stability of this perception over time and changing representations at the sense organs. The characteristics of various kinds of spatial reference systems will be outlined as a standard against which to compare infants' coordination of notions of where objects are in relation to themselves and other objects. These findings are derived mainly from two sources: eye–head coordination during visual search following change in observer position, and visual–manual coordination during manual search following change in observer position. The results of our own experiments will be compared with the findings derived from these two sources. We conclude that infants as young as 6 months are not restricted to the use of systems that define object position only in relation to themselves. Infants apprehend their own position and the position of objects more readily than has been suggested previously. We base this conclusion on our finding that infants take into account the direction and extent of their own movements in locating a target from a new point in space. Our knowledge and interpretation of the kinds of spatial reference systems used by infants is closely tied to the nature of the experimental conditions provided for its assessment.

II.   DO INFANTS PERCEIVE OBJECTS?

That objects appear separate from background is a basic prerequisite for spatial organization. Unless the sensory array is segregated into units that have internal coherence and boundaries of lasting stability there can be no spatial organization, since the elements to be organized would be brief, fluctuating, sensory impressions. The concept of an organized space is meaningless unless it is composed of objects of some permanence. Do infants partition sensory impressions into units that correspond in some way to what adults perceive as objects? Is a cup, for instance, perceived as separate from the table on which it rests? Does it maintain its form, size, color, and solidity despite variation in its distance and orientation relative to the observer, its ambient lighting, and its movement from one position to another? If a bottle is interposed between the cup and the observer so that the boundaries and surfaces of the cup are partially occluded, are the two objects perceived as separate and distinct or is there a perceptual fusion of forms?

Evidence that neonatal and young infants perceive three-dimensional objects separately from their background comes from observations of visual following and manual reaching. Visual-following studies (Harris, Cassel, & Bamborough, 1974) have revealed differences in head–eye movements when an object moves relative to a stationary background, when the background moves relative to a stationary object, and when both background and object move. It is the relative motion of an object against a stationary background that promotes organized visual following, thereby indicating location of the object with respect to a spatial framework. Neonatal reaching for objects also clearly implies a perceptual separation of surfaces. Amiel-Tison and Grenier (1980) provide a particularly striking example of reaching and grasping in an infant of 17 days. In the course of a research program evaluating the neurological status of newborns, they describe a sequence of advanced motor behavior termed ''motricité liberée.'' This motor behavior, thought to be characteristic of older infants, was induced in newborns when they were firmly supported in a manner that freed them from the necessity of executing counterbalancing movements of the extremities associated with poor control of head position. Other, more systematic, studies of reaching suggest that this behavior is not restricted to these particular seated postures. Bower, Broughton, and Moore (1970) suggest that not only do newborn infants reach in the direction of objects, but they also show distress when anticipated tactile confirmation does not eventuate when reaching for virtual objects. Although there are several alternative explanations of this latter finding (Lockman & Ashmead, in press), it now seems clear that very young infants reach toward objects relatively accurately (McDonnell, 1979; Provine & Westerman, 1979; von Hofsten, 1977, 1979, 1980) and the reaching is adapted to object distance (Field, 1976) and to size (Bruner & Koslowski, 1972). Since visual following and reaching are controlled by the movement and position of objects, we conclude that the latter are perceived as separate from background.

Are object boundaries distinguished from those of adjacent objects or from those that are interposed between the observer and a target object? The occlusion of one object by another does not destroy adult perception of the unity and integrity of the partially hidden object. Is this ''amodal completion'' (Kanizsa, 1979) a feature also of object perception in infancy?

This problem has recently been investigated by Spelke (1980). This research clearly illustrates a method frequently employed in the study of infant perception. It will therefore be described in some detail. Spelke presented a group of 4-month-old infants with a vertical, black, wooden rod placed behind a tan-colored wooden block. Two control groups of infants were also included in the design: One group viewed the same rod in front of the block and the other two shorter rods separated by a gap arranged in front of the block. These displays were presented on successive trials until a criterion of habituation of looking time was achieved for each infant. In test trials subjects were presented with two displays in succession: a complete rod and a broken rod. Since a well-established finding in infant research is an increment in visual fixation on configurations that are perceived to be novel, it was expected that infants should look longer at the broken rod if they had perceived the occluded rod as being continuous. Contrariwise they should look longer at the complete rod if they had perceived the occluded one as discontinuous. The control groups responded clearly, looking longer at the display they had not previously seen. The experimental group looked equally at each display. Marked recovery to the discontinuous rod was not evident, thus implying that occlusion was registered. At the same time, since differential recovery to the discontinuous rod failed to occur, it cannot be said that the two ends were seen as continuous, even although in alignment and of the same color and texture. The Gestalt principles of similarity and good continuation thus appear not to be effective for 4-month-old infants when looking at stationary objects. More interestingly, further experiments showed that if the partially hidden rod were moved back and forth behind the block without ever becoming totally visible, the results were quite different. The experimental group looked longer on test trials at the broken rod, whereas a control group, having been habituated to another display and then shown the two test displays, looked equally at both. Spelke (1980) has found that the Gestalt principle of common fate obtains with young infants, even when the parts are dissimilar in color, texture, and alignment. Although adults rely on texture, color, alignment, and common movement to infer completeness of an object that is partially visible, young infants depend predominantly on common movement. Taken together with earlier findings that indicate the significance of movement in infant perception (Gibson, Owsley, & Johnston, 1978; McKenzie & Day, 1976; Ruff, 1980), this outcome strongly suggests that our estimates of perceptual capacities in infancy may need to be modified upon further investigation with moving three-dimensional objects. So far, mainly static two-dimensional patterns have been used as stimulus objects.

Given an array that is structured into surfaces and edges and sometimes perceived as continuous despite partial occlusion, we can ask whether these units maintain their identity despite variation in viewing conditions. The abstraction of invariant features by young infants has recently been reviewed by several authors (Cohen, De Loache, & Strauss, 1979; Day & McKenzie, 1977; Ruff, 1980, in press). Although there are many qualities of objects that have not yet been investigated, there is now substantial agreement that shape retains its constancy from at least 3 months (Caron, Caron, & Carlson, 1979), size from at least 4 months (Day & McKenzie, 1981), substance rigidity–elasticity from 3 months (Gibson, Owsley, Walker, & Megaw-Nyce, 1979; Walker, Owsley, Megaw-Nyce, Gibson, & Bahrick, 1980), and object motion from 5 months (Gibson, Owsley, & Johnston, 1978). Here we will be mainly concerned with constancy of perceived object position. The experimental findings related to this are reviewed in Sections IV, V, and VI.

III. FRAMES OF SPATIAL REFERENCE

There is a confusing array of terms in the literature describing the development of spatial reference systems. For the most part a dichotomous terminology has been used. This contrasts an egocentric, subject- or self-referent system with an objective, allocentric or geocentric system. Controversy has centered mainly on whether infants can or cannot take into account cues about spatial location other than those relating directly to their own body. The term "egocentric" is sometimes used in a spatial sense to define position relative to the self, but at other times it carries additional theoretical meaning in relation to Piagetian views of the concept of the object, where object position is defined by the infant's action.

A further complication is that cues other than self-referent ones may be referred to as external or object-referent. Lloyd, Sinha, and Freeman (1981) point out that cavalier treatment has generally been given to this kind of spatial information and they emphasize the particular significance of local cues, meaning the spatial relations entered into by the object at the point of search. An object may be, for example, in a container on a patterned background, or under a blue rather than a yellow cover. These spatial relations as well as the object's relation to more distant referents, such as the room frame, need to be considered.

Following O'Keefe and Nadel (1979), we distinguish between orientation and guidance systems of spatial reference. While orientation systems involve an egocentric framework to specify location or direction, guidance systems involve objects or cues in the environment as landmarks that should be approached or maintained at a fixed distance. We shall use the terms (a) *simple self-referent* to refer to spatial orientation systems of the type "on the left;" (b) *complex self-referent* to refer to spatial orientation systems involving positions relative to the self and to other objects, e.g., "second on the left;" (c) *local-guidance referent* to refer to cues at the point of hiding or of disappearance, e.g., the blue color of the cover under which an object is hidden; and (d) *distal-guidance referent* to refer to landmark cues not immediately associated with the object or event position, e.g., the yellow door of the laboratory.

In Sections IV, V, and VI we shall review the evidence relating to spatial reference systems derived from visual search for an object or event; in Section VII, those derived from manual search for an object. These reviews will be restricted to situations in which the object or event remains fixed while the infant moves. This is not to imply that other situations do not reveal characteristics of the spatial reference systems used by infants. However, our main interest is in the capacity to detect stability of environmental characteristics. We focus in this discussion on position constancy, that is, the perceived fixity of an object or event in space despite observer movement.

IV. VISUAL SEARCH FOR AN OBJECT OR EVENT

While visual following of a moving object is operative from birth, the ability to locate a stationary object when the observer moves from one point in space to another may be a much later development. The findings of several studies converge to suggest that young infants fail to differentiate self-movement from environmental stability. We shall review three relevant studies before describing our own experiments in the following section. The dependent variable throughout is the direction of visual looking following change in observer position. The subject is not required to search manually for the object as in the studies reviewed in Section VII. Infants first learn that an interesting object or event will appear at a particular place. The question at issue is whether this place can be relocated after the subject's position relative to it has changed.

Acredolo (1978) concludes that a simple self-referent spatial reference system becomes transformed into an objective reference system and that the age at which this transformation occurs depends on the salience of the cues surrounding the event (Acredolo & Evans, 1980). In a longitudinal study, subjects were tested at 6, 11, and 16 months of age. They learned to expect the appearance of a person at one of two identical but opposite windows. This event was always in a fixed position relative to the subjects, either on their right or left, and for half the subjects the critical window was marked by a distinctive local referent, a yellow star. A sound signal preceded the appearance of the person by a standard interval. After infants had anticipated this event, they were rotated through 180°, the signal was again given, and the direction of first visual orientation was noted. To locate the window that was previously on their right, they now had to turn to their left and vice versa. Only at 16 months of age did infants take cognizance of their rotation through 180° and turn reliably toward the true location of the event. Their performance was independent of the presence of the local referent. At 6 months, with or without this referent, infants oriented in the same direction as that prior to rotation. At 11 months, localization was somewhat improved when a distinctive cue marked the position of the event. In order to turn toward this position, infants had to coordinate the transformation produced by their movement with the original information concerning the event's location relative to themselves. It is interesting that at 11 months, but not at 6 months, the local-guidance referent aided localization but was insufficient for reliable specification of position. To examine further the role of local referents, Acredolo and Evans

(1980) studied the direction of looking after rotation when the distinctiveness and the location of landmarks were varied. In the absence of local referents, all infants responded in a self-referent fashion. However, the addition of a panel of flashing lights around the target window and stripes on its background wall enabled 9- and 11-month-old infants to orient correctly, while 6-month-old infants fluctuated in looking between the target and nontarget windows. No group looked consistently toward the true location of the event after rotation when the landmark was associated with the nontarget rather than the target window.

These results led Acredolo (1981) to conclude that there was a developmental sequence from responses guided by self-referents to those guided by external referents. When the event occurs, for example, on the right, younger infants continue to orient to their right after rotation, although the spatial array relative to themselves is reversed. The interpretation of this behavior is not unambiguous. Infants may turn in this direction because they can use only their body as a referent for spatial orientation. Alternatively, they may have learned that turning their heads to the right produces the event. When infants turn to the objective position after rotation, we can conclude that the place, and not the particular response, controls their behavior; but if repetition of the response—turning right—occurs, the infant might be simply repeating a response that has previously been reinforced. This possibility has been recently acknowledged by Acredolo (1981).

A further question concerns the nature of the spatial cues that were available. Training and testing were conducted in an enclosure free of distal referents excepting the two windows and the mother. The windows were sometimes marked by local referents, either a yellow star or stripes and flashing lights. The more distinctive the cue at the target window, the greater the number of infants who oriented toward it on test trials. Yet even the most distinctive cues did not ensure objective responding. These referents were located only at one or the other window. In the laboratory situation used by Acredolo (1978) and Acredolo and Evans (1980), the kinds of spatial cues normally used to find a way through an environment were radically reduced, although a distal cue, not recognized by the experimenters, was potentially available. Infants were tested with the mother located behind them, and moving so as to maintain this position after rotation. Presson and Ihrig (1980) tested 9-month-old infants in a similar situation with the mother moving when the subject moved, but for another group the mother maintained a stable position throughout training and testing. The proportion of correct responses was notably higher in the latter group. This outcome lends support to the conclusion that infants are capable of using other than simple orientation cues and, in some circumstances, are able to make use of guidance cues located at places other than the target or nontarget window. Before concluding that infants are initially limited to a self-referent system of spatial localization, their performance needs to be compared under a range of conditions. It is thus appropriate to examine behavior when local and distal referents are stable, salient, and located in a variety of positions.

Besides the ambiguity associated with interpretation of the dependent variable and the paucity of available spatial cues, yet another factor must be taken into consideration: the type and extent of the change in observer position. Rotation through 180° involves a reversal of the visual field. A reduced extent of change in observer position was used by Rieser (1979). Subjects aged 6 months were first trained to look toward one of four doors to see a display, and then tested from a new position 90° from the training position while either supine or seated and tilted laterally. No external referents were available in the testing situation apart from the presence or absence of different patterns on some of the doors. Subjects responded egocentrically when no local referent was available. Objective responses to the true location were observed when gravity cues were present and in some conditions involving local referents. On the whole, the pattern of results indicated that 6-month-old infants could sometimes guide their search by referring to visible landmarks, but that an egocentric code was used predominantly. When the extent of change in observer position is reduced, infants as young as 6 months of age are able to respond correctly under some circumstances. However, as in the experiments discussed earlier, repetition of the response that was reinforced prior to the change in position cannot be excluded. Furthermore, only guidance cues associated with possible target areas were provided.

Cornell and Heth (1979) sought to disentangle the role of place and response cues in spatial localization. In their first experiment they tested infants aged 4, 8, and 12 months in an environment rich in distal referents such as doors, windows, and pictures on the wall. For some infants, a series of novel slides was presented on their right while a single slide was presented repeatedly on their left; for others, the sides of novel and constant stimuli were reversed. All infants readily learned to turn 90° to the point where novel visual stimuli were presented. They were then rotated through 180°. Only responses in the initial trials after rotation are of interest here. The youngest group turned in the same direction as they had turned prior to rotation, whereas the two older groups turned equally often to the place of familiar or of novel stimulation. Thus no group relied primarily on place cues. Clearly the youngest group relied on response cues. The purpose of a second experiment was to examine the ability of subjects of different ages to learn to turn toward the novel stimuli under different experimental conditions. The conditions were (a) novel stimuli always at the same objective location with the infants faced in different directions so that they sometimes had to turn right and sometimes left to view them; (b) infants faced in different directions but the objective location of the novel stimuli varied so that it was always in a constant direction relative to them, either on their right or left; and (c) infants faced in one direction and the novel stimuli remained at the one objective location and thus in a constant position relative to them. The last condition was essentially the same as the training condition in the first experiment except that subjects were rotated through 360° in between trials in order to control for the movement that was necessary in the other conditions. The subjects were aged 4, 8, 12, and 16 months. There was clear evidence of successful response acquisition in conditions b and c but not in condition a. All age groups were able to acquire the discrimination when they had to turn in a constant egocentric direction, but none succeeded when they had to turn in different directions to the same objective location. It is conceivable that the older groups (12 and 16 months) would have succeeded had more training trials been allowed. Nevertheless, it is clear that while infants aged from 4 to 16 months can use response cues equally efficiently in such a learning task, only older infants sometimes use place cues, and then only after extensive training. Cornell and Heth (1979) concluded that older infants can use a variety of spatial cues but that younger infants cannot.

Several conclusions emerge from this review:

First, behavior following a change in subject position may not be independent of earlier training. Moreover, *what* has been learned may differ between age groups. Repetition of the response that has been reinforced in training may have little relevance to the infant's notions of spatial localization. Training effects can be estimated by deliberate manipulation, as in the second experiment of Cornell and Heth (1979). However, since there may be differences in rate of learning within and between age groups, the use of a criterion of learning rather than a fixed number of trials is preferable. Alternatively, the training phase may be eliminated, as in some studies using manual search.

Second, it has been clearly shown that behavior varies with the distinctiveness of local cues. The role of distal cues is less clear. Infants may use cues that are not restricted to either the objective position or the position to which the infant would orient if using only self-referent cues. The findings of Presson and Ihrig (1980) suggest that distal cues such as the position of the mother may be an aid to objective responding if they are near, salient, and stable.

Finally, while it appears that cues associated with place are difficult for young infants, this conclusion is based on studies that have involved an extreme change in observer position. Rotation through 180° necessarily involves a complete reversal of the visual array: Objects that were on the left are now on the right and vice versa. Rieser's (1979) results suggest that, after rotation through smaller angles, young infants have some ability to guide visual search by reference to visible landmarks.

V. SOME RECENT EXPERIMENTS[1]

We report here five experiments involving adaptation of the conditions under which object localization is assessed. The first two were similar to those of Acredolo (1978) and involved rotation of the subjects through 180°. However the procedure was modified in an attempt to render the response less ambiguous. This was achieved by incorporating training of anticipatory responses to *both* side windows prior to testing in order to rule out the possibility that a particular response was repeated because it had previously been reinforced. This procedure was also used in the final three experiments. These were primarily concerned with the effect of the extent of change in observer position, with and without distinctive local referents. In each experiment the target, test, and training positions were all contained in the frontal visual field, within the area in which infants who are not yet crawling can engage in active interchange with their surroundings.

Localization with Control for Response Reinforcement

It seems clear that older infants have usually responded to place information since they orient to a place following a transformation in their own position relative to it. However, young infants could have learned that a head turn to the right (or left) is instrumental in producing the occurrence of the event. Under these circumstances, there would be no reason to expect that they should change their direction of turn when they are faced in a different direction. We therefore modified our procedure so that responses to both the left and the right were acquired prior to testing. Consequently, after a change in position, the responses were equivalent in terms of reinforcement history. Our subjects were required to learn a conditional discrimination problem, viz., when the experimenter went out of sight to the infant's right, she would reappear at the right window; when she went out of sight to the infant's left, she would reappear at the left window. After the acquisition of anticipatory responses in both directions, the experimenter disappeared to the right or to the left, the infant was rotated, and the direction of the first visual orientation was observed. While the experimental logic was similar to that of Acredolo, the procedure differed in four ways. First, rather than a simple discrimination, subjects had to learn a conditional discrimination. Second, the discriminative stimulus was presented prior to, rather than after, rotation. Third, the windows were made distinctively different by the color of the curtains rather than by added patterns. Fourth, infants were seated on their mother's lap. While these modifications might have made the task more difficult, they rendered the results more clearly interpretable. In the first experiment only infants aged between 12 and 14 months were included.

Complete data records were obtained from 20 infants: 10 aged 12 months and 10 aged 14 months. Subjects were tested individually inside a plain wooden enclosure 3 m long and 2 m wide. The side walls were 1.8 m high, each with a .5 × .45-m window centrally positioned with the lower edge 1.3 m from the floor. The windows were curtained with unpatterned material, one in red, the other in blue. The end walls were 1.3 cm high so that the head and shoulders of the experimenter were visible from the center of the enclosure. Babies were seated on their mother's lap on a chair in the middle of the enclosure, with their eyes at midwindow level. Two video cameras were fixed to the metal frame of the enclosure, one in the center of each end wall, at a height of 1.8 m. Infant behavior was videotaped for later scoring. Apart from the inside wooden walls of the enclosure, the video cameras, and the curtained windows, infants could see the plain white walls of the laboratory and two strips of fluorescent ceiling lights that were parallel to the side walls and positioned symmetrically above. One experimenter acted as the discriminative stimulus and reinforcer, and another monitored the experimental sessions from an adjacent control room. The experimental arrangement is pictured in Figure 1.

Training began with the experimenter attracting the subject's attention from the center of one of the end walls. She then walked to the right or to the left, making sure that infants visually followed her movement. Three seconds after reaching the corner of the enclosure she appeared at the nearer window. In the first stage of training, these trials were repeated to one side until the infant anticipated the experimenter's appearance on two consecutive trials by turning to look at the appropriate window before the experimenter appeared. Mothers were instructed to rotate the chair—sometimes to the right, sometimes to the left—between trials to accustom the infant to the rotatory movement that would later occur in the test trials. In the second stage of training, trials to the other side were given until two successive anticipations were again achieved. The third stage of training, with side of trial randomized, continued until there were two successive anticipations, one for each side.

The final experimental phase consisted of two test and two control trials, each of 9-sec duration. In the test trials the experimenter walked out of sight once in each direction and did not reappear. The subject was rotated through 180° after

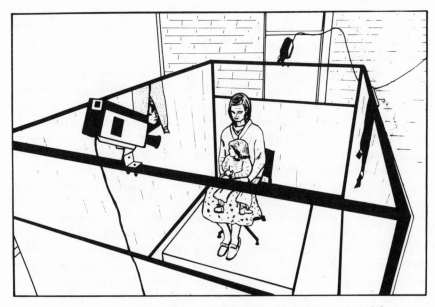

Figure 1.   Experimental arrangement for Experiments 1 and 2.
(See text for details.)

the experimenter was out of view. The direction and duration of visual fixation were observed. Control trials were the same except that the subject was not rotated. These control trials were included as a check on retention of responses learned during training. Curtain color, side of first training, direction in which the infant faced, direction of rotation on test and control trials, and order of test and control trials were all counterbalanced.

Five analyses of the data were made. The first was concerned with whether there were age differences in the attainment of the conditional discrimination as measured by the number of trials to reach criterion at each stage of training; the second, with whether rotation of the subject influenced the direction of first fixation. In the latter analysis, the number of infants looking first to the target window on test and control trials was compared. The third analysis was concerned with whether the number of infants responding correctly on test trials differed from chance expectation. The difference between test and control trials, and performance on test trials were examined in the fourth and fifth analyses, with duration of looking as the dependent variable.

The mean number of trials to criterion in each of the three stages of training for the two subject groups is given in Table 1. Analysis of variance with age groups (12 and 14 months) as a between-subjects factor and stage of training (Stages 1, 2, and 3) as a within-subjects factor showed that there was no difference between the groups in the rate at which the discriminative responses were acquired. Despite the apparent difficulty of the conditional discrimination task, the infants reached criterion in fewer trials than the number provided by Cornell and Heth (1979) in a simple discrimination task.

The direction in which infants looked on trials following their change in position was the matter of primary interest. The number of subjects looking first at the correct and the incorrect window is given in Table 2 for test and control trials.

To examine the effect of the change in subject position, we compared the number of infants looking first to the correct window on test and control trials. For each age group these numbers did not differ (Wilcoxon matched-pairs signed-rank test). We then checked whether the number of infants responding correctly on test trials differed from chance expectation on the basis of the binomial distribution. For neither age group was this so.

The duration of looking toward the correct and incorrect window for each

Table 1. The Mean Number of Trials to Criterion for Each Age Group During Training in Experiment 1

Group	Stage 1	Stage 2	Stage 3
12 months	4.6	3.4	5.2
14 months	3.1	2.9	2.8

Table 2.   The Number of Infants Looking First to the Correct and the
Incorrect Window on Test and Control Trials, Experiment 1

	Test 1		Test 2		Control 1		Control 2	
Group	Correct	Incorrect	Correct	Incorrect	Correct	Incorrect	Correct	Incorrect
12 months (n = 10)	7	1	4	1	8	2	7	0
14 months (n = 10)	7	0	8	1	8	0	8	1

group during test and control trials was then considered and is summarized in
Table 3. The duration of looking at the correct window was expressed as a
proportion of the total possible looking time (18 sec). These proportions were
transformed by means of an arcsin transformation. An analysis of variance
showed no difference in the duration of looking at the correct window between
test and control trials. Infants of both ages looked at the correct window for the
same duration, whether rotated or not. On test trials, subjects looked longer at
the correct window, $F(1,18) = 12.98$, $p < .01$. Neither the main effect for age
nor the interaction proved to be significant.

Thus, subjects in both age groups acquired the conditional discrimination
during training. Although they looked longer at the correct than the incorrect
window following rotation, the number of infants looking first to the correct
window did not differ from chance expectation.

Localization with Increased Distinctiveness of the Local Referent

In order to establish whether more distinctive local referents would enhance
performance, we tested another subject sample. The windows were curtained in

Table 3.   The Mean Duration of Fixation (sec) for Each Group in Test and
Control Trials, Experiment 1

	Test trials		Control trials	
Group	Correct	Incorrect	Correct	Incorrect
12 months				
Trial 1	1.8	0.3	2.3	0.6
Trial 2	0.9	0.3	1.3	0.7
14 months				
Trial 1	2.0	0.5	3.3	0.6
Trial 2	1.6	0.5	2.6	0.2

Table 4. The Mean Number of Trials to Criterion for Each Age Group
During Training in Experiment 2

Group	Stage 1	Stage 2	Stage 3
10 months	3.4	3.2	2.7
12 months	2.1	3.5	3.1

red and blue material as in the preceding study. As well, one side wall was
papered in green and white stripes and the other in a yellow irregular pattern on a
purple background. There were 10 infants aged 10 months and 10 aged 12
months. The training and testing procedures were the same as those described for
the first experiment.

The number of trials to criterion is given in Table 4. The subject groups did not
differ at any stage of training. The number of infants looking first at the correct
and incorrect windows on test and control trials is given in Table 5. Again, while
there was no difference in the performance of either age group on the test and
control trials, the number of infants looking first toward the correct window on
test trials did not exceed chance expectation.

The duration of looking is presented in Table 6. The same analysis as in the
preceding experiment showed no significant differences between the times spent
looking at the correct window during test and control trials. For test trials there
was no difference in the proportion of time fixating the correct and incorrect
window.

Thus, in both experiments infants performed similarly on test and control
trials; the number of infants looking first to the correct window and the duration
of looking at the correct window was not significantly affected by the change in
their position. However the number of infants looking first toward the correct
window after rotation did not exceed chance expectation for any age group, i.e.,
10, 12, and 14 months. The addition of distinctive local referents had little
effect. Nevertheless, the number of infants looking toward the correct window

Table 5. The Number of Subjects Looking First at the Correct and the
Incorrect Windows in Test and Control Trials, Experiment 2

Group	Test 1 Correct	Test 1 Incorrect	Test 2 Correct	Test 2 Incorrect	Control 1 Correct	Control 1 Incorrect	Control 2 Correct	Control 2 Incorrect
10 months (n = 10)	7	3	6	2	8	2	7	3
12 months (n = 10)	6	4	5	2	8	0	8	0

Table 6.   The Mean Duration of Fixation for Each Group in Test and Control
Trials, Experiment 2

	Test trials		Control trials	
Group	Correct	Incorrect	Correct	Incorrect
10 months				
Trial 1	2.8	1.8	2.7	0.8
Trial 2	1.8	1.0	2.1	1.0
12 months				
Trial 1	1.5	1.8	2.7	0.7
Trial 2	1.3	1.3	2.8	0.2

was at least equivalent to that reported in the studies reviewed above involving
reinforcement of one particular response during training.

If infants were able only to localize objects or events with reference to their
own body, chance responding would have been predicted on test trials following
rotation. That another frame of reference may have been utilized is suggested by
the similarity of performance on test and control trials.

Localization in the Frontal Visual Field

The extent of change in subject position was reduced from a rotation through
180° to a maximum rotation through 60° to either side of the target in two
experiments (Experiments 3 and 4) and 90° to either side in a third (Experiment
5). In order to avoid the problem of response perseveration, more than one
direction of response was reinforced during training but only one target position
was involved. Infants were trained to look toward the fixed target position when
it was on their left and when it was on their right. After achieving a criterion of
correct anticipation from these two training positions, the direction and duration
of looking from a third, novel orientation were tested. We reasoned that if infants
should look toward the target position when their position relative to it had
changed and they had had no prior training from this new position, they must be
using cues specifying target position that are not exclusively body centered.

We tested subjects younger than those in Experiments 1 and 2 since the task
was one of simple, rather than conditional, discrimination. As noted earlier,
Rieser (1979) found that 6-month-old infants could orient correctly under certain
conditions when their change in position was 90°. In Experiment 3, complete
records were obtained for 15 6-month-old and 15 8-month-old infants. The
experimental arrangement is shown schematically in Figure 2.

Infants were seated on their mother's lap at the center of a semicircular
enclosure, 2 m in diameter and 1.3 m high. The target event, the experimenter
playing peek-a-boo with the subject, took place at *one* of three possible positions;

throughout training and testing, it was at the same position for any one subject. Its position was marked by a white ball decorated with a schematic face and hanging just below the top of the enclosure. For each subject, three other positions were marked by dangling balls of different colors: one ball indicated the first training position; the second, the second training position; and the third, the novel test position. Each ball was suspended from the perimeter of the enclosure at one of five positions 30° apart (see Figure 2).

Mothers were asked to face toward one of the colored balls, either 30° or 60° to the right or to the left of the target position. This was the starting point for the first training phase. The ball that was immediately ahead was jiggled up and down by an experimenter hidden from view behind the enclosure. Movement of the ball ceased as soon as the infant looked at it, and 2 sec later the experimenter appeared above the wall of the enclosure at the target position. After infants had anticipated this event by looking toward it before the end of the 2-sec period on two successive occasions, mothers were asked to face toward another differently colored ball, 30° or 60° from the target position, but on the opposite side of the target from that of first training. This was the starting point for the second training phase. Trials continued until two successive correct anticipations occurred. The third phase of training was then begun: The two starting points that had previously been used were selected randomly and training proceeded until the infant achieved four successive correct anticipations. After these three phases

Figure 2.   Experimental arrangement for Experiments 3 and 4.
(See text for details.)

of training, there were two test trials followed by two control trials. In the test trials, the mother faced toward the remaining ball that had not been used during training trials. After the infant had looked at the moving ball it was made stationary, and the infant's direction and duration of looking were observed for the next 5 sec. In the control trials, also of 5-sec duration, the retention of the correct direction of looking from each of the two training positions was measured. The position of the target (one of the three intermediate positions), the starting point for the first and second training phases (30° or 60° to the right or left of the target), and the color of the balls indicating training and test positions (red, blue, and green) were counterbalanced.

Infant behavior throughout was recorded by two video cameras. One was situated at the target position, and the other was placed so that direction of gaze from the training and test positions was visible to the experimenter on the monitor located outside the enclosure.

The mean number of trials to criterion in each phase of training for each age group are shown in Table 7. Both age groups readily reached criterion for each phase of training and the course of training did not differ between age groups. Our primary interest was where infants first looked following their change in position on test trials. We counted the number of infants whose first fixation was toward the target position on test and control trials. These results are given in Table 8. There was no significant difference between the number of infants whose first fixation was to the target position on test and control trials. Although memory for the responses acquired during the training phase was not perfect, most subjects looked in the appropriate direction and the standard of performance was not affected by the change to a novel position. Binomial tests were used to assess whether the number of infants looking first at the target on each of the test trials exceeded chance expectation. Since there were three possible balls to fixate, the white target ball and the two colored training balls, it was considered that there was a probability of .33 of looking first to the target. For each group on each test trial, performance was greater than might be expected by chance, $p < .01$ in each instance.

The duration of fixation on the target position over the two test trials and the two control trials was summed and expressed as a proportion of the total possible looking time of 10 sec. For test trials the mean proportions for the 6- and 8-

Table 7. The Mean Number of Trials to Criterion During Training for Each Age Group, Experiment 3

	Phase 1	Phase 2	Phase 3
6 months	5.1	5.3	7.1
8 months	4.3	3.8	6.1

Table 8. The Number of Infants in Each Age Group Whose First Fixation Was at the Target Position in Test and Control Trials, Experiment 3

	Test trials		Control trials	
	1	*2*	*1*	*2*
6 months	10	11	11	11
8 months	11	12	14	13

month group were .28 and .48, respectively, and for control trials, .25 and .40. Analysis of variance following an arcsin transformation of these proportions showed that the older infants persisted longer in looking at the target position, $F(1,28) = 9.65$, $p < .01$. Whereas the young infants, like the older ones, looked first toward the target position, they fixated on that position for a shorter period.

Our data show that infants as young as 6 months of age may be trained to localize a target from two different starting points. Following this training and without prior reinforcement, they were able to locate the target despite a change in their position relative to it. Age differences were not pronounced, except that older infants persisted longer in looking toward the target. These results suggest that infants are able to register the place of a target and monitor the direction and extent of their own movements so that the target can be located from a different position. In these terms, position constancy appears to be present at an earlier age than has been previously reported.

Our investigation differs from earlier ones in two major ways. The first is the form of training and the second is the extent of change in observer position. In regard to the first, we wished to avoid the priming of one specific response that might be simply repeated during testing. Turning to the right and to the left were therefore reinforced during the training phase. From this training, infants abstracted a position in space that is not defined by means of a simple self-referent hypothesis, e.g., "on the right." Cornell and Heth (1979) however, found that infants from 4 to 16 months were unable to acquire a discriminative response to place. Their subjects did not learn to turn to the source of novel stimulation when it was always in the one objective location and the infant was faced in different directions. But it is to be noted that the change in subject position was 180°. Our results lead to the prediction that a place response could have been acquired had the extent of change in subject position been reduced.

In order to examine further the effect of our training procedure, we tabulated the direction of first fixation on the first and second trials of the second training phase. Subjects had already learned to anticipate the target from a starting point 30° or 60° to the right or left of the target. They were then induced to fixate the moving ball on the opposite side of the target—for some subjects, at the same degree of eccentricity; for others, at a different degree of eccentricity. They were allowed 2 sec in which to respond. The number of 6-month-old infants looking first toward the target on the first and second trials of the second training phase was 7 and 8, and for 8-month-old infants, 11 and 10, respectively. For 8-month-old infants, anticipation of the target position was as accurate after training from one starting point as it was after extended training. The performance of younger infants, however, was improved by further training. At least for 8-month-old infants, the difference in training procedure would seem not to be the major variable accounting for the difference between our findings and those of others.

The second and more important difference was in the extent of change in subject position between training and test trials. Apart from the experiment of Rieser (1979), earlier studies involved turning the subject through 180°, whereas we turned subjects through a maximum of 60° to either side of the target. The target, training, and test positions in our experiment were in front of the body, with the fixed target sometimes on the subject's right and sometimes on the left. It seems feasible that the mapping of objects into objective space may well occur first for those within a limited frontal field, possibly extending later to include more peripheral objects and, later still, to the space behind the subject.

Localization Without a Distinctive Local Referent

As in Acredolo's studies, our event was marked by a distinctive local referent, a white ball decorated with a schematic face. Is it possible that its color or pattern was detected in the peripheral field and subjects simply searched for it? Although Acredolo and Evans (1980) had shown that even more distinctive cues were not sufficient to ensure target localization, we decided to examine further the importance of distinctive local referents. An additional and comparable group of 15 8-month-old infants was tested in Experiment 4. The conditions of training and testing were the same as in Experiment 3, except that identical unpatterned, white balls indicated target, test, and training positions so that no distinctive local referent was available. During training, the mean number of trials to criterion for the first, second and third stages were 6.1, 2.6, and 6.0, respectively. It is worth noting that the total number of trials to reach the final criterion did not differ for the two groups of 8-month-old infants in Experiments 3 and 4, $t(28) <$ 1. As in Experiment 3, the number of infants fixating first on the target position in test and control trials was not different. The number of infants locating the target was 10 and 13 on the test trials, and 11 and 10 on the control trials. In each instance, performance exceeded chance expectation. The direction of looking in the second phase of training was compellingly similar to that obtained with colored markers, 11 infants responding correctly on the first trial and 12 on the second. The mean proportional duration of fixation on target during test trials was .36, and during control trials, .36. Overall, the elimination of a distinctive local referent made remarkably little difference to the outcome.

Localization in an Extended Frontal Field

In order to examine the effect of increasing the extent of the change in position between training and test phases, we adapted our apparatus for Experiment 5 so that infants were centered in a circular enclosure. Eight identical white balls were suspended from the top of the enclosure at equally spaced intervals. Our procedure was similar to that of the preceding experiments, except that the eight balls remained in position throughout training and testing. Thus the target ball was not, as earlier, the only ball that did not move. The order of test and control trials in the final phase was counterbalanced, and the maximum change in position of the subject between training and test trials was extended to 90° on either side of the target. Fifteen comparable 8-month-old infants completed the experiment. The mean number of trials to reach criterion in phases 1, 2, and 3 of training were 5.0, 3.1, and 5.7, respectively. The number of infants directing their first fixation to the target on the two test trials was 10 and 8, and on the two control trials, 11 and 9, respectively. From the first and second trials of the second training phase, these frequencies were 10 and 11. The mean proportional duration of looking at the target on test trials was .31, and on control trials, .31. Thus, although infants acquired the correct anticipations during training, their performance on test trials was somewhat inferior to that of the earlier experiments. We have yet to determine whether this was due to the increased position change or to other experimental modifications.

VI. VISUAL SEARCH AS AN INDEX OF SPATIAL LOCALIZATION

Transformation in observer position changes the relation between the object and the observer, but not the relation between the object and its surrounding environment. That the young infant first relies on an orientation system where object position is defined in relation to the self, and later relies on a guidance system where object position is defined in relation to other objects has been supported by the findings of Acredolo (1978, 1981), Cornell and Heth (1979), and Rieser (1979). Additional support comes from experiments involving manual search as the dependent variable. These will be briefly reviewed in the following section.

Our findings suggest that other than simple self-referents may be used earlier than has been suggested thus far. Whether infants use these cues depends on the behavioral task and the context in which it is set. Several factors influence young infants' localization of a target when their own position, but not that of the target, changes. These include the type of training, the availability of local and distal referents in the testing environment, and the degree of change in observer position.

In most studies, training has consisted of priming one response. It has therefore been difficult to distinguish a response based on an orientation hypothesis from mere response perseveration. The latter tells us little about the infant's ability to locate objects in space. To avoid this ambiguity, we trained infants to look both to their right and to their left prior to testing. Neither of these responses was reinforced differentially so that it was possible to exclude an interpretation involving response repetition. Developmental changes may consist of differing interpretations of the behavioral task rather than a switch from a subjective to an objective frame of reference. Our results show that it was only the 6-month-old infants whose performance improved after extended training, even though both groups were at the same level after the first phase. Since the total number of training trials did not differ between age groups, younger infants were equally able to learn the position of the target. Moreover, they could locate the target after their position relative to it had been changed. It seems likely that our method of training helped them to define the problem in spatial terms. This possibility warrants careful consideration and further experimentation.

Acredolo and Evans (1980) have convincingly shown that the distinctiveness of local referents in the region of the target augments the frequency of its localization following rotation of the subject. Yet even the most distinctive referents did not aid target localization in their younger subjects. In contrast, we have shown that 8-month-old infants are not dependent on distinctive local referents. While infants sometimes have difficulty in locating a target after they have been rotated through 180°, it is not clear that they are restricted to the use of simple orienting hypothesis to guide their search. In appropriate conditions, they are able to make use of other than simple self-referent cues. Even 6-month-old infants do not search in some constant place relative to themselves, and from at least 8 months of age localization is not dependent on cues provided by distinctive local referents.

VII.   MANUAL SEARCH AS AN INDEX OF SPATIAL LOCALIZATION

Since our primary concern is with the localization of objects following movement of the subject, the many studies that have involved manual search following movement of the object will not be reviewed here. However, some of these (Acredolo, 1979; Bremner, 1978b) have included conditions involving subject movement, and therefore it is of interest briefly to compare these findings with those described above.

In a series of studies, Bremner (Bremner, 1978a, 1978b, in press; Bremner & Bryant, 1977) examined the manner in which 9-month-old infants code for spatial position when searching manually for an object. In the experiment most relevant to this discussion, Bremner (1978b) placed infants at a table with two hiding places, one on the infant's right and one on the left. These hiding places were marked by covers that were distinctively different. One was "baited" with a toy while the infant watched. The infant was then moved to the opposite side of the table and allowed to search for the object. Under these conditions, few 9-month-old infants made errors. In general, when the object did not change position and infants were rotated through 180°, their first search was directed toward the correct object position. Bremner (in press) interprets his findings and those of Acredolo (1979) to mean that there is a gradual progression from using self-referent systems to using external reference systems between 6 and 16 months, and that distinctive local cues enhance the use of the latter system for infants in the middle of this age range. But we have found that even the youngest infants in this age range are not dependent on simple self-referent systems.

Bremner's findings, like those of Acredolo and Evans (1980), demonstrate the differential effectiveness of local referents: Distinctive covers are more helpful than distinctive backgrounds. Nevertheless, additional cues must be involved, since performance improved when the infant rather than the array was rotated. Fixation on the target during movement may be the relevant factor accounting for this difference, but it would require an explanation of why it should be differentially associated with subject- rather than object-movement. It seems likely that infants may have used spatial cues provided by the surroundings. Testing was conducted in the infants' homes and was therefore likely to be rich in cues that were familiar to the infant. It may also be noted that the infant's mother and the experimenter were present—the experimenter opposite and moving with the infant, while the mother remained in a fixed position. Bremner attributes a special role to subject movement in the organization of manual search and, more generally, to the developing capacity to code spatial position.

Acredolo (1979) found that infants were much less likely to search in a self-referent manner when tested in their homes than when tested in a landmark-free laboratory or a strange office with landmarks. In this investigation there were no training trials; hence, the effect of priming of one response was eliminated. Her findings are in accord with those of Bremner (1978b) in showing that under some circumstances 9-month-old infants use other than simple self-referent cues, but the importance of the familiarity of the testing environment rather than the nature of the local referent at the point of search is emphasized.

Consider the possible spatial reference systems that could have been involved in our in our experiment with 8-month-old infants using identical markers. Local referents—that is, the color, form, size, and pattern of the markers—were not distinctive. Neither the mother nor the experimenter could have been used as a distal referent, since position relative to the mother was identical throughout and the experimenter was not visible during testing. A constant position relative to the body cannot have been used, since infants oriented correctly whether the target was on their left or right. Implicit directives such as "Look to the ball that is second from the right" would be appropriate. This would imply the coding of position using an orientation system in which objects are located relative to other objects in terms of their mutual relation to the observer. This is certainly a more complex code than the usual self-referent system with which infants of this age are credited. Alternatively, infants in our experiment could have used a directive such as "Look to the ball that is near the window," i.e., a guidance hypothesis with a distal referent. We cannot, as yet, choose between these interpretations. In either case, other than an entirely self-referent system must be involved.

In short, findings from manual search studies have shown that 9-month-old infants can reach correctly even when rotated through 180°, providing that there is a distinctive local referent, testing is conducted in a familiar environment presumably rich in distal referents, and that one response is not extensively primed. In contrast, our results for 8-month-old infants show that one response can be primed, a distinctive local referent is not necessary, the testing environment need not be familiar, and performance is not dependent on infants becoming self-mobile.

VIII.   CONCLUSIONS

At least from 6 months, infants perceive the stability of a fixed environmental event over changes in their position relative to it. In a series of experiments involving eye–head coordination of visual orientation to an anticipated event, we have shown that infants are by no means entirely dependent on a self-referent spatial coding system in which position is defined solely by its relation to the whole body or part of it. In contrast to earlier studies using the same dependent variable, our subjects were able to locate the position of an event after their position relative to it had changed. Several factors have contributed toward this difference in outcome. First, by training responses both to the right and to the left, the problem of response repetition has been avoided. This procedure may be particularly important for younger subjects. While older infants readily interpret initial training in terms of place, younger infants may not do so. Their tendency to repeat the reinforced response does not imply an inability to use an objective code of spatial reference. Rather, it reflects ambiguity in the test situation. Second, the mapping of objects or events into objective space may be difficult following a complete about-face of the subject. Observer movement changes the relation between a fixed environmental feature and the observer. What remains constant is the relation between this feature and other stable referents or landmarks. Infants perceive this invariant relation earlier for arrays in front of the body, within a spatial field encompassing their own range of active movements. While position constancy may develop later than the constancies of object features such as size, shape, and rigidity, it is already clear that it waits neither on the maturation of self-mobility nor on the attainment of those characteristics that define Stage IV of sensorimotor development.

In summary, within the first half-year, infants perceive the stability of fixed objects or events in space across transformations in their own positions. The main constraint on this perception of constancy of position is that it seems to be limited initially to transformations that the frontal visual array. The major problem in the development of spatial localization of objects is not the substitution of a subjective reference system by an objective one, but rather the specification of conditions under which several different systems are used separately or in combination. The specification of these conditions is clearly dependent on the manner and the setting in which this behavior is assessed. Having established the spatial coding systems that are used by infants at different ages and under different conditions, it will then be possible to examine individual variation in their use.

ACKNOWLEDGMENTS

The research reported in this chapter was supported by a grant from the Australian Research Grants Committee to B. E. McKenzie and R. H. Day. The report was written while the first author was on an Outside Studies Program at the Laboratoire de Psychologie, Centre National de la Recherche Scientifique, Maternité de Montpellier, France. We thank Dr. Scania de Schonen for helpful discussion and critical comment and Elfriede Ihsen for research assistance.

NOTE

1. A more detailed report of Experiments 3, 4, and 5 is in preparation.

REFERENCES

Acredolo, L. P. Development of spatial orientation in infancy. *Developmental Psychology,* 1978, *14,* 224–234.

Acredolo, L. P. Laboratory versus home. The effect of environment on the nine-month-old infant's choice of spatial reference system. *Developmental Psychology,* 1979, *15,* 666–667.

Acredolo, L. P. Small- and large-scale spatial concepts in infancy and childhood. In L. S. Liben, A. H. Patterson, N. Newcastle (Eds.) *Spatial representation and behaviour across the life span: Theory and application.* New York: Academic Press, 1981, pp. 63–81.

Acredolo, L. P. & Evans, D. Developmental changes in the effects of landmarks on infant spatial behavior. *Developmental Psychology,* 1980, *16,* 312–318.

Amiel-Tison, Claudine & Grenier, A. *Evaluation neurologique du noveau-né et du nourrisson.* Paris: Masson, 1980.

Bower, T. G. R., Broughton, J. M. & Moore, M. K. Demonstration of intention in reaching behavior of neonate humans. *Nature,* 1970, *228,* 679–681.

Bremner, J. G. Spatial errors made by infants: Inadequate spatial cues or evidence of egocentrism? *British Journal of Psychology,* 1978, *69,* 71–84. (a)

Bremner, J. G. Egocentric versus allocentric spatial coding in nine-month-old infants: Factors influencing the choice of code. *Developmental Psychology,* 1978, *14,* 346–355. (b)

Bremner, J. G. Object localization in infancy. In M. Potegal (Ed.), *The neural and developmental bases of spatial orientation.* In press.

Bremner, J. G. & Bryant, P. E. Place versus response as the basis of spatial errors made by young infants. *Journal of Experimental Child Psychology,* 1977, *23,* 162–171.

Bruner, J. S. & Koslowski, B. Visually preadapted constituents of manipulatory action. *Perception,* 1972, *1,* 3–14.

Caron, A. E., Caron, R. F. & Carlson, V. R. Infant perception of the invariant shape of objects varying in slant. *Child Development*, 1979, *50*, 716–721.

Cohen, L. B., De Loache, J. S. & Strauss, M. S. Infant visual perception. In J. D. Osofsky, (Ed.). *Handbook of infant perception*. New York: Wiley, 1979, pp. 393–438.

Cornell, E. H. & Heth, C. D. Response versus place learning by human infants. *Journal of Experimental Psychology: Human Learning and Memory*, 1979, *5*, 188–196.

Day, R. H. & McKenzie, B. E. Constancies in the perceptual world of the infant. In W. Epstein (Ed.) *Stability and constancy in visual perception*. New York: Wiley, 1977, pp. 285–320.

Day, R. H. & McKenzie, B. E. Infant perception of the invariant size of approaching and receding objects. *Developmental Psychology*, 1981, *17*, 670–678.

Field, J. Relation of young infants reaching behavior to stimulus distance and solidity. *Developmental Psychology*, 1976, *12*, 444–448.

Gibson, E. J., Owsley, C. J. & Johnston, J. Perception of invariants by five-month-old infants: Differentiation of two types of motion. *Developmental Psychology*, 1978, *14*, 407–415.

Gibson, E. J., Owsley, C. J., Walker, A. & Megaw-Nyce, J. Development of the perception of invariants: Substance and shape. *Perception*, 1979, *8*, 609–619.

Gratch, G. Recent studies based on Piaget's view of object concept development. In L. B. Cohen & P. Salapatek (Eds.) *Infant perception: From sensation to cognition*, Vol. II. New York: Academic Press, 1975.

Harris, P. L., Cassel, T. L. & Bamborough, P. Tracking by young infants. *British Journal of Psychology*, 1974, *65*, 345–349.

Kanizsa, G. *Organization in Vision*. New York: Praeger, 1979.

Lockman, J. J. & Ashmead, D. H. Discontinuities in the development of manual behavior. In L. P. Lipsitt (Ed.) *Advances in infancy research*, Vol. 2. (In press)

Lloyd, S. E., Sinha, C. G. & Freeman, N. H. Spatial reference systems and the canonicality effect in infant search. *Journal of Experimental Child Psychology*, 1981, *32*, 1–10.

McDonnell, P. M. Patterns of eye-hand co-ordination in the first year of life. *Canadian Journal of Psychology*, 1979, *33*, 253–267.

McKenzie, B. E. & Day, R. H. Infants' attention to stationary and moving objects at different distances. *Australian Journal of Psychology*, 1976, *28*, 45–51.

O'Keefe, J. & Nadel, L. Precis of O'Keefe and Nadel's The hippocampus as a cognitive map. *Behavioral and Brain Sciences*, 1979, *2*, 487–533.

Presson, C. C. & Ihrig, L. *Using mother as a spatial landmark: Evidence against egocentric encoding in infancy*. Unpublished manuscript, 1980.

Provine, R. R. & Westerman, J. A. Crossing the midline. Limits of early eye-hand behavior. *Child Development*, 1979, *50*, 437–441.

Rieser, J. Spatial orientation of six-month-old infants. *Child Development*, 1979, *50*, 1078–1087.

Ruff, H. A. The development of perception and recognition of objects. *Child Development*, 1980, *51*, 981–992.

Ruff, H. A. The development of object perception in infancy. In T. Field (Ed.), *Review of human development*. New York: Wiley, in press.

Spelke, Elizabeth. *Perceptual knowledge of objects in infancy*. Paper presented at the Cognition Conference, Royaume, June, 1980.

von Hofsten, C. Binocular convergence as a determinant of reaching behavior in infancy. *Perception*, 1977, *6*, 139–144.

von Hofsten, C. Development of visually directed reaching: The approach phase. *Journal of Human Movement Studies*, 1979, *5*, 160–178.

von Hofsten, C. Predictive reaching for moving objects by human infants. *Journal of Experimental Child Psychology*, 1980, *30*, 369–382.

Walker, A. S., Owsley, C. J., Megaw-Nyce, J., Gibson, E. J. & Bahrick, L. E. Detection of elasticity as an invariant property of objects by young infants. *Perception*, 1980, *9*, 713–718.

DEVELOPMENTAL ASSESSMENT OF SOCIAL-COMMUNICATION SKILLS FOR EARLY INTERVENTION:

TESTING A COGNITIVE STAGE MODEL

Jeffrey M. Seibert, Anne E. Hogan and
Peter C. Mundy

I. INTRODUCTION

Research reported in this chapter begins from the premise that the objectives of basic research and practical application need not be incompatible. Pessimistic conclusions about their inevitable independence or lack of a common focus (Phillips, 1980) are overstated. The research, conducted in an early intervention setting, is testing a cognitive stage model through the development of a set of assessment scales for analyzing early social-communication development. The

Advances in the Behavioral Measurement of Children, Volume 1, pages 55–92.
Copyright © 1984 by JAI Press Inc.
All rights of reproduction in any form reserved.
ISBN: 0-89232-282-9

scales, based on the stage model, are useful for testing its theoretical predictions. At the same time, they have immediate implications for educational intervention decisions. The need for such an instrument has been apparent to both practitioners and researchers. The dual focus of the research on theory and practice adds new dimensions to the issues raised by either in isolation.

An ironic twist to the research is that the population most likely to benefit directly from the research is also the most appropriate research population for answering some of the stage-related questions raised by the theory. Research to test the model has employed a heterogeneous group of handicapped and high-risk infants and toddlers. The rationale for this sampling strategy will be considered later.

Before reviewing theoretical issues, the research needs to be placed in its applied context. The next section illustrates how practical concerns can suggest a course of action that is compatible with basic research objectives.

II. THE ASSESSMENT-INTERVENTION MODEL

Implicit in the applied goals of research is an assumption about what is a desirable approach to the early detection and prevention of developmental disabilities. This approach, called the *Assessment-Intervention Model* by Scott (1978), asserts that desired outcomes of intervention should be reflected in the content of the assessment instruments. Instruments should include skills or concepts laid out according to developmental sequences or task analyzed into components. These component skills and sequences become the objectives of intervention, the behaviors to be facilitated. Effective use of the Assessment-Intervention Model requires that all or most outcomes are known, that the sequences of developmental prerequisites can be specified, and that this information is reflected in the developmental assessments available to the interventionist. The approach also requires that appropriate facilitating experiences to foster development are known. Based on current knowledge, these requirements cannot be met, but they suggest areas of programmatic research.

In considering appropriate assessment tools for the Assessment-Intervention Model, Carver's (1975) distinction between psychometric and edumetric measures is useful. Psychometric measures, such as the Bayley Scales of Infant Development (Bayley, 1969) or the Cattell Infant Intelligence Test (Cattell, 1966), are empirically derived tests that have been constructed and norm referenced primarily to detect individual differences in developmental status. They also typically have been developed to predict future relative developmental status. Edumetric measures, in contrast, comprise items that are intended to serve as the objectives for educational intervention. Their function is neither classification nor prediction of the individual's future status based on his current developmental status. Rather, they specify a content domain that is important for mastery. Skills and concepts tapped by edumetric measures typically have face validity. Their acquisition, at least with a handicapped population, cannot always be taken for granted. Relative rates of mastery of these skills are not necessarily predictive of future relative ranking in the population at large. Items reflect skills that a competent peer will have mastered and that are important for adaptive functioning. Sound edumetric instruments are grounded in a theory of development that can elucidate both the mechanisms and interrelationships of development. Edumetric rather than psychometric measures are the more appropriate tools for planning intervention.

However, few edumetric measures of infant development exist. As a result, many intervention projects use psychometric tests such as the Bayley scales, or instruments derived from them, as if they were edumetric measures. However, there may be major obstacles to employing the results of psychometric tests as the basis for intervention because of the very different objectives underlying their construction. Items have been included primarily for their ability to discriminate among individuals at different ages. Explicit developmental links among items are not specified, because they are irrelevant to the purpose of psychometric tests. Consequently, the interventionist must make several unspecified steps in order to translate results from psychometric tests into a meaningful plan for arranging intervention. Training the scales' developmental milestones, without understanding which skills are interrelated and what underlying processes and concepts they index, may be an inefficient or even counterproductive use of time and resources. For example, *stacking cubes* is a common milestone on many infant assessments, commonly targeted as an intervention objective. It is often taught by physically prompting the child to stack the cubes. Such an intervention strategy may be appropriate if the focus is on the fine motor skills involved in voluntary release and the perceptual–motor skills involved in placing one object directly above another. But stacking blocks is not an essential skill in itself. It reflects the spontaneous behavior typically observed in children of a certain age who are mastering concepts about spatial relationships among objects and the effects of gravity on objects. Stacking cubes will probably be taught in a different manner if it is regarded as a conceptual as well as a motoric achievement. However, nothing in the psychometric test suggests what the nature of this accomplishment may be, other than the typical age at which it appears.

The experienced interventionist may acquire an understanding over time of the developmental significance of items from psychometric tests and their relationship to other test items. However, more efficient than this trial-and-error process of learning would be the availability of an edumetric instrument, based on a well-articulated theory of development and organized to make meanings and relationships explicit. The Piagetian-based sensorimotor scales of Uzgiris and Hunt (1975) or Escalona and Corman (unpublished) represent instruments of this type. Their application in intervention settings is slowly increasing (Seibert, in press). However, no such instrument has existed for assessing early social-communication development, an area of obvious concern to early interventionists. The practical objective of the research to be reported is the development of such an instrument. A cognitive stage model provides the theoretical framework on development guiding scale construction. The model posits that developments in the social-communication and object cognitive domains are related through a series of underlying cognitive structures. The next section reviews theoretical and empirical issues related to validation of a stage model, for the sensorimotor period in particular.

III.   ISSUES AND RESEARCH ON COGNITIVE STAGE MODELS

A number of different uses of the term "stage" can be found in the developmental literature. In this chapter, the term's definition is similar to Piaget's (1960) meaning, elaborated on by other cognitive theorists (e.g., Fischer, 1980; Flavell & Wohlwill, 1969; Pinard & Laurendeau, 1969; Wohlwill, 1973). The term in this sense has explanatory as well as descriptive value. However, consensus about the empirical implications of the concept has been difficult to obtain, even among those sympathetic to the potential theoretical value of the construct. Our use of the term reflects a *synthesis* of the ideas of these various theorists, in particular, Wohlwill (1973) and Fischer (1980). The reader interested in the range of debate generated by the concept of "developmental stages" is referred to Brainerd's (1978) critical review of the stage question. His review is followed by commentaries, both pro and con, from over two dozen theorists and researchers.

As an explanatory construct, stages have been proposed "to unify a set of otherwise quite disparate and seemingly unrelated behaviors" (Flavell & Wohlwill, 1969, p. 92) and "to account for systematic forms of *interpatterning* among sets of developing responses" (Wohlwill, 1973, p. 191). Most commonly, the concept has been applied to sets of developing *cognitive* behaviors for which it is assumed there exists a common underlying organizational base or structure that changes with development. The presence of a behavior indicative of a particular stage structure leads to a prediction that other behaviors, also representative of that stage, are likely to be in the individual's repertoire, or to be acquired soon. This gives the construct potential explanatory power. Correlational analysis becomes the methodology of choice for developmental stage research (Wohlwill, 1973).

Five criteria, originally proposed by Piaget (1960), are relevant to the validity of the stage construct. Briefly, these include:

1. *Hierarchization* or *invariant sequence*—stages emerge in a fixed developmental order.
2. *Integration*—each stage incorporates behaviors and structures of the previous stage.

3. *Consolidation*—each stage includes a phase of achievement of behaviors representative of that level and a phase of preparation for developments of the next stage.
4. *Structure*—behaviors characteristic of a stage are interrelated by shared cognitive structure, and therefore should develop concurrently.
5. *Equilibration*—stages of development are characterized by a series of alternating periods of disequilibrium and stability.

Most research on the stage construct has focused on the developmental periods of middle childhood and adolescence, the concrete and formal operational periods, respectively. However, the sensorimotor period has advantages over the other periods (Wohlwill, 1973). The number of different series of responses to trace is fewer, and many of the sequences of steps have already been articulated. In addition, the time span for observing typical longitudinal development is shorter for this period. A few studies examine the evidence for stages during the sensorimotor period. Because of their relevance to the research to be reported here, they will be briefly reviewed. For more detailed reviews, the reader is referred to Uzgiris (1976) and McCall (1979).

In support of the hierarchization or invariant sequence criterion, evidence comes from a variety of studies (e.g., Kahn, 1976; Kopp, Sigman, & Parmelee, 1973, 1974; Kramer, Hill, & Cohen, 1975; Rogers, 1977; Uzgiris, 1973). These investigators used various instruments, such as the Casati–Lezine scales and the Uzgiris–Hunt scales, designed to elicit behaviors originally described by Piaget (1951, 1952, 1954) as characteristic of the different stages of sensorimotor development. Research has been conducted with normal infants and toddlers (Kopp et al., 1973; Uzgiris, 1973) as well as with severely retarded adolescents and adults (Kahn, 1976; Rogers, 1977). In general, the evidence supports the ordinality of the proposed sequences, with occasional inversions in the order in which items were acquired reported in the longitudinal studies (Kopp et al., 1973, 1974; Uzgiris, 1973). In studies in which these items were assigned to stages, inversions occurred within but not between stages. In other words, the stage sequencing was nearly perfect, which is what is critical to the construct (Uzgiris, 1978).

The integration criterion is more difficult to verify empirically. Piaget was not specific in proposing successive structures for the stages of the sensorimotor period. Uzgiris (1976, 1977a), based on her own observations using a Piagetian framework, has proposed a four-stage sequence of changing behavioral organization for the sensorimotor period, leaving open the possibility of an initial reflexive-like stage. The organization characteristic of the actions of each stage becomes incorporated into the subsequent stages, in accordance with the integration criterion. The child's approach to his world moves from simple, indiscriminate, but voluntary actions, to complex, coordinated, and differentiated but fairly rigid actions, with a beginning distinction between means and ends. This organization is superseded by a level of differentiated actions, immediately modifiable to feedback through trial and error. At the final level, actions are adjusted prior to execution as a result of symbolic anticipatory regulation. Other researchers (notably Fischer, 1980; McCall, 1979; and McCall, Eichorn, & Hogarty, 1977), have proposed sequences of stages involving a similar integrative progression of organization from one level to the next.

Verification of both the consolidation and equilibration criteria requires analysis of the patterns of acquisition of behaviors across the different stages. Individual longitudinal data need to be examined for alternating periods of change and quiescence. The expected pattern of performance for the transition period is one of low intertask consistency, in which the child displays only some behaviors at a higher level. For the period of consolidation, the pattern becomes one of high intertask consistency at the same stage. Some investigators (e.g., Brainerd, 1978; Fischer & Bullock, 1981; Pinard & Laurendeau, 1969; Uzgiris, 1977a) have speculated that rate of development should show bursts of rapid acquisition over short periods of time, corresponding to a transitional phase. These bursts should be followed by plateaus of slower development, representing the period of achievement or consolidation. The main problem in an evaluation of these predictions is the relativity of the judgment required. What represents high vs. low intertask consistency? How brief should the time span be for the acquisition of new behaviors to constitute a burst? How long should a period of consolidation last if it is to represent a stage in development? In addition, if the child's rate of development is retarded, how should the time frame be altered? The only individually analyzed longitudinal data bearing directly on any of these issues are those gathered by Uzgiris (1973). With the development of new skills in object permanence as the reference point, she observed periods of divergence and convergence of scale scores in other areas (Understanding of Means–Ends, Object Relations in Space and Understanding of Causality) in a sample of 12 children. The four-level sequence Uzgiris (1976) proposed is based on these observed phases of transition and consolidation.

McCall et al. (1977) analyzed cross-age correlations for the items derived from principal-components analyses of the 3-year longitudinal data of the Berkeley Growth Study. They were looking for patterns in the group data that might index stages. Despite Uzgiris's (1977b) cautions about the limitations of atheoretical, psychometrically based group data for examining the stage question, the results of McCall and co-workers' (1977) analysis are suggestive. There appear to be periods when the rank-order correlations for the sample remain stable, followed by transitions when the rank order appears to be undergoing shifts. These shifts occur at times when the nature of the items loading on the principal component is changing. The alternating periods of rank-order stability and instability correspond approximately to the four stages that Uzgiris (1976) has delineated. McCall's interpretation of the organization underlying the items in the principal component at each stage is similar to Uzgiris's (1976) characterization of her levels. Because an analysis of the Fels longitudinal data yielded similar results (McCall, Hogarty, & Hurlburt, 1972) McCall concludes that the shifting correlations are real and not merely random fluctuations. Although the relationship between individual patterns of divergence and convergence and rank-order correlations for a *group* of individuals may not be a simple one, McCall's interpretation of the pattern as indicative of stages is reasonable. Had the group patterns not been observed, however, no conclusions about the stage hypothesis could be drawn, since analysis of individual patterns is necessary for disconfirmation. These patterns in the group data only suggest that stage transitions and consolidation may be happening at the individual level.

Kagan, Kearsley, and Zelazo (1978) observed similar patterns of intraindividual stability and instability in their longitudinal study of attentiveness, vocalization, and smiling to visual and auditory events. They report major psychological changes at 8 months and shortly after 1 year of age, two of the transition periods reported by McCall et al. (1977).

The structure criterion is concerned with what mediates the hypothesized interrelationships among behaviors at each stage. Transition and consolidation presuppose the existence of structure. Pinard and Laurendeau (1969) propose that a stage structure should produce almost complete synchrony in the appearance of behavioral developments at the same stage. This strict definition is based on Piaget's notion of the *structures d'ensemble,* or total structures. However, such congruence almost certainly does not occur in development, at least not for the individual stages of the sensorimotor period (Uzgiris, 1977b; Wohlwill, 1973). Fischer and Bullock's (1981) looser criterion, requiring what they call interval rather than point synchrony for developments at the same stage, is probably a better reflection of actual events. Two related developments need not emerge at the same point in time, but only within some specifiable interval of time.

An evaluation of this criterion requires tasks to be analyzed for similarity of structure to allow predictions about which behaviors should develop in synchrony (Uzgiris, 1977b). Piaget's (1951, 1952, 1954) own writings provide the primary source for this analysis of the task domains. Any test of the structure criterion assumes that stage-level assignments are accurate, but this assumption is open to challenge. There are a number of instances of different stage assignments for the same item in the available literature. For example, success on the single invisible displacement task of the Object Permanence scale has been assigned to either stage V or stage VI, depending on the interpretation of the investigator. Fortunately, agreements far outweigh disagreements. Nevertheless, consensus should be reached on the decision rules for stage assignment.

One of the more direct tests of the structure criterion comes from a study of severely retarded children and adolescents (Woodward, 1959). Considerable consistency in stage of functioning was observed for these individuals across a range of sensorimotor tasks. In contrast, Rogers (1977) observed a much lower level of stage congruence for a similar sample. Two studies, reviewed by Uzgiris (1976), using the Casati–Lezine scales with normal infants, also revealed a relatively high percentage of stage concordance across domains. However, as Wohlwill (1973) remarks, even such an apparently straightforward analysis of concordance can have problems, when cross-sectional data on normally developing children are used. Some subjects may be in transition, as predicted by the equilibration criterion, and would be expected to display a lack of stage consistency across tasks. If the periods of incongruence could be demonstrated to occur only at certain points in development, the case for the structure criterion would be supported.

Structure has also been investigated by examining the patterns of correlations among scale scores for infants matched for chronological age. In some cases, scores are gathered at regular intervals and data for each age level are analyzed separately. In her review of this research, Uzgiris (1976) reports that reported correlations are typically low and not significant. However, how *correlations* should reflect *stage congruence* at single points in development is not clear. If the single age sampled includes subjects at different stages of development, high interscale correlations may be predicted. However, it is not apparent why the correlations should be high if the age group sampled includes subjects primarily *within* a single stage. Such a sample would evidence little of the between-stage variance needed to observe significant correlations. In an extreme example, a sample of subjects, nearly all of whom are consolidated at the same stage across domains, would display strong individual patterns of concordance but very low intercorrelations among scales. Correlational analyses of restricted age ranges without analyses of individual patterns of performance therefore can be misleading, if the question being addressed is validation of global structures characterizing major stages. The research by Bates and her colleagues (Bates, Benigni, Bretherton, Camaioni, & Volterra, 1979) illustrates how sampling narrow developmental ranges (9–13 months) yields information about specific, local, structural relationships between various cognitive and communicative developments, but says little about general stages.

Sampling a much broader developmental age span, encompassing several stages, may ensure reasonable sample variance, but raises other problems. According to Wohlwill (1973), it is most appropriate for demonstrating that two or more sets of variables share a common structural base, but only when there is reason to believe that the extent and mode of the relationship between the variables remain constant over time. Such a research strategy may, therefore, be most applicable to the sensorimotor period, when structures should be most global and undifferentiated and mediate a broad array of behaviors over an extended period of time.

Fischer (1978) has pointed out dangers in using correlational analyses of synchrony in development across extended time intervals to demonstrate shared structure. The main problem is that although the variables of interest may be highly correlated with each other, they often are highly correlated with other measures, such as shoe size or height, that do not reflect cognitive structural mediation. Kagan et al. (1978) observe that typically observed relationships may not be necessary relationships. Bates et al. (1979) argue that patterns of nonsignificant as well as significant relationships among variables must be examined if conclusions about mediating structures are to be drawn. Researchers employing this strategy generally want to prove that the relationship between the cognitive variables exists independent at least of chronological age to ensure that factors other than very general noncognitive ones are mediating the relationship. Using a statistical control, partialling out the effects of age, however, seems to "amount to throwing out the baby with the bath water" (Wohlwill, 1973, p. 203). For example, Uzgiris and Hunt (1975) report strong correlations, ranging from .80 to .93, among all of their sensorimotor scales for a large cross-sectional sample. However, when chronological age was partialled out to look for specifically cognitively based relationships, all interscale correlations dropped dramatically, with only 2 of 21 possible correlations above .50. If this research strategy is to be employed to evaluate the evidence for structure, other ways of controlling for or eliminating the typically observed correlations between the cognitive variables and noncognitive factors must be found.

In summary, considering the bulk of evidence from the sensorimotor period relevant to the various stage criteria, the following conclusions can be reached: Various studies support the invariant sequence of a number of developments in the sensorimotor period. Proposed models of organizational levels appear to meet the integration criterion. However, the evidence both for periods of transition and consolidation and for congruent stage developments mediated by changing cognitive structures is inconclusive. Considering the obvious centrality of the structure criterion to the stage construct, additional research to assess its validity should be a priority.

IV. APPLICATIONS OF THE STAGE MODEL FOR INTERVENTION

Several reviews are available on the implications of Piaget's theory of cognitive development for educational practice (e.g., Furth & Wachs, 1974; Lawton & Hooper, 1978; Sigel, 1969; Sullivan, 1969). Flavell (1963) proposed a number of years ago that theoretically based assessments could be developed from the model. More recently, he has suggested that information on invariant sequences could be useful for establishing measures of readiness (Flavell, 1977). Brainerd (1978), however, has cautioned against using the stage construct as a basis for evaluating readiness to learn, if it leads to a decision *not* to train certain skills or *not* to provide certain experiences because the child is judged to be at a stage that indicates lack of readiness. On the other hand, not everything can be taught at the same time and the stage construct may provide a coherent framework for determining what is likely to be learned more easily at a given point in development.

Uzgiris and Hunt (1975) developed their infant scales as an alternative to psychometrically based infant tests. One of their goals was that such a conceptually based instrument would find practical application by indicating sequences of acquisition and suggesting environmental circumstances that might facilitate cognitive development.

Of the various stage-related criterion, invariant sequence has probably received the most widespread consideration for intervention during the sensorimotor period (e.g., Bricker & Bricker, 1973; Robinson & Robinson, 1978). Its implications for determining training sequences, coupled with its substantial empirical support, make its practical relevance obvious. Application has been less widespread for the notion of horizontal organization or structure. In a few instances, a stage analysis has been employed to organize sensorimotor assessment scales in order to be able to describe the child's stage of functioning in different task domains (e.g., Chatelanat & Schoggen, 1980; Dunst, 1980). With this information, a picture of a child's relative strengths and weaknesses across task domains or scales can be created. In addition, the series of stages has been used as a basis for proposing curricula for early intervention (e.g., Dunst, 1977; Smith, unpublished; Stephens, 1977). However, the full range of implications of a cognitive stage model for making early-intervention decisions is only beginning to be explored (e.g., Seibert, in press; Seibert & Hogan, in press). Caution is to be advised. Wholesale acceptance of the stage construct by practitioners would be inappropriate, since its validity is still being assessed. Consequently, a practical plan of action is to conduct stage-related intervention in a context that simultaneously yields theoretically relevant data. Such a strategy of research and application will be described in the remainder of this chapter.

V.   THE THEORETICAL MODEL

The structure criterion is central to any assertion about the validity of the stage construct, but it has only received tentative empirical support. A direct test of the predictions generated by the structure criterion therefore appears to be the obvious next research step. Verification of the other criteria is secondary to the more fundamental question of shared cognitive structures.

In evaluating the structure criterion, it is essential to establish which domains of behaviors are expected to be related. From the perspective we are adopting, cognition is broadly defined as control over sets of skills that enables the individual to engage in adaptive interactions with both his physical and his social environments (Fischer, 1980). This broad conceptualization of cognition to encompass interactions with persons as well as objects is consistent with Piaget's theory, but has received more explicit emphasis in the recent writings of cognitive developmentalists such as Uzgiris (1977a), Flavell (1977), McCall (1979), and Fischer (1980). Adaptive interactions with objects include the traditional Piagetian sensorimotor skills involving concepts such as object permanence and causality. Adaptive interactions with persons involve concepts and skills related to communication and language development. A cognitive conceptualization of the basis of communication and language is compatible with developmental psycholinguistics' recent focus on pragmatics—the study of the rules governing language *use* (e.g., Bates, 1976; Dale, 1980; Seibert & Oller, 1981). The organizational structure is hypothesized to underlie both early social-communication skills (as cognitive skills focused on people), and object-focused cognitive skills. The changing underlying cognitive structures mediate developments in both domains. The term *domain* refers to the focus of the developing adaptive behaviors, either on persons or on objects.

Following Wohlwill's (1973) proposals for conducting developmental research, the next step is to determine the set of developmental dimensions that comprise each domain. These dimensions provide the basis for generating a set of developmental measurement scales. Wohlwill (1973) distinguishes between quantitative and qualitative developmental dimensions. For the former, a quantitatively continuous variable that develops over time, such as height or efficiency of processing time to recognition, can be hypothesized. For the qualitative developmental dimensions, the behaviors that develop over time appear to be related conceptually but no underlying quantitatively continuous variable can be identified. Sequential development of motor skills leading to walking is an example of the latter. The concept of developmental dimensions is similar to Fischer's (1980) concept of task domains. For the analysis of the cognitive domains, development is best represented by *qualitative* developmental dimensions involving sequences of conceptually related behaviors. The identity of the dimensions is arbitrary, reflecting the particular developmental level that is the reference point for describing the developmental sequences. The transition between the end of the sensorimotor period and the onset of symbolic or representational thought is the reference point for our own research. Developmental dimensions for each domain are defined in terms of the adaptive skills and concepts of the competent, normally developing 2-year-old.

Most of the conceptual work to define dimensions and construct measurement scales has already been accomplished for the object domain. The developing sensorimotor concepts described by Piaget (1951, 1952, 1954) are readily translatable into developmental dimensions. These include concepts of object permanence, means–ends relationships, cause–effect relationships, spatial relationships among objects, and the functional and socially influenced use of objects. The scales developed by Uzgiris and Hunt (1975), noted earlier, provide a reliable means for measuring these dimensions. The scales have been modified for our research by excluding items of a social nature (such as appeals to adults for assistance) from the causality scale and from both imitation scales. They have been adapted for conceptual and methodological reasons, to ensure that their item content does not overlap with the social-communication scales. Organization of the scale items into levels also represents an adaptation of the scales, to be discussed later.

In the social domain, no major analysis and synthesis of developmental concepts comparable to Piaget's for the object domain was available to direct the delineation of developmental dimensions across the sensorimotor period. There is a wealth of both data and theoretical speculation on maternal–infant interaction, on the emergence of communication skills, and on prerequisites to language. The dimensions we have derived from a review of this literature will be presented in the next section.

After dimensions have been identified and delineated, the behavioral items comprising each scale must be analyzed a priori for structural organization so that items can be assigned to stages (Uzgiris 1977b; Wohlwill, 1973). The specific stage model adopted in our research is the four-level sequence proposed by Uzgiris, with an initial reflex level added to produce a five-level sequence. More details of the sequence will be presented in the next section.

The structural assumptions are consistent with Wohlwill's (1973) Model IV Stage approach and Fischer's approach (1980) rather than with the stronger version of the model implied by *structures d'ensemble* (Pinard & Laurendeau, 1969). Development of same-stage skills across the different dimensions is expected to occur typically in interval synchrony, and only rarely in perfect congruence. The order of emergence of new skills is not always predictable. A child may display skills at different levels at certain points in time, and each child may present a relatively unique profile of skills across the developmental dimensions. This is the most complex stage model and the most difficult to validate, but it probably most closely approximates psychological reality.

According to Fischer (1980), asynchrony in the acquisition of behaviors across scales is expected because a skill will be present in a child's repertoire only if he is at the requisite level of development *and* has had the opportunity for experiences relevant to the mastery of that skill. Different patterns of acquisition of new skills for different individuals are predicted by the model, based on the expectation that different children will have different patterns of experience. Hunt, Mohandessi, Ghodssi, and Akiyama (1976) have documented that experiences can differentially affect the patterns of acquisition of behaviors across the Uzgiris–Hunt scales. Fischer (1980) postulates an upper limit in level of functioning, called an optimal level, that shifts with development. This represents the level beyond which immediate opportunity for experience will have little effect. The optimal level probably represents a limit imposed by the child's current level of neurological organization, reflecting physiological and maturational factors.

Before turning to the research based on the structural predictions, a brief overview of the social-communication scales is presented. The discussion reviews how the social-communication dimensions were identified and translated into scales which were then organized into structural stages in common with the object dimensions. For a more detailed discussion, see Seibert and Hogan (1982).

VI. THE SOCIAL DIMENSIONS: THE EARLY SOCIAL-COMMUNICATION SCALES

In line with our practical objectives, the scales have been developed with an awareness of both their potential function as an edumetric instrument to guide the interventionist and their role in evaluating the structure criterion. Therefore, selection of developmental dimensions and scale item content reflects practical as well as theoretical considerations. Consistent with the structural stage model, the assessment instrument has a vertical organization, corresponding to the developmental dimensions or scales, and a horizontal organization, reflecting the five structural levels.

The Vertical Organization

The social-communication dimensions represent concepts and skills that the literature indicates the normally developing child has mastered by 24 months. The typical 2-year-old has a practical communication system which is transitional into a symbolic or representational communication system, that is, language. The dimensions reflect the development of communication skills to the point just prior to the emergence of language as a syntactic, rule-governed symbol system.

From a practical perspective, the scales are intended to operationalize communicative intent by analyzing it into developmental dimensions and tracing their origins to the very earliest level of social awareness after birth. The scales therefore are working hypotheses about prerequisites to language and about sequences of acquisition. Our analysis of this domain is based on a review of recent literature in developmental psycholinguistics, maternal–infant interaction, attachment, and early social-cognitive development. The scales incorporate most behaviors typically considered in the area of infant social development, organized from a linguistic pragmatic orientation (Seibert & Oller, 1981).

Table 1 provides an overview of the categorization system used to analyze the social domain into component dimensions. The three column headings represent three broad pragmatic functions of early interaction with persons abstracted from the literature review. *Social Interaction* encompasses behaviors that have as their primary objective and function the establishment of attention to self, with no goal in mind except playful interaction between self and other. *Joint Attention* refers to interactions for which one communicative partner is attempting to direct the other partner's attention to an object, person, or event. The primary purpose is sharing attention, that is, looking at the same thing together. At the higher levels,

Table 1.   Matrix for Generating the Social-Communication Dimensions

Roles	Functions		
	Social Interaction	*Joint Attention*	*Behavior Regulation*
Responding	RSI	RJA	RBR
Initiating	ISI	IJA	IBR
Maintaining	MSI	MJA	—

joint-attention activities lead into linguistic communicative functions focused on information exchange, or shared attention about details of entities, events, and situations. *Behavior Regulation* includes behaviors for which one communicative partner is attempting to direct or regulate the other's behavior, typically to achieve an external goal. Often, behavior regulation occurs in the form of enlisting the assistance of another in order to have a need met. The goal of the interaction may also be either to restrict the activity or to elicit a compliant action from the partner.

The three rows in Table 1 represent role aspects of communicative interaction that intersect the three functions just described. Persons are interactive and either partner may be in the role of *initiator* or *responder*. These complementary roles are represented in the first two rows. For the Social Interaction and Joint Attention functions, the child should be able to participate in an interaction *sequence* in a dialogue-like manner. He must become skillful at *maintaining* these interactions, represented as a separate role in the third row. Each role-by-function category, resulting from the intersection of the columns and the rows, represents a social developmental dimension upon which a measurement scale has been based. The eight scales together represent a single assessment instrument for evaluating early social-communicative competencies, called the Early Social-Communication Scales (ESCS).

Language can be used to achieve all of the functions reflected in the scales, but these functions can be accomplished in other ways prior to the development of language (Bates et al., 1979; Bruner, 1975a; Sugarman-Bell, 1978). This organization represents one way of conceptualizing distinct but interrelated social dimensions. Occasionally, the assignment of a skill to one scale may seem arbitrary when the skill is related to another developmental dimension as well. However, in order to avoid artifactual congruences in stage scores between scales, each item is assigned to only a single scale.

An extensive literature review provides the basis for much of the content of the scales. Sources for the content of the Social Interaction scales include Bruner's (1975a, 1975b, 1977) observations on turn-taking, including object-exchange games, and Uzgiris and Hunt's (1975) Operational Causality scale, in particular, items that involve appeals for repetition of physically and socially interactive games between the child and the adult. Also relevant to the social dimensions are reports by Brazelton, Koslowski, and Main (1974) and Trevarthen (1979) of the very young infant's early social responsivity, and Bowlby's (1969) and Ainsworth's (1969, 1972) discussions of the development of means for gaining attention, proximity, and physical contact.

For the Joint Attention scales, Bruner's insight (Bruner, 1975a, 1975b; Ninio & Bruner, 1978; Scaife & Bruner, 1975) into the social nature of the development of object-reference has been especially influential. Labeling an object in order to direct another's attention to it can accomplish the same function as either pointing to the object with one's index finger or directing another's attention to the object with one's gaze. Some degree of understanding involved in following another's line of regard appears to be an immediate prerequisite to the development of object-label comprehension (Hogan, Seibert, & Mundy, 1980; Seibert, 1979). Werner and Kaplan (1963) and, subsequently, Bates (Bates, Bretherton, Shore, & Carpen, 1979; Bates, Camaioni, & Volterra, 1975) have proposed that there is a continuity between gestural and verbal acts of reference and that nonsocial as well as social pointing has a role in the development of object-reference. The observations and speculations of Huttenlocher (1973), Nelson (1974), and Reich (1976) have also contributed to the development of the Joint Attention scales.

For the Initiating Behavior Regulation scales, Bates's (Bates et al., 1975) discussion of the child's use of adults as social intermediaries or agents has been of value. Items have also been adapted from Uzgiris and Hunt's (1975) Operational Causality scale. The original scale includes socially mediated solutions to simple problems: The child uses the adult to activate objects that he himself cannot successfully manipulate. Bruner's (Bruner, Roy, & Ratner, 1979) analysis of the emergence of the request function parallels the sequence represented in the Initiating Behavior Regulation scale. Nelson (1973), Benedict (1979), and Miller, Chapman, Branston, and Reichle (1980) have proposed categories for the analysis of action comprehension and following simple commands that have contributed to the development of the Responding to Behavior Regulation scale. Also relevant is Macnamara's (1977) discussion of the role of gestures and context in fostering the development of comprehension of verbal directives.

The Horizontal Organization

The structural analysis of the scale items is critical to the test of the structure criterion. Failure to determine the appropriate structure underlying individual items could obscure the relationship between domains although a relationship exists. Guiding the decision-making process are the stage descriptions provided by Piaget (1951, 1952, 1954) and the recent empirical efforts of several investigators, including Uzgiris (1973, 1976, 1977a), McCall (McCall et al., 1977) Fischer (1980; Fischer & Corrigan, 1979), and Sugarman-Bell (1978). The general characterization of the changing organization of the five levels is from Uzgiris (1976, 1977a). However, decisions about level assignment of items are based on a synthesis of the ideas of all of these structurally oriented researchers.

Decisions were made by seeking group consensus among the research staff in applying the structural descriptions for each level to an analysis of individual items. Each item was analyzed for level of organization or understanding implied either in its acquisition or in its performance in a functional context. Available developmental age estimates for some behaviors were *not* used. The process is an inferential one, and not simply a reading off of structure from behaviors. Verification of structural analysis for individual items is not open to any direct and immediate test. It can be assessed only over time through a series of related studies that test the validity of the structure criterion itself. The process is susceptible to error, in particular because the structural level that a behavior of a specific topography represents may vary as a function of how the skill has been acquired (e.g., acquired through trial and error vs. foresight). In such cases, since the child's learning history is typically not observable, a conservative tack has been adopted. The behavior is assigned to the lowest level at which it reasonably could have been acquired.

The following descriptions embody some of the criteria employed for organizing the content of both the social and the object scales into horizontal levels.

Level 0 (approximately birth to 2 months) can be described as *responsive* or *reflexive*. The infant's actions are primarily *reactions* to the changing physical and social stimulation around him.

Level 1 (approximately 2–7 months) is characterized by *simple, undifferentiated actions*. It marks the beginning of voluntary activity by the infant. Although capable of making visual and auditory discriminations, the infant at this level does not coordinate them systematically with his actions toward persons and objects. His actions on objects are simple and repetitive. Her social interactions imply recognition of people (e.g., the social smile), but there is little evidence that he actively differentiates among persons.

Level 2 (approximately 8–13 months) corresponds to the development of *complex, differentiated actions*. The child's perceptual discriminations among objects and people in his environment become coordinated with his actions toward them. But actions toward objects and actions toward people are not coordinated with each other. Desires and goals related to objects are evident in the child's behavior, but the social partner, perceived as a source of social interaction, is not yet understood as a means to achieving object goals.

At level 3 (approximately 14–21 months), characterized by *regulation* of one's own behavior *using differentiated feedback,* a flexibility emerges in the infant's actions. This flexibility is observed in his immediate modification of his actions in subtle ways when confronted with lack of success in problem-solving situations. The child discovers solutions through deliberate trial and error. She begins to show an understanding both of what works and what does *not* work in simple problem situations. This level marks the appearance of conventionalization of signals and the ability to coordinate attention simultaneously to both objects and people. People are used to solve "object-problems" (e.g., people can get desired objects for the child). Objects are used to solve "people-problems" (e.g., by giving an object to someone, the child can gain that person's attention). Level 3 initiating skills usually involve the coordination of a gesture or action on an object with eye contact to the adult. Once a child is using single words in addition to or as a substitute for gestures, social-communication skills are classified at sublevel 3.5. The earliest conventionalizations of sounds as words are not symbolic. Typically, referent objects are perceptually present and context still helps carry the word's meaning. Consequently, the earliest words are considered to be level 3 developments.

Level 4 (approximately 22 months and on) is characterized by *anticipatory regulation*. The child's problem solving shifts to a symbolic mode, as he becomes capable of mental action or thought. Trial and error is at times replaced by foresightful problem solving. Symbolic or representational abilities are hypothesized to provide the foundation for a number of developments related to language, pretend play, and delayed observational learning (Piaget, 1951). Communication begins to occur solely through linguistic means at this level, as some words are combined generatively and are used to refer to nonpresent objects, indexing their new status as symbols rather than perceptually bound signals.

This overview only touches on the range of developments that characterize each cognitive level. The interested reader is referred to Uzgiris (1976, 1977a), McCall (McCall, 1979; McCall et al., 1977), and Fischer (1980) for their discussions of the levels.

Table 2 presents the results of the process of level assignment applied to a single scale from each domain. Profiles encompassing the total item content of both the Adapted Uzgiris–Hunt Scales (AUHS) and the ESCS, organized into dimensions and structural levels, are available from the authors.

VII.　TESTING THE STRUCTURAL PREDICTIONS

According to the structure criterion, development during the sensorimotor period in both the object cognitive domain and the social-communication domain should be mediated by an underlying, shared, *specifically cognitive* organization. Empirically, evidence for such a relationship should be indexed by high correlations between both measures for a cross-sectional sample of infants and toddlers spanning the sensorimotor period. High correlations enable one to predict with reasonable accuracy a child's level of development in one domain from knowledge of his level of development in the other. But merely confirming the relationship at this level is inadequate as a test of the structure criterion. As noted in the

Table 2. Examples of Scales from the Object Domain and the Social-Communication Domain, Organized According to the Five Structural Levels (from Uzgiris, 1976)

Levels	Object Domain: Schemes for Relating to Objects	Social-Communication Domain: Responding to Another's Attempt at Behavior Regulation (RBR)
0 (0–2 mos.) Responsive	Holds or grasps object placed in hand	Can be soothed
1 (2–7 mos.) Simple Voluntary Undifferentiated Actions	Uses only simple action patterns on all objects (e.g., mouthing, banging, waving)	a. Turns to other's voice b. Resists releasing object pulled by other
2 (8–13 mos.) Complex Differentiated Actions	Uses different actions for different objects (e.g., stretches elastic, rubs cotton)	a. Inhibits action to "No" or other sharp vocalization b. Looks to other and protests as other takes object away
3 (14–21 mos.) Regulation by Feedback	Uses objects in socially influenced ways (e.g., combs hair, wears necklace)	Comprehends at least two simple commands accompanied by gestures
	As objects are presented, spontaneously names them without looking to other	Comprehends at least two simple commands in context, without accompanying gestures
4 (22 mos. +) Anticipatory Regulation	Uses objects in symbolic play (e.g., pretends block is car, or banana is telephone)	Follows a series of simple contrastive commands presented without accompanying gestures and with minimal context

earlier review, if noncognitive variables correlate as strongly with the cognitive measures of interest, problems of interpretation arise. If chronological age or level of motor development, for example, predict equally well to either cognitive measure, no empirical grounds exist for asserting that the observed relationship between the cognitive measures is mediated by cognitive structures. The observed correlations could be a function of general opportunity for experience or could be mediated by specifically motoric rather than cognitive factors. The patterns of correlations among all potentially relevant variables need to be considered before conclusions about the nature of observed relationships can be drawn.

As Uzgiris and Hunt's (1975) analyses of scale intercorrelations, with and without age partialled out, illustrate, such problems of interpretation are very likely to arise in a cross-sectional sample of normally developing children. There is little evidence for a specifically cognitive relationship among the Uzgiris–Hunt scales in a normal sample when the statistical contribution of age to the correlations is removed. This does not necessarily mean that the high interscale correlations, without age removed, are mediated primarily by noncognitive experiential and maturational factors associated with chronological age. However, Uzgiris and Hunt's (1975) data provide no basis for distinguishing between typical and necessary developmental relationships.

Generally, experiments are the preferred methodology to separate typical from necessary relationships and to demonstrate causal links among variables. If there were some way to manipulate broad categories of opportunities for experiences or to intervene and modify dramatically the rate of motor development and to observe the effects of such manipulations on the cognitive variables, perhaps more definite conclusions could be drawn. It hardly deserves comment that such experimental interventions with humans are neither feasible nor ethical. However, there is an alternative. Unfortunate cases of deviant and delayed development constitute natural experiments of sorts. It is well established, for example, that chronological age is not always a good predictor of mental status in samples of retarded children. Furthermore, motor development and mental development in brain-damaged individuals are not always correlated. Many persons with severe congenital motor handicaps, such as cerebral palsy, are of normal intelligence as children and adults (Flavell, 1977). Contrastively, many severely mentally retarded individuals display motor skills at higher developmental levels than their mental skills. However, little data exist on the effects of these deviations from typical development on the predicted relationship between cognitive variables during the sensorimotor period. If developmental disturbances in these other areas in turn alter the strength of the observed relationship between the cognitive variables, the case for a necessary cognitive relationship will be seriously weakened. If, however, correlations among cognitive variables remain high within deviant samples, the case for the cognitive structural base will be strengthened. In other words, the potential for either confirmation or disconfirmation of predictions of the structure criterion exists—powerful conclusions to be drawn from strictly correlational analyses. Of course, these ''natural experiments'' do not always allow a precise statement of the nature of the ''manipulation.'' One cannot always know or understand all of the ramifications of a particular handicap. Fortunately, this is not critical to the proposed analyses. If the various handicapping conditions produce deviations from the typically observed relationships among at least some of the variables, the goal of the ''manipulations'' will have been achieved. Necessary relationships should become distinguishable from typical ones.

The sampling strategy is more likely to be effective in altering typical correlations among developmental measures in a group of handicapped infants than in infants classified only as at risk for developmental disabilities. The high-risk group's development may be expected more closely to approximate normal development, with greater likelihood that all developmental measures will be statistically confounded. The attenuation of typical correlations would be expected to be observed most readily in a heterogeneous group of individuals displaying various handicapping conditions of varying degrees of severity.

To gain as much information as possible from the data gathered on various samples, two types of analyses will be conducted. A series of pairwise, zero-order, product–moment correlational analyses between all of the measures of interest will provide a picture of the relationships between all pairs of variables, without considering the potential contribution of the other variables to the observed Pearson's. A technique called the hierarchical model of the multiple regression/correlation (MRC) analysis (Cohen & Cohen, 1975) will enable more precise mathematical statements of the strength of the relationships among measures, controlling for some of the variables. The hierarchical MRC involves a series of multiple regression/correlation analyses with one dependent variable and a set of independent variables. Selection of the dependent variable and the order in which the independent variables are entered is determined by the research question. The most important piece of information generated by this technique for our purposes is the *unique* proportion of the *total* variance in the dependent measure shared with each new independent variable entered. At each step in the analyses, the variance shared with previously entered variables is removed. The change in the proportion of variance accounted for by each new independent variable is analogous to the square of the semipartial correlation between that variable and the dependent variable, controlling for the "effects" of all previously entered variables. The result is a statistically conservative estimate of the unique proportion of the total variance shared between the two measures. For our own purposes, this means that the proportion of variance shared between the two cognitive measures can be determined, with variance shared with chronological age (CA) and a measure of motor development first removed. The theoretical question dictates that CA and the motor variable be entered into the analyses prior to the independent cognitive variable, to control for their contribution to the variance in the dependent cognitive measure. Such an analysis, with a deviant population, may allow a powerful statement of the strength of the relationship between the cognitive measures, if the sampling strategy effectively reduces the correlations of either of these variables with CA or level of motor development. The MRC analyses also generate a multiple correlation coefficient and a combined total of the proportion of variance in the dependent measure accounted for by all of the independent variables entered into the analyses up to that point.

It may be expected that the statistically conservative MRC analyses will yield little information of value in a normal population. The statistical removal of the variance shared with the typically highly correlated CA and motor measure may leave little variance to be accounted for by strictly cognitive factors. The analyses, if the sampling strategy is effective, should achieve greatest power with the most deviant samples. Deliberate strategies to partition the handicapped sample into subsamples can be pursued to reduce further the typical relationships of CA and motor development to measures of mental development (i.e., mental age or cognitive level).

The emphasis thus far has been on correlational techniques. However, should the predicted pattern of relationships be confirmed, descriptive analyses at an individual level would be required to demonstrate stage congruence between cognitive domains. High correlations do not necessarily imply congruence. For example, one domain may systematically lead the other by a full level throughout development. The correlation between measures for the two domains would be very high but level congruence nearly nonexistent. A descriptive analysis involving a comparison of individual scores for each cognitive domain must supplement the correlational analyses. If the results confirm predictions and suggest the need for such an analysis, it will be described in the *Results* section, below.

It may be observed that our sampling strategy is at odds with a recently advocated approach to research with handicapped populations. Kopp and Krakow (1980) argue for more careful specification of handicapped sample characteristics, with greater effort to restrict and subcategorize samples. The differences are not irreconcilable, but they reflect different strategies for different research questions. Our goal is to evaluate global or universal aspects of development, independent of disability. Kopp and Krakow (1980) address questions of individual differences in patterns of development across different well-defined subsets of high-risk and handicapped groups. Their goal is to determine how each type of disability differentially affects developmental progress in the various domains. However, for research questions about universals in development, a heterogeneous sample is an asset, not a liability. Understanding the developmental similarities across different disability groups can provide a better perspective for evaluating group and individual differences.

Method

Subjects

A sample of 90 high-risk and handicapped infants and toddlers served as subjects in the research to be reported. They were accessible sometime during the past 3 years through their participation in a daily center-based program of early intervention directed by the senior author. Some children who participated in the intervention project were excluded from the study. A minimal criterion for inclusion in the study was enough functional vision and motor ability to demonstrate successful reach and grasp for an object. A wide range of developmental levels is represented in the sample. Means and standard deviations for CA (corrected for prematurity, when necessary) and for the developmental measures administered to each child are presented in Table 3 for 20 high-risk children (first

Table 3. Means and Standard Deviations for High Risk and Handicapped
Samples and Subsamples

Measure		High Risk $n = 20$	Total Handicapped $n = 70$	Handicapped with CA $\geq$ 30 mos. $n = 33$	$|MA\text{-}PA|\geq$ 4 mos. $n = 29$
CA	$\bar{X}$	22.25	24.21	33.54	29.76
(mos.)	SD	8.17	9.47	2.93	6.09
BAYLEY					
PA	$\bar{X}$	18.65	12.26	17.03	17.66
(mos.)	SD	6.85	7.49	7.11	8.07
BAYLEY					
MA	$\bar{X}$	20.00	11.83	16.06	18.07
(mos.)	SD	7.22	6.57	6.32	7.69
MEAN					
AUHS	$\bar{X}$	3.08	2.11	2.78	2.94
(level)	SD	.72	1.06	.89	.76
MEAN					
ESCS	$\bar{X}$	3.01	2.03	2.51	2.71
(level)	SD	.60	.95	.96	.84

column) and 70 handicapped children (second column). Of the 20 high-risk
children, 15 are male, as are 32 of the 70 handicapped children. Within the
handicapped sample, 16 have Down syndrome; 4 have a visual impairment as
their primary handicap; 4 have a hearing impairment; 7 are emotionally disturbed, with accompanying mental retardation; 5 have significant physical handicaps (cerebral palsy, arthrogryposis); 14 have multiple handicaps that include
mental retardation and some physical or sensory impairment; and 20 others have
some degree of retardation with various (e.g., hydrocephalus, anoxia, fetal alcohol syndrome) or unknown etiologies. The great majority of the children are
from families of low socioeconomic status.

Procedures

Each child was assessed on the AUHS, the ESCS, and the Bayley Mental
Scale for construct validation, and on the Bayley Motor Scale as an index of level
of motor development. Administration of the total test battery for a child was
completed within 3 weeks. Except for minor modifications, the procedures for
the AUHS are contained in Uzgiris and Hunt (1975). A draft of procedures for
the ESCS is being revised for publication (Seibert & Hogan, in preparation).

The data for each child include CA, Bayley mental age (MA) and psychomotor age (PA), a mean object level score for the AUHS, and a mean social level
score for the ESCS. The mean level scores are computed in the following way.

For each scale from each cognitive assessment instrument, the highest level at which a child passes an item in a scale is the score the child receives for that scale. For example, if a child passes at least one item at level 3, but none any higher, in the Responding to Joint Attention scale, a score of 3 is given to the child for that scale. A mean level score is then determined for each child by computing the average level score for all the scales for that assessment instrument. In the object domain, this average is based on the five AUHS. In the social-communication domain, the mean ESCS level score is based on either seven or eight scales. Because the Maintaining Joint Attention scale was developed recently, the majority of test sessions did not generate a score for this scale. If a score was available, it was included in the calculation of the mean. In the earliest testing sessions, when the ESCS was first being developed, scores for one or two scales were occasionally missing. When this happened, the mean was computed using the five or six remaining scales. Mean scores based on only five or six ESCS scores constitute less than 3% of the total data pool.

ESCS and AUHS test administrations were carried out independently for each child and rated without knowledge of performance in the other domain. Seven testers administered the ESCS and seven testers administered the AUHS. Only three testers (the authors) were trained on both instruments, but none administered both sets of scales to the same subject. All testing sessions for both sets of scales were videotaped and independently scored by two raters, neither of whom had information on the child's performance on the other assessment. Interrater discrepancies for both the ESCS and the AUHS were resolved by recourse to the videotaped records of the testing sessions.

Interrater and test–retest reliabilities were computed for a subset of specially collected data, as part of a study of the reliability of the ESCS. Spearman's rank-order correlation coefficient for interrater reliability for mean ESCS level was .93 (n = 56, p < .001). The correlation coefficient for the mean ESCS level for test–retest reliability was .88 (n = 28, p < .001). For the mean AUHS level, interrater and test–retest reliabilities were determined for a smaller subset of the scores. The scales' reliability has already been demonstrated across a number of studies with different populations (e.g., Kahn, 1976; Uzgiris & Hunt, 1975). The analysis for interrater reliability for mean AUHS level produced a Spearman's rank-order correlation coefficient of .98 (n = 41, p < .001). An analysis of test–retest reliability for mean AUHS level yielded a correlation coefficient of .98 (n = 8, p < .01).

Results

Two types of analyses, described earlier, were performed on the data. For both the high-risk and handicapped samples, a series of pairwise, zero-order, product–moment correlational analyses was carried out for all of the measures. This allows an examination of the strength of the relationships among each pair of variables, without considering effects of the other variables. The results are presented in the top half of Table 4 for the high-risk sample and the top half of of Table 5 for the handicapped sample.

In addition, a series of hierarchical MRC analyses was conducted, with mean ESCS level as the dependent measure. The PA, CA, and mean AUHS level were entered into the analyses as independent variables, in that order. Mean ESCS level was chosen as the dependent measure because it is the novel measure in the battery, for which a cognitive base is being evaluated. The order for entering the independent variables allows a determination of the unique contribution of the AUHS scores to the total variance in the ESCS scores, with the variance shared with PA and CA removed. Results of the hierarchical MRC analyses are present-ed in the bottom half of Table 4 for the high-risk sample and the bottom half of Table 5 for the handicapped sample. Variances are reported as adjusted R^2. Adjusted R^2 is an unbiased estimate of R^2, used to correct for the overestimate of R^2 that may occur when the number of subjects is small relative to the number of independent or predictor variables in the regression analyses. Throughout the rest of this paper, all variances will be reported as adjusted R^2. The MRC analyses produce a multiple R (not adjusted) and a total adjusted R^2 for all of the variables,

Table 4. Results of Correlational Analyses Between All Measures and Summary of Hierarchical Multiple Regression/Correlation Analyses with Mean ESCS as Dependent Variable, for High Risk Sample (N = 20)

	*Correlational Analyses for All Measures**			
	CA	*PA*	*MA*	*Mean AUHS*
PA	.91			
MA	.97	.90		
Mean AUHS	.85	.87	.85	
Mean ESCS	.78	.76	.78	.93

Note:
*all correlations significant (p < .001)

	Hierarchical Multiple Regression/Correlation Analyses with Mean ESCS Level as Dependent Variable		
Independent Variable	*Multiple R*	*Adjusted R^2*	*Change in Adjusted R^2*
PA	.76	.56	.56
CA	.79	.58	.02
AUHS	.93	.84	.26

Table 5. Results of Correlational Analyses Between All Measures and Summary of Hierarchical Multiple Regression/Correlation Analyses with Mean ESCS as Dependent Variable, for Total Handicapped Sample (N = 70)

| | *Correlational Analyses for All Measures**| | | |
	CA	PA	MA	Mean AUHS
PA	.61			
MA	.63	.82		
Mean AUHS	.65	.77	.91	
Mean ESCS	.44	.62	.85	.89

Note:
*all correlations significant (p < .001)

| | *Hierarchical Multiple Regression/Correlation Analyses with Mean ESCS Level as Dependent Variable* | | |
Independent Variable	Multiple R	Adjusted R^2	Change in Adjusted R^2
PA	.62	.38	.38
CA	.63	.37	− .01
AUHS	.91	.83	.46

in addition to the change in adjusted R^2 as each new independent variable is entered.

All of the correlations for the high-risk sample in Table 4 are greater than chance (p < .001). The correlations of greatest interest to the structural hypothesis are those of the ESCS with the other variables. The correlation of ESCS with AUHS for the high-risk sample (r = .93) is significantly greater than the correlation of ESCS with the other variables (p < .005). This indicates a shared cognitive base to the relationship between ESCS and AUHS, even for the relatively normally developing high-risk sample. The hierarchical MRC reported in the bottom half of Table 4 reinforces this interpretation. A significant proportion of the total variance in the ESCS scores for the high-risk sample is shared with AUHS scores [a change in adjusted R^2 = .26, F(1,16) = 26.23, p < .001], with PA and CA accounted for. Psychomotor age, analyzed first, accounts for a significant proportion of ESCS variance [change in adjusted R^2 = .56, F(1,18) = 22.72, p < .001], but the effect of CA is negligible [change in adjusted R^2 = .02, F(1,17) = .976, ns].

It may appear, from these results, that the sampling strategy is not needed to demonstrate a strictly cognitive relationship between the ESCS and the AUHS.

Nevertheless, as predicted, the degree of that relationship becomes even clearer when the results from the handicapped sample are examined. All of the correlations in the top of Table 5 are significantly greater than chance ($p < .001$). The correlation of ESCS with AUHS is virtually the same as that observed with the high-risk sample. However, the correlations of ESCS with CA and PA are considerably lower in comparison. The correlations of ESCS with AUHS and MA are not significantly different from each other, but both are significantly greater ($p < .001$) than the correlations of ESCS with both CA and PA. With the variance attributable to PA and CA removed, the change in adjusted R^2, when AUHS is entered into the hierarchical MRC analyses to predict ESCS, is .45 [$F(1,66) = 173.20$, $p < .001$]. This represents nearly half of the total variance in the ESCS scores. In comparison, for the high-risk sample, AUHS scores uniquely accounted for only about one-fourth of the variance. Psychomotor age, entered first, shares 38% of the variance with ESCS [$F(1,68) = 40.97$, $p < .001$]. Chronological age does not account for any additional variance. The total amount of ESCS variance accounted for by the three variables (the second column) is virtually the same for both samples. For the high-risk sample, total adjusted $R^2 = .84$; for the handicapped sample, total adjusted $R^2 = .83$.

The analyses conducted with the handicapped sample amplify the relationships observed in the high-risk sample. However, it remains ambiguous to what extent general maturational and experiential factors, as indexed by PA and CA, mediate the relationship observed between ESCS and AUHS, since all measures are significantly correlated with each other, even in the handicapped sample. Therefore, a deliberate subject selection strategy was pursued to create subsamples for which the observed relationships of both PA and CA to the cognitive measures are further attenuated. Effects of such a sampling strategy on the ESCS–AUHS relationship may clarify the contribution of motor- and age-related factors to the correlation, relative to cognitive structural factors.

Two sampling strategies were adopted, creating two subsamples. The criterion for the first is that the subject is handicapped and at least 30 months of age chronologically. Requiring a CA of 30 months controls for opportunity for experience, since normally developing children should be at ceiling on all of the developmental measures by 30 months. This sampling strategy is intended to reduce the correlations of CA to the other developmental measures, by restricting the variance in CA.

The criterion for the second subsample is that the subject evidence at least a 4-month difference *in either direction* between his MA and PA. By including only subjects with such discrepancies, the correlation between MA and PA should be reduced, along with the correlation of PA with the other cognitive measures. This strategy should minimize the confounding statistical effects of PA, as a general index of motor development, on the cognitive relationships. For either sampling strategy to be of value, adequate numbers of subjects must meet each criterion and the developmental range of scores should approximate that observed in the other samples. Table 3 reports the means and standard deviations of all of the variables for the 33 handicapped subjects with a CA of 30 months or greater, and for the 29 subjects with absolute MA-PA discrepancies of 4 months or greater. With the exception of CA in both subsamples, the means and standard deviations are similar to the other samples; means lie between those for the high-risk and the total handicapped samples.

The results of the series of pairwise correlational analyses and the hierarchical MRC analyses for the two subsamples are presented in Tables 6 and 7. The sampling strategies have effectively reduced the correlations of the cognitive measures with PA and CA. Of greater significance, the correlation of ESCS with AUHS remains unaffected in both subsamples.

For the subsample with the restricted CA range, the correlations of ESCS with both MA and AUHS are greater than chance ($p < .001$). The correlation of ESCS with PA is also significant ($p = .05$). The correlation of ESCS with CA is nonsignificant, as anticipated. The correlations of ESCS with both AUHS and MA are not significantly different from each other, but both are significantly different from the correlations of ESCS with CA and PA ($p < .001$).

Table 6. Results of Correlational Analyses Between All Measures and Summary of Hierarchical Multiple Regression/Correlation Analyses with Mean ESCS as Dependent Variable, for Handicapped Sub-sample with CA 30 Months or Greater (N = 33)

	Correlational Analyses			
	CA	*PA*	*MA*	*Mean AUHS*
PA	.23			
MA	.29*	.65**		
Mean AUHS	.34*	.56**	.87**	
Mean ESCS	.12	.40*	.84**	.85**

Notes:
*p < .05
**p < .001

Hierarchical Multiple Regression/Correlation Analyses with Mean ESCS Level as Dependent Variable

Independent Variable	*Multiple R*	*Adjusted R^2*	*Change in Adjusted R^2*
PA	.40	.13	.13
CA	.40	.10	−.03
AUHS	.87	.73	.63

Table 7. Result of Correlational Analyses Between All Measures and Summary of Hierarchical Multiple Regression/Correlation Analyses with Mean ESCS as Dependent Variable for Handicapped Sub-sample with Absolute Difference Between MA and PA of at least 4 months (N = 29)

Correlational Analyses

	CA	PA	MA	Mean AUHS
PA	.35*			
MA	.35*	.55**		
Mean AUHS	.05	.54**	.85**	
Mean ESCS	.08	.26	.81**	.87**

Notes:
*p < .05
**p < .001

Hierarchical Multiple Regression/Correlation Analyses with Mean ESCS Level as Dependent Variable

Independent Variable	Multiple R	Adjusted R^2	Change in Adjusted R^2
PA	.26	.04	.04
CA	.26	.00	−.04
AUHS	.91	.81	.81

According to the hierarchical MRC analyses for the restricted CA range sub-sample in Table 6, the unique contribution of AUHS to the total variance in ESCS is .62 [F(1,29) = 66.53, p < .001]. A significant but very small proportion of the variance in ESCS is shared with PA [change in adjusted R^2 = .13, F(1,31) = 4.76, p < .05], when PA is entered first into the analyses. CA has no significant additional effect [change in adjusted R^2 = −.03, F(1,30) = 0.00, ns].

For the subsample with the |MA-PA| split of at least 4 months, the correlations of ESCS with both MA and AUHS, reported in Table 7, are significant (p < .001). Neither correlation between ESCS and CA or PA is significantly greater than chance. The goal of the sampling strategy has been achieved. The correlations of ESCS with MA and AUHS are not significantly different from each other. Both are significantly greater than the correlations of ESCS with CA and PA (p < .001). Consistent with the pattern of correlations, the hierarchical MRC analyses indicate nonsignificant proportions of variance in ESCS are attributable to PA (change in adjusted R^2 = .04, F(1,27) = 0.98, ns) and CA [change in adjusted R^2 = −.04, F(1,26) = 0.00, ns]. The AUHS scores for this subsample account for 81% [F(1,25) = 108.69, p < .001] of the total variance in ESCS. This value is nearly identical to the combined variances for PA, CA, and AUHS in the high-risk and total handicapped samples.

With statistical support for the structure criterion in the group data, a descriptive analysis of the individual data is needed to determine the degree of stage congruence between the ESCS and AUHS. A data point to evaluate that congruence was generated for each child by subtracting his mean AUHS score from his mean ESCS score. If there is congruence between domains, the mode for the distribution of these discrepancies should be at zero. In addition, since skill acquisition can be accelerated in either domain as a function of opportunities for experience, discrepancies should be distributed symmetrically on either side of the mode. The distribution should approximate a normal distribution, with decreasing frequency the larger the discrepancy. The frequency histogram for the combined sample (n = 90) of high-risk and handicapped subjects is presented in Figure 1. Scores are collapsed into four-tenths of a stage interval. Discrepancy scores within one-fifth of a stage of each other therefore are scored at the zero point in the distribution, to allow for measurement error. Data points to the right of the mode represent mean ESCS scores superior to mean AUHS scores; points to the left represent superior AUHS scores. The distribution conforms to the prediction. When individual mean level scores were inspected, it was found that discrepancies of various magnitudes are distributed across all levels. Therefore, the results cannot be merely an artifact of ceiling or floor effects. In addition, congruent scoring cannot have resulted from experimenter bias, or halo effects, since testing and rating were carried out independently for each instrument by different testers and raters.

VII. DISCUSSION

The results are consistent with predictions based on the stage structure criterion. The relationship between the social-communication domain and the object cognitive domain, as indexed by the correlational analyses, remains strong and nearly identical across all of the samples and subsamples. Observed correlations of these variables with CA and PA vary widely across samples, dropping in some instances to nonsignificant levels near zero. From a strictly empirical perspective, only the AUHS score consistently and reliably provides a strong index of the level of social-communication performance across samples.

The hierarchical MRC analyses demonstrate that for all of the samples, a unique part of the variance in the ESCS scores is shared with the AUHS scores. What becomes evident as the analyses are repeated across the handicapped sample and the subsamples is that the strength of the observed relationship between the two cognitive measures is only minimally a function of their relationship to chronological age and level of motor development. The total proportion of variance in ESCS scores shared with the combined variables, PA, CA,

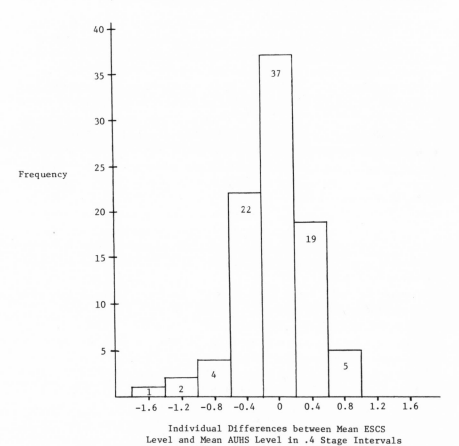

Individual Differences between Mean ESCS
Level and Mean AUHS Level in .4 Stage Intervals
(Positive difference indicates higher ESCS score)

Figure 1. Distribution of Differences between Mean ESCS Level and Mean
AUHS Level (n = 90)

and AUHS scores, remains nearly the same across all samples. However, the
proportion attributable solely to the AUHS scores increases dramatically as the
different sampling strategies reduce the statistical relationship between the social-communication scores and both PA and CA. This leads to probably a more
valid index of the real strength of the relationship between the two cognitive
measures. The minimal degree of mediation by CA and PA is empirically, if not
theoretically, unexpected. When a number of different variables are all typically
highly intercorrelated with each other, it is often assumed that each variable is
contributing in a *theoretically* meaningful way to some part of the variance in
each of the other variables. When the relationship of one of these variables to the
others is reduced for a certain subsample, the correlations among the other
variables are expected to drop correspondingly. In addition, the multiple *R* in the

regression analyses may be expected to drop. This did not occur for the correlations between ESCS and AUHS. Therefore, we conclude that the high correlations of the cognitive measures with CA and PA in the normal (high-risk) sample represent typically observed but not necessary relationships. Only the stable correlation between the AUHS and the ESCS indexes a necessary developmental relationship, that is, a cognitive structural relationship.

In any attempt to replicate these results, two issues must be considered. First, failure to find reduced relationships of PA and CA with the cognitive measures for handicapped samples does not disconfirm the hypothesis. For example, when data for only Down syndrome infants, a more homogeneous subsample of the total sample, are examined, the correlation of PA with the ESCS score is as high as that observed in the high-risk sample. Critical to the hypothesis is that the relationship *between the two cognitive measures* remains strong across all samples, provided the same developmental range is represented in the samples. Correlations with other variables, not cognitively mediated, may be expected to fluctuate as a function of sample characteristics. To the extent that another measure assesses cognitive factors, its correlation with the ESCS and AUHS may be expected to remain high. The consistently strong correlations of MA with ESCS and AUHS, for all the samples, illustrate this point.

The second issue is that a similar breadth of scores, representative of the different developmental levels, must be included in a replication sample. If scores cover a shorter developmental time span, the observed correlations between the cognitive measures may drop because the sample variances have been reduced.

The frequency histogram indicates that the two domains, as represented by the two sets of scales, are structurally equivalent. This supports the model, because level equivalency for scale items was established a priori, on conceptual grounds, and not empirically. Although either domain may be accelerated for some children, there is a tendency for the AUHS scores to be the accelerated measure in more instances. The histogram reflects this in the greater number of discrepancies to the left of the zero point and by the longer tail to the left of the distribution. Consistent with the information provided by the histogram, the group means in Table 3 indicate a slight numerical superiority for the average AUHS mean level, compared to ESCS mean level, for all samples and subsamples. The differences in the means, however, are not significant for the high-risk sample [$t(19) = 1.26$, ns] or the total handicapped sample [$t(69) = 1.37$, ns]. The differences are significant for the above-30-months-CA subsample [$t(28) = 3.01$, $p < .01$] and the |MA-PA| split-greater-than-4-months subsample [$t(32) = 3.04$, $p < .01$]. The AUHS advantage, if replicated, should be explained. It may reflect differences in testing procedures between the two sets of scales, errors in level assignment for a few scale items, or differences in typical opportunities for experiences relevant to mastery of skills in the two domains. The fact that the differences reach significance only in the subsamples suggests that social-communication development may be more vulnerable to disruption than object cognitive development in instances of more extreme deviation. Despite the minor perturbations in the pattern of the data from the model's predictions, the overall picture is remarkably consistent with expectations. The mode is clearly at zero and discrepancies are distributed almost equally on either side of the mode.

Other patterns in the data, not germane to the structure criterion, are worth noting. Although the relationship between the object cognitive and social-communication domains apparently exists relatively independent of motor development for these samples, level of motor development apparently contributes in a meaningful way to the variance in the object scores. For every analysis across subsamples, the relationship between PA and AUHS remains at least moderate and highly significant. This suggests that the assessment of object cognitive skills is more dependent on level of motor development than is the assessment of social-communication skills. Intuitively, this makes sense. Many communication skills can be demonstrated merely by eye contact, vocalizations, and gross body movements. In contrast, AUHS skills require a greater degree of motor control to manipulate objects. Despite the dependence of AUHS performance on motor skills, its relationship to the social-communication scales can exist quite independent of the child's level of motor development. Apparently, two relatively orthogonal components contribute to variance in the object cognitive scores: a motor component and a cognitive component. The ESCS appears to be a more motor-independent measure of cognition, possibly better suited for assessing cognitive capacities in physically handicapped children. Such a conclusion is consistent with the finding (Mundy, Seibert, Hogan, & Fagan, in press) that the ESCS correlated more strongly than MA with a simple visual recognition measure. The recognition measure assesses preference for novelty, as an index of cognitive processing skills, almost completely independent of motor skills. In addition, it has a strong visual component, like the ESCS.

Any conclusion about the role of a motor component in the measures studied should be qualified. The level of motor development in the samples did not bear a necessary relationship to the social-communication measure. However, visually directed reach and grasp was established as a minimal entry criterion. This skill may be central to the acquisition *during the sensorimotor period* of many of the basic cognitive concepts. In addition, although motor development was not significantly correlated with the social-communication measure in one of the subsamples, this does not mean that it plays no role in the development of those skills in normally developing children. The only reasonable conclusion is that its role is not a necessary one. In addition, severe motor impairments may prevent normal rates of development in both cognitive domains, without affecting the observed correlations between the cognitive measures. Both social and object skills may develop in concordance, but at a slower than normal rate. The data from this study cannot address these issues. Observation of physically handicapped infants with no indication of organic retardation could provide the answer. Longitudinal data gathered by our project on a single child with congenital arthrogryposis (fusion of the knee, ankle, elbow, and wrist joints) suggest that reach and grasp may be necessary for normal rates of cognitive development during infancy. Like other severely physically handicapped children reported in the literature (e.g., Decarie, 1969; Kopp & Shaperman, 1973), this child was nearly normal on most language and cognitive measures at 3 years of age (adapting for his motor deficit). However, the child had demonstrated significant delays during the first 2 years of life in achieving cognitive and communicative milestones, even those not dependent on motor skills for their performance. Whether such a delay in infancy has significance for later intellectual development is an entirely different question, but evidence suggests that it may not (Kopp, 1979).

With support for the existence of global structural levels, other structural issues need to be addressed. The decision rules for assigning scale items to structural levels must be better operationalized. Developing and applying these rules is not always straightforward. Factors such as how a particular skill has been acquired or how context-specific it is may affect the decision about level assignment.

Empirical analyses may augment theoretical efforts at level assignment. Older, severely handicapped adolescents and adults, retarded at a sensorimotor level of functioning, have been observed to show high stage congruence across cognitive dimensions (Woodward, 1959). The stage model predicts that such retarded individuals should be capable of acquiring new skills only at or below their arrested level of development. If individuals functioning at a particular level of sensorimotor development demonstrate or acquire a skill assigned to a higher level of development, the decision rules that led to level assignment of that item should be reevaluated.

A training study strategy, adapted from Wohlwill (1973), can be used with developing infants and children to test other structural relationships among scales. The strategy involves constructing a sample of children matched for the same developmental level on a targeted scale. Despite the match on the targeted scale, subjects typically are at different developmental levels on other scales, considered to be closely related. A child's pretest performance on a related scale may be at the same level, a lower level, or a higher level than his performance on the targeted scale. Each child is trained on higher items from the targeted scale. The number of items mastered on the targeted scale following training should correlate with the child's pretest score on the related scale, if the scales are structurally related. Pilot data using this design have been gathered on a small number of subjects, matched and trained on self-recognition skills. Children's pretest performances on the related Object Permanence scale were at various levels. Posttest scores on self-recognition following training correlated moderately and significantly with initial object permanence levels.

The other stage criteria also need to be addressed in future research. Full validation of the assessment scales depends on such efforts. Because of their hypothesized structural link to the items of the AUHS, for which ordinality has been demonstrated, and because of the apparent hierarchical nature of many of the ESCS items at successive levels, ordinality of the ESCS was assumed. Nothing in the pattern of results challenges that assumption. Nevertheless, their ordinality, as a reflection of the hierarchization and integration criteria, should be assessed rather than assumed.

Longitudinal observations of the development of skills from both sets of cognitive scales need to be gathered and evaluated for periods of transition and consolidation. In addition, stage congruence across the individual scales at predicted points of consolidation needs to be examined. Research also is needed to examine relationships among skills from different scales, both within and between domains. A skill or concept from one scale may index a concept that is prerequisite to a skill from another scale. The abstraction of component dimensions into separate scales should not be interpreted to mean that development of a new skill within a scale depends only on the skills listed earlier in that scale. For example, pilot data suggest that the concepts indexed by socially appropriate use of objects (from the object scales) and the ability to follow another's pointing gesture are prerequisites to the comprehension of referential labels (Hogan, Seibert, & Mundy, 1980). Other relationships among the scale dimensions, at the same point in time and across periods of several months or more, also need to be explored. These analyses can yield information about changes in the interpatterning of cognitive structures across development.

Intervention implications of the ESCS and the cognitive stage model have been discussed in depth elsewhere (Seibert, in press; Seibert & Hogan, 1982). Our research has started from the premise that development of better, conceptually based assessment instruments can make both theoretical and practical contributions. In this chapter, we have emphasized theoretical issues, but we remain concerned about their applied relevance. We have attempted to expand on a framework suggested by others for looking at how the very young child adapts to his physical and social environments and how his ability to adapt changes with development. If this framework and the scales are useful in stimulating additional research on the stage question and the nature of early cognitive development, and if they provide the practitioner with a basis for more effective intervention, our primary objectives for conducting this research will have been achieved.

ACKNOWLEDGMENTS

Some of the data reported in this chapter were presented at the Biennial Meetings of the Society for Research in Child Development, Boston, April 1981. Research was supported in part by the Mailman Foundation and in part by OSE Grant No. G007802091. The authors wish to thank Keith Scott and Mary Hale-Haniff for comments on earlier drafts of this paper.

REFERENCES

Ainsworth, M. D. S. Object relations, dependency, and attachment: A theoretical review of the infant-mother relationship. *Child Development*, 1969, *40*, 969–1025.

Ainsworth, M. D. S. Attachment and dependency: A comparison. In J. L. Gewirtz (Ed.), *Attachment and dependency*. Washington, D.C.: V. H. Winston, 1972.

Bates, E. *Language and context: The acquisition of pragmatics*. New York: Academic Press, 1976.

Bates, E., Benigni, L., Bretherton, I., Camaioni, L., & Volterra, V. *The emergence of symbols: Cognition and communication in infancy*. New York: Academic Press, 1979.

Bates, E., Bretherton, I., Shore, C., & Carpen, K. *The emergence of symbols in language and action: The role of contextual support*. Paper presented at the meeting of the Society for Research in Child Development, San Francisco, March 1979.

Bates, E., Camaioni, L., & Volterra, V. The acquisition of performatives prior to speech. *Merrill-Palmer Quarterly*, 1975, *21*, 205–226.

Bayley, N. *Bayley Scales of Infant Development*. New York: Psychological Corporation, 1969.

Benedict, H. Early lexical development: Comprehension and production. *Journal of Child Language*, 1979, *6*, 183–200.

Bowlby, J. *Attachment and loss (vol. 1): Attachment*. New York: Basic Books, 1969.

Brainerd, C. J. The stage question in cognitive developmental theory. *The Behavioral and Brain Sciences*, 1978, *2*, 173–213.

Brazelton, T. B., Koslowski, B., & Main, M. The origins of reciprocity: The early mother-infant interaction. In M. Lewis & L. A. Rosenblum (Eds.), *The effect of the infant on its caregiver*. New York: John Wiley & Sons, 1974.

Bricker, D., & Bricker, W. Infant, toddler and pre-school research and intervention project: Report-year III. *IMRID Behavioral Science Monograph No. 23*, Institute of Mental Retardation and Intellectual Development, George Peabody College for Teachers, Nashville, Tennessee, 1973.

Bruner, J. S. From communication to language—A psychological perspective. *Cognition*, 1975, *3*, 255–287. (a)

Bruner, J. S. The ontogenesis of speech acts. *Journal of Child Language*, 1975, *2*, 1–19. (b)

Bruner, J. S. Early social interaction and language acquisition. In H. R. Schaffer (Ed.), *Studies in mother-infant interaction*. London: Academic Press, 1977.

Bruner, J., Roy, C., & Ratner, N. *The beginnings of request*. Unpublished manuscript, University of Oxford, Oxford, 1979.

Carver, R. P. The Coleman Report: Using inappropriately designed achievement tests. *American Educational Research Journal*, 1975, *12*, 77–86.

Cattell, P. *The measurement of intelligence of infants and young children*. New York: Psychological Corporation, 1966.

Chatelanat, G., & Schoggen, M. Issues encountered in devising an observation system to assess spontaneous infant behavior-environment interactions. In J. Hogg & P. Mittler (Eds.), *Advances in mental handicap research, vol. 1*. New York: John Wiley & Sons, 1980.

Cohen, J., & Cohen, P. *Applied multiple regression/correlation analysis for the behavioral sciences*. Hillsdale, N.J.: Lawrence Erlbaum Associates, 1975.

Dale, P. Is early pragmatic development measurable? *Journal of Child Language*, 1980, *7*, 1–12.

Decarie, T. G. A study of the mental and emotional development of the thalidomide child. In B. M. Foss (Ed.), *Determinants of infant behavior (Vol. 4)*. London: Metheun, 1969.

Dunst, C. J. *An early cognitive-linguistic intervention strategy*. Unpublished manuscript, Western Carolina Center, Morganton, N.C., 1977.

Dunst, C. J. *Manual for the clinical and educational use of the Uzgiris and Hunt Scales of Infant Psychological Development.* Baltimore, M.D.: University Park Press, 1980.

Escalona, S., & Corman, H. *Albert Einstein Scales of Sensorimotor Development,* Unpublished manuscript.

Fischer, K. Commentary on C. J. Brainerd's "The stage question in cognitive-developmental theory." *The Behavioral and Brain Sciences,* 1978, *2,* 186–187.

Fischer, K. W. A theory of cognitive development: The control and construction of hierarchies of skills. *Psychological Review,* 1980, *87,* 477–531.

Fischer, K. W., & Bullock, D. Patterns of data: Sequence, synchrony, and constraint in cognitive development. In K. W. Fischer (Ed.), *Cognitive development: New directions for child development.* San Francisco: Josey-Bass, 1981.

Fischer, K. W., & Corrigan, R. *A skill approach to language development.* Paper presented at the Johnson Conference on Language Behavior in Infancy and Early Childhood, Santa Barbara, October 1979.

Flavell, J. H. *The developmental psychology of Jean Piaget.* Princeton: D. Van Nostrand Co., Inc., 1963.

Flavell, J. H. *Cognitive development.* Englewood Cliffs, N.J.: Prentice-Hall, 1977.

Flavell, J. H., & Wohlwill, J. F. Formal and functional aspects of cognitive development. In D. Elkind & J. H. Flavell (Eds.), *Studies in cognitive development.* New York: Oxford University Press, 1969.

Furth, H., & Wachs, H. *Thinking goes to school: Piaget's theory and practice.* London: Oxford University Press, 1974.

Hogan, A. E., Seibert, J. M., & Mundy, P. C. *The emergence of object labels in developmentally delayed toddlers: Implications for intervention and for a theory of early reference.* Paper presented at the Fifth Annual Boston University Conference on Language Development, Boston, October 1980.

Hunt, J.McV., Mohandessi, V., Ghodssi, M., & Akiyama, M. The psychological development of orphanage-reared infants: Interventions with outcomes (Tehran). *Genetic Psychology Monographs,* 1976, *94,* 177–226.

Huttenlocher, J. The origins of language comprehension. In R. L. Solso (Ed.), *Theories in cognitive psychology.* Hillsdale, N.J.: Lawrence Erlbaum, 1973.

Kagan, J., Kearsley, R. B., & Zelazo, R. R. *Infancy: Its place in human development.* Cambridge, Mass.: Harvard University Press, 1978.

Kahn, J. Utility of the Uzgiris and Hunt scales of sensorimotor development with severely and profoundly retarded children. *American Journal of Mental Deficiency,* 1976, *80,* 663–665.

Kopp, C. B. Perspectives on infant motor system development. In M. H. Bornstein & W. Kessen (Eds.), *Psychological development from infancy: Image to intention.* Hillsdale, N.J.: Lawrence Erlbaum Associates, 1979.

Kopp, C. B., & Krakow, J. B. *Research on biologically at-risk/handicapped infants: The issue of sample characteristics.* Unpublished manuscript, UCLA, Los Angeles, 1980.

Kopp, C. B., & Shaperman, J. Cognitive development in the absence of object manipulation during infancy. *Developmental Psychology,* 1973, *9,* 430.

Kopp, C. B., Sigman, M., & Parmelee, A. H. Ordinality and sensory-motor series. *Child Development,* 1973, *44,* 821.

Kopp, C. B., Sigman, M., & Parmelee, A. H. Longitudinal study of sensorimotor development. *Developmental Psychology,* 1974, *10,* 687–695.

Kramer, J. A., Hill, K. T., & Cohen, L. B. Infants' development of object permanence: A refined methodology and new evidence for Piaget's hypothesized ordinality. *Child Development,* 1975, *46,* 149–155.

Lawton, J. T., & Hooper, F. H. Piagetian theory and early childhood education: A critical analysis. In L. Siegel & C. Brainerd (Eds.), *Alternatives to Piaget.* New York: Academic Press, 1978.

Macnamara, J. From sign to language. In J. Macnamara (Ed.), *Language learning and thought*. New York: Academic Press, 1977.

McCall, R. B. Qualitative transitions in behavioral development in the first two years of life. In M. H. Bornstein & W. Kessen (Eds.), *Psychological development from infancy: Image to intention*. Hillsdale, N.J.: Lawrence Erlbaum, 1979.

McCall, R., Eichorn, D., & Hogarty, P. Transitions in early mental development. *Monographs of the Society for Research in Child Development*, 1977, *42*(3), No. 171.

McCall, R. B., Hogarty, P. S., & Hurlburt, N. Transitions in infant sensorimotor development and the prediction of childhood IQ. *American Psychologist*, 1972, *27*, 728–748.

Miller, J. F., Chapman, R. S., Branston, M. B., & Reichle, J. Language comprehension in sensorimotor stage V and VI. *Journal of Speech and Hearing Research*, 1980, *23*, 284–311.

Mundy, P. C., Seibert, J. M., Hogan, A. E., & Fagan, J. Novelty responding and behavioral development in developmentally delayed children. *Intelligence*, in press.

Nelson, K. Structure and strategy in learning to talk. *Monographs of the Society for Research in Child Development*, 1973, *38*(1–2), No. 149.

Nelson, K. Concept, word, and sentence: Interrelations in acquisition and development. *Psychological Review*, 1974, *81*, 267–285.

Ninio, A., & Bruner, J. The achievement and antecedents of labelling. *Journal of Child Language*, 1978, *5*, 1–15.

Phillips, D. C. What do the researcher and the practitioner have to offer each other? *Educational Researcher*, 1980, *9*(11), 17–24.

Piaget, J. *Play, dreams, and imitation in childhood*. New York: Norton, 1951.

Piaget, J. *The origins of intelligence in children*. New York: International Universities Press, 1952.

Piaget, J. *The construction of reality in the child*. New York: Basic Books, 1954.

Piaget, J. The general problems of the psychobiological development of the child. In J. M. Tanner & B. Inhelder (Eds.), *Discussions on child development*, Vol. 4. London, Tavistock, 1960.

Pinard, A., & Laurendeau, M. "Stage" in Piaget's cognitive-developmental theory: Exegesis of a concept. In D. Elkind & J. H. Flavell (Eds.), *Studies in cognitive development*. New York: Oxford University Press, 1969.

Reich, P. A. The early acquisition of word meaning. *Journal of Child Language*, 1976, *3*, 117–123.

Robinson, C. C., & Robinson, J. Sensorimotor functions and cognitive development. In M. Snell (Ed.), *Systematic instruction of the moderately and severely handicapped*. Columbus, OH: Charles F. Merrill Publishing Co., 1978.

Rogers, S. J. Characteristics of the cognitive development of profoundly retarded children. *Child Development*, 1977, *48*, 837–843.

Scaife, M., & Bruner, J. The capacity for joint visual attention in the infant. *Nature*, 1975, *253*(5489), 265–266.

Scott, K. G. The rationale and methodological considerations underlying early cognitive and behavioral assessment. In F. D. Minifie & L. L. Lloyd (Eds.), *Communication and cognitive abilities—early behavioral assessment*. Baltimore: University Park Press, 1978.

Seibert, J. M. *A model for analyzing the development of early communication skills, based on levels of cognitive organization*. Paper presented at the Fourth Annual Boston University Conference on Language Development, Boston, September 1979.

Seibert, J. M. Use of the scales of psychological development in early intervention programs. To be published in I. C. Uzgiris & J.McV. Hunt (Eds.), *Research with scales of psychological development in infancy*. Urbana, Ill.: University of Illinois Press, in press.

Seibert, J. M., & Hogan, A. E. A model for assessing social and object skills and planning intervention. In D. McClowry, A. Guilford, & S. Richardson (Eds.), *Infant communication: Development, assessment and intervention*. New York: Grune and Stratton, in press.

Seibert, J. M., & Hogan, A. E. *Administration manual for the Early Social-Communication Scales*, in preparation.

Seibert, J. M., & Oller, D. K. Linguistic pragmatics and language intervention strategies. *Journal of Autism and Developmental Disorders,* 1981, *11,* 75–88.

Sigel, I. E. The Piagetian system and the world of education. In D. Elkind & J. Flavell (Eds.), *Studies in cognitive development: Essays in honor of Jean Piaget.* New York: Oxford University Press, 1969.

Smith, M. *Project A.D.A.P.T.: Cognitive development.* Unpublished curriculum, Santa Barbara, Calif.

Stephens, B. A Piagetian approach to curriculum development. In E. Sontag, J. Smith & N. Certo (Eds.), *Educational programming for the severely and profoundly handicapped.* Reston, Va.: Council for Exceptional Children, 1977.

Sugarman-Bell, S. Some organizational aspects of pre-verbal communication. In I. Markova (Ed.), *The social context of language.* New York: Wiley & Sons, 1978.

Sullivan, E. V. Piagetian theory in the educational milieu: A critical appraisal. *Canadian Journal of Behavioral Science,* 1969, *3,* 1.

Trevarthen, C. Communication and cooperation in early infancy: A description of primary intersubjectivity. In M. Bullowa (Ed.), *Before speech: The beginning of interpersonal communication.* Cambridge: Cambridge University Press, 1979.

Uzgiris, I. C. Patterns of cognitive development in infancy. *Merrill-Palmer Quarterly,* 1973, *19,* 181–204.

Uzgiris, I. C. Organization of sensorimotor intelligence. In M. Lewis (Ed.), *Origins of intelligence.* New York: Plenum, 1976.

Uzgiris, I. C. Plasticity and structure. In I. C. Uzgiris & F. Weizman (Eds.), *The structuring of experience.* New York: Plenum, 1977. (a)

Uzgiris, I. C. Commentary on R. B. McCall, D. H. Eichorn & P. S. Hogarty, "Transitions in early mental development." *Monographs of the Society for Research in Child Development,* 1977, *42*(3), No. 171, 95–102. (b)

Uzgiris, I. C. Commentary on C. J. Brainerd's "The stage question in cognitive-developmental theory." *The Behavioral and Brain Sciences,* 1978, *2,* 204–205.

Uzgiris, I.C., & Hunt, J.McV. *Assessment in infancy: Ordinal scales of psychological development.* Urbana, Ill.: University of Illinois Press, 1975.

Werner, H., & Kaplan, B. *Symbol formation.* New York: Wiley, 1963.

Wohlwill, J. F. *The study of behavioral development.* New York: Academic Press, 1973.

Woodward, M. The behavior of idiots interpreted by Piaget's theory of sensorimotor development. *British Journal of Educational Psychology,* 1959, *29,* 60–71.

ASSESSMENT OF INSTITUTIONALIZED MENTALLY RETARDED CHILDREN

Alan D. Poling, Carol Parker and
Stephen E. Breuning

I. INTRODUCTION[1]

The present chapter is concerned with the appropriate assessment of mentally retarded children institutionalized in allegedly therapeutic facilities. We begin with a brief history of institutionalization, proceed to a general coverage of intelligence tests, measures of adaptive behavior, and treatment evaluation, then conclude with a discussion of legal and ethical issues. Our intent is to consider general assessment strategies, not to exhaustively analyze the specific assessment instruments used with the mentally retarded.

Advances in the Behavioral Measurement of Children, Volume 1, pages 93–136.
Copyright © 1984 by JAI Press Inc.
All rights of reproduction in any form reserved.
ISBN: 0-89232-282-9

II.   INSTITUTIONALIZATION OF THE MENTALLY RETARDED

It has been recognized throughout recorded history that there are significant behavioral differences across individuals, and stigmatization of the mentally retarded, who lack the adaptive and intellectual responses of their peers, has a long and depressing history. Spartans and Romans destroyed the severely handicapped at birth, while less severely debilitated youth served as objects of amusement for wealthy Greek and Roman families. This latter practice was revived centuries later by the French, German, and English courts, who delighted in the use of retarded persons as *bouffons, hofnarren,* and *jesters* (Kanner, 1964).

The first known organized attempts to care for the mentally retarded came with the advent of Christianity. Soon after Christ's death, converts from the Institutes of Justinian opened an asylum for the mentally retarded and other handicapped persons at the religious shrine of Gheel, in Brabant. This edifice, where clothing, food, and shelter were provided, is a likely candidate for the first institution serving the mentally retarded.

Unfortunately, the precedent of providing humanitarian care for the mentally retarded established at Gheel did not persist into the Middle Ages, a time that was marked by gross inconsistencies in the treatment of the handicapped. Early in this period, the mentally retarded were widely acknowledged as "infants of God," and their garbled speech regarded as a divine revelation. Such individuals generally were treated kindly, although no attempts at habilitation are known to have occurred.

Later in this era, ironically in the "Age of Enlightenment," treatment of the mentally retarded worsened. During this period, it was rather widely accepted that the mentally retarded were not filled with the spirit of God, but rather demonically possessed. The famed church reformer Martin Lurther echoed this position in arguing that a young retarded boy be drowned: "Such changelings are merely a mass of flesh, a *massa cornis,* with no soul . . . the devil sits in such changelings where their sould should have been . . ." (Kanner, 1964). Despite such contentions, the mentally retarded were rarely drowned, although they were frequently tortured under the guise of exorcisms and purgations.

Following and overlapping this time of exorcisms and purgations, a period of protection for the mentally retarded ensued, with various religious sects providing care in institutions similar to Gheel. The Hospice des Bicêtre in Paris, established about 1650 by St. Vincent de Paul and the Sisters of Charity, is a well-known example of such institutions. Although well intentioned, these institutions did nothing to habilitate the mentally retarded and certainly provided less than optimal care. Philippe Pinel, widely acclaimed as the "father of modern psychiatry," in 1792 toured the two main French institutions, Bicêtre and Salpêtrière, and found them to be crowded and unclean, with the patients maintained at the mercy of brutal keepers (Nowrey, 1945). Pinel astutely observed that behavior usually deteriorated, rather than improved, under these conditions.

In the 1700s, Pereire, Hauy, and Dodere initiated work with the nonretarded handicapped that was to have a tremendous impact on subsequent treatment of the mentally retarded. Itard drew on their findings in his work with Victor, the renowned "wild boy of Aveyron." Itard's efforts represent one of the first, and best publicized, attempts to enhance the repertoire of the mentally retarded. Seguin, the French "father of mental retardation," continued work in the vein opened by Itard and his predecessors, and did much to develop systematic methods for educating the mentally retarded. In 1838, Seguin established an experimental program for habilitating the mentally retarded at Salpêtrière; the success of this program led to the initiation of a similar program at Bicêtre in 1841. These programs represent the first documented attempts at educating and habilitating the institutionalized mentally retarded.

Similar efforts were begun at about the same time in Switzerland under the direction of Guggenbuhl. Guggenbuhl established the first major residential facility (institution) solely for the mentally retarded in 1841, and is considered by many as the "father of institutional care." His first institution, Abendberg, was located near Berne, Switzerland. Abendberg emphasized education and habilitation and was widely acclaimed as successful soon after opening. The early success of Abendberg led to the establishment of similar facilities in Berlin (1842) and Leipzig (1846), Germany; in Bath, England (1848); and in Boston, Massachusetts (1848). Although Guggenbuhl's work initially was highly regarded, conditions in institutions soon came to be vehemently criticized. Much of this criticism came from the British minister to Berne, who described conditions at Abendberg as being absolutely deplorable, with patient abuse common and deaths passing unnoticed for extended periods. Following a complete governmental investigation, the Swiss Association of Natural Sciences withdrew its support and Abendberg was closed. Other Continental institutions remained open, however, and grew in size.

Probably the first institution for the mentally retarded in the United States can be attributed to a Hervey Wilbur, who in 1848 began taking mentally retarded children into his home in Barre, Massachusetts, for the purpose of education and habilitation. Another important historical happening occurred in this year and state, as the Massachusetts legislature under the goading of Samuel Howe established the first American school for the mentally retarded at the Perkins Institute for the Blind in Boston. In 1855, this school was moved to south Boston and renamed the Massachusetts School for Idiotic and Feeble-minded Youth. This school, which first served 10 students, was generally considered a success. Due in part to this success, coupled with tireless lobbying by Howe, 25 additional state institutions for the mentally retarded were in operation; by 1875 they contained over 15,000 patients (Maloney & Ward, 1979).

While treatment was the initial intent of American (and other) institutions, as early as 1925 institutions were beset by a wealth of problems and were providing only custodial care, or serving as detention centers. As we discuss elsewhere (Poling & Breuning, in press):

> When institutions first opened in the United States, they were spacious and well-staffed. However, despite educational success, placement of the residents into the community was occurring infrequently. Also, because of the educational success, more and more mentally retarded individuals were being placed *into* the institutions. Thus, institutions became over-crowded. To make matters worse, additional financial support was rarely provided. This resulted in the dilution of programs and services and eventually the providing of only custodial care.

> Only providing custodial care resulted not only in a loss of educational success with the residents, but also increased pessimism and concern as to the purposes of these institutions. Society was no longer sending individuals to institutions for habilitative reasons but rather to segregate its undesirable elements. The mentally retarded were now being viewed as a menace to society, incapable of learning, and spreaders of idiocy, crime, and disease. Institutions were moved or created away from large urban areas.

One factor that contributed greatly to the change in attitude regarding the mentally retarded was the infamous eugenics movement of the late 1800s and early 1900s. This movement, championed by Francis Galton, proclaimed that ability was inherited and fixed, and that the way to improve humanity was through selective breeding. This claim was supported by "data" garnered by Goddard (of "Kallikak" fame), Dugdale, Tredgold, and others. Although subsequently proven false, the notion that allowing the mentally retarded to reproduce would deleteriously affect future generations powerfully influenced their treatment. Specifically, sterilization or institutionalization were advocated to "protect society." Habilitative programs were alleged to be useless, since intelligence and other characteristics were genetically determined and largely unchangeable. Segregation via institutionalization became the vogue by the 1930s, and massive numbers of individuals were wrongly placed in institutions; nearly half of the states also passed legislation permitting involuntary sterilization of the mentally retarded (Krischell, 1972).

From the 1930s to 1950s, institutions continued to provide primarily custodial care, although faith in the eugenics movement died with its most fervent advocate, Adolph Hitler. Several important happenings in the 1950s were responsible for a new era of optimism concerning the mentally retarded, which led eventually to changes in institutional care. Maloney and Ward (1979) describe these events in detail, but a partial list includes the following: (1) The foundation of the National Association of Parents and Friends of Retarded Children, forerunner of the National Association for Retarded Citizens, which has consistently demanded that the constitutional rights of the mentally retarded not be infringed. (2) The widespread recognition of mild retardation, which came with the massive intelligence testing of World War II inductees. The mildly retarded were, in many cases, obviously contributing members of society and not serious menaces. (3) Publication of Masland, Sarason, and Gladwin's book, *Mental Subnormality* (1958), which emphasized the social, psychological, and cultural, as opposed to genetic, determinants of mental retardation. (4) The passage, in 1958, of Public Law 85-926, which provided for the training of teachers in special education.

Optimism concerning habilitation of the mentally retarded continued into the 1960s as the federal government under the leadership of President Kennedy increased support for the study of mental retardation. In this decade, important strides were taken in understanding etiological factors (e.g., phenylketonuria, maternal rubella), and behavior-management procedures based on the principles of operant conditioning came into widespread use. Data collected during the 1960s and 1970s indicated that such procedures were of significant value in treating a variety of behavioral problems characteristically associated with mental retardation (e.g., Poling & Breuning, in press; Whitman & Scibak, 1979).

Concern for the constitutional rights of the mentally retarded, as well as scientific interest in procedures for improving their behavior, was a hallmark of the 1970s. Several landmark court decisions did much to set forth these rights and to establish safeguards for their protection. Perhaps the most famous case, Wyatt v. Stickney (1972), was responsible for the influential "Minimum Constitutional Standards for Adequate Habilitation of the Mentally Retarded." Among other provisions, these standards specified that the mentally retarded have "the right to habilitation including medical treatment, education and care, according to their need, regardless of age, degree of retardation, or handicapped condition . . . right to the least restrictive condition necessary to achieve the program of habilitation" (Wyatt v. Stickney, 1972, p. 396).

In part due to a desire to protect the rights of the retarded, coupled with abundant data suggesting that institutionalization generally did little to improve patients in any regard (e.g., Goldfarb, 1943, 1947; Klaber, 1969; Provence & Lipton, 1962; Quilitch & Gray, 1974; Thormalen, 1965), a call for deinstitutionalization arose from many quarters during the past 15 years (e.g., Kugel & Wolfensberger, 1969). As defined by Madle (1978), deinstitutionalization involves "(1) the prevention of admission to institutions by finding and developing community methods of care and training, (2) the return to the community of all residents who have been prepared through programs of habilitation and training to function adequately in appropriate local settings, and (3) the establishment and maintenance of a responsible residential environment which protects human and civil rights and contributes to the return of the individual to the community, whenever possible" (p. 348).

From 1915 to 1935, the number of mentally retarded persons living in institutions skyrocketed, followed by a more gradual increase that persisted into the late 1960s when, in 1969, approximately 190,000 mentally retarded persons were housed in public institutions, 33,000 resided in private institutions, and 32,000 lived in state mental hospitals not formally designed to treat the retarded (Office of Mental Retardation Coordination, 1972). More recent data are not available, but it is estimated that 3–4% of the over 7 million mentally retarded citizens in the United States are currently institutionalized (Poling & Breuning, in press). This number may decrease somewhat as the faltering American economy makes it increasingly difficult for states to maintain large therapeutic institutions. It is beyond our purposes to discuss this or other aspects of deinstitutionalization; Wolfensberger (1972) does so nicely. However, it is safe to say that deinstitutionalization will never become a viable alternative for all mentally retarded people. As Robinson and Robinson (1976) note, "It is generally agreed that there are some children who can profit from residential placement and that there are families for whose welfare it is essential that a child be removed from the home. It is also agreed that even if it were economically feasible, a practice of institutionalizing all or even most retarded children would frequently ignore the welfare of the child and family" (p. 433).

In general, the retarded child's parents (or guardians) are responsible for the decision to institutionalize. This decision inevitably involves some assessment of the child. In general, the likelihood that a given child will be placed in an institution varies directly with the degree of retardation (Robinson & Robinson, 1976). Behavioral problems are also an important factor in the decision to institutionalize (e.g., Fotheringham, 1970; Fotheringham, Skelton, & Hoddinott, 1971), as is a lack of adaptive behavior (e.g., Fotheringham, 1970; Kershner, 1970), the presence of serious medical problems (e.g., Smith, Decker, Herberg, & Rupke, 1969), or other handicapping conditions beyond mental retardation (see Robinson & Robinson, 1976). That these factors increase the likelihood of institutionalization is not surprising. Institutions traditionally have served to manage the mentally retarded individual who could not be readily cared for in other, less restrictive, environments. These include the ill, the multiply handicapped, and the persistent misbehavers.

Beyond contributing to the decision as to whether a particular child should be given institutional care, formal assessment plays an important part in determining what treatments a retarded citizen should receive, and in evaluating their efficacy. The termination of institutionalization also rests upon assessment data in most cases. The specific behavioral domains evaluated in the institutionalized mentally retarded vary widely, as do the individual assessment devices used. During the early 1900s, global clinical evaluations, perhaps supplemented by anecdotal reports, constituted the primary mode of assessing the institutionalized retarded. More recently, intelligence testing has become standard practice, as has determination of adaptive functioning. Direct observation of specified behaviors, both undesired and desired, has also become increasingly popular, especially in the area of treatment evaluation. Innumerable standardized tests, differing widely in form and logic, have also been developed to assess specific functions, e.g., perceptual–motor skills and sensory acuity.

In the following pages, we discuss several assessment procedures that are commonly used with institutionalized mentally retarded children. Tests of intelligence and adaptive behavior will be considered initially, followed by a discussion of general procedures for behavioral assessment. The final sections will focus on treatment evaluation, an important area inextricably linked with assessment, and ethical and legal issues in assessment. With the exception of the evaluation of drug effects, we will not attempt to cover medical assessment. Nor will we discuss procedures for collecting historical data concerning institutionalized children. The former omission reflects our own training—we are not physicians, and could offer only a cursory overview of medical assessment. It should, however, be apparent that ascertaining the general health, sensory/motor function, and neurological disorders (if any) of institutionalized patients is an integral and invaluable part of the evaluation process. The latter omission reflects our belief that, the collection of historical data in institutions is usually adequate, although irrelevant information is occasionally included in an individual's records, and clinicians all too often show a remarkable inability to learn from the recorded mistakes of their predecessors.

Before continuing, we must strongly emphasize that assessment of an institutionalized person is a multifaceted enterprise, usually involving physicians, educators, psychologists, and administrators. No single chapter can do justice to the contribution of each of these disciplines, nor provide more than a capsule summary of the assessment process, along with some general guidelines intended to improve its quality.

III. INTELLIGENCE TESTING

Assessment procedures typically serve one of two purposes: an identification function or an intervention planning and programming function (Oakland & Matuszek, 1976). Since the onset of the twentieth century, tests of intelligence have played an increasingly important role in identification of the mentally retarded. In response to a search for methods of identifying and educating subnormal children in Parisian schools, Alfred Binet and Theodore Simon published the first Binet–Simon scale in 1905. This scale consisted of 30 items whose difficulty was determined empirically through administration of the items to 3- and 11-year-old normal and retarded children. The scale covered a wide range of skills, emphasizing judgment, comprehension, and reading. No standardized method of scoring the scale was developed, however, and thus the scale was of limited utility.

Subsequent revisions in 1908 and 1911 expanded the number of items included, categorized them into age groups, and extended the coverage to adults. With the categorization of the items into age groups came the popular introduction of mental age, the chronological age on a normal child who could pass particular items, and norm-referenced intelligence tests.

Attracting worldwide attention, the Binet–Simon scales were translated and adopted for use in many countries, including the United States. Louis Terman, working at Stanford University, published the Stanford–Binet revision in 1916. It was in this publication that the intelligence quotient (IQ), the ratio between mental age and chronological age, was first introduced.

While the number and use of IQ tests has grown, no one has defined or observed any entity called intelligence; it is a construct inferred from various observed behaviors. This construct is used to explain differences between individuals and predict future behavior.

Like any other test, whether it be in mathematics, history, or English, an intelligence test represents a sample of behavior. Exactly which behaviors are sampled, to what extent they are sampled, and the manner in which they are sampled is largely dependent on a particular test author's conception of intelligence. Salvia and Ysseldyke (1981) describe 13 kinds of behaviors sampled by intelligence tests: discrimination, generalization, motor behavior, general information, vocabulary, induction, comprehension, sequencing, detail recognition, analogies, abstract reasoning, memory, and pattern completion.

Although intelligence tests allegedly allow for the quantification of differences between normal and subnormal individuals, definitions of mental retardation historically have been vague and imprecise (for a review see Blanton, 1975, or Robinson & Robinson, 1976). Some definitions have focused on etiology and biological determinants, others on psychological, environmental, social, or academic aspects (Oakland & Goldwater, 1979).

Currently, the most commonly accepted definition, that of the American Association of Mental Deficiency (AAMD; Grossman, 1977), combines several of the above focal points in one definition. The AAMD defines mental retardation as "significantly subaverage intellectual functioning existing concurrently with deficits in adaptive behavior and manifested during the developmental period" (Grossman, 1977). Worthy of particular attention in the present context is "significantly subaverage intellectual functioning." This refers to performance on an individually administered intelligence test of two or more standard deviations below the mean. Thus scores on intelligence tests have become a major component in the diagnosis of mental retardation. It should be noted, however, that all three of the components of the above definition must be met in order for an individual to be classified as mentally retarded. Thus it is recognized that the intelligence test only samples a limited range of behavior, and decisions based on that sample alone are inadequate. Some authors, in fact, have argued against the use of intelligence test data for any purpose, as is apparent in the following quote from an article by Reschly (1979):

> IQ tests measure only a portion of the competencies involved with human intelligence. The IQ results are best seen as predicting performance in school, and reflecting the degree to which children have mastered middle class cultural symbols and values. This is useful information,

but it is also limited. Further cautions—IQ tests do not measure innate-genetic capacity and the scores are not fixed. Some persons do exhibit significant increases or decreases in their measured IQ (p. 224)

Utility aside, intelligence tests are an integral component in the diagnosis of mental retardation and, in conjunction with measures of adaptive behavior, are used to identify the degree or severity of mental retardation (Grossman, 1977). The four degrees of mental retardation and the corresponding IQ scores are as follows: (1) mild mental retardation, the degree of retardation present when intelligence test scores range from two to three standard deviations below the mean (52 to 67 on the Stanford–Binet and 55 to 69 on the Wechsler Scales); (2) moderate mental retardation, the degree of retardation present when intelligence test scores range from three to four standard deviations from the mean (36 to 51 on the Stanford–Binet and 40 to 54 on the Wechsler Scales); (3) severe mental retardation, the degree of retardation present when intelligence scores range from four to five standard deviations below the mean [20 to 35 on the Stanford–Binet and 25 to 39 on the Wechsler Scales (extrapolated)]; and (4) profound mental retardation, the degree of retardation present when intelligence test scores fall more than five standard deviations below the mean [19 and below on the Wechsler Scales (extrapolated)].

A different classification system based on severity, learning ability, and IQ scores is used in educational settings. The first category consists of the educably mentally retarded/impaired (EMR or EMI), or those with IQs between 50–55 and 70–75 (varies with particular school). The second category consists of the trainably mentally retarded/impaired (TMR or TMI), or those with IQs between 25/35 and 50/55. The third category consists of the severely and profoundly mentally retarded/impaired (SMI or PMR), or those with IQs below 25/35.

Although their history is a lengthy one, intelligence tests have been surrounded by continuing controversy. Psychologists, educators, philosophers, and laymen have all failed to generate a universally accepted definition and explanation of intelligence, although theories of intelligence abound. Significantly, the State of California and the New York Board of Education have both limited the use of intelligence tests in public schools in response to the problems associated with the construct of intelligence and its measurement. Although intelligence tests continue to be widely used, it has become apparent that the interpretation of an IQ score is more complicated than examining a single number. Several points should be kept in mind when using tests of intelligence for purposes of assessment.

First, an IQ score is highly amenable to change. Depending on test content, examiner, fatigue, medication state, or any number of environmental variables, a score can vary up or down by as many as 20 points. For example, the importance of motivational factors in determining the IQ of the institutionalized mentally retarded has been convincingly demonstrated in a number of studies showing that reinforcement of correct responses significantly increases the tested systematic IQ of mentally retarded, but not "normal," individuals (e.g., Breuning & Davidson, 1981; Breuning & Davis, in press; Breuning & Zella, 1978; Clingman & Fowler, 1976).

Second, as Anastasi (1968) points out, IQ has become synonomous with intelligence to most laymen and to many professionals as well. It is crucial to regard IQ as a descriptive, rather than an explanatory, concept (see Liverant, 1960, for a further discussion of this point). The IQ does not represent an attribute but rather a score derived from performance on one test, under specific conditions, and in relation to a particular reference population. As pointed out above, testing under various conditions can dramatically change this score.

Third, the standard deviation and the mean of a particular test have direct bearing on the interpretation of a test score (any elementary statistics book can be consulted for calculation of these values; see Anastasi, 1968, or Salvia & Ysseldyke, 1981, for a thorough discussion of their relevance to psychometrics). Most intelligence tests have a mean of 100 and a standard deviation of 15 or 16, placing the cutoff for mental retardation at 68 or 70. The Slosson Intelligence Test (Slosson, 1971), however, has a mean of 100 and a standard deviation of approximately 24, placing the cutoff score at 52. Knowledge of a test's mean and standard deviation are essential for accurate interpretation of a score.

Finally, technical adequacy should never be assumed when administering a test of intelligence, or any assessment device. Three factors are crucial in the determination of the technical adequacy of these instruments: (1) the reference group to whom a comparison is made, (2) the reliability of the instrument used, and (3) the validity of the instrument used.

All IQ tests are norm referenced, that is, an individual's performance is compared to that of a reference group's (the norm population). In order for meaningful comparisons to be made, the reference group must be representative of the population and similar to those tested on all important variables (e.g., education, socioeconomic status). If comparisons are made when systematic differences occur between the individual tested and the norm population, they are invalid. Examples of this abuse of norm-referenced tests can be found in the administration of intelligence tests written in the English language to non-English-speaking immigrants to the United States, whose performance cannot be meaningfully compared to the English-speaking population.

Related to this issue is standardization of test administration. The person whose performance is being compared to a norm group must be tested under equivalent conditions. In many instances, the instructions presented in test manuals are not followed when these tests are administered to the mentally retarded (Salvia & Ysseldyke, 1981). When this happens, no meaningful statement can be made based on the standard test norms. Quite simply, one must follow prescribed administration procedures exactly, or avoid any normative statements based on test results.

One must also examine the currency of the norms reported by a test manual. For example, it has been shown that average performance on several intelligence tests today exceeds average performance on those same tests 40 years ago (Thorndike, 1973). Thus an average performance today would yield an above-average IQ when compared to older norms.

The second factor to be examined in assessing the technical adequacy of an instrument is its reliability. Reliability refers to the consistency of measurement, or freedom from error. Although error is always present (Newland, 1971), the extent to which it is present is of major concern. The reliability of a test is expressed in terms of a reliability coefficient, the value of which ranges from .00 to .99 (for an excellent coverage of reliability and its calculation, see Salvia & Ysseldyke, 1981). This coefficient can be thought of as the proportion of variability accounted for by true differences in individuals. The lower the reliability coefficient, the more error can be assumed reflected by an obtained score on an IQ test. Nunnally (1967) presents an equation for estimating the true score, the score which would be obtained if the test instrument were free of error, based on the reliability. The lower the reliability, the closer the true score estimate will be to the mean of the population.

Salvia and Ysseldyke (1981) provide general guidelines for the interpretation of the size of the reliability coefficients for tests to be used for educational decisions:

> When important educational decisions, such as tracking and placement in a special class, are to be made for the student, the minimum standard should be .90. When the decision being made is a screening decision, such as recommendation that a child receive further assessment, there is still a need for high reliability. For screening devices, we recommend a .80 standard. (p. 98)

The technical adequacy of a test depends on a third factor, its validity. Validity refers to the extent to which a test measures what is purports to measure; test validity allows appropriate inferences based on those test results.

Validity is of several interdependent types; content, criterion related, and construct. These are not measured but rather are judged both by the test author and test user based on a variety of information. Content validity is based on expert judgment of the appropriateness of test items, the adequacy of the items in covering the domain sampled, and the manner in which the items are sampled. Criterion-related validity refers to the correlation between a test and some criterion measure. A test is said to have criterion-related validity if performance on a present or future criterion measure can be accurately predicted based on the test score. Construct validity refers to the extent to which a test is measuring some specified construct (e.g., intelligence). This aspect of validity is shown through indirect evidence and inference. If the construct is poorly defined or vague, this type of validity is difficult to confirm: The only person who may be convinced is the test author, whose view of the construct is reflected in the test.

Several intelligence tests are described below in varying detail. At the onset, the reader should be cautioned that the appropriateness of these tests for use with mentally retarded institutionalized children, both in terms of validity and reliability, is questionable.

Prior to the administration of an individual intelligence test for purposes of diagnosis, group intelligence tests are occasionally administered to certain higher functioning individuals as a screening device for those requiring further assessment. These include the Culture Fair Intelligence Tests (Cattell, 1950; Cattell & Cattell, 1960, 1963), the Cognitive Abilities Test (Thorndike & Hagen, 1971), the Goodenough–Harris Drawing Test (Harris, 1963), the Otis–Lennon Mental Ability Test (Otis & Lennon, 1969), and the Primary Mental Abilities Test (Thurstone & Thurstone, 1965).

Standardization procedures are the source of a number of difficulties which severely limit the inferences which can be made based on these tests. Most group intelligence tests designate different versions for use with different grade levels (for example, level A for kindergarten through third grade, level B for fourth through sixth grades). Each test level is normed only on students in those grades and thus on a limited age group. However, a child may earn the mental age of an individual who was never tested, that mental age having been obtained through extrapolation.

The manner in which the standardized samples are obtained almost certainly precludes their being representative of the population. Most group tests are typically standardized on representative districts, rather than on representative individuals. The districts included in the sample may not necessarily include a representative sample of individuals. In addition, the samples included in the norming are obtained on a volunteer basis. If a randomly chosen district refuses to participate, an attempt is made to replace it with a comparable one, but this process cannot replace true random selection in guaranteeing the representation of the population.

In determining the usefulness of group intelligence tests, it is necessary to examine the type of individuals composing the norm sample. If the test is standardized in public schools, it should be noted that individuals excluded from public schools have also been excluded from the norm sample. Severely retarded and disturbed students are among those excluded, which results in the introduction of systematic bias in the norms. Although group tests may occasionally be administered, in order to assess the presence and severity of mental retardation, public law (93-380, 94-142) mandates than an individual intelligence test be administered. In addition to specifying that the test be individual, public law also requires it to be administered according to the standardized test procedure and to be validated for the purpose for which it is used. Several commonly used individual intelligence tests are described and evaluated in the following sections.

The Stanford–Binet Intelligence Scale

The Stanford-Binet Intelligence Scale (Terman & Merrill, 1973) currently in use is the third revision of the test, developed through a renorming of the second revision of the original 1916 Stanford–Binet.

The items on the test range in difficulty from the 2-year-old level to the superior-adult level. Behavior samples vary at each age level, but a list of representative areas of emphasis includes manipulation, vocabulary, language comprehension, language usage, memory, perceptual discrimination, verbal discrimination, verbal reasoning, nonverbal reasoning, and numerical reasoning (Poling & Breuning, in press). Both a mental age and a deviation IQ ($\bar{X} = 100$, SD $= 16$) score are obtained from the Stanford–Binet.

The standardization sample of the 1972 Stanford–Binet included 2100 subjects in seven communities. The test manual includes no data concerning the demographic characteristics of the sample. Salvia, Ysseldyke, and Lee (1975) indicate that, with the 1972 renorming, although the norms of the test changed, placement of items at appropriate age levels did not. Thus, an "average" child must now perform above grade level to earn an average IQ score.

No reliability or validity data are included in the test manual regarding the 1972 edition. The authors report data on earlier versions, assuming the data apply to the current version.

Given the inadequate description of the normative sample, the bias introduced with the renorming, and the absence of adequate reliability and validity data, the 1972 Stanford–Binet has questionable merit for use in making major educational, treatment, or placement decisions.

The Wechsler Scales

Three distinct scales have been developed by David Wechsler for use in assessing intelligence at different age levels: the Wechsler Preschool and Primary Scale of Intelligence (WPPSI), for use with children 4 to 6½ years of age (Wechsler, 1967); the Wechsler Intelligence Scale for Children–Revised (WISC–R), for use with children ages 6 through 16 (Wechsler, 1974); and the Wechsler Adult Intelligence Scale (WAIS), for use with individuals over 16 years of age (Wechsler, 1955). All three scales assess similar behaviors: information, comprehension, similarities, arithmetic, vocabulary, digit span, memory of sentences (only in WPPSI), picture completion, picture arrangement, block design, object assembly, coding, mazes (except WAIS), and geometric design (only in WPPSI). The Wechsler scales yield scaled scores ($\bar{X} = 10$, SD $= 3$) for each of the subtests, which are then transformed to yield Verbal, Performance, and Full-Scale IQ scores ($\bar{X} = 100$, SD $= 15$).

The WAIS was standardized on 1700 subjects, the WISC–R on 2200, and the WPPSI on 1200. All samples were stratified based on age, sex, geographic region, urban–rural residence, race, education, and occupation (or occupation of head of household), and proportion of individuals included was commensurate with the 1950 U.S. census.

The test manuals present extensive reliability data for the WPPSI, WISC–R, and WAIS. The split-half reliability estimates for the Verbal IQ scores range from .91 to .96; the Performance IQs, from .89 to .95, with only one estimate below .90; and the Full-Scale IQs, from .95 to .97.

Various studies (Salvia & Ysseldyke, 1981) have established the concurrent validity of the Wechsler scales by correlating scores with other intelligence test scores. Correlations range from .82 to .95 for Full-Scale IQs.

The reliability data provided by the Wechsler test manuals suggest that they are sufficiently high for major educational, treatment, and placement decisions. Limited validity data suggest the same. The tests have the advantage of providing subtest scores as well as Verbal, Performance, and Full-Scale IQ scores.

Slosson Intelligence Test

The Slosson Intelligence Test (Slosson, 1971) is a short test patterned after the Stanford–Binet, containing many highly similar items, and thus sampling a similar range of behaviors. The items range in difficulty from the .5 month through the adult level. The test provides an age score which is in turn transformed into a ratio IQ. The means for the IQ scores range in difficulty from the .5 month through the adult level. The test provides an age score which is in turn transformed into a ratio IQ. The variability of the mean and standard deviation of the test scores across age levels should be noted. The means for the IQ scores range from 91.7 at age 15 to 114.6 at age 4. The standard deviations range from 16.7 at age 17 to 31.2 at age 18 and older.

The normative sample is composed of various groups of individuals, inadequately described in the test manual, from New York State. No data concerning the proportion of individuals making up the classes included in the sample are provided.

The only reliability data provided consist of a test–retest reliability coefficient obtained in 139 persons ranging in age from 4 to 50 years. The sampling procedure does not prevent the confounding of true-score variance and chronological age variance, possibly resulting in a spuriously high coefficient (Salvia & Ysseldyke, 1981).

Correlations between the Slosson and the Stanford–Binet constitute the validity data. The values range from .90 to .98; however, it should be remembered that the items on these two particular tests are highly similar.

Although this test was designed as a screening device, care should be taken in its use and interpretation due to variable mean and standard deviation values and limited reliability and validity data.

McCarthy Scales of Children's Abilities

The McCarthy Scales of Children's Abilities (MSCA; McCarthy, 1972) consist of 18 subtests for use with 2½- to 8½-year-olds, which sample block building, puzzle solving, pictoral memory, word knowledge, number questions, tapping sequence, verbal memory, right–left orientation, leg coordination, arm coordination, imitative action, draw-a-design, draw-a-child, numerical memory, verbal fluency, counting and sorting, opposite analogies, and conceptual grouping. These 18 tests make up the Verbal, Perceptual-Performance, Quantitative, Memory, Motor, and General Cognitive Scales. The test yields a scaled score ($\bar{X}$ = 100, SD = 16) for the General Cognitive Scale, as well as separate scores ($\bar{X}$ = 50, SD = 10) for the five remaining scales.

The MSCA was standardized on 100 children at each age level, stratified on the basis of sex, age, race, geographic region, father's occupation, and urban–rural residence, with proportions reflecting the 1970 U.S. census data.

The reliability coefficients reported were all calculated using the split-half method, with the exception of those for three subtests, which were calculated using the test–retest method. The coefficients range in value from .79 to .93 for the six major scales.

The test manual presents limited predictive and concurrent validity data based on studies correlating MSCA scores with various other intelligence test scores. Although the studies provide some support for the concurrent validity of the device, the samples in these studies were small; thus they provide limited information.

In summary, the standardization of the MSCA appears to be very good, the reliability better than average. The validity, however, has not been conclusively shown. As Salvia and Ysseldyke (1981) point out, no exceptional children were included in the sample, thus invalidating the use of this test with those populations.

Intelligence tests have been an integral component in the assessment of mental retardation and will likely remain so well into the future. Their value in this capacity, however, is highly questionable in light of current standardization practices and a marked lack of information concerning their reliability and validity with this population. Kamin (1974) has written a highly readable discussion of historical problems and abuses associated with the use of intelligence tests.

Tests of Receptive Skills

Each of the above-mentioned tests provides information concerning both verbal and performance skills. However, with many individuals, particularly those with limited ability to emit vocal or gestural (i.e., sign language, symbol system) responses, the use of scales designed for special populations may be warranted. These tests primarily assess receptive language skills and should not be considered as comprehensive tests of so-called intelligence. Only a very small sample of behavior is examined, and these tests are of limited use in assessment when used alone. Nonetheless, these tests are widely used with the mentally retarded and often provide the only applicable method of norm-referenced assessment.

Two of the more frequently used tests with the mentally retarded are the Pictorial Test of Intelligence (French, 1964) and the Leiter International Performance Scale (adapted by Grace Arthur in 1950). The French Pictorial views six domains: Picture Vocabulary, Form Discrimination, Information/Comprehension, Similarities, Size/Number, and Immediate Recall. This test is appropriate for individuals between the ages of 3 and 8, has a mean of 100 and a standard deviation of 16, is adequately normed, has acceptable measures of reliability and validity, and scoring is fairly simple.

The Arthur adaptation of the Leiter assesses analogies, discrimination, generalization, pattern completion, and sequencing. This test is reported appropriate for individuals between the ages of 2 and 18 and has a mean of 95 and SD of 16. Because of the mean of 95, the scoring instructions require that five free points be added to the score. Results from the Leiter must be viewed cautiously as there are no normative data, reliability is unknown, and validity is low to nonexistent. Administration and scoring are awkward—many of the test items require color discriminations, while the scoring manual is illustrated in black and white.

Other, less appropriate, tests include the Quick Test (Ammons & Ammons, 1962), Peabody Picture Vocabularly Test (Dunn, 1965), and Columbia Mental Maturity Test (Burgemeister, Blum, & Lorge, 1972). These are discussed in detail by Salvia and Ysseldyke (1981).

IV.   ADAPTIVE BEHAVIOR AND ITS MEASUREMENT

Primarily due to the problems associated with intelligence testing, and in an attempt to reduce the disproportionate labeling of minorities as retarded, the AAMD in 1961 expanded its definition of mental retardation to include deficits in adaptive behavior as one of the criteria for its diagnosis (Heber, 1961). At that time, the AAMD proposed a definition in which adaptive behavior referred to "the effectiveness with which the individual copes with the natural and social demands of his environment . . . (Heber, 1961, p. 61).

Several theoreticians (Leland, Nihira, Foster, Shellhaas, & Kagin, 1968; Mercer, 1979; Nihira, 1976; Robinson & Robinson, 1976), as well as a number of governmental agencies and committees (Office of Civil Rights, 1976; President's Committee on Mental Retardation, 1975), have subsequently offered definitions for the term adaptive behavior. The definitions are similar, and all place varying emphasis on independent functioning, personal responsibility, and social responsibility. Currently the most widely accepted definition is that of the AAMD (Grossman, 1977), which defines adaptive behavior as "the effectiveness or degree with which the individual meets the standards of personal independence and social responsibility expected of his age or cultural group."

Although a general definition for adaptive behavior seems to be agreed upon, it is somewhat vague and imprecise, and data from the empirical measurement of adaptive behavior are few. The various behaviors which comprise those classified as adaptive are often not easily specified, nor are they easily observed or measured. The specific behaviors considered as "adaptive" will always be socially determined and, as with indices of intelligence, will to some extent reflect the view of the particular test author.

Current attempts to devise tests of adaptive behavior typically have emphasized one of the two roles of assessment, identification/placement or intervention/treatment, in the construction of the instruments.

In 1965, a cooperative project between Parsons State Hospital in Kansas and the AAMD was begun, one of the objectives being to develop an instrument to assess adaptive behavior as an independent entity. Leland, Shellhaas, Nihira, and Foster (1967) expressed the purpose of measuring adaptive behavior in the project as an aid in the remediation of deficit behaviors in the institutionalized retarded. The work at Parsons State Hospital eventually culminated in the AAMD Adaptive Behavior Scale (ABS), 1975 revision (Nihira, Foster, Shellhaas, & Leland, 1975).

In 1954, the Pacific State Hospital in California began a study (Coulter & Morrow, 1978) designed to identify the mentally retarded in the community. An extension of this study in 1969 produced the System of Multicultural Pluralistic Assessment (SOMPA; Mercer, 1979), which includes a scale for the allegedly nonbiased assessment of adaptive behavior.

The distinction between tests of adaptive behavior for identification of the mentally retarded and those for planning intervention programs is an important one. A norm-referenced interpretation (i.e., comparison of performance to that of a reference group) of test results is required for identification, while criterion-referenced interpretation (i.e., comparison of performance to an arbitrarily set criterion level) is required for treatment planning.

At present, public law (94-142) mandates the assessment of both intellectual functioning and adaptive behavior before an individual can be diagnosed as mentally retarded. Given this requirement and the increased interest in the "normalization" of retarded individuals (Nirje, 1969), careful attention is due both norm- and criterion-referenced assessment of adaptive behavior. It is essential that the administrator of adaptive behavior tests be aware of the purposes for which they were designed, and to use them accordingly (for a detailed discussion of adaptive behavior and other issues surrounding its assessment, interested readers are referred to Coulter & Morrow, 1978).

Like intelligence tests, all devices used to assess adaptive behavior should be evaluated for technical adequacy. The same general issues (norms, realiability, and validity) should be considered in evaluating measures of adaptive behaviors as in evaluating intelligence tests. However, the assessment of adaptive behavior requires a few specific comments, most directed at particular measurement devices, described below.

Vineland Social Maturity Scale

The Vineland Social Maturity Scale (VSMS; Doll, 1965) is possibly the most widely known and used instrument for the assessment of adaptive behavior. Like all major scales of adaptive behavior, the VSMS is not administered directly to the individual being assessed. Rather, it follows an interview format in which a third person, the respondent, who is thoroughly familiar with the individual being assessed, answers questions concerning that individual. The administrator must be skilled at interview techniques and capable of integrating the information to determine whether or not the subject habitually and customarily performs a task, not whether the subject can perform a task. The test comprises 117 items appropriate to assess social competence from birth to 30 years of age. The VSMS is an age scale, so various items appears at each age level and are grouped into eight areas: self-help general, self-help eating, self-help dressing, locomotion, occupation, communication, self-direction, and socialization.

Each item can be scored in one of five ways based on the subject's performance of the task. The composite score yields a social age (SA) which can be transformed to a social quotient (SQ). The means and standard deviations of these values vary with age; Doll (1965) provides a table containing these values for both SA and SQ at each age.

The norms for the VSMS were collected in 1935 and consist of 620 white, middle-class individuals from greater Vineland, New Jersey. Both children with educational or mental retardation and those with physical handicaps were excluded.

Test–retest reliability estimates are provided in the test manual. The test–retest correlation for SA is .98; for SQ, .57. Salvia and Ysseldyke (1981) suggest that the SQ correlation is probably a better estimate of reliability since it is not affected by chronological age. The manual also provides interinterviewer and interrespondent correlations; the pooled test–retest correlation is .92 for SA.

The validity of the VSMS is estimated to be over .80 when scores are correlated with subjective ratings of social competence made by those familiar with the subject. The content validity, however, must be questioned since the items and their placement at appropriate levels were determined over 40 years ago.

Although reliability and validity estimates are above average for a testing instrument, the VSMS is a dated scale. A revision of the scale is necessary before its value for use today can be assessed.

Cain–Levine Social Competency Scale

The Cain–Levine Competency Scale (Cain, Levine, & Elzey, 1963), administered in an interview format to one who is thoroughly familiar with the subject, was designed to assess the independence of trainable mentally retarded children between the ages of 5 years and 13 years 11 months.

The 44 items are grouped into four subscales: self-help, initiative, social skills, and communication. Instructions are provided to rate 38 items on a 4-point scale, the remaining 6 on a 5-point scale. One represents the lowest level of performance, while 4 represent the highest level. The raw scores are summed and a constant (specified for each age level) added if the subject is a boy (since boys typically perform at a lower level than girls). These scores can then be converted to percentile ranks.

The scale was normed on 716 boys and girls, whose IQs ranged from 25 to 49, residing in California. Data presented in the manual indicate a representative bias toward lower-class families as defined by occupational level of parents or guardians.

Reliability estimates were computed using the odd–even internal consistency method based on total score. Correlations ranged from .75 to .91. Test–retest reliability estimates were also computed; a total score correlation of 198 is reported.

Content validity is based on expert opinion. Items were chosen based on discussion with parents and professionals, curriculum guides for the TMR, and an evaluation of other scales. Correlation of scores with chronological age range from .4 to .5, with IQ, from .09 to .30, providing limited evidence for criterion-related validity.

Reliability estimates suggest the Cain–Levine is adequate for screening the mentally retarded; the reader is cautioned that the validity is questionable and that the restricted norm sample provides information concerning California residents only.

The AAMD Adaptive Behavior Scale

The AAMD Adaptive Behavior Scale (ABS; Nihira, Foster, Shellhaas, & Leland, 1969) was developed for the measurement of adaptive behavior in the mentally retarded, disturbed, and developmentally disabled. As was mentioned previously, the emphasis was on an aid to planning remedial programs.

The two-part test is administered to a third individual who is questioned concerning the behavior of the subject. Part 1 is designed to assess adaptive behavior and contains 66 items grouped into 10 domains: independent functioning, physical development, economic activity, language development, numbers and time, domestic activity, vocational activity, self-direction, responsibility, and socialization. Part 2 is designed to assess maladaptive behavior and consists of 44 items grouped into 14 domains: violent and destructive behavior, antisocial behavior, rebellious behavior, untrustworthy behavior, withdrawal, stereotyped behavior and odd mannerisms, inappropriate interpersonal manners, unacceptable vocal habits, unacceptable or eccentric habits, self-abusive behavior, hyperactive tendencies, sexually aberrant behavior, psychological disturbance, and use of medication.

In Part 1 the respondent is required to check statements which apply to the subject; in Part 2 the respondent is required to rate the subject's behavior. Raw scores are obtained for each part, and tables are provided which convert the scores to decile ranks.

The norms provided are based on evaluations of approximately 4000 institutionalized individuals ranging in age from 3 to 69 years. The mean IQs of these persons ranged from 28 at age 3 to 45.8 at ages 16–18. The test manual does not specify who performed the evaluation or what test was used.

Only interrater agreement data are presented in the manual in the form of correlation coefficients between ratings by attendants for 133 subjects. The mean reliability estimates ranged from .71 to .92 in Part 1 and from .37 to .77 in Part 2.

Minimal validity data are presented by the test authors in the manual. A factor analysis indicates three factors are present: personal independence, social maladaption, and personal maladaption. No evidence of content validity is provided by the authors.

Although ABS was purportedly developed to aid in planning remedial programs, it is a norm-referenced device, usually thought to be inappropriate for such uses. Reliability estimates are low, and little data support the validity of the instrument. The AAMD ABS does not appear adequate for use in making major decisions concerning the three groups of handicapped persons for which it was designed. However, this scale is currently being revised in an attempt to alleviate its shortcomings.

The System of Multicultural Pluralistic Assessment

Although the System of Multicultural Pluralistic Assessment (SOMPA; Lewis & Mercer, 1978; Mercer, 1979) was developed to provide a comprehensive assessment of public school children, ages 5 through 11, this group does not exclude the mentally retarded, and therefore will be summarized here. SOMPA contains eight tests designed to assess three different areas: medical, social-system, and pluralistic (intelligence).

The social-system model of SOMPA assesses role performance through two tests: the WISC–R (reviewed in Section III) and the Adaptive Behavior Inventory for Children (ABIC). The ABIC contains 242 questions grouped into six subtests: family, peer relations, nonacademic school roles, earner/consumer, and self-maintenance. As with other adaptive behavior scales, a respondent who is familiar with the subject is interviewed. The respondent can score each question in one of five ways based on the subject's level of performance. The raw scores for each of the six scales are transformed to standard scores ($\bar{X} = 50$, SD = 15), and an average scale score is calculated on the basis of the six subscale scores.

The great majority of the split-half estimates of reliability for the subtests are below .9, although the correlation for the average scale scores is approximately .97. Statistical errors in computing interrater agreement preclude evaluation of those data. The test manual provides no data concerning validity.

The reliabilities reported in the SOMPA test manual for the ABIC are generally too low for use in making a major decision concerning the mentally retarded. The lack of validity data and limited norm sample requires the test user to exercise caution in administering and interpreting this newly developed test.

Like intelligence, adaptive behavior is a nebulous and ill-defined concept. Those who are required to administer measures of adaptive behavior and make identification or treatment decisions concerning the mentally retarded based on the results must carefully examine the test for technical adequacy and the validity for the purpose for which it is to be used.

Behavioral Assessment

To this point, we have emphasized that considerable effort has been expended in developing devices for assessing the level of intelligence and adaptive behavior of the mentally retarded. In a real sense, the use of such devices constitutes behavioral assessment insofar as they provide information about the overt actions of the person to whom they are administered. However, in recent years the term "behavioral assessment" has come to represent a unique approach to assessment. "At its heart the goals of behavioral assessment are to identify meaningful response units and their controlling variables (both current environment and organismic) for the purposes of understanding and altering behavior" (Nelson and Hayes, 1979, p. 1). It is impossible for us to do more than summarize some of the most salient features of behavioral assessment. Four recent books (Ciminero, Calhoun, & Adams, 1977; Cone & Hawkins, 1977; Haynes, 1978; Hersen & Bellack, 1976) are devoted entirely to the topic, as are the journals *Behavioral Assessment* and the *Journal of Behavioral Assessment*.

In essence, behavioral assessment involves two major components (Lutzker & Martin, 1981). The first is determination of the exact nature of a clinical problem; the second is determination of potentially useful strategies for altering that problem. Some authors (e.g., Ciminero, 1977) have considered treatment evaluation as a third component of behavioral assessment; we discuss this topic separately in Section V. We also consider the techniques of behavioral assessment to be useful for quantifying behaviors that are not "problems" in any obvious sense, and consider them in this light.

It has become somewhat conventional to categorize behavioral measures into three broad categories or domains. Hersen and Barlow (1976), for example, differentiate motoric, physiological, and self-report measures. Lutzker and Martin (1981) retain this tripartite system, which they describe in the following way: "Rather than restricting behavioral assessment to observable behavior, it may frequently be necessary to gather information from three separate channels (Lang, 1968, 1971; Cautela, 1968; Hersen, 1976). The channels are motoric (e.g., the actions or movements of a person), physiological (e.g., a person's heart rate, blood pressure, and so on), and cognitive (e.g., what a person thinks or says to himself)'' (p. 19). Note that an independent observer's only access to the cognitive channel is through the client's self-report, thus Lutzker and Martin's three categories are essentially identical to those described by Hersen and Barlow.

Behavioral assessment begins with the definition of the response to be measured. As noted above, this response often constitutes a problem for someone—the client, his or her peers or family, the clinician, or society at large—although occasionally data are taken purely to provide normative information, or as an aid in making administrative (e.g., placement) decisions concerning an individual. If a particular behavior is problematic, it may be so by virtue of occurring too frequently (as when an institutionalized boy regularly assaults his peers), not frequently enough (as when an institutionalized girl fails to respond to her name), or in inappropriate circumstances (as when a child fails to confine toileting to a bathroom). Irrespective of why, or even if, a behavior constitutes a problem, its definition must be clear and include an unambiguous description of the topography (physical form) of the behavior. Further, the dimension of behavior of concern must be precisely specified—is it the rate, latency, magnitude, or some other aspect of responding which is significant—as well as the exact techniques used in its measurement. Considerable care is required to establish adequate definitions, whose worth ultimately is determined by the accuracy, reliability, and validity with which behavior is measured when these definitions are employed.

Reliability and validity were introduced in the context of intelligence tests, but are equally important when other assessment devices are considered. These include the techniques that are characteristic of behavioral assessment. Salvia and Ysseldyke (1981) emphasize the worthlessness of an unreliable instrument by comparing it to a stretchable rubber ruler. Such a ruler would not produce consistent measurements, even if a single board was repeatedly measured under seemingly consistent conditions; the length obtained would depend mostly on how hard the ruler was stretched, not the physical dimensions of the board. To continue the ruler analogy, an invalid test would be exampled by the use of a solid ruler to measure weight. Such a ruler might be perfectly adequate for assessing length, but this dimension would have no necessary relation to weight, and it would be most unfortunate if weight and length measures were confused. Accuracy is a dimension of measurement that includes components of both reliability and validity: ''A measure is accurate to the extent to which it reflects the 'true value' of that which is being measured'' (Wysocki & Fuque, in press). Unless these dimensions are considered, and a measurement procedure can clearly be shown to be accurate, valid, and reliable, its use with the institutionalized mentally retarded simply cannot be defended. Too often, these considerations are ignored and assessment devices are chosen on the basis of precedent or rhetoric, nor reason or empirical evaluation. In considering the various assessment devices that have been, and are being, used with the mentally retarded, the reader should hold this thought in mind.

The specific behaviors which should be assessed in a given institutionalized mentally retarded child depend upon a number of factors, including age and the severity of retardation. In general, as discussed previously, residents entering an institution are at minimum evaluated with respect to general health, intelligence, and level of adaptive behavior. Futher assessment typically is individualized, and often occurs as a necessary precursor to the development and evaluation of habilitative programs. Oftentimes, a child is nonsystematically observed by staff to be deficit with respect to some desired behavior or to frequently engage in an inappropriate action. Systematic assessment of the child is then begun to quantify the response of concern and to attempt to identify the factors controlling it.

This quantification may involve any of all of several techniques. As Lutzker and Martin (1981) note, behavioral assessment encompasses six general techniques. While not of equal merit when institutionalized mentally retarded children are considered, each of these techniques merits brief coverage.

One procedure of relatively little value is the *interview,* where the clinician meets with the child, his family, or other knowledgeable individuals. While the interview is a useful source of historical data and forms the data base for the tests of adaptive behavior reviewed in the preceding section, the value of the interview as an index of current behavior is limited insofar as verbal reports often bear little relation to actual measures of overt behavior. Linehan (1977) and Morganstern (1976) comprehensively consider the role of the interview in behavioral assessment.

With the exception of the tests previously outlined, *standardized tests* are not commonly used with the mentally retarded. However, an incredibly wide range of personality and achievement inventories are available and are occasionally incorporated into the assessment process. Results generally are less than satisfactory, since most of these devices have not been developed for nor systematically evaluated with the handicapped, and provide only indirect, inferred indices of actual behaviors of concern. Salvia and Ysseldyke (1981) carefully discuss the use of a variety of standardized tests with handicapped populations.

Checklists seemingly are of somewhat greater utility than standardized tests for evaluating institutionalized mentally retarded children. In general, checklists require an observer to report after the fact whether a child emitted a particular response during a given time period (e.g., Did Johnny make his bed today?) or, more generally, to specify whether a particular response is in an individual's repertoire (e.g., Can Susie independently use a fork and knife in self-feeding?). A variety of standardized checklists suitable for use with the mentally retarded have been developed; these are presented ably by Walls, Werner, Bacon, and Zane (1977). The one essential requirement when checklists are used is correspondence between raters' evaluations of an individual and that person's actual behavior. Such correspondence should not be assumed, but rather proven by comparing the results of direct observations of behavior with checklist ratings of the same response. When it can be convincingly demonstrated that checklists do provide accurate measures of important behaviors, they represent a simple, uniform, and cost-effective means of assessment.

Questionnaires are much like checklists, although they are not necessarily designed to elicit simply yes/no responses. In general, administering questionnaires to mentally retarded children is of no value, although questionnaire data provided by other individuals may be of some interest. Nonetheless, the same information most often can be obtained through more direct, and consequently more believable, modes.

Physiological assessment involves directly monitoring bodily function. This can often be done via automated equipment which, although costly and sometimes prone to break, increases the overall objectivity and accuracy of measurement. For example, sensors have been developed for measuring bed-wetting; these have profitably incorporated into programs for treating enuresis (e.g., Foxx & Azrin, 1973).

In institutionalized children, physiological indices are most important with respect to health-related behaviors, although physiological indices have been used to measure anxiety and other clinical states in adults. It is of considerable interest that when physiological, motoric, and self-report data are collected simultaneously to index a particular clinical problem (e.g., a phobia), treatment often fails to produce equivalent changes across the three dimensions (Hersen & Barlow, 1976). As Paul (1967) contends, "While multiple measures of outcome are necessary, the dependent variable in any outcome evaluation must be . . . change in the disturbing behavior which brought the client to treatment" (p. 112).

Self-monitoring is a method of assessment that cannot be generally recommended with institutionalized mentally retarded children, many of whom lack the necessary skills to count and record counts of their own actions. Even if a child possesses such skills, unless other, independent indices can be found which allow the accuracy and reliability of self-report data to be determined, such measures are inevitably suspect. An individual's report of his or her actions may be affected by any of a number of factors (e.g., the consequence of reporting a particular level of behavior), such that their believability is far less than optimal. Despite this, self-reports of perceived changes in behavior can be a valuable part of the evaluation of an intervention if, and only if, the self-report data are supported by other, more objective measures. Mahoney (1977) and Bellack and Schwartz (1976) comprehensively describe the problems associated with self-reports and offer some suggestions for their solution.

Analog methods involve behavioral assessment outside the environment in which an individual's behavior is of importance. Analog methods simulate the environment of concern in a way which allows behavior to be easily controlled and monitored. The essential problem with analog methods is generalizability of findings: Is the level of behavior observed in the analog situation an accurate reflection of that same behavior in the actual situation of concern? When it is, analog methods can be quite useful, although to date they have been rarely used with institutionalized mentally retarded children. Laboratory indices of short-term memory have, however, been profitably employed in the assessment of drug effects (e.g., Davis, Poling, Wysocki, & Breuning, in press; Sprague & Sleator, 1977; Wysocki, Fuqua, Davis, & Bruening, 1981). McFall (1977) and Nay (1977) review the use of analog measures.

Direct observation of behavior (or its outcome) is an especially useful method for assessment with most institutionalized populations; it has been used to assess an incredibly wide range of responses ranging from appropriate toileting to academic performance. Unfortunately, direct observation which is accurate and reliable is seldom easily or cheaply accomplished. In some instances, automated equipment makes it relatively simple to record a particular behavior, and can be substituted for direct observation. The time a child spends seated during an educational session may, for instance, be readily determined by affixing a con-tact-operated microswitch to the chair's seat and having this switch, when oper-ated, activate a running time meter. Automated recording has been used in a number of reported studies (e.g., Hollis & St. Omer, 1972; Sprague & Toppe, 1966), and certainly has much to recommend it. However, as discussed else-where (Poling, Cleary, & Monaghan, 1980):

> Human observers are required when complex behaviors are not easily detected in meaningful ways by machines are of interest, or where the costs of automated recording are too great. . . . As transducers, humans are invariably suspect. Folklore suggests that lay observa-tions are an imperfect reflection of actual happenings, and a large and growing body of data indicates that allegedly scientific observations sometimes provide an inaccurate index of the variables being considered (Bailey, 1977; Johnson & Bolstad, 1973; Johnston & Pennypacker, 1980). Among the factors demonstrated to influence reported observations are the observer's motivation and expectations (e.g., Rosenthal, 1966), the specifics of the observational situa-tion (e.g., Johnson & Bolstad, 1973), the observational and data recording techniques that are used (e.g., Repp, Roberts, Slack, Repp, & Beckler, 1976), and the characteristics of the behavior being monitored (e.g., Johnston & Pennypacker, 1980). (p. 243)

Literally thousands of pages have been written concerning strategies for mini-mizing the problems associated with the use of human observers; much of this voluminous literature is reviewed in the books listed previously as sources of information concerning behavioral assessment and in the books listed in the following section as overviews of within-subject designs. What follows is a capsule summary of some generally accepted guidelines for the use of human observers. These guidelines are intended to be of practical, quite as much as heuristic, value.

1. In some instances, behavior produces a lasting product, the presence or absence of which can be readily detected. In these cases, it makes perfect sense to measure the number of products produced, rather than to directly monitor the

behaviors which produced them. For example, institutionalized individuals often engage in prevocational tasks involving the assembly of components into complete units—bendix brakes, for instance. Here, the number of brakes assembled by an individual in a given time period would be a tenable and straightforward index of his or her prevocational skills. Unfortunately, many significant behaviors of institutionalized mentally retarded children leave no permanent products.

2.   It rarely is possible to monitor a given individual constantly. Nonetheless, the closer to continuous that observation can be made, the greater the likelihood that the level of behavior recorded is an accurate general reflection of that behavior. Intermittent time sampling, an observational procedure where an individual is monitored only occasionally, for brief time periods (e.g., for 20 sec at hourly intervals), is especially unlikely to provide an accurate, generalizable measure of behavior, particularly if observations are widely separated in time.

3.   The person responsible for the design of observational procedures should be aware of the range of procedures commonly employed and their characteristics. For instance, in continuous time sampling, the total observational period (e.g., the lunch hour) is divided into small observational intervals (e.g., 10 sec), and the observer records whether or not the response of concern (e.g., screaming) occurred during each of these intervals. There are two variations of continuous time sampling, differentiated on the basis of the criteria used to determine whether a target behavior is scored as having occurred during a given observational interval. In partial-interval time sampling, an interval is "scored" (i.e., the target behavior is said to have occurred) if the behavior was observed at any time during the interval. In contrast, in whole-interval time sampling, an interval is scored only if the response of concern occurred throughout the interval. These two techniques do not necessarily yield equivalent results or results that are in accordance with those obtained using other observational procedures (e.g., simple frequency counts) or duration measures. Logic, not caprice or precedent, should determine the general observational procedure used, and its parameters as well.

4.   Observers must be adequately trained and monitored. Training involves providing observers with definitions of the target behavior(s), acquainting them with the specifics of the observational procedure, and giving them extensive practice in actually monitoring responding and recording data. Typically, two (or more) observers are trained simultaneously, and training continues until their correspondence in independently scoring responding reaches or exceeds some criterion level across a predetermined number of days. While this approach is reasonable, it is necessary not only to show that two observers can agree in their rating of behavior, but also to demonstrate that their ratings are accurate: A high degree of interobserver agreement, as correspondence between observers is termed, does not ensure a high level of observer accuracy. Further, even if accuracy is adequate at the end of training, it cannot be assumed that observation will remain accurate indefinitely. This must be empirically determined, which

can be done by having observers score a set of criterion videotapes at various points in time—perhaps at the end of training and at 2-week intervals thereafter. If observers consistently evaluate the tapes in accordance with the criterion scores, which represent the way in which the person desiring the assessment data would like them scored, and can agree with one another's ratings, observation can be assumed to be accurate. However, it should be noted that interobserver agreement can be calculated in a variety of ways, and seemingly high indices of interobserver agreement are in some cases misleading (see Johnson & Bolstad, 1973).

Consider a situation in which the frequency of seizures in a young girl, Sally, is to be determined. Seizures are duly defined, the time and location of observation is selected, a simple frequency count is chosen as the method for collecting data, two observers are trained, and assessment begins. Charlie is the primary observer and each day monitors Sally throughout the 4-hour observational period. Every third day, on average, a second observer, Joe, also determines Sally's frequency of seizures. Joe and Charlie work independently and, after 5 days of joint observation, a measure of interobserver agreement is determined by calculating the correlation (Pearson r) between the number of seizures recorded each day by Joe, and by Charlie. The correlation is found to be 1.0, which might seem to indicate that the two observers accurately, and coincidentally, responded to the occurrence of seizures. In fact, it does not do so: Such a high correlation does not necessarily imply that either observer was accurate in his observations, nor that the two observers ever agreed with respect to a given seizures, but only that there was a direct and proportional relationship between the number of seizures reported by Joe and by Charlie. In actuality, Joe may have observed only 20% of the seizures that actually occurred, while Charlie may have counted every seizure and recorded a number of other behaviors as seizures as well. As long as their ratings were proportional, these discrepancies in their actual mode of observation would not be apparent in the correlation coefficient, which would be high.

A related problem occurs when data are collected via time-sampling procedures and interobserver agreement is calculated according to the formula:

$$\text{Percentage agreement} = \frac{A}{A + D} \times 100$$

where A = intervals in which the ratings of the two observers agreed and D = intervals where the ratings of the two observers disagreed. Here, if the behavior of interest occurred very infrequently, overall agreement can be quite high even when the observers rarely agree in those intervals in which one or the other observer reported the occurrence of the target behavior. The solution, obviously, is to calculate interobserver agreement separately for scored intervals (those in which one or both observers reported the occurrence of the target behavior) and for unscored intervals (those in which one or both observers reported the absence of the target behavior). For observations to be acceptable, scored interval and unscored interval agreement should be high. How high?

There is no set answer; above 80% appears to be somewhat conventional, but there is nothing magical about this value. It is theoretically possible to mathematically compare obtained levels of interobserver agreement with "chance" levels (e.g., Yelton, Wildman, & Erickson, 1977), and some authors argue that acceptable levels of interobserver must be "significantly" (e.g., at the .05 probability level) above chance levels.

It is beyond our scope to address this or further issues concerning human observers in assessment; other have done so quite competently (e.g., Johnson & Bolstad, 1973). If we have but alerted readers to some potential difficulties in the use of human observers, our purpose is fulfilled.

Thus far, we have emphasized the manner in which behavior can be quantified through the techniques of behavioral assessment. Behavioral assessment involves another, related component, which is the specification of the relationship between behavior and environmental events.

The use of any assessment device requires that environmental conditions be controlled (as when intelligence tests are administered under standardized conditions) or that the conditions under which behavior is assessed be clearly specified. This is required so that users of the assessment data can judge their generalizability. In behavioral assessment, the general physical environment in which the client is observed is described and, in most instances, an attempt is made to disclose specific environmental events (stimuli) which precede and follow the response of interest. Physiological, or "organismic," variables relevant to the client's functioning are also specified in what Goldfried and Sprafkin (1976) have termed the "SORC" model of assessment. In this model, "S" refers to antecedent stimuli, which precede the response of interest ("R") in time. Consequence stimuli ("C") follow, and are usually produced by, the response of interest. These stimuli, like antecedent and organismic variables, assumedly affect the rate of occurrence of the target behavior. The SORC model is consistent with learning theory analyses of behavior, and having information about events which reliably precede and follow a problem behavior may provide a clinician with profitable hunches about the factors which control the response, as well as procedures that might be successfully employed in its treatment.

For example, we once worked with a mentally retarded institutionalized boy brought to our attention because of an alleged problem of "exposing himself." Systematic observation revealed that he was perfectly decorous throughout most of the day. But each time a particular female aide came near, his trousers were faithfully lowered. This inevitably evoked the aide's anguished retreat. Although the etiology of the boy's undressing was never determined, its treatment was straightforward: The aid was reacquainted with the concept of operant extinction and was requested to ignore the child's disrobing, which she was eventually able to do. Within 2 weeks after the aide's behavior changed, the boy's "problem" had disappeared.

This somewhat facetious example indicates the potential worth of determining antecedents and consequences of behavior, although in fairness it must be noted that effective treatment of a behavioral problem does not require specification of the variables which control the response prior to treatment. This caveat aside, detailed specification of the environment in which behavior is observed is an invaluable part of the assessment process, if only because any observation represents only a sample of behavior, whose generalizability to another situation depends crucially on the similarity of that situation to the one in which behavior was actually monitored.

In general, the environmental antecedents and consequences of behavior are determined through the same techniques used to quantify the response itself. It should, however, be noted that simple observation is never adequate for determining a causal, or functional, relation between a response and an environmental event. This requires manipulation of a variable, which is the hallmark of treatment evaluation, described in the following section.

V. ASSESSING TREATMENT EFFECTS

The assessment of treatment effects refers to all systematic attempts to determine whether a therapeutic intervention has produced a desired outcome. In the nomenclature of science, the therapeutic intervention is an independent variable, the outcome is a dependent variable, and the analytic procedures used to determine their relationship are known collectively as research methodology. While the goals of the researcher may differ somewhat from those of the practicing clinician or administrator, the techniques used to evaluate the effects of their interventions are one and the same. This point is all too often overlooked in clinical practice, where shoddy and haphazard evaluations abound.

Two general strategies can be adopted in treatment evaluation. The first general strategy involves group, or between-subjects, comparisons where at least two sets of subjects are assumed, or preferably determined, to be equivalent with respect to characteristics relevant to the treatment being evaluated. In the simplest form of group comparison, one set of subjects (the experimental group) is exposed to the independent variable (treatment), while the second set of subjects (the control group) is treated identically in all respects save exposure to treatment. If differences are found between the two groups on measures of the dependent variable (the behaviors assessed), this effect is attributed to treatment. Evaluation of the difference between groups usually entails the use of inferential statistics, which allow one to determine the likelihood that an obtained difference in group means or other measures of central tendency would occur through sampling error ("chance") alone when the groups were actually representative of a single population. If this likelihood, termed the significance level, is less than some arbitrarily chosen value (usually .05), then the difference is assumed to be real and, if the difference is in the appropriate direction, the treatment is deemed effective.

The second general strategy for treatment evaluation involves within-subjects comparison. Here, each client serves as his or her own control: Performance of a given individual is simply compared under conditions where the treatment of interest is and is not present. Control (treatment-absent) and experimental (treatment-present) conditions can be arranged in any of a number of logical configurations, or designs, which will be discussed subsequently. Inferential statistics have not typically been used to evaluate the outcome of within-subject designs, although some have advocated their use in this capacity (e.g., Gentile, Roden, & Klein, 1972; Kazdin, 1976). Rather, data are typically presented graphically for each individual and the significance of a treatment determined by the evaluation of the clinician or researcher and his or her peers.

Both within- and between-subjects comparisons require that certain conditions be met if conclusions are to be meaningful. Obviously, regardless of how a treatment is evaluated, its outcome must be reflected in a measure that is valid, reliable, and sensitive. We have discussed these topics previously, although treatment evaluation raises some issues not usually covered in discussions of assessment. For example, evaluations of treatments that are intended to suppress undesired behaviors may be inadequate if only undesired behaviors are monitored. An intervention, such as administration of a behaviorally active drug, might well reduce such behavior; however it is also likely that desired behaviors will be reduced. To evaluate such a treatment as successful simply because no data were collected on the occurrence of desirable behaviors is at best misleading, and at worst tragic. Those interested in treatment evaluation would be well to emphasize the totality of its impact and not to focus on one criterion or measure, however important.

Beyond ensuring that the dependent measure is adequately measured, any worthwhile evaluation must make certain that the intervention is actually implemented as planned, and that unknown extraneous variables acting coincidentally with the independent variable (treatment) are not wholly or partially responsible for changes in behavior assigned to the intervention. Research methodology is intended to provide assurance that extraneous variables do not confound treatment effects, and researchers or clinicians can take a number of precautions to ensure that interventions are actually implemented as planned. Barber (1976) provides a detailed coverage of these precautions as well as a highly worthwhile overview of the errors that can be made in any form of treatment evaluation. Though obvious, it is worth reiterating that any person involved in evaluation can fabricate or misrepresent findings, or commit other, more subtle errors that lead to findings which cannot be independently replicated. For this reason, undue weight should not be placed on the outcome of any one evaluation, regardless of design and apparent rigor.

While certain conventions are shared in between- and within-subjects designs, the logic of the two approaches differs, as do the problems and advantages associated with each. For these reasons, the two approaches are considered separately in the following section. Spatial requirements demand that our coverage be brief and selective; the reader interested in fuller coverage of treatment evaluation may consult any of a number of sources discussing between-subjects (e.g., Campbell & Stanley, 1966; Keppel, 1973; Kirk, 1968; Myers, 1972) and within-subjects (e.g., Bailey, 1977; Hersen & Barlow, 1976; Johnston & Pennypacker, 1980; Sidman, 1960) designs.

Between-subjects designs. There are innumerable variations on the simple two-group design discussed above, including factorial designs which allow for the evaluation of two or more treatments and their interaction. Two variations that have proven useful in treatment evaluation, especially with respect to pharmacotherapies, are the crossover design and the counterbalanced design (Chassan, 1960; Sprague & Werry, 1971).

Wysocki and Fuque (in press) nicely summarize these designs and their strengths and weaknesses as follows:

> In the crossover design, two groups of subjects are typically used. Subjects are randomly assigned to groups and receive conditions in a different order. In drug-related crossover designs the most common conditions are drug and placebo. One group begins with the drug condition and the other group with the treatment condition. At the same point in time the groups are changed from drug to placebo and vice versa. There are several advantages and disadvantages in using crossover designs. First, ethical considerations are minimized as no subjects are denied treatment. Second, fewer subjects are needed than in most group designs. And third, this design is relatively sensitive to drug effects (e.g., Sprague & Werry, 1971). However, the design is dependent on the reversibility of drug (or other treatment) effects and the assumption that any effects obtained prior to the crossover will not carry over and influence effects obtained following the crossover.
>
> In the counterbalanced design, there are typically several conditions being compared by having different randomly determined groups receive each condition in a different order. For example, a counterbalanced design could be used to compare placebo, Drug 1, Drug 2, and Drug 3. In this situation four groups would typically be used with each group receiving the conditions in a different sequence. The following diagram represents one possible random arrangement of conditions:
>
> Group 1:   Drug 1, Drug 3, Placebo, Drug 2
> Group 2:   Drug 2, Placebo, Drug 3, Drug 1
> Group 3:   Drug 3, Drug 2, Drug 1, Placebo
> Group 4:   Placebo, Drug 1, Drug 2, Drug 3
>
> The same advantages and disadvantages presented for the crossover design pertain to the counterbalanced design.

Beyond the advantages and disadvantages associated with specific between-subjects designs are a number of general characteristics which many have described as shortcomings (e.g., Sidman, 1960). One of these concerns is the large number of individuals required for most between-subjects comparisons. It is, for example, nearly impossible in a given institution to find more than a few children with similar behavior problems requiring similar treatments.

Another problem involves the loss of information concerning individuals that inevitably occurs when groups are compared. Few treatments produce consistent effects across clients; some typically improve, some worsen, and others fail to change. Knowing that group data representing some number of people exposed to a given treatment differ in a statistical sense from data representing a control group provides scant little information concerning behavior change in individuals, and less concerning the factors responsible for any differences that do occur across clients. From a clinical perspective, it is more useful to understand the factors responsible for variability in treatment effects than to know how to statistically evaluate this variability. Unfortunately, the latter tract is usually associated with between-subjects evaluations. Beyond this, statistically significant differences in behavior may not be clinically significant. That is, even though an inferential statistic may indicate that a given treatment has produced an effect, the absolute magnitude of that effect might be so small as to be of no therapeutic importance. Clinical, as opposed to statistical, significance is usually determined in one of three ways: (1) *By comparing obtained levels of behavior during treatment with criterion levels set before treatment*—These criterion levels (treatment objectives) define solution of the behavioral problem which treatment is designed to ameliorate. (2) *By comparing the performance of individuals undergoing treatment with that of similar individuals who do not manifest the behavioral problem for which treatment was instituted*—Such norm-referenced comparison is simple enough in principle but difficult to arrange in practice when mentally retarded institutionalized children are considered. The problem here, obviously, is determination of an appropriate peer group. (3) *By having those who defined the problem evaluate the success of its treatment*—This approach, although intuitively appealing, requires that evaluations actually reflect changes in the behavior of the client. A variety of factors unrelated to clients' actions may lead to diagnoses of improvement, including the observer's expectations and the demand characteristics of the situation (Johnson & Bolstad, 1973). Because of this, all determinations of clinical significance must rest primarily on data indicating the level of performance of treated individuals, and secondarily on skilled interpretation of these data. This caveat, by the way, holds true regardless of whether between- or within-subjects designs are used in treatment evaluation.

Beyond obscuring individual variability and placing perhaps undue emphasis on inferential statistics as means of evaluating the success of treatment, between-subjects evaluations tend to be somewhat inflexible, since the outcome of a treatment cannot be determined until all of the data are collected and analyzed statistically. The problem here is twofold: First, treatment cannot be changed for an individual even if his or her performance is worsening without violating the design of the evaluation. Second, since the outcome of the evaluation cannot be known until all of the data are in, the clinician often fails to interact with the data on a day-to-day basis (Michael, 1974). Thus, worsening clients may be overlooked and, less obviously, the clinician may not observe trends in the data that provide valuable clues as to why treatment is or is not working.

In view of the foregoing, between-subjects designs cannot be generally recommended for treatment evaluation in mentally retarded institutionalized children, although they may be invaluable in some instances and are required in certain research applications. Among these are situations where the cost-effectiveness of broad-spectrum programs are to be compared, and situations where the behavior of groups of individuals per se is of importance (e.g., littering by all members of an institution). When between-subjects designs are employed, it is crucial that they be used correctly. Two common errors involve the inappropriate use of inferential statistics and the nonrandom assignment of subjects to groups, each of which renders conclusions invalid.

Within-subject designs.   In contrast to most between-subjects designs, within-subjects designs always involve repeated measures of the performance of individuals. The simplest form of within-subjects evaluation is the A-B design, where A designates a baseline condition in which treatment is not in effect and B designates the treatment condition. This design, however, is not adequate for demonstrating functional relations between an independent and dependent variable (see Hersen & Barlow, 1976; Wolf & Risley, 1971). The A-B design may suggest that a treatment is effective but, as Risley and Wolf (1972) note, "The weakness in this design is that the data in the experimental (treatment) condition are compared with a forecast from the prior baseline data. The accuracy of an assessment of the role of the experimental procedure in producing the change rests on the accuracy of that forecast. A strong statement of causality therefore requires that the forecast be supported. A strong statement of causality is accomplished by elaborating the A-B design" (p. 5).

This elaboration may be accomplished by repeatedly introducing and withdrawing treatment, as in the A-B-A-B design, one member of a large family of so-called withdrawal designs. (These designs are also commonly referred to as ,"reversal" designs, although this designation may be misleading as Hersen and Barlow [1976] have contended.) The A-B-A-B design is quite powerful in disclosing treatment effects and has been profitably employed in evaluating a variety of interventions in many different populations. The logic of the design is unimpeachable: If behavior is consistently better during treatment than during baseline, and if this effect is repeatable, it seems likely that treatment is actually responsible for the observed improvement in behavior.

Despite the advantages of withdrawal designs, they meet with two major difficulties: (1) To document that an intervention is effective, such designs require that behavior change in a countertherapeutic direction when treatment is terminated. Such countertherapeutic behavior changes may not be ethically defensible. (2) Withdrawal designs cannot be used to evaluate treatments that produce irreversible effects. Because of these limitations, alternatives to withdrawal designs have been developed, among them the multiple-baseline and multielement-baseline design.

In the multiple-baseline design, baseline data are taken across two or more behaviors, individuals, or situations. The effects of an intervention are demonstrated by introducing the intervention across baselines at different points in time (all of the dependent measures must require change in the same dirction), and showing that a given behavior improves relative to the baseline condition only when treatment is introduced for that behavior. Thus, the multiple-baseline design represents a series of A-B designs staggered in time and attempts to control for the effects of extraneous variables by showing that specific changes in behavior occur only with the onset of treatment for that behavior.

The multiple-baseline design has grown in favor as a technique for evaluating behavior change interventions (Kazdin, 1975), probably because it is adequate for demonstrating a treatment's effectiveness but does not require countertherapeutic behavior change to do so. Kazdin and Kopel (1975) discuss this design at length and provide some excellent suggestions concerning its appropriate use.

The final design to be considered is the multielement-baseline design, which is fully described by Ulman and Sulzer-Azaroff (1975). They summarize it as follows:

> The multielement baseline involves the repeated measurement of a behavior under alternating conditions of the independent variable. In contrast with multiple-baseline and reversal designs, the multi-element baseline design does not consist of experimental phases where one behavior modification procedure is applied during several consecutive sessions until stability is achieved within that condition. Rather, experimental and baseline conditions are presented in alteration—on either a constant or an unpredictable schedule—within sessions and/or from one session to the next. . . . The experimental conditions of a multielement baseline procedure are alternated independent of changes in behavior. A distinctive (potentially discriminable) stimulus is correlated with each condition and the effects of the treatment procedure(s) can be observed by comparing differential performances. Thus, if different patterns of responding develop, and each pattern is observed to be unique to a particular experimental condition . . . then experimental control has been demonstrated. (p. 379)

The primary advantages of the multielement-baseline design involve its suitability for rapidly comparing treatments, its ability to demonstrate the utility of a treatment without terminating treatment or inducing countertherapeutic behavior change, and the large amount of useful information which can be gathered in a short time when this design is used. Treatments which interact cannot be readily evaluated with this design, nor can treatments which produce long-lasting or irreversible effects.

The preceding certainly does not exhaust the list of useful within-subjects designs: Multiple-probe techniques enable one to evaluate treatments designed to improve lengthy sequences of behavior (Horner & Baer, 1978), while changing-criterion designs (Hartmann & Hall, 1976) are especially well suited to evaluate interventions that specify a stepwise change in the target behavior [e.g., a weight-control program that requires a client to lose 4.5 kg a week]. It is far beyond our scope to consider these designs; books have been devoted to the topic of within subjects evaluation. However, we should note that when such designs are used appropriately they are fully capable of assessing both the reliability of a treatment's effects within an individual or group of individuals and the extent to which the outcome of a particular intervention generalizes across individuals, situations, and behaviors. These issues are addressed in the general sources listed above.

Unique issues in evaluating drug effects. One general area of treatment evaluation that merits special consideration is the evaluation of pharmacotherapies, an area where methodological errors abound as indicated by a number of recent reviews (e.g., Breuning & Poling, in press-a, in press-b; Freeman, 1970; Klein & Davis, 1969; Lipman, DiMascio, Reatig, & Kirson, 1978; Marholin & Phillips, 1976; Sulzbacher, 1973; Wysocki & Fuqua, in press). At minimum, it seems that any acceptable drug evaluation must meet the following six criteria, first advanced by Sprague and Werry (1971):

1. *Placebo control.* An inactive substance as close as possible to the drug in physical characteristics should be administered during all or most nondrug conditions. This prevents biases and expectations on the part of clients and observers alike from influencing obtained results (see Breuning, Ferguson, & Cullari, 1980). In order to evaluate any placebo response that might be occurring (i.e., a response to an inert substance administered as a drug), it is often wise to include a condition in which neither active drug nor placebo is included.

2. *Double blind.* As a further control for expectations and biases, neither clients nor observers should know when drug and placebo are being given. The use of blind observers should, in fact, be standard procedure regardless of whether drugs or other interventions are being evaluated (see Breuning, Ferguson, & Cullari, 1980).

3. *Standardized doses.* In any evaluation, the dose of drug given (mg/day or, perferably, mg/kg/day) must be clearly specified, along with the schedule of administration. With some drugs (e.g., lithium chloride), blood levels are of crucial importance and should be reported. Drug regimens should be in effect long enough for behavior to stabilize and for the effects of prior regimens to abate. All drugs that a client receives should be specified and, whenever possible, only the drug being evaluated should be given during the evaluation period. Breuning (in press), and Ferguson and Breuning (in press) discuss dose-related issues in detail.

4. *Standardized evaluation.* The procedures used to assess drug effects must be reliable, valid, and sensitive. It is crucially important that the measures used to evaluate a drug's effectiveness have a direct and obvious relationship to the condition the drug is prescribed to treat.

5. *Appropriate statistical evaluations.* As noted previously, when inferential statistics are employed, they must be used appropriately and reported in a clear and unambiguous fashion. It is of some interest that, in 1971, Sprague and Werry reported that only 21% of the studies they evaluated met this criterion.

6. *Random assignment to groups.* Related to objective 5, when randomized groups designs are used, assignment must be truly random. If not, a fundamental assumption of most inferential statistics is violated.

Since 1971, Sprague and Baxley (1978) have added a seventh requirement, to wit, that pharmacotherapy be compared to some alternative, less restrictive, treatment. This requirement seemingly was added in consideration of a plethora of data (e.g., Breuning, in press; Breuning, O'Neill, & Ferguson, 1980; Breuning & Poling, in press-a, in press-b) indicating that the great majority of behaviorally active drugs produce undesired side effects.

Beyond the criteria listed above, a methodologically adequate clinical drug evaluation must utilize an acceptable design, either within- or between-subjects, which can raise a number of vexing legal and ethical issues. These are considered in the next section.

Obviously, evaluating a drug treatment is no mean task. Nonetheless, it is not impossible to adequately evaluate pharmacotherapies, and some methodologically sound reports of such evaluations have recently appeared in the literature. It is to be hoped that this number will rapidly increase, for over half of all institutionalized mentally retarded individuals receive behaviorally active drugs (Breuning and Poling, in press-b).

Litigation and Legislation

In the past decade the rights of the mentally retarded have come under careful legal and legislative scrutiny (see The Mentally Retarded Citizen and the Law, 1976; and the Developmental Disability Bill of Rights Act–P.L. 94-103 for a thorough orientation). As a result, all mentally retarded individuals are to receive basic constitutional rights. While a discussion of how each right may relate to the issue of assessment is beyond the scope of this chapter, a brief presentation of a few global issues will be provided.

Central to any point of contention relating to the rights of the mentally retarded are the issues of labeling and fairness in diagnosis. The right to an accurate diagnosis and classification is likely one of the most violated rights of the mentally retarded. As stated earlier, IQ is sometimes used as the sole indicator of retardation. Futher, IQ "cutoffs" are typically derived using an upper limit of 68–70 and then deviations of 15–16 points per cutoff. There is usually no use of the "number of standard deviations below the mean" formula for cutoff scores. Thus, one is tempted to conclude that many individuals labeled as being mentally retarded are labelled inappropriately. This issue is further confounded by the fact that even when standard deviation cutoffs are used, the tests were most likely not designed or standardized with the mentally retarded, resulting in possible bias, and there were no analyses of many possible confounding variables (e.g., motivation, drug state). Finally, even when an "intellectual" assessment takes these factors into account, it must be remembered that the test was designed to predict success or failure in the school, not necessarily in society. While perhaps not generally practiced, it is generally well voiced that because of the stigmatisms and concerns attached to the mental retardation label, a comprehensive diagnosis is a priority right.

Assuming that an individual is appropriately classified with respect to degree of mental retardation, the right to the most appropriate treatment in the least restrictive setting comes into play. Detailed assessment rather than the more commonly used "conjecture" is the only way to ensure that this right is met. Individualized program plans (also a right) should be developed using the treatment precursor assessment methods mentioned earlier. Once treatment goals are derived and implemented, the methods of assessing treatment effectiveness previously described need to be utilized. If these methods are used, one can accurately assess the appropriateness of the treatment. While these technologies exist, the assessment of least restrictive setting is more complex.

The term "less restrictive" is not a precisely defined concept and often refers merely to comparisons of institutional and noninstitutional settings or of normal and specialized classroom settings. It must be remembered that there will likely be a continuum of restrictions across all rights of the individual and within any institutional and noninstitutional setting.

From a treatment standpoint, to argue "restrictiveness" is largely to argue environmental suitability. And while most legal and legislative decisions call for assessment to determine which individuals can be treated in a less restrictive setting, a priori determinations are rarely more than speculation. Unfortunately, the only data-based method of assessing environmental suitability is to (1) determine an environment which allows the individual less restrictions of basic rights, (2) move the individual into this environment, (3) implement the treatment plan, and (4) assess the effectiveness of the treatment plan. If these is evidence of progression, or possibly no regression, one might argue the appropriateness/suitability of the less restrictive setting.

VI. CONCLUDING REMARKS

In the foregiong pages, we have described a number of assessment procedures and devices commonly used with institutionalized mentally retarded children, and raised several general issues relevant to the assessment process. Although our coverage was by no means exhaustive, it should be apparent that assessment of this population as currently practiced leaves much to be desired. Intelligence tests and measures of adaptive behavior, while ubiquitously employed, are of debatable validity, reliability, and practical utility. However, their use in the identification and classification of the mentally retarded undoubtedly will continue. Direct observation of significant behaviors, through the techniques of behavioral assessment, has much to recommend it, although the use of human observers to quantify behavior is associated with a large and perplexing array of potential methodological errors. The problems of assessment are compounded in treatment evaluation, which not only requires behavior to be validly and reliably quantified, but demands as well that changes in behavior be potentially attributable to an intervention.

Despite these difficulties, it is possible to conduct assessments which yield valid, reliable, and meaningful data. Such data increase the likelihood that initial decisions concerning a child will be appropriate, and allow inappropriate decisions to be recognized and modified. Unfortunately, in closing we must emphasize that even the best assessment information ultimately is nothing more than a set of numbers to which someone—an administrator, parent, clinician, or the child—responds. The nature of this response depends on several factors beyond the actual data, and even the best assessment information can be ignored or misused: Appropriate assessment of a mentally retarded institutionalized child does not, in and of itself, ensure proper treatment. However, it may make errors that do occur apparent to the person responsible for them, or to concerned others. Further, inappropriate or inaccurate assessment data practically ensure inappropriate treatment. For these reasons, as well as the dictates of public law, adequate assessment is nothing less than mandatory.

ACKNOWLEDGMENTS

We thank Kathy Krafft and the other members of the Behavioral Pharmacology Laboratory at Western Michigan University for their comments on an earlier version.

NOTE

1. Unfortunately, a variety of terms have been used to label each of the several observational procedures we shall discuss. Thus, what we describe as intermittent time sampling is sometimes referred to as time sampling, while the general procedure we call continuous time sampling is also termed interval recording (e.g., Lutzker & Martin, 1981). There presently is no consensus with respect to appropriate terminology in this area, and confusion can be avoided only when authors describe as well as name particular procedures.

REFERENCES

Ammons, R. B., & Ammons, C. H. The Quick Test (QT): Provisional manual. *Psychological Reports*, 1962, *11*, 111–161.
Anastasi, A. *Psychological testing.* New York: Macmillan, 1968.
Bailey, J. S. *A Handbook of research methods in applied behavior analysis.* Tallahassee: Florida State University Press, 1977.
Barber, T. X. *Pitfalls in human research.* New York: Pergamon, 1976.

Bellack, A. S., & Schwartz, J. S. Assessment of self-control programs. In H. Herson & A. S. Bellack (Eds.), *Behavioral assessment: A practical handbook*. New York: Pergamon, 1976.

Blanton, R. L. Historical perspectives on classification of mental retardation. In N. Hobbs (Ed.), *Issues in the classification of children*, Vol. 2. San Francisco: Jossey-Bass, 1975.

Breuning, S. E. An applied dose response curve for thioridazine with the mentally retarded: Aggressive, self-stimulatory, intellectual, and workshop behaviors—a preliminary report. *Psychopharmacology Bulletin*, in press.

Breuning, S. E., Ferguson, D. G., & Cullari, S. Analysis of single-double blind procedures, maintenance of placebo effects, and drug induced dyskinesia with mentally retarded persons. *Applied Research in Mental Retardation*, 1980, *1*, 175–182.

Breuning, S. E., & Davidson, N. A. Effects of psychotropic drugs on intelligence test performance of institutionalized mentally retarded adults. *American Journal of Mental Deficiency*, 1981, *85*, 575–579.

Breuning, S. E., & Davis, V. J. Reinforcement effects on the intelligence test performance of institutionalized retarded persons: Behavioral analysis, directional control, and implications for habilitation. *Applied Research in Mental Retardation*, in press.

Breuning, S. E., O'Neill, M. J., & Ferguson, D. G. Comparison of psychotropic drug plus response cost procedures for controlling institutionalized mentally retarded persons. *Applied Research in Mental Retardation*, 1980, *1*, 253–268.

Breuning, S. E., & Poling, A. (Eds.). *Drugs and mental retardation*. Springfield, IL: Charles C. Thomas, in press. (a)

Breuning, S. E. and Poling, A. Pharmacotherapy with the mentally retarded. In J. L. Hatson & R. P. Barrett (Eds.), *Psychopathology of the mentally retarded*. New York: Brunner/Mazel, in press. (b)

Breuning, S. E., & Zella, W. F. Effects of individualized incentives on norm-referenced IQ test performance of high-school students in special education classes. *Journal of School Psychology*, 1978, *16*, 220–226.

Burgemeister, B. B., Blum, L. H., & Lorge, I. *Columbia Mental Maturity Scale* (3rd ed.). New York: Harcourt Brace Jovanovich, 1972.

Cain, L., Levine, S., & Elzey, F. *Cain-Levine Social Competency Scale*. Palo Alto: Consulting Psychologists Press, 1963.

Campbell, D. T., & Stanley, J. C. *Experimental and quasi-experimental designs for research*. Chicago: Rand-McNally, 1966.

Cattell, R. B. *Culture Fair Intelligence Test: Scale I*. Champaign, IL: Institute for Personality and Ability Testing, 1950.

Cattell, R. B., & Cattell, A. K. S. *Culture Fair Intelligence Test: Scale III*. Champaign, IL: Institute for Personality and Ability Testing, 1963.

Cattell, R. B., & Cattell, A. K. S. *Culture Fair Intelligence Test: Scale III*. Champaign, IL: Institute for qoPersonality and Ability Testing, 1963.

Cautela, J. R. Behavior therapy and the need for behavioral assessment. *Psychotherapy, Research and Practice*, 1968, *5*, 175–179.

Chassan, J. B. Statistical inference and the single case in clinical design. *Psychiatry*, 1960, *23*, 173–184.

Ciminero, A. R. Behavioral assessment: An overview. In A. R. Ciminaro, K. S. Calhoun, & H. E. Adams (Eds.), *Handbook of behavioral assessment*. New York: Wiley, 1977.

Ciminero, A. R. Calhoun, K. S., & Adams, H. E. (Eds.). *Handbook of behavioral assessment*. New York: Wiley, 1977.

Clingman, J. M., & Fowler, R. L. The effects of primary reward on the IQ performance of grade-school children as a function of initial IQ level. *Journal of Applied Behavior Analysis*, 1976, *9*, 19–23.

Cone, J. D., & Hawkins, R. P. (Eds.). *Behavioral assessment: New directions in clinical psychology*. New York: Brunner/Mazel, 1977.

Coulter, W. A., & Morrow, H. W. *Adaptive behavior: Concepts and measurements.* New York: Grune and Stratton, 1978.

Davis, V. J., Poling, A., Wysocki, T., & Breuning, S. E. Effects of phenytoin withdrawal on matching to sample and workshop performance of mentally retarded persons. *The Journal of Nervous and Mental Disease,* in press.

Doll, E. *Vineland Social Maturity Scale.* Circle Pines, MN: American Guidance Service, 1965.

Dunn, L. M. *Peabody Picture Vocabulary Test.* Circle Pines, MN: American Guidance Service, 1965. (Originally published 1953).

Fotheringham, J. B. Retardation, family adequacy and institutionalization. *Canada's Mental Health,* 1970, *18,* 15–18.

Fotheringham, J. B., Skelton, M., & Hoddinott, B. A. *The retarded child and his family: The effects of home and institution.* Toronto: Ontario Institution for Studies in Education, 1971.

Foxx, R. M., & Azrin, N. H. *Toilet training the retarded: A rapid program for day and nighttime independent training.* Champaign, IL: Research Press, 1973.

Ferguson, D. G., & Breuning, S. E. Antipsychotic and antianxiety drugs. In S. E. Breuning & A. D. Poling (Eds.), *Drugs and mental retardation.* Springfield, IL: Charles C. Thomas, in press.

French, J. L. *Pictorial Test of Intelligence.* Boston: Houghton Mifflin, 1964.

Freeman, R. D. Psychopharmacology and the retarded child. In N. J. Menslascino (Ed.), *Psychiatric approaches in mental retardation.* New York: Basic Books, 1970.

Gentile, R. R., Roden, A. H., & Klein, R. D. An analysis-of-variance model for the intrasubject replication design. *Journal of Applied Behavior Analysis,* 1972, *5,* 193–198.

Goldfarb, W. The effects of early institutional care of adolescent personality. *Journal of Experimental Education,* 1943, *12,* 106–129.

Goldfarb, W. Variations in adolescent adjustment of institutionally-reared children. *American Journal of Orthopsychiatry,* 1947, *17,* 457–499.

Goldfried, M. R., & Sprafkin, J. N. *Behavioral personality assessment.* Morristown, NJ: General Learning Press, 1974.

Grossman, H. J. (Ed.). *Manual on terminology and classification in mental retardation.* Washington, DC: American Association on Mental Deficiency, 1977.

Harris, D. *Children's drawings as measures of intellectual maturity.* New York: Hourcourt Brace Jovanovich, 1963.

Hartmann, D. P., & Hall, R. V. The changing criterion design. *Journal of Applied Behavior Analysis,* 1976, *9,* 527–532.

Haynes, S. N. *Principles of behavioral assessment.* New York: Gardner, 1978.

Heber, R. A. A manual on terminology and classification in mental retardation. *American Journal of Mental Deficiency* (Monograph Supplement), 1961, *66.*

Hersen, M. Historical perspectives in behavioral assessment. In M. Hersen & A. S. Bellack (Eds.), *Behavioral assessment: A practical handbook.* New York: Pergamon, 1976.

Hersen, M., & Barlow, D. *Single case experimental designs: Strategies for studying behavior change.* New York: Pergamon Press, 1976.

Hersen, M., & Bellack, A. S. *Behavioral assessment: A practical handbook.* New York: Pergamon, 1976.

Hollis, J. H., & St. Omer, V. V. Direct measurement of psychopharmacologic response: Effects of chlorpromazine on motor behavior of retarded children. *American Journal of Mental Deficiency,* 1972, *76,* 397–407.

Horner, R. D., & Baer, D. M. Multiple-probe technique: A variation of the multiple baseline. *Journal of Applied Behavior Analysis,* 1978, *11,* 189–196.

Johnson, S. M., & Bolstad, O. D. Methodological issues in naturalistic observation: some problems and solutions for field research. In L. A. Hammerlynck, L. D. Handy & E. J. Mash (Eds.), *Behavior changes: Methodology, concepts, and practice.* Champaign, IL: Research Press, 1973.

Johnston, J. M., & Pennypacker, H. S. *Strategies and tactics of human behavioral research.* New York: Lawrence Elbaum Associates, 1980.

Kamin, L. *The science and politics of IQ.* New York: Wiley, 1974.

Kanner, L. *A history of the care and study of the mentally retarded.* Springfield, IL: Charles C. Thomas, 1964.

Kazdin, A. E. Characteristics and trends in applied behavior analysis. *Journal of Applied Behavior Analysis,* 1975, *8,* 332.

Kazdin, A. E. Statistical analyses for single-case experimental designs. In M. Hersen & D. H. Barlow (Eds.), *Single case experimental designs.* New York: Pergamon Press, 1976.

Kazdin, A. E., & Kopel, S. A. On resolving ambiguities of the multiple-baseline design: Problems and recommendations. *Behavior Therapy,* 1975, *6,* 601–608.

Keppel, G. *Design and analysis: A researcher's handbook.* Englewood Cliffs, NJ: Prentice-Hall, 1973.

Kershner, J. R. Intellectual and social development in relation to family functioning: A longitudinal comparison of home vs. institutional effects. *American Journal of Mental Deficiency,* 1970, *75,* 276–284.

Kirk, R. E. *Experimental design: Procedures for the behavioral sciences.* Belmont, CA: Brooks/Cole 1968.

Klaber, M. M. The retarded and institutions for the retarded—a preliminary report. In S. B. Sarason & J. Doris (Eds.), *Psychological problems in mental deficiency.* New York: Harper and Row, 1969.

Klein, D., & Davis, J. *Diagnosis and drug treatment of psychiatric disorders.* Baltimore: Williams and Wilkins, 1969.

Krischell, C. H. State laws on marriage and sterilization of the mentally retarded. *Mental Retardation,* 1972, *10,* 36–38.

Kugel, R. B., & Wolfensberger, W. (Eds.). *Changing patterns in residential services for the mentally retarded.* Washington, DC: Superintendent of Documents, 1969.

Lang, P. J. Fear reduction and fear behavior: Problems in treating a construct. In J. M. Schlein (Ed.), *Research in psychotherapy,* Vol. III. Washington, DC: American Psychological Association, 1968. Lang, P. J. The application of psychophysiological methods to the study of psychotherapy and behavior modification. In A. E. Bergin & L. L. Garfield (Eds.), *Handbook of psychotherapy and behavior change.* New York: Wiley, 1971.

Leland, H., Nihira, K., Foster, R., Shellhaas, M., & Kagin, E. *Conference on Measurement of Adaptive Behavior.* Carsons, KS: CArsons State Hospital and Training Center, 1968.

Leland, M., Shellhaas, M., Nihira, K., & Foster, R. Adaptive behavior: A new dimension in the classification of the mentally retarded. *Mental Retardation Abstracts,* 1967, *4,* 359–387.

Lewis, J. R., & Mercer, J. R. The system of multicultural pluralistic assessment: SOMPA. In W. A. Coulter & H. W. Morrow (Eds.), *Adaptive behavior: Concepts and measurements,* New York: Grune and Stratton, 1978.

Linehan, M. M. Issues in behavioral interviewing. In J. D. Cone & R. P. Hawkins (Eds.), *Behavioral Assessment: New Directions in Clinical Psychology.* New York: Brunner/Mazel, 1977.

Lipman, R. S., DiMascio, A., Reatig, N., & Kirson, T. Psychotropic drugs and mentally retarded children. In M. A. Lipton, A. DiMascio & K. F. Killman (Eds.), *Psychopharmacology: A generation of progress.* New York: Raven Press, 1978.

Liverant, S. Intelligence: A concept in need of re-examination. *Journal of Consulting Psychology,* 1960, *24,* 101–110.

Lutzker, J. R., & Martin, J. A. *Behavior Change.* Monterey, CA: Brooks/Cole, 1981.

Madle, R. A. Alternative residential placements. In J. T. Neisworth & R. M. Smith (Eds.), *Retardation Issues, Assessment, and Intervention.* New York: McGraw-Hill, 1978.

Mahoney, M. J. Some applied issues in self-monitoring. J. D. Cone & R. P. Hawkins (Eds.),

Behavioral Assessment: New directions in clinical psychology. New York: Brunner/Mazel, 1977.

Maloney, M. P., & Ward, M. P. *Mental retardation and modern society.* New York: Oxford, 1979.

Marholin, D., & Phillips, D. Methodological issues in psycho-pharmacological research. *American Journal of Orthopsychiatry,* 1976, *46,* 477–495.

McCarthy, D. *Manual for the McCarthy Scales of Childrens Abilities.* New York: Psychological Corporation, 1972.

Masland, R., Sarason, S., & Gladwin, T. *Mental subnormality.* New York: Basic Books, 1958.

McFall, R. M. Analogue methods in behavioral assessment: Issues and prospects. In J. D. Cone and R. P. Hawkins (Eds.), *Behavioral assessment: New directions in clinical psychology.* New York: Brunner/Mazel, 1977.

Mercer, J. *System of multicultural pluralistic assessment: Technical manual.* New York: Psychological Corporation, 1979.

Michael, J. Statistical inference for single organism research: Mixed blessing or curse? *Journal of Applied Behavior Analysis,* 1974, *1,* 647–653.

Morganstern, K. P. Behavioral interviewing: The initial stages of assessment. In M. Hersen & A. S. Bellack (Eds.), *Behavioral assessment: A practical handbook.* New York: Pergamon, 1976.

Myers, J. L. *Fundamentals of experimental design.* Boston: Allyn and Bacon, 1972.

Nay, W. R. Analogue measures. In A. R. Ciminero, K. S. Calhoun, & H. E. Adams (Eds.), *Handbook of behavioral assessment.* New York: Wiley, 1977.

Nelson, R. O., & Hayes, S. C. Some current dimensions of behavioral assessment. *Behavioral Assessment,* 1979, *1,* 1–16.

Newland, T. E. Psychological assessment of exceptional children and youth. In W. Cruickshank (Ed.), *Psychology of Exceptional Children and Youth.* Englewood Cliffs, NJ: Prentice-Hall, 1971.

Nihira, K., Foster, R., Shellhaas, M., & Leland, H. *AAMD Adaptive Behavior Scale.* Washington, DC: American Association on Mental Deficiency, 1969.

Nihira, K., Foster, R., Shellhaas, M., & Leland, H. *American Association on Mental Deficiency Adaptive Behavior Scale, 1975 revision.* Washington, DC: President's Committee on Mental Retardation, 1975.

Nirje, B. The normalization principle and its human management implications. In R. B. Kugel & W. Wolfensberger (Eds.), *Changing patterns in residential services for the mentally retarded.* Washington, DC: President's Committee on Mental Retardation, 1969.

Nowrey, J. E. A brief synopsis of mental deficiency. *American Journal of Mental Deficiency,* 1945, *49,* 319–357.

Nunnally, J. *Psychometric theory.* New York: McGraw-Hill, 1967.

Oakland, T., & Goldwater, D. L. Assessment and interventions for the mildly retarded and learning disabled children. In G. D. Phye & D. J. Reschly (Eds.), *School psychology perspectives and issues.* New York: Academic Press, 1979.

Oakland, T., & Matuszek, P. Using tests in nondiscriminatory assessment. In T. Oakland (Ed.), *With bias toward none: Non-biased assessment of minority group children.* Lexington, KY: Coordinating Office for Regional Resource Centers, 1976.

Office of Civil Rights. Memorandum from OCR to state and local education agencies on elimination of discrimination in the assignment of children to special education classes for the mentally retarded. In T. Oakland (Ed.), *With bias toward none: Non-biased assessment of minority group children.* Lexington, KY: Coordinating Office for Regional Resource Centers, 1976.

Office of Mental Retardation Coordination. *Mental retardation source book.* Washington, DC: U.S. Government Printing Office, 1972.

Otis, A. S., & Lennon, R. T. *Otis-Lennon Mental Ability Test: Technical handbook.* New York: Harcourt, Brace and World, 1969.

Paul, G. L. Strategy of outcome reserach in psychotherapy. *Journal of Consulting Psychology,* 1967, *31,* 104–118.

Poling, A. D., & Breuning, S. E. An overview of mental retardation. In S. E. Breuning & A. D. Poling (Eds.), *Drugs and Mental Retardation.* Springfield, IL: Charles C. Thomas, in press.

Poling, A., Cleary, J., & Monaghan, M. The use of human observers in psychopharmacological research. *Pharmacology Biochemistry and Behavior,* 1980, *13,* 243–246.

President's Committee on Mental Retardation. *Mental retardation: The known and the unknown.* Washington, DC: Superintendent of Documents, 1975.

President's Committee on Mental Retardation. *The mentally retarded citizen and the law.* New York: The Free Press, 1976.

Provence, S., & Lipton, B. D. *Infants in institutions.* New York: International Univeristy Press, 1962.

Quilitch, R., & Gray, J. Purposeful activity for the PMR: A demonstration project. *Mental Retardation,* 1974, *12,* 28–29.

Risley, T. R., & Wolf, M. M. Strategies for analyzing behavioral change over time. In J. Nessebroade & H. Reese (Eds.), *Life-span developmental psychology: Methodological issues.* New York: Academic Press, 1972.

Repp, A. C., Roberts, D. M., Slack, D. J. Repp, C. F., & Beckler, M. S. A comparison of frequency, interval, and time-sampling methods of data collection. *Journal of Applied Behavior Analysis,* 1976, *9,* 501–508.

Reschly, D. J. Nonbiased assessment. In G. D. Phye & D. J. Reschly (Eds.), *School Psychology Perspectives and Issues.* New York: Academic Press, 1979.

Robinson, N. M., & Robinson, H. B. *The mentally retarded child.* New York: McGraw-Hill, 1976.

Rosenthal, R. *Experimenter effects in behavioral research.* New York: Appleton-Century-Crofts, 1966.

Salvia, J., & Ysseldyke, J. E. *Assessment in special and remedial Education.* Boston: Houghton Mifflin, 1981.

Salvia, J., Ysseldyke, J., & Lee, M. 1972 revision of the Stanford-Binet: A farewell to the mental age. *Psychology in the Schools,* 1975, *12,* 421–422.

Sidman, M. *Tactics of scientific research.* New York: Basic Books, 1960.

Slosson, R. L. *Slosson Intelligence Test.* East Aurora, NY: Slossen Educational Publications, 1971.

Smith, D. C., Decker, H. A., Herberg, E. N., & Rupke, L. K. Medical needs of children in institutions for the mentally retarded. *American Journal of Public Health,* 1969, *59,* 1376.

Sprague, R. L., & Baxley, G. B. Drugs for behavior management, with comment on some legal aspects. In J. Wortis (Ed.), *Mental retardation and developmental disabilities: Volume X.* New York: Brunner/Mazel, 1978.

Sprague, R. L., & Sleator, E. K. Methylphenidate in hyperkinetic children: Differences in dose effects on learning and social behavior. *Science,* 1977, 1274–1276.

Sprague, R. L., & Toppe, L. Relationship between activity level and delay of reinforcement in the retarded. *Journal of Experimental Child Psychology,* 1966, *3,* 390–397.

Sprague, R. L., & Werry, J. S. Methodology of psychopharmacological studies with the retarded. In N. Ellis (Ed.), *International review of research in mental retardation: Volume 5.* New York: Academic Press, 1971.

Sulzbacher, S. I. Psychotropic medication with children: An evaluation of procedural biases in results of reported studies. *Pediatrics,* 1973, *51,* 513–517.

Terman, L., & Merrill, M. *Stanford-Binet Intelligence Scale, 1972 norms edition.* Boston: Houghton Mifflin, 1973.

Thormalen, P. W. A study of on-the-ward training of trainable mentally retarded children in a state institution. *California Mental Health Research Monograph, No. 4,* 1965.

Thorndike, R. L. Dilemmas in diagnosis. In *Assessment problems in reading.* Newark, DE: The International Reading Association, 1973.

Thorndike, R., & Hagen, E. *Cognitive Abilities Test*. Boston: Houghton Mifflin, 1971.

Thurstone, L., & Thurston, T. *Primary Mental Abilities Test*. Chicago: Science Research Associate, 1965.

Ulman, J. D., & Sulzer-Azaroff, B. Multielement baseline design in educational research. In E. Ramp & G. Semb (Eds.), *Behavior analysis: Areas of research and application*. Englewood Cliffs, NJ: Prentice-Hall, 1975.

Walls, R. T., Werner, T. J. Bacon, A., & Zane, T. Behavioral checklists. In J. D. Cone and R. P. Hawkins (Eds.), *Behavioral assessment: New directions in clinical psychology*. New York: Brunner/Mazel, 1977.

Wechsler, D. *Manual for the Wechsler Adult Intelligence Scale*. New York: Psychological Corporation, 1955.

Wechsler, D. *Manual for the Wechsler Preschool and Primary Scale of Intelligence*. New York: Psychological Corporation, 1967.

Wechsler, D. *Manual for the Wechsler Intelligence Scale for Children—Revised*. New York: Psychological Corporation, 1974.

Whitman, T. H., & Scibak, J. W. Behavior modification research with the severely and profoundly retarded. In N. R. Ellis (Ed.), *Handbook of mental deficiency: Psychological theory and research*. Hillsdale, NJ: Erlbaum, 1979.

Wolf, M. M., & Risley, T. R. Reinforcement: Applied research. In R. Gloser (Ed.), *The nature of reinforcement*. New York: Academic Press, 1971.

Wolfensberger, W. *Normalization: The principle of normalization in human services*. Toronto: National Institute on Mental Retardation, 1972.

Wyatt v. Stickney. 344 Federal Supplement 387, 1972.

Wysocki, T., & Fuqua, R. W. Methodological issues in the evaluation of drug effects. In S. E. Breuning & A. D. Poling (Eds.), *Drugs and mental retardation*. Springfield, IL: Charles C. Thomas, in press.

Wysocki, T., Fuqua, R. W., Davis, V. J., & Breuning, S. E. Effects of Thioridazine on titrating delay matching to sample performance in the mentally retarded. *American Journal of Mental Deficiency*, 1981, *85*, 539–547.

Yelton, A. R., Wildman, B. G., & Erickson, M. T. A probability-biased formula for calculating interobserver agreement. *Journal of Applied Behavior Analysis*, 1977, *10*, 127–131.

ASSESSMENT OF PSYCHOLOGICAL CONSEQUENCES OF HEAD INJURY IN CHILDREN

Thomas J. Boll

I. INTRODUCTION

These observations suggest that as a result of concussion of any degree there may be permanent loss of neural function, the amount of such loss being in proportion to the severity of the concussive effects. They suggest also that diffuse loss of neurons may be present after concussion without any symptoms being apparent either to the subject or to experienced observers.

It is reasonable to assume that the number of available cerebral neurons is obviously greater than that required for functional efficiency. We may therefore surmise that in the patient who has been concussed and recovered, some function of his reserve neurons has been lost; and, if the process is repeated, it will only be a question of the number and severity of the injuries before the reserves are exhausted and permanent symptoms appear. The earliest symptoms to

Advances in the Behavioral Measurement of Children, Volume 1, pages 137–157.
Copyright © 1984 by JAI Press Inc.
ISBN: 0-89232-282-9

be expected from such a diffuse cerebral loss would be of the kind most difficult to measure—
subjective difficulty over intellectual problems, and slight personality changes. In this connection, it is worth noting how often after apparent recovery from severe concussion, the near
relatives may state that the patient has never been quite the same person since the accident. It
is, I think, questionable whether the effects of concussion, however slight, are ever completely reversible. (Sir Charles Symonds, 1962)

Head injury is a diffuse term that can be applied to anything from insignificant
bruises or lacerations of the scalp resulting in no changes in brain functioning and
integrity to massive intracranial hemorrhage or direct invasion of brain tissue by
foreign objects so extensive as to be unavoidably fatal. Most obviously superfi-
cial injuries involving self-limiting and easily repairable bruises and cuts to the
skin and underlying tissue are managed at home and never find their way into
statistical compilations of individuals who have sustained injuries to the head.
Slightly more severe injuries resulting from falls, participation in sports, or
minor vehicular accidents producing no dramatic initial symptoms, such as unconsciousness, are also, more commonly than not, managed without involvement of any aspect of the health-care system. One can extend injuries involving
the head one step further and still easily avoid becoming an official statistic.
Many, if not most, injuries to the head resulting in dizziness, nausea, vomiting,
and questionable or exceedingly brief period of unconsciousness are handled
relatively informally by a phone call or visit to the family pediatrician whose
activities typically involve a discussion of the injury, observation of the patient, a
brief physical examination, and reassurance to parent and child alike that unless
further difficulties develop all is well and the child will be ready for a full range
of activities, if not immediately, then certainly within the next day or two.

From an acute-care medical viewpoint, the treatment typically received by the
aforementioned victims of head injury is both appropriate and sufficient. This is
true because only rarely do such minor injuries result in other than perfectly self-
limiting and spontaneously recovering physical effects. The fact that, at least in
some percentage of these cases, long-term behavioral sequelae may well result
from actual changes to brain tissue not visible to the naked eye, much less
ascertainable on the basis of physical examination, will be discussed later in this
chapter with respect to the evidence for such injuries and the data suggesting
their implications for day-to-day human performance.

II. STUDIES OF PATIENTS WITH HEAD INJURIES

The recounting of the number of patients who avoid official recognition as
having sustained a head injury makes all the more impressive the number of
patients who actually do become officially identified as having received a head
injury. In 1975 the U.S. Census Bureau reported 9,759,000 head injuries (Cavaness, 1977). While the majority of these head injuries were relatively mild, at
least from the medical point of view, additional data developed in this chapter

will suggest that terms such as mild and moderate when applied to the medical aspects and surgical requirements of the head injury may mean very different things than when utilized to describe change to brain tissue and subsequent functional effect from the point of view of human behavior.

Published epidemiologic data on acute head injuries in children continue to be generally inadequate despite some significant efforts toward improvement in this area. In 1980, Annegers, Grabow, Kurland, and Laws states "although head trauma is a major cause of morbidity and mortality, the epidemiologic study has lagged because of difficulties in identifying and classifying cases and lack of standardized definition of the injuries." Despite the fact that children enjoy better survival and long-term medical outcome than do adults, accidents cause more deaths to infants and children between the ages of 1–14 years than the four most common fatal diseases in childhood combined (Klonoff & Robinson, 1967). There is general agreement that the incidence of head injury in males outnumbers that for females at a rate of approximately 2:1. For children in the preschool years, falls inside the home and while at play outside account for the largest number of head injuries. This is followed by vehicle-related accidents (as passenger or pedestrian), accidents resulting from use of some form of cycle, and assaults. Among school-age children, vehicular accidents are followed by falls, sports injuries, cycle accidents, and assaults. Age factors related to risk of head injury appear to vary from sample to sample. Mannheimer, Dewey, and Melinger (1966) placed the highest incidence of head injuries at ages 3–5 with a slight decrease each year until age 12. Burkinshaw (1960) reported 8 to be the modal age for head injuries in his study. Still other reports suggest a slight increase in injury incidence at the time children begin formal schooling. With regard to seasonal variations, spring and summer account for the greatest number of visits to the emergency room and admissions to the hospital for children in both preschool and school-age years. The highest percentage of visits occurred in the emergency room on Sundays followed by a typical weekday and Saturday. Admissions to the hospital, however, were greatest on Saturday and lowest during the week. Time of day has also been investigated with data consistently implicating afternoon and early evening hours as the time during which children are at greatest risk (Jennett, 1972; Klonoff, 1971; Klonoff & Robinson, 1967; Rune, 1970). Head injuries tend not to occur when the child is alone, but predictably, the type of companion was very different in the preschool and school-age groups. Typically, children prior to attending school received a head injury in or around the home when parent or relative was present. In only 14% of the instances in one major study were the children actually alone (Klonoff, 1971). For the school-age groups, children were alone 19% of the time, parents were in attendance 25% of the time, and school authorities, 20%. Not surprisingly, children who were injured while alone sustained rather more serious injuries than did those being observed by parent or school authority.

While any bump, bruise, or cut to the head qualifies as a "head injury," what we are really talking about are those injuries which may have implication for the organ of the mind: the brain. The most common and possibly most commonly misunderstood brain injury is the concussion. Concussion results from shock, jar, or actual blow to the head. A shock or jar may result from sudden acceleration/deceleration or rotation and does not require the head to be struck. Tissues are injured by shearing, tension, or compression. It has been traditional to diagnose concussion following a period of loss of conciousness (no matter how brief) or in the presence of cerebral symptoms without loss of consciousness. Cerebral symptoms which can be, and often are, present without loss of consciousness include mental confusion, apathy, dizziness, headache, nausea, vomiting, strabismus, and sleep at abnormal times of day. Concussion is most typically defined as the cessation or paralysis of brain functions following a shock, jar, or blow to the head. The period of unconsciousness is usually brief and spontaneously reversible. Such injury has been (and in some circles continues to be) considered as possible not only in the absence of physical and mental residuals, but also without structural damage to the brain (Merritt, 1967). Other writers, at least in the last two decades, recognize "that this cannot occur without damage to nerve cells and it is doubtful if any physiological or anatomical distinction should be drawn between concussion as just defined and more prolonged states of unconsciousness resulting from head injury" (Brain & Walton, 1969). Ward (1966) pointed out that the reticular activitating system which is involved in the maintenance of alertness and consciousness can be reversibly blocked by acceleration concussion. In fact, recent animal studies of head injuries induced by acceleration (without any blow to the head at all) and resulting in a very brief loss of consciousness and accompanying physiological reactions (such as blood pressure and heart rate changes and corneal reflex absence for less than 30 sec) produced degenerative changes in axons and their terminal arborizations in locations, including reticular nuclei, vestibular nuclei, and dorsal regions of the medulla (Gennarelli, Adams, & Graham, in press; J. A. Jane, personal communication). Such brains, it should be noted, not only subserved superficially normal posttraumatic behavior but were, on gross and even microscopic inspection, normal, without evidence of edema, herniation, or tissue destruction. It seems as increasingly obvious maxim in neuropsychology that if careful and sophisticated procedures are required to identify and appreciate the very real physical damage in the human brain, then it is only reasonable to apply careful and sophisticated procedures in attempting to identify and appreciate the presence of mental impairment underlying subtle change in the human behavior.

In the preceding century, Lashley stated, "It should be a fundamental principle of neural interpretation of psychological functions that the nervous activities are as complex as psychological activities which they constitute" (Cobb, 1960, p. X). Examination procedures reflecting the condition of the brain in neurologically broad terms (CAT-scan, physical neurological exam) or in psychologically broad terms (IQ, perceptual quotient) are unlikely to be equal to the task of measuring the degree and significance of brain changes and behavioral changes produced by disruption of minute internal brain structures following sudden compression, deceleration, and/or rotation common in nonimpact concussions.

Cerebral contusion and laceration are characterized by edema, capillary hemorrhages, degeneration of cortical and subcortical nerve cells, and, on occasion, a visible alteration in the integrity of brain substance. Such damage may be focal or diffuse. A prolonged period of unconsciousness may result. Headache, vomiting, lethargy, drowsiness, vertigo, ataxia, and amnesia are frequent signs of such disorder in its early phase. Both concussion and contusion produce varying periods of amnesia, later-occurring irritability and short-lived headache, sensitivity to movement, nausea, dizziness, and motor unsteadiness in varying degrees of severity. Eventual or even rapid resolution of these difficulties is not a guarantee of a sequelae-free course in the areas of more complex cognitive and emotional functioning.

Intracranial hematomas refer to bleeding inside the skull which may be subdural, epidural, or intracerebral. Epidural bleeding due to rupture of the middle meningeal artery, frequently caused by skull fracture (which may not be initially detected) compresses the brain from its location between the dura and the skull. It is a neurosurgical emergency with symptoms of increasing headache, motor impairment, unilateral or uneven pupillary dilation, and decline in mental alertness progressing to coma. Subdural hematoma resulting from rupture of veins bleeding in the subdural space produces usually slowly progressing symptoms related to increased intracranial pressure.

Skull fractures produce a wide variety of difficulties secondary to the actual fracture. Any small opening can serve as an entry for infecting agents. The fractured bone may tear the dura, and a depressed fracture may actually invade and damge brain tissue directly. While it certainly appears to be a clear index of severity of head injury, presence or absence of skull fracture has not been found to be a useful marker of future medical-neurological or mental recovery (Burkinshaw, 1960; Kløve & Cleeland, 1972; Selley & Frankle, 1961). In fact, according to Jennett (1972), "What is clear is that the most obvious lesions, cortical contusions and lacerations, are almost certainly the least important of all. Careful studies suggest that shearing of fibers, fat embolism and secondary ischemic damage are much more common than was previously believed and, because each of these lesions is apt to be widespread throughout the brain, they seem likely to account for many of the features associated with severe injuries" (p. 138). Sir Charles Symonds's comments suggesting that recovery is less than it might superficially seem are consistent with a type of brain injury producing more significant damage than initially seemed to be the case.

From the vantage point of most psychologists, recovery from head injury involves return of mental and emotional competence and stability following a mild or moderate head injury. Children suffering severe head injuries are far less common than those with milder injuries, and the degree of deficit experienced is so obvious that identifying its presence is rarely an issue. Certainly, even for the severely injured group, documentation of degree of deficit and understanding of residual and recovered competencies is an essential part of care. Heiskanen and Kaste (1974) followed a group of children for from 4 to 10 years following severe head injury. The median length of posttraumatic coma was 9 days. All patients suffered cerebral contusion and 25% had either intracranial hemorrhages or depressed skull fractures. Of the 34 children followed for this unusual length, 12 had persisting hemiparesis, another 10 had significant mental defect without motor impairment, and 5 developed a seizure disorder. They concluded that "after a coma lasting two weeks, a child is rarely able to succeed even moderately well in school. Even a coma lasting for a few days may lead to severe deterioration of intellectual capacity." Brink, Garret, Hale, Woo-Sam, and Nickel (1970) found a majority of their severely injured patients (comatose to 1 week or more) had IQs in the retarded range, with only a small percentage ever attaining average IQ scores. Even among these children, more extensive mental testing may have identified persisting deficits. Levin and Eisenberg (1979) found frequent, persistent, and serious intellectual deficits in children with loss of consciousness lasting more than 24 hours. Among those children in the severe and even in the more mildly injured groups, average IQ was no guarantee of adequate memory functioning nor was memory well assessed by standard IQ tests.

From the beginning of the twentieth century, a series of reports on children with lesser but widely varying degrees of severity of head injury (as measured by duration of coma but often including skull fracture) have been published. All have reported some degree of mental (cognitive or emotional) deficit as a permanent sequela in some proportion of the patients followed, in spite of the fact that in many studies purely observational, self- and other report data were available without direct objective measurement of the patient. Formal measurement, when obtained at all, was limited to some form of IQ measure and occasional academic data, along with an occasional mental-status-type examination of personal functioning.

Emotional and behavioral sequelae were commonly reported, including motor unrest, anxiety, irritability, uncontrollable behavior, lying, sleep disturbances, memory problems, loss of stamina, inability to handle stress, social isolation, and decline in academic performance (Ireland, 1972). In several of these studies, fewer than half of the head injuries were accompanied by a period of unconsciousness. The incidence of reported psychiatric symptoms ranged from 2 to 60%. The nature of the deficits found showed remarkable overlap, even when the percentage of patients found to experience them differed considerably. From 1950 onward, the amount of actual data gathered increased, as did (not surprisingly) the reported incidence of mental symptoms. Rowbotham, MacIever, Dicksson, and Bousefield (1954) found incidence of multiple behavioral changes to be 30%. Similar percentage of deficit was reported largely from parent questionnaire response by Burkinshaw (1960) and Hjern and Nylander (1962). Not only are these symptoms and incidence statistics quite consistent across time and differing national and cultural groups, but they correspond well to the prevalence of mental deficits reported for brain-damaged children regardless of etiology reported by Shaffer, Chadwick, and Rutter (1975) on the Isle of Wight. That head injury incidence fits the other groups of brain-damaged children is germane to the argument that head injury produces brain damage and that such brain damage results, in turn, in direct mental changes which are not simply attributable to nonneurological aspects of the injury.

The sequelae of head injury are not perfectly linked to severity of cerebral contusion, presence of skull fracture, or even length of unconsciousness, except in instances of coma exceeding 2 weeks. One factor influencing the outcome is the presence of posttraumatic complications. The most obvious of these is intracranial bleeding. Kløve and Cleeland (1972) demonstrated a decrease in long-term quality of recovery in the presence of subdural, epidural, and intracranial hematomas. Extradural hematomas may occur in association with extremely mild head injuries and brief loss of consciousness. The patient may appear reasonably well shortly after injury and only hours later show signs of increased intracranial pressure and reduced mental alertness.

The second postinjury occurrence associated with generally less favorable outcome is seizures. Posttraumatic seizures are commonly grouped into those occurring very shortly after injury and those which develop a week or more (in some instances, years) later. According to Jennett (1972), seizures are far more frequent (30 times more) in the first week than later. Twenty-five percent of patients with seizures in the first week have seizures after that. In contrast, 70% of patients with later-occurring seizures experience a recurrence. Only about 5% of children with head injury experience seizures, most commonly after a relatively severe injury. Young children (under 5), however, seem to require only a relatively mild injury to be at risk for posttraumatic seizures. The long-term significance of such an event is understood by the fact that even early occurring seizures, which have a comparatively low incidence of recurrence, still increase the risk of later-appearing epilepsy fourfold over cases with no prior seizures.

Adding to the complex of factors which must be considered in all discussions of risk is age at occurrence of the head injury. From a medical-neurological standpoint, children fare considerably better in all aspects of their recovery than do adults. Using seizures as an example of the age at occurrence, Black, Shepard, and Walker (1975) demonstrated that ''the overall incidence of early seizures in children appears to be a good deal higher than that of adults, whereas the late occurrence of seizures in children appears to be lower than that of adults.'' Within the broad category of childhood, however, infants show a different pattern from that of older children. Infants (0–2 years) show a low incidence of early seizures but a relatively high incidence of late attacks. This is the reverse of that seen in older children (2–15) but quite like the adult pattern. Black et al. (1975) conclude "It may be said that the response of the maturing nervous system to trauma is such that babies cannot be regarded as simply small children or older chldren as small adults." Epilepsy developing after head injury tends to persist. Eighty percent of the patients with seizures have seizures for 2 years independent of whether epilepsy being months or even years postinjury. Jennett (1975) postulates that posttraumatic epilepsy requires both focal and diffuse brain damage. Black et al. (1975) report that generalized seizures are more common in patients with persisting posttraumatic fits. Age of occurrence is related to a wide range of head injury variables. Many of these have been analyzed in considerable detail by Klonoff and Paris (1974). The epidemiological data reported earlier suggest that younger and older children experience somewhat different circumstances. The sequelae of these accidents also differ with age. Amnesia is difficult to document in children due to limitations of verbal report. Nevertheless, younger children show a higher incidence of loss of preaccident events than do older children. Younger children have a higher incidence of skull fractures. Risk factors also weigh against the younger child. Younger children, especially boys, have a higher preaccident history of developmental anomalies. Among the severely injured, serious intellectual deficit was more common in the younger than in the adolescent age groups (Brink et al., 1970). Children with mild and moderate injuries showed personality change, headaches, irritability, academic problems, and memory and attention deficits 2 years after accident. This was true for both younger and older groups. While young healthy individuals certainly seem more able to tolerate severe physical trauma than do older ones, the continued optimism regarding mental recovery based on an outmoded notion of plasticity in the young is misguided at best. Such optimism leads children away from proper evaluation, understanding, and treatment. Worse still, it leads them to be too quickly returned to activities such as school where continuing high demand for use of memory, language, and information processing are the nature of the tasks. These are the very skills most susceptible to damage—the ones requiring longest for recovery, and the ones most likely to be overlooked due to the child's appearance of health in other, more readily observable, areas of performance. Teuber and Rudel (1962) indicated with clarity the complexity of the relationship between age and type of mental ability deficit. Boll (1973) confirmed the Teuber and Rudel data and indicated that for diffusely damaged children, at least, the longer one can live with a normal brain, the more satisfactory one's overall quality of survival is likely to be. Kinsbourne (1974) very ably pointed out that certain focal, circumscribed lesions in childhood are compatible with an essentially normal (at least average) development of the full repertoire of human abilities. With the exception of the relatively uncommon penetrating injury without diffuse effect, however, the vast majority of children's head injury represents generalized insult to the brain. Isaacson (1975) presented a forceful and readable rebuttal to the simplistic plasticity notion, and Boll (1983) has reviewed a series of studies documenting the more impairing influence of generalized over focal damage despite its initially less dramatic appearance. As mental development is every bit as core to the overall maturing process as is physical change, the monitoring of this aspect of a child's life following head injury must be considered mandatory in any situation where the index of suspicion regarding possible sequelae has been raised. As will become obvious—if it is not obvious already—the type of head injury that appropriately raises such suspicion in order to provide for timely appreciation of developmental events in need of intervention is significantly less severe than has conventionally been held to be the case.

The emotional consequences, while arguably secondary to ability deficiencies resulting in reduced capacity to cope with one's world, are nonetheless the most visible and at the same time most disputed consequences of mild head injury. No one denies the relationship between very severe brain injury and acute psychotic and confused states which tragically become chronic for a small percentage of children and adults. Because the injury was obviously serious and because, too, in many instances physical sequelae accompany such types of injury, the role of damage to the brain in the destruction of personality as it was premorbidly is easily accepted. Such is not the situation at the mild end of the continuum of consequences of head injury, however. A patient who was mildly injured in terms of requirements for medical-neurological treatment and who has enjoyed good—even complete—physical recovery must, it is surmised, be mentally well also. If such is not the case, causes and even motivations aside from the injury are sought to explain the aberrant behavior. This is true despite that fact that, throughout the twentieth century, descriptions of notable personality change and even significant psychological-behavioral disorder following head injury have been published many times. As early as 1903, Meyer described "the anatomical facts and clinical varieties of traumatic insanity." Other studies have proceeded from conditions of known personality deficits backward in search of a cause. Strecker and Ebaugh (1924), Strauss and Kephart (1965), and Blau (1936) all utilized patients who presented with unacceptable behavior and were found to have a history of brain trauma. The most salient characteristics pointed to in these children were poor attention, poor impulse control, difficulty managing any form of stress of frustration, oversensitive irritability, and mental inconsistency. Despite the compelling consistency of such reports, the data were usually selectively drawn, lacking in quantitative rigor, and limited in content. Perhaps for this reason, and due in part to the tendency to adopt a nonphysical explanation for behavior when possible, such data have intruded little on the routine management of children with head injury. Nevertheless, more recent and more adequately controlled studies suggest two findings: (1) Young children have no relative advantage over older children in mental recovery. (2) Children as a group experience a rather higher frequency of psychological disturbance following head injury, while adults most commonly complain of headache and somatic symptoms (Black, Blumer, Wellner, Jeffries, & Walker, 1970).

The precise neurological tie to psychological disturbance has not been identified. While Lishman (1973) has found some limited relationship between site of lesion and personality expression in adults, such specific data with children have yet to be obtained. Nonneurological factors prior to and following head injury must be considered. This can be accomplished without in any way diminishing the nonspecific role played by the damaged brain in the overall behavioral outcome. Harrington and Letemendia (1958) and Hjern and Nylander (1962) found that disruptive family backgrounds produced a higher incidence of psychological disturbance following head injury. Additionally, Shaffer et al. (1975) found that children from unhappy and uncaring homes were at greater risk for head injury in the first place. Craft, Shae, and Cartlidge (1973) found that children presenting problems in behavior in school were more likely to have had a head injury, and Sobel (1970) found children with depressed mothers were at higher risk of accidental poisoning. The child's reaction to the event of the head injury itself has rarely been studied. Klonoff and Paris reported that children more commonly react with anxiety and denial. Denial (minimal concern that any harm could have been done) was far and away the most frequent reaction. Parents, on the other hand, showed far more persistent anxiety and a more cautious, protective attitude toward the child. For parents of both older and younger children, anxiety diminished significantly at 1 and 2 years after injury, but persistent anxiety was found in fully 25% of parents 2 years after head injury. Parents of younger children tended toward overprotection, while parents of older children showed denial more frequently. Half of the parents placed blame for the accident on themselves and 25% blamed the child. Parents blamed boys more often than girls.

The consequences of brain injury may well make a child more difficult to live with. This in turn further could increase his risk of mistreatment and induce negative experiences inside and outside the family. Children with brain damage are often distractable and irritable. They often have difficulty delaying gratification and can be easily frustrated, as well as acting impulsively and uncritically. Such behavior is bound to generate hostility, rejection, and avoidance in others, thus setting up a circle of negative action and reactions. Rutter (1977) convincingly rejected a vulnerability model as explanatory of increased incidence of psychological disorders following brain damage. He postulates instead that the simple additive effects of the brain damage are sufficient to account for the incidents observed. Furthermore, the additive model does not require a premorbid susceptibility within the patient or his environment. Such a model is adequate not only in cases of risk and disadvantage, but also in those well-documented instances when psychological disturbance emerges in the absence of premorbid environmental, familial, or behavioral deficits. Rutter points to five factors which may have a negative influence on a brain-injured patient's overall psycho-social adjustment. They are (1) the abnormal brain activity itself which, when present, can clearly disrupt all aspects of psychological functioning; (2) cognitive deficits produced by the brain damage reducing general coping and specific academic capabilities; (3) direct effects such as irritability and lowered frustration tolerance on personality; (4) effects of treatments such as hospitalization, drugs, and restrictions on activities; (5) responses of the environment, especially the family, due to long-standing stereotypes about the characteristics and needs of a head-injured person.

A significant component of personality difficulties could be due to changes in cognitive capacity that alter the patient's overall functional interaction with the environment. This notion is consistent with Rutter's five sources of psychological difficulties. Eson and Bourke (1980) claim that "psychodynamic changes are the result of the individual ways of coping with a disturbance in the generative information processing function and if the patient is helped with these early in the recovery process, the personality changes might be more moderate."

The implications of the comments by Sir Charles Symonds used to begin this chapter are nowhere more provocative than for patients with mild head injury requiring little or no medical-neurological attention. Data supporting his concern about the effect on the elderly (while not relevant in a chapter on children) have been recently reviewed (Boll, 1982). The suggestion that the effects of more than one head injury are cumulative has received recent support from the investigations of Gronwall and Wrightson (1975). They found that students required longer to recover from a second injury than from the first. Almost 40 years ago Windle, Groat, and Fox (1944) demonstrated that even without loss of consciousness it was possible to produce as much actual change in brain tissue with two lesser injuries as with a single more serious one. Multiple sports-related blows to the head, none of which produced loss of consciousness, were demonstrated by Roberts (1969) to produce documentable mental deficits, including some cases of permanent disability.

The degree of severity of head injury required to produce documentable changes in mental functioning is minimal. Levin and Eisenberg (1979) have shown that patients with loss of consciousness for over 24 hours enjoyed encouraging but far from total recovery. For these patients and ones with loss of consciousness less than 24 hours, permanent memory deficits were the rule. More startlingly, however, patients without evidence of loss of consciousness who were alert upon arrival in the emergency room and whose IQs were in the average range also showed deficits in complex memory tasks.

The most comprehensive investigation of the effects of mild head injury over time was conduced by Klonoff and his colleagues, who followed both preschool and school-age children for 5 years after head injury (Klonoff, Low, & Clark, 1977). Klonoff et al. studied both patients admitted to the hospital and those seen in the emergency room only. Their five categories of head injury were as follows: (1) *minor*—patients without evidence of loss of consciousness; (2) *mild*—no evidence of loss of consciousness but cerebral symptoms such as vomiting, dizziness, lethargy, and nausea indicating concussion; (3) *moderate*—concussion with loss of consciousness less than 5 min; (4) *severe*—skull fracture or concussion with loss of consciousness 5 to 30 min; (5) *serious*—concussion with loss of consciousness greater than 30 minutes or depressed and/or compound skull fracture and/or other symptoms of serious injury such as aphasia or posttraumatic psychosis. It is apparent that his study omits children with the most serious types of head injury. In fact, in a medical-neurological sense, groups 1 and 2 would be unlikely to receive more than phone consultation and reassurance from many physicians, group 3 might be hospitalized overnight; and, without unexpected complications, most patients in group 4 would endure relatively brief hospitalization as well. Certainly the first two groups would be routinely reassured that no brain damage had occurred and that sequelae beyond brief headaches was not to be expected. Groups 3 and 4 would be expected to enjoy full if slightly more gradual recovery, and, amazingly, even patients in group 5 are commonly treated and released from care without any serious effect at evaluation of short-term, much less long-term, mental consequences. Not uncommonly, in even serious head injury, physical, neurological and electroencephalographic results are, or quickly become, normal, giving unfounded support by optimistic prognostications.

Klonoff et al. (1977) used a nueropsychological battery which included the Wechsler Intelligence Scale for Children (the Stanford–Binet Form L-M for children under 5 years of age). For children under 9 years of age, the battery was made up of the Reitan–Indiana Neuropsychological Test Battery for Children—14 tests and 28 variables, two of Benton's tests, and a lateral dominance test. For children age 9 and over, the tests included the Halstead Neuropsychological Test Battery for Children, two of Benton's tests, a lateral dominance measure, and the Kløve Motor Steadiness Battery, for a total of 23 tests and 48 variables. These well-recognized and standarized procedures provide a broad sample of simple and complex psychological functions utilized in a routine fashion to maximize the opportunity for between- as well as within-patient performance comparisons. Such a battery provides an emphasis on patient strength as well as deficit and ensures that an inclusive rather than selective sample of the patients' behavioral capabilities is obtained.

In contrast to the normality of the medical-neurological exam findings, Klonoff et al. (1977) reported that for children under 9 years of age impairment was noted on 28 or 32 neuropsychological tests immediately following head injury. One year later 20 neuropsychological tests showed impairment. Follow-up continued with the following number of impaired performances in neuropsychological examination: 13 at 2 years, 5 at 3 years, 4 at 4 years, and 1 fully 5 years after head injury. Among children in the 9–15-year age range, 48 neuropsychological tests were performed. At time of head injury, 42 showed impairment for the group as a whole. In subsequent years the results were 31 at 1 year, 15 at 2 years, 12 at 3 years, 8 at 4 years, and 6 at 5 years. These figures clearly suggest that our index of suspicion is far too low and that our estimates not only of completeness but also of rate of recovery are too optimistic. These investigators noted that among the younger children, 24.7% failed a grade or were placed in a remedial or slow-learner classroom after the head injury. At year 5, fully 23.7% of the head-injured children in both younger and older groups continued to demonstrate measurable neuropsychological deficits. If one includes electroencephalographic and physical-neurological results, two-thirds of these children (66.7%) were found to have residual deficits in at least one area 5 years after their head injury. This is true despite the fact that in most cases the degree of severity of head injury was far from life threatening. It was instead quite compatible with relatively quick physical recovery and anticipation of complete and rapid return of all mental functions.

It should be noted that far from being a "worse case" estimate of the situation, the data of Klonoff and his colleagues, however excellent, are likely to represent something of an underestimate of the actual problems which frequently occur in the lives of children following head injuries. The data presented by Klonoff and his colleagues were gathered through careful and skillful administration of batteries of neuropsychological tests. These tests are given in structured, often encouraging, situations designed to elicit the patient's maximum effort and performance. This is as it should be. Nevertheless, we know that yet another difficulty besets the neurologically impaired patient: reduction in tolerance for stress. Such stresses as physical illness, fatigue, alcohol, medications, and emotional upset will exacerbate deficits not readily apparent under more quiescent circumstances. Any normal or environmental upset then is just that much more disruptive to a child already hindered by neurological compromise. Thus, even persons who are performing quite well may, during a stressful period, show a surprising dip in competence and a vicious cycle of stress → failure → stress which may produce additional coping difficulties. In a careful demonstration of this phenomena, Ewing, McCarthy, Gronwall, and Wrightson (1980) examined students shortly after head injury and followed them for several years. While initially impaired in complex tasks, these students appeared to return to normal and in fact completed a university curriculum for 3 years. Examination of these students under the stresses of artificial altitude [3800 ft. (1158.25 m) in a hyperbaric chamber] produced a disproportionately large decrement in memory and mental vigilance in comparison to other students whose backgrounds were quite the same except for the head injury sustained 3 years previously. Sir Charles Symonds's (1962) comment, "it is, I think, questionable whether the effects of concussion, however slight, are ever completely reversible" has yet to be refuted.

If children with even relatively mild head injury are at risk and deserve more careful consideration of their "mental status" than is currently given, what sort of examination is likely to provide an appreciation of posttraumatic behavioral sequelae? Almost 20 years ago, I. S. Wechsler insisted "no neurological status exam is complete without a mental examination" and "a complete mental examination takes several hours" (Wechsler, 1963). It is possible to lay out some guidelines for the choice of a battery of tests. A description of the most widely recognized and commonly used set of procedures will also be provided, with some recommended extensions that were found to have considerable clinical utility, particularly for evaluating the complaints of injured patients. Obviously, any selection msut be able to claim scientific validity for the purpose at hand. The simple jury rigging of tests or the use of ad hoc combinations of tests outside their usual context is a matter of sheerest speculation. It is only acceptable for the purpose of a research undertaking, not for clinical practice—no matter what the independently established validity of each single procedure may be.

III. ASSESSMENT OF PSYCHOLOGICAL CONSEQUENCE OF HEAD TRAUMA

Two types of overall guidelines can be added to the specific ones regarding generalizability, validity, and recognized utility for the task at hand. (1) Maximize the complementary use of multiple inferential methods. (2) Examine a reasonably broad sample of mental *Contents,* i.e., Verbal Knowledge, perceptual skill; *Processes,* i.e., Attention, memory; across several *Modalities* (Visual, Auditory, Tactile); and employing Linguistic and figural *Materials.*

Inferential Methods

Level of Performance

The quantity of one's performance, whether it be a number of IQ points amassed or the grade level achievement attained on an academic measure, is most commonly relied upon by psychologists to assess a person's performance. This is true despite the fact that all psychologists realize there are numerous reasons for an individual's poor performance that have nothing to do with the problem at hand—whether that problem is neurological or otherwise. Problems in motivation, background and experience, and peripheral and environmental difficulties—both of an immediate as well as an ongoing nature—can influence a person's performance with respect to his or her level of achievement in a testing situation. Despite the fact that this method does have limitations, it is clearly an important one as well. It provides the opportunity to look developmentally at an individual who may do exceedingly well or exceedingly poorly. This is quite in contrast to many methods which do not allow an individual to perform in an above-average manner, but only to appear either as impaired or not imparied. Cutoff scores and ranges of scores, while appearing to add something to level of performance, really do little more than draw a line somewhere in the middle of the level which the child is attempting to achieve and provide labels on either side of that line. While level of performance provides a great deal of information about how a child is currently performing, it provides very little information about how he or she has performed in the past, what performance will be like in the future, or the reasons for the attainment of that particular level. This method of inference is insufficient when utilized by itself.

Pattern of Performance

Intratest patterns of behaviors, such as those derived from Wechsler Verbal and Performance IQs or the Scales within the Verbal and Performance sections, are typically attended to by psychologists in evaluating that data. Additional information provided by performance on other, somewhat different, tests, such as those of visual perception, auditory processing, or academic accomplishment, are also utilized comparatively to determine whether the child is functioning in a consistent or inconsistent manner and where relative and unusual degrees of strength and weakness lie. When this form of pattern analysis is utilized explicitly rather than implicitly, it provides a second and a fresh look at the same data and allows for an increase in the number of data points that are attended to formally prior to coming to an overall conclusion about an individual child's adequacy of performance. It also allows for an increase in the advantage gained by utilizing additional tests due to the rapid increase in number of comparisons that can be made when each new test is compared to all others already administered. This by itself provides a relatively potent argument for utilizing a broad sample of psychological measures when examining a child for the presence or absence of subtle as well as obvious behavioral difficulties.

Specific Signs of Behavioral Difficulty

Certain behaviors are essentially incompatible with normality at any time. This tends to be more true for adults than for children, as the developmental phase of childhood allows for great variations in personal competence within a single chronological age. Nevertheless, obvious linguistic, perceptual, motor, and sensory deficits should never be present. Subtle difficulties which occur in individuals who, on the basis of other achievements, should have no trouble in these areas represent a kind of evidence that does not require complex scaling in order to be appreciated for its significance. Many tests utilized during the physical examination of the chi;d by a physician, such as reflexes, are of this nature and provide important additions to the overall results of a comprehensive examination.

Right–Left Comparisons

Particularly for children in whom developmental inconsistency and unpredictability is the norm, certain types of comparisons can be counted upon to be relatively constant. Even during childhood, the relative efficiency of the two sides of the body remains roughly the same. On nonpracticed motor tasks, children and adults tend to perform about 10% better with their preferred than with their nonpreferred hand and are essentially comparably skilled in sensory–perceptual tasks. Children who deviate significantly in either directly on these measures are displaying some sort of difficulty which requires explanation. The additional advantage of these measures is that they add still more data points to one's pattern analysis and provide tests dealing with simple psychological functions from which level of performance information can also be derived and which provide information about coordination and tactile–sensory intactness; such data are quite relevant to remedial educational programs and social activities in which children are likely to engage and which can be influenced by the neurological consequences of a head injury.

Composition of a battery which maximizes the complementary use of these multiple inferential methods can maximize as well the amount of information that is provided by a minimum number of psychological tests, if these tests are selected for evaluation from the maximum number of points of view.

When dealing with head-injured children, it is also critical that whatever evaluation battery be chosen, it should be designed in such a way that repeated examinations are not only possible, but an essential and routine part of the overall treatment package. Baseline data to assess the degree of impairment and the child's current status clearly should be derived as quickly as possible after a child has sustained a head injury from which some suspicion of damage has developed. Retesting at approximately 6-month intervals will document the frequently encouraging amount of recovery that occurs, and will document the actual nature of the damage that occurred to the child's premorbid skills which is difficult to delineate during the first examination. This will aid in modifying intervention programs in and outside of school to fit the child's actual strengths and weaknesses rather than simply his clinically apparent improvement, which is easy to overestimate.

There are certain areas that can be recognized to be necessary for inclusion in a psychological battery, but which can be used in a complementary fashion with multiple inferential methods to determine the actual tests which will be chosen. These areas include psychometric intelligence, academic achievement, language functions, perceptual functions, memory, attention, motor functions, information processing, and personality functions.

Certainly for any child of school age a measure of *psychometric intelligence* is appropriate. The most adequate of these are the Stanford–Binet Form L-M, the Wechsler Preschool and Primary Scale of Intelligence, or the Wechsler Intelligence Scale for Children–R. Measurements of *academic levels*, while potentially a full-day process in itself, can at least be surveyed as to the basic acquisitional level by such measures as the Wide Range Achievement Test or the Peabody Individual Achievement Test.

Language functions, essential to all aspects of school performance, can be assessed qualitatively and quantitatively in several ways. Receptive tests such as token tests and measures of auditory–verbal discrimination such as the Speech Sounds Perception Test from the Halstead Battery can be utilized along with full language pathology examinations by appropriately trained experts. A minimum screening procedure such as the Halstead–Wepman Aphasia Screening Battery, usually utilized in conjunction with other measures but not representing a complete language examination, can be useful in the context of other tests requiring language competence.

Assessment of *perceptual functions* of a visual receptive and expressive nature, and auditory and tactual perceptual capacities as well, can give valuable clues to areas of deficits and pathways for potential remedial activity. Multimodal interventions without multimodal assessment result in trial-and-error learning for the teacher which can be as puzzling as it is for the student.

Motor coordination and *persistence,* often disrupted by brain injury, play a important roles in the actual expression of other psychological abilities and need to be assessed directly and not merely inferred from more complex psychological tests with (usually minimal) motor requirements such as those seen in standard psychometric intelligence measures. *Memory, attention,* and *information processing,* all requisites for efficient use of other mental abilities, are the most sensitive to brain impairment and cannot be assumed to be intact simply because IQ is "normal." Direct measurement by such tasks as the Trail Making Test, the Digit Symbol Test from the Wechsler Scale, and the Selective Reminding Task (Buschke, 1973) modified for children by using animal names to be remembered provides examples of tests tapping these types of mental processes. *Personality* assessment–whether derived from clinical interview, projective techniques, or paper-and-pencil questionnaires—represents a last but definitely not least area of need for measurement. Any experience with children following head injury reveals the presence of anxiety, uncertainty, and lowered self-esteem due to recognized and unrecognized difficulties which are an intimate part of the recovery package. These require every bit as much understanding, attention, and intervention, as any cognitive deficit following neurological impairment of any sort, including traumatic head injury.

Prior to any such formal undertaking, some determination of who should undergo more than a cursory observation must be made. At this stage it is unfortunate to say that it must be made without adequate, fixed guidelines, particularly for those children with relatively mild head injury. On the other hand, it is quite certain that the earliest possible initial assessment is optimal. It provides the best point from which recovery can be observed and recommendations for various interventions made. It also provides the child and family with an understanding of likely difficulties before their unanticipated appearance can be misunderstood and allowed to develop into even greater problems than the head injury itself.

On the other hand, the practical issues of cost, time, and professional resources do not allow for blanket examination of every child with a head injury, no matter how cost-effective in economic and psychological terms such an approach might actually turn out to be. Certainly, children in Klonoff's severity grades 3, 4, 5, and beyond do deserve such attention. If parents of children with head injuries falling into severity grades 1 and 2 could be provided with some guidelines for monitoring their child's behavior instead of routine and not necessarily correct reassurances, the likelihood is that those children who do experience behavioral difficulty would be identified and appropriate referrals made. It is also likely that if parents were informed of the nature of the head injury and the subsequent behavioral changes resulting from such injury, their own increased ability to handle these frequently short-term problems would be sufficient. Behavior such as irritability, apathy, social withdrawal, decreased attention and concentration, distractability, decreased frustration tolerance, and fatigue commonly produce disapproval reactions in others. Such reactions may raise anxiety and lower self-esteem in a child already burdened with a somewhat lessened adequacy of mental functioning. Recognition that these negative behaviors are due to the head injury and are not under the child's control is more likely to result in tolerance and support at a time when the child's reduced coping capacity requires aid, not isolation or attack.

Idle reassurance that "no damage was done" leaves caretakers to conclude that a change in the child is unrelated to the head injury. This leaves the parents, teachers, and child to provide their own explanation while explicitly removing the most likely one from consideration. Such removal of the correct diagnosis of the behavior almost ensures incorrect treatment, thus again causing more mischief than can be credited to the head injury itself.

Such failure to recognize the potentially harmful effects of relatively mild head injury also reduces the enthusiams for available preventative action. As vehicular accidents become increasingly predominant among the causes of head injury in children, the value of use of seat belts increases. Because no treatment is available to enhance the rate or eventual completeness or recovery, emphasis must be on prevention.

IV. A FINAL COMMENT

It is naive (occasionally fatally so) for an adult to assume, despite the concussive shock and abrupt commotion of an accident, that he or she will not only hold onto the child is his lap but protect it from injury in the process. Such protection is unlikely even if the adult is not instantly injured and thus rendered immobile for a second or two. Even a second of stunned immobility or weakness is more than enough for the child to be jerked out one's grasp and into the dashboard, windshield, or other internal parts of the car. Only a fixed restraining device holds any realistic hope of providing protection for the child under 50 lb. (22.7

kg). Tension-sensitive devices are adequate for adults and older children but not for children under age 6. Children in the driver's lap or roaming free about the car are vulnerable even to sudden stops which may avoid a collision yet maim the child.

When prevention fails, enhancement of coping and reduction of psychological morbidity due to the recovery process is the next available approach. The cornerstone of this treatment strategy is early and adequate evaluation of the patient's areas of deficit so that all concerned can deal with them for what they are: the neurobehavioral sequelae of brain trauma. If the patient is maximally tolerated in his environment, then his reaction to reduction in cognitive adequacy is more likely to be adaptive and consequent reductions in functional proficiency are likely to be minimized. In like fashion, the availability of the patient to retraining procedures designed to enhance utilization of permanently impaired or recovering abilities is far better when secondary emotional disruptions are understood in the same context, rather than being viewed as an unrelated annoyance for which the patient is responsible. Rimel, Giordani, Barth, Boll, and Jane (1981) found a 33% unemployment rate among previously employed, mildly injured patients 3 months after injury. Bond (1976) and Oddy, Humphrey, and Uttley (1978) report that psychosocial consequences represent the greatest economic and personal danger from head injury. The importance of increased appreciation of the actual behavioral sequelae may have finally emerged as integral to the routine management of this all-too-common childhood disorder.

REFERENCES

Annegers, J. F., Grabow, J. D., Kurland, L. T., & Laws, E. R. The incidence, causes and secular trends of head trauma in Olmstead County, Minnesota, 1935–1974. *Neurology,* 1980, *30,* 912–919.

Bailey, P. Fracture at the base of the skull: Neurological and medico-legal considerations. *Medical News,* 1903, *82,* 918.

Beekman, F. Head injuries in children: Analysis of 331 cases with special reference to end results. *Annals of Surgery,* 1928, *87,* 355.

Black, P., Blumer, D., Wellner, A., Jeffries, J. J., & Walker, A. L. An interdisciplinary perspective study of head trauma in children. In C. R. Angle, & E. A. Bering (Eds.), *Physical trauma as an etiological agent in mental retardation.* Bethesda, MD: U.S. Department of Health, Education and Welfare, 1970.

Black, P., Shepard, R. H., & Walker, A. L. Outcome of head trauma: Age and post-traumatic seizures. In R. Porter & D. FitzSimmons (Eds.), *Outcome of severe damage to the central nervous system.* Siba Foundation Symposium, *34.* North Holland, Amsterdam: Elsevier, Excerpta Medica, 1975.

Blau, A. Mental changes following head trauma in children. *Archives of Neurology and Psychiatry,* 1936, *35,* 723.

Boll, T. J. Behavioral sequelae of head injury, In P. R. Cooper (Ed.) *Head Injury.* Baltimore: Williams and Wilkins Company, 1982, pp. 363–375.

Boll, T. J. Neuropsychological assessment of the child: Myths, current status and future prospects. In C. E. Walker & M. C. Roberts (Eds.) *Handbook of Clinical Child Psychology.* New York: John Wiley and Sons, 1983, pp. 186–208.

Boll, T. J. The effect of age at onset of brain damage on adaptive abilities in children. *Proceedings of the American Psychological Association,* 1973.

Bond, M. R. Assessment of psychosocial outcome of severe head injury. *Acta Neurochurgica,* 1976, *34,* 57–70.

Brain, W. R., & Walton, J. N. *Brain's diseases of the nervous system.* London: Oxford University Press, 1969.

Brink, J. D., Garret, A. L., Hale, W. R., Woo-Sam, J., & Nickel, V. L. Recovery of motor and intellectual function in children sustaining severe head injuries. *Developmental Medicine and Child Neurology,* 1970, *12,* 565–571.

Burkinshaw, J. Head injuries in children. Observations on their incidence and causes with an inquiry into the value of routine skull X-rays. *Archives of Diseases of Childhood,* 1960, *35,* 205.

Buschke, H. Selective reminding for analysis of memory and learning. *Journal of Verbal Learning and Verbal Behavior,* 1973, *12,* 543–550.

Cavaness, W. Incidence of cranial cerebral trauma in the United States. *Trans-American Neurological Association,* 1977, *102,* 136–138.

Cobb, S. A salute from neurologists. In F. A. Beech, D. O. Hebb, C. T. Morgan, & N. W. Nissen (Eds.), *The neuropsychology of Lashley.* New York: Mac-Graw-Hill, 1960.

Craft, A. W., Shae, T. A., & Cartlidge, M. E. F. Bicycle injuries in children. *British Medical Journal,* 1973, *4,* 146–147.

Eson, M. E., & Bourke, R. S. *Assessment of information processing deficits after serious head injury.* Presented at the eighth annual meeting of International Neuropsychological Society, 1980.

Ewing, R., McCarthy, C., Gronwall, D., & Wrightson, P. Persisting effects of minor head injury observable during hypoxic stress. *Journal of Clinical Psychology,* 1980, *2,* 147–155.

Gennarelli, T. A., Adams, G. H., & Graham, D. I. Acceleration induced head injury in the monkey: The model, its mechanical and physiological correlate. *Acta Neuropathological, Supplement,* in press.

Gronwall, D., & Wrightson, P. Cumulative effects of concussion. *Lancet,* 1975, *2,* 995–997.

Gronwall, D., & Wrightson, P. Duration of post-traumatic amnesia after mild head injury. *Journal of Clinical Neuropsychology,* 1980, *2,* 51–60.

Harrington, J. A., & Letemendia, F. J. J. Persistent psychiatric disorders after head injuries in children. *Journal of Mental Science,* 1958, *104,* 1205–1218.

Heiskanen, O., & Kaste, M. Late prognosis of severe brain injury in children. *Developmental Medicine and Child Neurology,* 1974, *16,* 11–14.

Hjern, B., & Nylander, I. Later prognosis of severe head injuries in childhood. *Archives of Diseases of Childhood,* 1962, *37,* 113.

Ireland, J. Fracture of the skull in children. *Archives of Surgery,* 1972, *24,* 23.

Isaacson, R. L. The myth of recovery from early brain damage. In H. R. Ellis (Ed.), *Aberrant development in infancy: Human and animal studies.* New York: Halstead Press, 1975.

Jennett, B. Head injuries in children. *Developmental Medicine in Child Neurology,* 1972, *14,* 137–147.

Jennett, B. Late effects of head injury. In M. Kirtchley, J. L. O'Leary, & B. Jennett (Eds.), *Scientific foundation of neurology.* London: Heinemann, 1972.

Jennett, B. Scale, scope and philosophy of clinical problems. In R. Porter & D. FitzSimmons (Eds.), *Outcome of severe damage to the central nervous system.* Siba Foundation Symposium, *34,* North Holland, Amsterdam: Elsevier, Excerpta Medica, 1975.

Kinsbourne, M. *Mechanisms of hemispheric disconnection and cerebral function.* Springfield, IL: Charles C. Thomas, 1974.

Klonoff, H. Head injuries in children: Predisposing factors, accident conditions, accident proneness and sequelae. *American Journal of Public Health,* 1971, *61,* 2405–2417.

Klonoff, H., Low, M. D., & Clark, C. Head injuries in children: A prospective five year follow-up. *Journal of Neurology, Neurosurgery, and Psychiatry*, 1977, *40*, 1211–1219.

Klonoff, H., & Paris, R. Immediate, short-term and residual effects of acute head injuries in children: Neuropsychological and neurological correlates. In R. Reitan & L. Davison (Eds.), *Clinical neuropsychology: Current status and applications*. Washington, DC: V. H. Winston & Sons, 1974.

Klonoff, H., & Robinson, G. C. Epidemiology of head injuries in children. *Canadian Medical Association Journal*, 1967, *96*, 1308–1311.

Kløve, H., & Cleeland, C. G. The relationship of neuropsychological impairment to other indices of severity of head injury. *Scandinavian Journal of Rehabilitation Medicine*, 1972, *4*, 55–60.

Levin, H. S., & Eisenberg, H. N. Neuropsychological outcome of closed head injury in children and adolescents. *Child's Brain*, 1979, *5*, 281–289.

Levin, H. S., & Grossman, R. G. Storage and retrieval. *Pediatric Psychology*, 1976, *1*, 38–42.

Lishman, W. A. The psychiatric sequelae of head injury: A review. *Psychological Medicine*, 1973, *3*, 304–318.

Mannheimer, D. I., Dewey, J., & Melinger, G. D. Fifty thousand child-years of accidental injuries. *Public Health Reports*, 1966, *81*, 519.

Merritt, H. H. *A textbook of neurology*, (4th Edition). Philadelphia: Lea & Febiger, 1967.

Meyer, A. The anatomical facts and clinical varieties of traumatic insanity. *American Journal of Insanity*, 1903–04, *60*, 373.

Oddy, M., Humphrey, M., & Uttley, D. Subjective impairment and social recovery after closed head injury. *Journal of Neurology, Neurosurgery, Psychiatry*, 1978, *41*, 611–616.

Rimel, R. W., Giordani, B., Barth, J. T., Boll, T. J., & Jane, J. A. Disability caused by minor head injury. *Journal of Neurosurgery*, 1981, *9*, 221–228.

Roberts, A. H. *Brain damage in boxers*. Pittman: London, 1969.

Rowbotham, G. F., MacIver, I. N., Dicksson, J., & Bousefield, N. E. Analysis of 1400 cases of acute injury to the head. *British Medical Journal*, 1954, *1*, 726.

Rune, V. Acute head injuries in children. *Acta Paediatrica Scandinavica, Supplement*, 1970, *209*, 1–119.

Rutter, M. Brain damage syndromes in childhood: Concepts and findings. *Journal of Clinical Childhood Psychology and Psychiatry*, 1977, *18*, 1–21.

Selley, I., & Frankel, F. B. Skull fracture in infants: A report of fifty cases. *Acta Chir Scandinavica*, 1961, *122*, 30.

Shaffer, D., Chadwick, O., & Rutter, M. Psychiatric outcome of localized head injury in children. In R. Porter & D. FitzSimmons (Eds.), *Outcome of severe damage to the central nervous system*. Siba Foundation Symposium, *34*. North Holland, Amsterdam: Elsevier, Excerpta Medica, 1975.

Sobel, R. The psychiatric implications of accidental poisoning in childhood. *Pediatric Clinics of North America*, 1970, *17*, 653–685.

Strauss, A. A., & Kephart, N. C. *Psychopathology and education of the brain injured child*, (Vol. I & II). New York: Grune and Stratton, 1965.

Strecker, E. A., & Ebaugh, F. G. Neuropsychiatric sequelae of cerebral trauma in children. *Archives of Neurology and Psychiatry*, 1924, *12*, 443.

Symonds, C. Concussion and its sequelae. *Lancet*, 1962, *1*, 1–5.

Teuber, H. L., & Rudel, R. G. Behavior after cerebral lesions in children and adults. *Developmental Medicine in Child Neurology*, 1962, *4*, 3–20.

Ward, A. A. The physiology of concussion. *Clinical Neurosurgery*, 1966, *12*, 95–111.

Wechsler, I. S. *Clinical Neurology*. Philadelphia: Strauss, 1963.

Windle, W. F., Groat, R. A., & Fox, C. A. *Surgery, Gynecology and Obstetrics*, 1944, *79*, 561.

Young, W. M. Poverty, intelligence, and life in the inner city. *Mental Retardation*, 1969, *7*, 24.

AGE NORMS FOR THE REITAN–INDIANA NEUROPSYCHOLOGICAL TEST BATTERY FOR CHILDREN AGED 5 THROUGH 8

Roland D. Maiuro, Brenda D. Townes,
Peter Paul Vitaliano and Eric W. Trupin

I. INTRODUCTION

During recent years interest in clinical neuropsychological evaluation procedures has risen markedly. The information provided by neuropsychological test batteries has been reliably used to identify the type or location of brain lesions in adults (Boll, 1981), to classify children as normal, learning disabled, or brain damaged (Reitan & Boll, 1973), to identify children at risk for reading dis-

Advances in the Behavioral Measurement of Children, Volume 1, pages 159–173.
Copyright © 1984 by JAI Press Inc.
ISBN: 0-89232-282-9

abilities (Fay, Trupin, & Townes, 1981; Rourke, 1981), and to predict academic success (Townes, Trupin, Martin, & Goldstein, 1980). Despite the proven utility of the Halstead–Reitan neuropsychological measures, the interpretation of such measures has largely remained a sophisticated clinical art rather than a clearly normed psychometric science. Most test norms published to date have consisted of general cutoff scores based upon collective categories of subjects (e.g., "adults," "children 5 through 8," or "children 9 through 14") which may be used to differentiate significantly brain-damaged from normal protocols. Refined interpretation of data for the individual case, which may vary significantly in terms of a host of factors including basic demographics such as age and sex, has remained dependent on the interpreter's exposure to raw scores derived from a large number and variety of clinical and normal cases.

While a number of references exist which aid the interpretation of neuropsychological test results for adults (Adams & Jenkins, 1981; Reitan & Davison, 1974) and older children (Selz & Reitan, 1979), few references exist for the use of such measures with young school-aged children (Fisk & Rourke, 1979). Spreen and Gaddes (1969) published developmental norms for a number of neuropsychological tests based on a sample of normal children ranging in age from 6 to 15. While their paper provides a useful description of a variety of test measures appropriate for children, it is of limited use as a reference source for the Reitan–Indiana Battery. The authors report normative results for a nonstandard mix of tests drawn from various neuropsychological batteries, with some age groups not consistently assessed and others represented by very small samples. Hughes (1976) reported norms for both the Halstead Neuropsychological Test Battery for Children and the Reitan–Indiana Neuropsychological Test Battery for Children based on data collected at the University of Chicago. While this paper includes a useful comparison of normal and clinical samples of children for both test batteries, the results reported for some age groups on the Reitan–Indiana are also based upon extremely small subject samples (e.g., n = 1, n = 3). As a result, the data are collapsed into grossly defined categories of "ages 9 to 14" and "ages 5 to 9" with no differentiation by sex. In a carefully performed and useful series of studies, Robert Knights and his associates have provided normative data on a variety of neuropsychological tests for children, including many drawn from the Halstead–Reitan and Reitan–Indiana test batteries (Knights & Moule, 1967; Knights & Tymchuk, 1968; Knights & Watson, 1968). Much of Knights's comprehensive normative data, however, are also limited by small sample size across some age groups and are generally retrievable only in bulletin or manuscript form directly from the author (Knights, 1966; Knights & Norwood, 1980).

One possible source of data which could aid in the interpretation of neuropsychological test results for young children is a breakdown of normative raw scores based upon a large number of subjects. Given the rapid developmental and maturational changes associated with young children, separate breakdowns by age would appear to be indicated. Breakdowns by sex, unless sex differences are shown to be negligible, would also be desirable. The purpose of the present chapter is to present such norms for the Reitan–Indiana Neuropsychological Test Battery for Children Aged 5 Through 8 Years (Reitan, 1969; Reitan & Davison, 1974). The norms were derived from a larger study which evaluated the relationship between neuropsychological functioning and academic performance in young school-aged children (Townes et al., 1980). Although the subject sample has some generalizability limitations associated with the distribution of IQ and socioeconomic variables, the data were systematically collected from a large number of children and should be useful to clinicians and researchers working with similar populations.

II. METHOD

Subjects

Subjects were 451 children drawn from elementary schools in the Lake Washington School District, a suburb of Seattle, Washington. Letters were sent to the homes of approximately 800 normally programmed kindergarten and second-grade children in four schools requesting permission for the children to participate in a study of adaptive abilities among normal elementary school children. All regular class children who were permitted to participate were included in the present data analyses, with the exception of five children whose ages fell above or below the cutoff points of 5.0 and 8.9 years. In addition, questionnaires were mailed to the parents of all subjects to obtain background information about the children and their families. With the exception of two Asian-American children, all subjects were identified as white and primarily middle class according to the Hollingshead and Redlich (1958) Index of Social Class, and the subject sample was found to be representative of the general school district population (cf. Townes et al., 1980).

Four age groups of children were formed according to year, with 128 children included within the 5.0–5.9 range, 106 within the 6.0–6.9 range, 128 within the 7.0–7.9 range, and 89 within the 8.0–8.9 age range. The distribution of males and females was similar across the four age groups, with 61, 58, 68, 47, and 67, 48, 60, 42 males and females, respectively (see Table 1). The mean full-scale IQ as measured by the Wechsler Intelligence Scale for Children (WISC; Wechsler, 1949) was 114.94 for the sample and within the bright–normal range for all age groups.

Procedure

The Reitan–Indiana Neuropsychological Test Battery for Children Aged 5 Through 8 (Reitan, 1969; Reitan & Davison, 1974) was individually administered to each subject by one of four experienced psychometrists, all of whom

Table 1. Age and Sex Breakdowns of Subject Sample

	Age Group			
	5.0–5.9	6.0–6.9	7.0–7.9	8.0–8.9
Mean Age (years)	5.6	6.3	7.6	8.3
Number of Males	61	58	68	47
Number of Females	67	48	60	42
Total N	128	106	128	89

were trained in the standard procedures for administering the tests. Given the difficulty of the Tactual Performance Test for some younger age children, a time limit of 10 min was observed for the dominant-hand, nondominant-hand, and both-hands trials so as to not unnecessarily overwhelm or frustrate the subject. Hand dominance was established for each subject by observing the preferred hand used by the child for the name-writing task. In instances where "right–left differences" are analyzed, a dominant–nondominant classification was imposed and the scores of right handers and left handers were combined. To prevent examiner and order effects from influencing the data, the psychometrists were rotated among the four participating elementary schools, and subjects were tested on a randomly assigned basis.

For purposes of organization, the test variables are listed according to the method of inference commonly used in the clinical interpretation of neuropsychological test results. These categories include level of performance, pathognomonic signs, patterns of performance, and right–left differences (Boll, 1978; Reitan, 1967; Reitan & Davison, 1974). All test variables were analyzed in terms of the appropriate raw score indices (e.g., number of items correct, number of errors, number of absolute responses, performance in time in seconds or minutes). Combinations of lateralization indices were also computed in the "right–left differences" section for purposes of simplification, since such variables were previously reported separately in the "level of performance" section.

The variable scores for males and females were combined within each age group to analyze the effects of age as there were no sex-by-age interactions. However, separate norms are listed for those tests shown to be subject to sex differences by previous analyses (Townes et al., 1980). Separate norms for males and females were thus reported for select tests of verbal reasoning (Matching Pictures), language skills (Verbal Aphasia items), serial perceptual matching (Matching Figures and Matching V's), as well as on tests of spatial memory (Target) and motor performance (Grip Strength and Tapping Speed). Means and standard deviations were computed and univariate analyses of variance ANOVAs; df = 3 and 447) were performed on all variables to examine the significance of age upon neuropsychological performance (see Table 2).

III. RESULTS

Of the 60 test variables investigated, 49 were found to be significantly related to age. Significant differences were found among measures related to subject's level of performance, pathognomonic signs, patterns of performance, and right–left differences. Of the 9 variables not found to be significantly affected by age, most were measures of rarely occurring responses (e.g., imperceptions or suppressions) or test items with a limited range as dictated by either examiner or criterion termination of the task (e.g., number of errors in Marching Test II).

In terms of level of performance, age-related differences are consistently seen across measures of abstract problem solving and flexibility (Category Test, Progressive Figures, Color Form), verbal reasoning and concept formation (Matching Pictures), visual–spatial expressive (Star, Concentric Squares) and receptive (Matching Figures, Matching V's) skills (Target Test), tactile–kinesthetic problem solving (TPT), motor strength and speed (Grip Strength, Tapping), and motor accuracy and coordination (Marching Tests I and II).

Inspection of the differences reported in the Table of Normative Comparisons (Table 2) indicates that some measures show a relatively regular and gradual progression across the age groups while others reflect a more irregular pattern of development. The mean performance on the Category Test in particular appears to change quite dramatically as the subject matures to 7 years of age, reflecting significantly more sophisticated abstraction abilities during this developmental period. This finding is strikingly consistent with the research findings of cognitive and developmental psychologists with respect to the attainment of concrete operations at this age (Elkind, 1976).

While statistical differences are found for the number of blocks placed on the TPT, differences are most apparent in terms of the relative efficiency (time) demonstrated in completing the task. Significant differences were observed on both time and error variables of the Marching Test I. However, the variables derived from the Marching II subtest appeared to have a number of significant limitations in the present study. For example, examination of the means and standard deviations for the "number of circles completed" reveals a tremendous amount of variability in performance among normal children aged 5 and 6, indicating that this measure may be unreliable for very young children. Children aged 7 and above, however, appear to be more proficient and less variable in their performance on this task. The lack of significant differences for the "number of errors" variable on this subtest would appear to be largely due to the low ceiling imposed by the criterion of three errors per page used to terminate the test.

Separate norms are provided for males and females on those level-of-performance measures shown to be susceptible to sex differences by previously reported analyses (Townes et al., 1980). These measures included Grip Strength, Tapping, Matching Pictures, Matching Figures, Matching V's, Aphasia Screen-

Table 2. Table of Normative Comparisons Means and Standard Deviations for Neuropsychological Test Variables

Test	Age								F	P<
	5.0–5.9		6.0–6.9		7.0–7.9		8.0–8.9			
	$\bar{X}$	SD	$\bar{X}$	SD	$\bar{X}$	SD	$\bar{X}$	SD		
LEVEL OF PERFORMANCE										
Category (total errors)	22.96	10.57	27.57	11.02	12.33	8.01	9.88	6.54	40.35	.001
TPT (time in minutes of dominant hand)	6.14	2.66	5.73	2.75	5.07	2.54	4.01	2.16	10.37	.001
TPT (dominant number of blocks)	5.43	1.27	5.57	1.05	5.74	0.89	5.93	0.45	3.89	.005
TPT (time in minutes of nondominant hand)	4.95	2.53	4.52	2.45	3.45	1.89	2.94	1.88	13.58	.001
TPT (nondominant number of blocks)	5.69	0.97	5.87	0.55	5.94	0.44	5.97	0.23	3.22	.01
TPT (time in minutes of both hands)	3.03	1.97	2.74	1.92	1.76	1.14	1.41	1.07	18.96	.001
TPT (both hands number of blocks)	5.93	0.48	5.98	0.20	5.98	0.26	6.00	0.00	0.83	ns
TPT (total time)	14.12	5.82	12.99	5.86	10.44	4.43	8.36	4.20	15.98	.001
TPT (memory)	3.24	1.43	3.91	1.38	4.61	1.04	4.82	1.06	29.03	.001
TPT (location)	1.55	1.42	2.21	1.71	3.26	1.77	3.82	1.65	32.38	.001
Marching I (time in seconds of dominant hand)	26.72	8.98	23.62	6.93	18.27	5.48	16.03	4.25	44.63	.001
Marching I (dominant hand number of errors)	2.51	2.24	2.34	2.58	1.58	1.78	1.28	1.51	6.60	.001
Marching I (time in seconds nondominant hand)	30.16	10.10	27.57	9.55	21.26	6.44	18.95	5.93	34.29	.001

164

Marching I (nondominant hand number of errors)	5.01	3.10	4.49	3.24	3.72	2.88	2.99	2.38	7.44	.001
Marching II (number of circles)	19.03	20.09	28.24	26.28	50.10	29.80	59.91	27.95	43.44	.001
Marching II (dominant hand number of errors)	1.68	1.18	1.87	1.27	2.05	1.46	1.95	1.45	1.38	ns
Marching II (nondominant hand number of errors)	2.05	1.30	2.03	1.32	2.07	1.42	1.85	1.25	0.41	ns
Star (accuracy)	3.37	2.41	4.50	2.28	5.67	1.01	5.76	0.95	34.44	.001
Star (time in seconds)	28.03	24.74	22.82	14.76	20.26	18.66	18.35	9.68	4.60	.001
Concentric Squares (accuracy)	1.80	1.91	2.75	2.28	4.26	2.76	5.10	2.54	31.54	.001
Concentric Squares (time in seconds)	38.55	23.57	33.40	15.12	32.11	18.71	31.25	16.55	3.13	.01
Progressive Figures (number of errors)	1.00	1.56	0.79	1.50	0.22	0.47	0.36	0.96	8.41	.001
Progressve Figures (time in seconds)	88.41	68.79	75.38	57.40	43.95	25.44	41.16	23.63	19.65	.001
Color Forms (number of errors)	1.58	1.83	0.98	1.51	0.43	1.05	0.36	1.05	14.07	.001
Color Forms (time in seconds)	39.69	24.01	32.17	21.59	18.91	10.82	17.67	10.11	30.40	.001
Grip Strength (kg.) (dominant hand: males)	9.19	2.04	9.50	2.48	13.06	2.49	13.64	2.53	9.63	.01
Grip Strength (kg.) (dominant hand: females)	7.68	1.89	8.54	1.88	11.85	2.28	11.74	2.93	"	"
Grip Strength (kg.) (nondominant hand: males)	8.17	2.07	8.68	2.34	12.06	2.49	12.51	2.19	21.76	.001
Grip Strength (kg.) (nondominant hand: females)	6.98	1.85	8.12	1.87	10.31	2.16	10.79	2.46	"	"
Tapping (dominant hand: males)	28.61	3.29	29.84	3.80	34.71	4.43	35.60	3.85	86.01	.001

(*continued*)

Table 2. (Continued)

Test	Age											
	5.0–5.9		6.0–6.9		7.0–7.9		8.0–8.9				
	$\bar{X}$	SD	$\bar{X}$	SD	$\bar{X}$	SD	$\bar{X}$	SD	F	P<
LEVEL OF PERFORMANCE (continued)										
Tapping (dominant hand: females)	28.70	3.13	28.95	2.89	33.67	4.70	35.43	3.68	"	"
Tapping (nondominant hand: males)	26.02	2.62	27.25	3.61	31.20	3.62	31.47	3.06	78.99	.001
Tapping (nondominant hand: females)	25.84	2.77	25.71	2.50	29.74	3.60	31.72	2.54	"	"
Matching Pictures (total number correct: males)	13.67	2.75	14.91	2.61	17.04	1.45	17.30	1.93	41.26	.001
Matching Pictures (total number correct: females)	14.83	2.30	15.02	3.22	17.43	1.60	17.45	1.60	"	"
Matching Figures (number of errors: males)	0.51	1.19	0.27	0.69	0.16	0.44	0.15	0.46	3.66	.001
Matching Figures (number of errors: females)	0.33	0.72	0.21	0.62	0.10	0.35	0.12	0.39	"	"
Matching Figures (time in seconds: males)	38.43	15.92	30.95	11.75	21.70	7.26	20.36	8.02	41.48	.001
Matching Figures (time in seconds: females)	31.42	10.91	32.02	12.71	19.75	5.87	19.71	8.28	"	"
Matching "V"s (number of errors: males)	2.51	1.86	1.72	1.36	1.22	1.35	1.45	1.39	10.47	.001

166

Matching "V"'s (number of errors: females)	2.19	1.76	1.92	1.62	1.25	1.59	1.02	1.46	"	"
Matching "V"'s (time in seconds: males)	46.18	18.00	41.14	16.59	29.57	12.96	25.68	8.09	22.60	.001
Matching "V"'s (time in seconds: females)	44.54	33.53	37.52	16.18	28.23	12.04	24.24	9.78	"	"
Target (number correct: males)	7.67	3.75	9.33	3.19	14.84	3.11	15.23	3.70	119.20	.001
Target (number correct: females)	6.95	2.73	8.00	2.73	13.43	3.83	15.02	2.97	"	"

PATHOGNOMONIC SIGNS

Aphasia (number of errors)

Aphasia Verbal (males)	5.48	2.05	4.33	2.69	1.00	1.09	0.72	0.99	136.89	.001
Aphasia Verbal (females)	4.93	1.84	3.48	2.34	0.68	1.14	0.60	1.01	"	"
Aphasia Figure Construction (males)	1.74	.95	1.29	0.91	0.44	0.63	0.57	0.68	37.13	.001
Aphasia Figure Construction (females)	1.55	.99	1.47	0.90	0.65	0.80	0.67	0.75	"	"

Imperceptions

Tactile Right	0.72	1.09	0.80	1.34	0.32	0.70	0.26	0.67	6.66	.001
Tactile Left	0.49	0.98	0.49	0.87	0.20	0.49	0.22	0.58	4.02	.01
Auditory Right	0.20	0.53	0.15	0.10	0.39	0.03	0.18	2.39	.05	
Auditory Left	0.39	0.70	0.25	0.53	0.16	0.51	0.17	0.40	3.74	.01
Visual Right	0.08	0.38	0.05	0.25	0.02	0.15	0.01	0.11	1.51	ns
Visual Left	0.10	0.41	0.05	0.21	0.05	0.23	0.02	0.15	1.24	ns

(*continued*)

Table 2. (Continued)

	Age									
	5.0–5.9		6.0–6.9		7.0–7.9		8.0–8.9			
Test	$\bar{X}$	SD	$\bar{X}$	SD	$\bar{X}$	SD	$\bar{X}$	SD	F	P<
PATHOGNOMONIC SIGNS (continued) Recognition Tasks										
Finger Recognition Right (number of errors)	3.04	2.31	2.56	2.31	1.39	1.68	1.25	1.67	16.20	.001
Finger Recognition Left (number of errors)	3.24	2.40	2.99	2.23	1.33	1.58	1.44	1.68	22.22	.001
Fingertip Symbol Right (number of errors)	2.00	2.05	1.55	1.76	0.65	0.93	0.43	0.86	21.16	.001
Fingertip Symbol Left (number of errors)	1.97	2.09	1.47	1.66	0.70	0.92	0.65	1.16	15.19	.001
Tactile Form Recognition Right (number of errors)	0.39	0.69	0.21	0.51	0.13	0.36	0.14	0.46	4.84	.001
Tactile Form Recognition Right (time in seconds)	18.30	5.99	18.07	6.39	15.84	4.92	14.95	5.92	6.75	.001
Tactile Form Recognition Left (number of errors)	0.30	0.67	0.12	0.38	0.04	0.19	0.07	0.25	6.89	.001
Tactile Form Recognition Left (time in seconds)	17.23	6.50	17.10	7.86	14.00	3.71	13.41	4.16	9.90	.001

PATTERNS AND RELATIONSHIPS/RIGHT–LEFT DIFFERENCES

Grip Strength (dominant–nondominant hand: males)	1.02	1.13	0.80	1.17	1.00	0.98	1.13	1.70	5.00	.01
Grip Strength (dominant–nondominant hand: females)	0.70	1.04	0.41	1.20	1.54	1.13	0.95	1.28	"	"
Tapping (dominant–nondominant hand: males)	2.59	2.53	2.59	1.98	3.51	3.20	4.13	2.52	4.41	.01
Tapping (dominant–nondominant hand: females)	2.86	2.51	-3.24	2.76	3.92	3.64	3.72	2.54	"	"

PATTERNS AND RELATIONSHIPS/RIGHT–LEFT DIFFERENCES (continued)

Namewriting (dominant–nondominant hand: time in seconds)	-11.73	10.75	-11.69	10.68	-7.66	-7.16	-6.36	6.03	7.64	.001
TPT (dominant–nondominant hand: time in minutes)	1.19	2.19	1.21	2.51	1.62	2.22	1.07	2.02	1.60	ns
Marching II (dominant–nondominant)	-0.37	2.17	-0.16	2.25	-0.01	2.38	-0.10	1.88	-0.74	ns
Total Imperceptions (right–left)	0.01	1.55	0.21	1.44	0.03	1.02	-0.11	0.83	0.81	ns
Tactile Form Recognition Errors (right–left)	0.09	0.63	0.08	0.55	0.09	0.40	0.07	0.49	0.10	ns
Tactile Form Recognition Time in Seconds (right–left)	1.06	4.25	0.97	5.31	1.84	3.95	1.37	4.47	1.09	ns
Total Recognition Errors (right–left)	-0.08	2.72	-0.27	3.07	0.10	2.23	-0.35	2.06	0.57	ns

ing Items, and the Target Test. In terms of motor functioning, it should be noted that sex differences are more apparent on measures of gross motor strength (Grip) where males consistently score higher, as compared to fine motor speed (Tapping) where sex differences appear to be less noteworthy. Also, sex-difference advantages in favor of females on Matching Pictures, Matching Figures, Matching V's, and Verbal Aphasia Items appear to be more prominent in the earliest age group, with an apparent trend toward more equal performance as the children grow older. While females generally performed better on the verbal reasoning items of the Aphasia Screening Test, males, specifically those 6 years and older, performed better on the figure-construction part of the test. Males also appeared to perform consistently better on the Target Test, a measure tapping both visual-spatial orientation and memory abilities. Thus, in terms of sex differences, males appear to have an advantage in the acquisition of spatial and motor skills, whereas females have a developmental advantage in the early acquisition of language-related abilities and perceptual matching skills.

The results of the present study indicate that many test variables commonly viewed as "pathognomonic signs" in adults must be interpreted differently and with considerable caution in young children. For example, on the Aphasia Screening Test, it would appear that up to five or six errors are not uncommon for a normal 5-year-old, with about four errors common for a 6-year old. However, by the age of 7, the children tested did not generally make more than one error. Similarly, a significant number of children in all age groups tended to draw at least one of the figures inaccurately on the Figure Construction subtest of the aphasia exam. Thus, the use of such an error as a clear-cut pathognomonic sign would not appear to be justified.

Tactile and auditory imperceptions/suppressions became increasingly rare with age in the sample of children studied. One sensory error in the tactile modality was not unusual in the 5- and 6-year-old groups but uncommon for the 7- and 8-year-old groups. While one auditory imperception was not unusual for a 5-year-old, it was relatively rare in 7- and 8-year-olds, as fewer than one in five children experienced such errors. Visual imperceptions/suppressions, however, were quite rare for all groups of children, regardless of age, occurring in less than 10% of the sample studied.

All Tactile Recognition tasks were significantly affected by age and appeared to function more as "level of performance" variables than as pathognomonic signs. In this sense, two or three errors were common for the 5- and 6-year-old groups in Finger Recognition and Fingertip Symbol measures, respectively, with less than two errors characteristic of the 7- and 8-year-old groups. Tactile Form Recognition errors were somewhat more unusual for 7- and 8-year-olds.

Age-related increases in dominant/nondominant hand differences were found for both Grip Strength and Finger Tapping measures. However, while the absolute level of performance increases with age across these measures, it should be noted that the dominant–nondominant ratio remains essentially the same (approximately 1.1:1.0 for both males and females). Such a pattern is consistent with the finding that lateral dominance is normally clearly established by the age of 5. Greater coordination and control of the nondominant side of the body also appears to occur, as evidenced by a relative decrease in the disparity of dominant–nondominant Handwriting Time (first name). No dominant/nondominant or "right–left" differences were found on measures of sensory recognition or sensory imperception across tactile, auditory, and visual modalities (Total Imperceptions, Total Recognition Errors).

IV. DISCUSSION

The overall results of the present study underscore the importance of taking age norms into account when interpreting neuropsychological test results on young children. The number of variables found to be significantly affected by age greatly exceeded the number that would be expected from a series of univariate analyses on the basis of chance. Thus, 49 out of 60 variables were significant as opposed to the approximate number of 3 that would have been expected by chance given a .05 minimum level of confidence. These age-related changes in cognitive, language, sensory–perceptual, and motor functions observed across the Reitan–Indiana neuropsychological test variables parallel the findings of a number of neurological studies of children. Such neurological studies have shown significant increases in the myelination and maturation of neural pathways as well as increased interhemispheric transfer in children aged 5 to 10 (Galin, Diamond, & Herron, 1977; O'Leary, 1980; Yakolev & Lecours, 1967).

Recent studies of a variety of neuropsychological measures have emerged which indicate that the failure to take developmental and demographic factors into account can result in diagnostic misclassification in adults (Adams, Boake, & Crain, 1982; Anthony, Heaton, & Lehman, 1980; King, Hannay, Masek, & Burns, 1978). The risk of making such misclassification errors would appear to be even higher when assessing younger age groups in which significant cognitive and maturational differences appear to exist (Fletcher & Satz, 1980). It is recommended that the present norms be used as a reference when interpreting neuropsychological test results in children aged 5 through 8 with premorbid characteristics similar to those of the normative sample. Caution should be exercised in the use of the norms with children whose premorbid and demographic characteristics differ significantly from the Caucasian, middle-class, and bright–normal children presently studied. It would appear that future studies should be performed to examine the relative influence of factors such as IQ, education, and socioeconomic status in order to further refine our understanding of variables affecting performance on these neuropsychological measures.

V. SUMMARY

The purpose of the present chapter was to present normative data for the Reitan–Indiana Neuropsychological Test Battery for Children Aged 5 Through 8 Years. Subjects were 451 children drawn from elementary schools in the Lake Washington School District, a suburb of Seattle, Washington. The large subject sample permitted breakdowns by age and sex, where significant, to be performed. Of the 60 test variables investigated, 49 were found to be significantly related to age. Significant differences were found among measures related to level of performance, pathognomonic signs, patterns of performance, and right–left differences. Of the 9 variables not found to be significantly affected by age, most were measures of rarely occurring responses (e.g., imperceptions or suppressions). Separate norms are reported for males and females on various measures of motor performance, verbal reasoning and concept formation, and visual-spatial orientation and memory. The overall results of the study underscore the importance of taking age norms and sex differences into account when interpreting neuropsychological test results on young children.

ACKNOWLEDGMENTS

This study was supported by Spencer Foundation Grant B-296 and National Institute of Child Health and Human Development Grant HDO-2274 to the Child Development and Mental Retardation Center of the University of Washington. The authors wish to thank Jane Eberle and Joan Russo for their help in organizing and analyzing the data, as well as the administrators, teachers, parents, and students of the Lake Washington School District for their assistance and support of the research program.

REFERENCES

Adams, R. L., Boake, C., & Crain, C. Bias in a neuropsychological test classification related to education, age, and ethnicity. *Journal of Consulting and Clinical Psychology,* 1982, *50* (1), 143–145.

Adams, R. L., & Jenkins, R. L. Basic principles of the neuropsychological examination. In C. E. Walker (Ed.), *Clinical practice of psychology.* New York: Pergamon Press, 1981.

Anthony, W. Z., Heaton, R. K., & Lehman, R. A. W. An attempt to cross-validate two actuarial systems for neuropsychological test interpretation. *Journal of Consulting and Clinical Psychology,* 1980, *48,* 317–326.

Boll, T. J. Diagnosing brain impairment. In B. B. Wolman (Ed.), *Clinical diagnosis of mental disorders.* New York: Plenum Press, 1978, pp. 601–675.

Boll, T. J. The Halstead-Reitan neuropsychological battery. In S. B. Filskov & T. J. Boll (Eds.), *Handbook of clinical neuropsychology.* New York: John Wiley, 1981, pp. 577–607.

Elkind, D. *Child development and education: A Piagetian perspective.* New York: Oxford University Press, 1976, pp. 85–93.

Fay, G., Trupin, E. W., & Townes, B. D. The young disabled reader: Acquisition strategies and associated deficits. *Journal of Learning Disabilities,* 1981, *14,* 32–35.

Fisk, J. L., & Rourke, B. P. Identification of subtypes of learning disabled children at three age levels: A neuropsychological, multivariate approach. *Journal of Clinical Neuropsychology,* 1979, *1,* 289–310.

Fletcher, J., & Satz, P. Developmental changes in the neuropsychological correlates of reading achievement: A six year longitudinal followup *Journal of Clinical Neuropsychology,* 1980, *2*(1), 23–37.

Galin, D., Diamond, R., & Herron, J. Development of crossed and uncrossed tactile localization on the fingers. *Brain and Language,* 1977, *4,* 588–590.

Hughes, H. E. Norms developed. *Journal of Pediatric Psychology,* 1976, *1,* 11–15.

Hollingshead, A. V., & Redlich, F. C. *Social class and mental illness.* New York: Wiley, 1958.

King, G. D., Hannay, H. J., Masek, B. J., & Burns, J. W. Effects of anxiety and sex on neuropsychological tests. *Journal of Consulting and Clinical Psychology,* 1978, *46*(2), 375–376.

Knights, R. M. *Normative data on tests for evaluating brain damage in children 5 to 14 years of age.* Research Bulletin No. 20, 1966, Department of Psychology, University of Western Ontario, London, Ontario.

Knights, R. M., & Moule, A. D. Normative and reliability data on finger and foot tapping in children. *Perceptual Motor Skills,* 1967, *25,* 717–720.

Knights, R. M., & Norwood, J. A. *Revised smoothed normative data on the neuropsychological test battery for children.* 1980, Department of Psychology, Carleton University, Ottawa, Ontario, Canada.

Knights, R. M., & Tymchuk, A. J. An evaluation of the Halstead-Reitan category tests for children. *Cortex,* 1968, *4,* 403–414.

Knights, R. M., & Watson, P. The use of computerized test profiles in neuropsychological assessment. *Journal of Learning Disabilities,* 1968, *1,* 6–19.

O'Leary, D. S. A developmental study of interhemispheric transfer in children aged five to ten. *Child Development,* 1980, *51*(3), 743–750.

Reitan, R. M. Psychological assessment of deficits resulting from cerebral lesions in subjects with normal and subnormal intelligence. In J. L. Khanna (Ed.), *Brain damage and mental retardation: A psychological evaluation.* Springfield, IL: Charles C. Thomas, 1967.

Reitan, R. M. *Manual for administration of neuropsychological test batteries for adults and children.* Privately published by the author, Indianapolis, 1969.

Reitan, R. M., & Boll, T. J. Neuropsychological correlates of minimal brain dysfunction. *Annals of the New York Academy of Sciences,* 1973, *205,* 65–88.

Reitan, R. M., & Davison, L. A. *Clinical neuropsychology: Current status and applications.* Washington, D.C.: V. H. Winston & Sons, 1974.

Rourke, B. P. Neuropsychological assessment of children with learning disabilities. In S. F. Filskov & T. J. Boll (Eds.), *Handbook of clinical neuropsychology.* New York: John Wiley, 1981, pp. 577–607.

Selz, M., & Reitan, R. M. Neuropsychological test performance of normal, learning disabled, and brain damaged older children. *Journal of Nervous and Mental Disease,* 1979, *167,* 298–302.

Spreen, O. & Gaddes, W. H. Developmental norms for fifteen neuropsychological tests: Age 6 to 15. *Cortex,* 1969, *5,* 171–191.

Townes, B. D., Trupin, E. T., Martin, D. C., & Goldstein, D. Neuropsychological correlates of academic success among elementary school children. *Journal of Consulting and Clinical Psychology,* 1980, *48*(6), 675–684.

Wechsler, D. *Wechsler Intelligence Scale for Children: Manual.* New York: Psychological Corporation, 1949.

Yakolev, P. I., & Lecours, A. R. The myelogenetic cycles of regional maturation of the brain. In A. Minkowski (Ed.), *Regional development of the brain in early life.* Philadelphia: Davis, 1967.

FROM TRAIT TO CATEGORY OF
CHILD BEHAVIOR DISORDER:
ADVANCES IN THE USE OF THE ADELAIDE
PARENT RATING SCALE

Roslyn A. Glow and Peter H. Glow

I. INTRODUCTION

A barrier to progress in the study of child psychopathology is the presence of two conflicting views of the nature of child behavior disorder.

In the first view, which originates in medicine and psychoanalysis and has its full expression in clinical psychiatry, behavior disorders are seen as distinct entities, discontinuous from normal behavior. This view is often, but not necessarily, accompanied by the belief that the behavioral system is an essentially unitary one, and possibly also that the etiology of the disorder is due to a distinct set of causal events. In its most characteristic form, the first view sees behavioral

Advances in the Behavioral Measurement of Children, Volume 1, pages 175–216.

abnormalities as distinct syndromes, if not diseases, each with a unique set of signs and symptoms, following a recognizable course, and potentially if not actually referable to a recognizable pathological process and susceptible to a distinct set of curative agents.

Although most working clinicians would not claim to espouse the full medical model, it pervades the area of child psychopathology, particularly child psychiatry. DSM III (*Diagnostic and Statistical Manual of Mental Disorders*, 3rd ed.; American Psychiatric Association, 1980), with its use of multiple axes, reflects this view less than do some previous systems, but the thinking underlying most of its diagnostic entities is very much influenced by the disease model.

The second tradition in systematic child psychopathology is that represented by the empirical approach of psychologists.

Although there are internecine disputes about the relative importance of traits (dispositions) and of the immediate impact of the environment, agreement on methodological behaviorism is complete. That is, there is commitment to measure behavior and it correlates as accurately and as objectively as possible and to rely upon conventional statistical criteria for interpreting data. Empirically oriented psychologists accept the view that behavior is multifaceted, that behavioral systems may be relatively distinct within one individual, that the same behavioral laws apply to normal and abnormal behavior, and that abnormal behavior is most usefully perceived as a quantitative rather than qualitative phenomenon (i.e., statistically extreme expression of one or more traits, or an excess or deficiency of various socially significant behaviors). Glow and Glow (1979) present a theoretical account of child hyperactivity that reflects this view.

The technological success of the measurement of intelligence and other generalizable behavior tendencies on the one hand, and of specific acts (target behaviors), reinforcing events, etc., on the other, has led to a new burst of activity in the measurement of child behavior disorders, also no doubt spurred on by the requirement to demonstrate the efficacy of new treatments.

This has led to a hiatus between clinical conceptualization and research measurement, with clinicians tending to use individualistic, particularistic, categorical systems, while researchers use multidimensional scaling techniques.

Child psychopathology, to a much greater extent than its adult counterpart, relies upon indirect methods for diagnosis and measurement. For adults, the main criteria for determination of mental disorder are discernible form the patient's behavior as observed or self-reported. The following are relevant criteria: The client seeks help (observed) for problems in behavior, feelings, etc. (self-reported). The client seeks to use (observed) or uses (self-reported) psychoactive medication in order to control or change his mood or behavior. The client is unable to perform tasks of daily living, working, or housekeeping as expected from previous performance (observed or self-reported; the ''expected'' level is generally easily ascertained from the history). The client is in serious conflict with important agencies or persons, e.g., the law, employer, close relatives, because of behavior (observed or self-reported). Once again this is usually easily ascertained.

In the case of children, these criteria are of little use, since children do not seek help on their own behalf, and they do not have access to, the means of seeking, or awareness of the role of psychoactive medication. The establishment of expectations for performance of self-help and other tasks is difficult in a developing system, and is complicated by variations in patterns and trajectories of growth and development. Further, the concept of conflict is inapplicable to those who are either highly dependent or so immature as to be absolved from legal responsibility.

The clinician is thus left to rely very much on the behaviors of parents, or other adults, in seeking help for children, and on adult report of the child's difficulties. Observation of the child's behavior provides useful data in the area of capacity to perform cognitive tasks, or if bizarre and striking psychotic behaviors are present, and many children can give a coherent account of their troubled feelings if asked appropriate questions. In many cases, though, direct assessment may be of little validity because of the novelty of the clinical setting and its apparent irrelevance to the child's normal setting, and because the child's cognitive or experiential limitations making communication difficult.

Report of the child's typical behavior, especially at home and at school, thus takes on particular importance. This is despite the fact that the intensity of adult complaint (which necessarily involves characteristics of the complaining adult as well as of the child) will partly determine whether or not a child behavior problem is recognized by the clinician and how severe it is judged to be.

Systematic parent and teacher report has often been used in treatment evaluation studies (see reviews by Barkley, 1976; Sroufe, 1975) and for selection or description of subjects for research, specifically into hyperactivity. However, it is often difficult to relate questionnaire data to the recognized entities that make sense to the working clinician or that are the focus of the child psychiatric literature. The difficulties of translation of information about individuals or groups of children from one mode to another exemplify the barrier between the two traditions referred to earlier.

This chapter presents an attempt to make this translation.

In a series of studies, the authors (Glow, 1979, 1980, 1981; Glow & Glow, 1980, 1981; Glow, Glow, & Rump, 1982) have carried out large normative studies of the Conners Teachers Rating Scale (Conners, 1969, 1976) and a revised 96-item version (Glow, 1980) of the Conners Parents Rating Scale (Conners, 1970, 1976). The revised version is hereafter referred to as the Adelaide Parent Rating Scale (APRS).

Studies of teacher–teacher agreement (Glow, 1979), parent–teacher agreement (Glow, 1981), peer–teacher–parent agreement (Glow & Glow, 1981), one-year repeated measure reliability (Glow et al., 1982), and prevalence of hyperactivity (attention deficit disorder with and without hyperactivity; Glow, 1980) have been reported.

This chapter presents data on the estimated prevalence of various child disorders as reported by parents, using the APRS. From a single data pool, both trait and categorical approaches to the determination of child behavior disorders are used as bases for prevalence estimates. The process of translation of data from one form (multidimensional scaled scores) to the other (a unique classification for each subject in the data pool) is the focus of the chapter. To the extent that this provides a model for solving the translation problem, the hiatus between the two approaches to child psychopathology may be reduced.

II. METHOD

Background to the Study

The study was carried out in primary (elementary) schools in Adelaide, South Australia, a city of about 900,000. The majority of primary schoolchildren are taught in government schools. Most of the remainder are in Catholic parochial schools, and a small number are in other private schools. Most children are taught in regular classes, including those with behavior problems and most of those with learning difficulties. Only the 1.5% of children with severe handicaps (such as mental retardation, blindness, or deafness) are taught in special classes or schools which were excluded from these studies. Children with less severe handicaps tend to be allocated to vertically grouped (composite) classes and to be taught basic subjects in smaller remedial groups. Such classes were included in the studies. Grouping is overwhelming on a mixed-ability basis, with high correspondence between age and grade placement. Children may attend school at age 5 and must at age 6. The initial "reception" half-year is integrated with grade 1 in many schools, so although the modal child receives 7½ years of primary schooling, for many purposes the system is more clearly perceived in terms of seven grades.

Construction of the APRS

A stratified random sample of 35 grade cohorts, in as many schools was selected, and a mail survey of the APRS was carried out. A pilot study with patients at the Department of Psychiatry, Adelaide Children's Hospital, had revealed a need to translate a few items of the Conners (1976) scale from American to Australian idiom, to rewrite negative items, to allow parents to respond in terms of frequency–severity rather than just frequency of child behaviors, and to add items concerned with disobedience, unreliability, and excessive thirst. Exact item wordings are given in Table 1. An additional complication of the study was that some of the samples contained high proportions of children with non-English-speaking parents (recent immigrants) and some schools maintain a policy of multilingual communication. Accordingly, translations into Greek, Italian, and Serbo-Croatian, the three most common languages of linguistically alienated parents of Adelaide schoolchildren, were prepared.

Parents were contacted through the school and replied anonymously. Three communications (letter and questionnaire, and two follow-up letters) were sent. The latter could not focus upon nonrespondents because of respondent anonymity. Although the sample was representative (age, sex, year of schooling, and school type), response rates differed greatly from school to school.

When a specific technique (Rosnow & Rosenthal, 1976) for assessing the effect of self-selection bias on the variables of main interest was used, this bias was found to be trivial. Only 1 of 13 behavioral measures showed an effect of respondent speed, indicating that although respondents differed from nonrespondents on some characteristics (English speaking, socioeconomic status), they were unlikely to differ more than marginally in the amounts of behavior disorder reported.

The overall response rate was 70.7% of the enrolled children in the sample, usable data being collected for 1919 children.

For the principal factor analysis, cases with incomplete item data were deleted, leaving 1454 cases. Communalities were iterated and the number of factors extracted was determined by Cattell's (1965) scree criterion at 13, accounting for 42.2% of variance. The Kaiser criterion would have resulted in 26 factors being extracted and is inappropriate when, as in this case, the number of items is large (Comrey, 1973). The factors were rotated with Kaiser normalization.

The item score distributions were very skewed, the modal item having 79% of responses in the zero category. The consequence of the very skewed distribution is mainly that the correlations and thus the factor loadings will be reduced, while there will be a tendency for items with similar degrees of skew to load on similar factors. This is probably desirable when data from a representative population are used to study psychopathology, provided that N is large enough to minimize the effects of any one individual.

Many items had material (≥.30) loadings on several factors, and 24 had only trivial (<.30) loadings. The criterion of ≥.30 was chosen empirically in order to maximize the number of items with one and one only loading. Rotated factor loadings are shown in Table 1.

In scale construction the 55 items with one only loading ≥.30 were allocated to the scales representing the relevant factor. Each item with more than one such loading was added into the scale in which there was the greatest increase in internal consistency (coefficient alpha) if it were included. No item was included in a scale if it reduced alpha.

In the scales with few items, additional items were added to see if the scale would become more stable; however, the result was that only a single item (81)

Table 1. Rotated Factor Solution for A.P.R.S. Items 1–96, N = 1454

						Factor							
	I	*II*	*III*	*IV*	*V*	*VI*	*VII*	*VIII*	*IX*	*X*	*XI*	*XII*	*XIII*
P1 Conduct Problem													
38 Carries a chip on his or her shoulder	42	18	05	18	-01	17	00	10	17	-05	05	16	-09
39 Bullying	60	09	13	11	08	11	18	10	03	01	-01	-02	12
40 Bragging and boasting	45	10	19	02	13	15	03	08	08	03	04	-15	22
41 Cheeky to grown-ups	43	08	21	-06	15	08	04	00	10	11	06	05	12
46 Feels cheated (with brothers and sisters)	49	06	05	24	10	07	07	-04	10	-03	11	09	-18
47 Mean (with brothers and sisters)	59	05	03	13	12	-03	02	04	08	05	06	17	-11
48 Fights constantly (with brothers and sisters)	50	10	09	07	10	01	11	05	07	06	07	15	-12
49 Disturbs other children	53	16	15	00	01	13	08	04	04	-03	03	04	23
50 Wants to run things	55	03	20	-01	-02	00	11	17	04	02	05	-09	05
51 Picks on other children	66	10	11	01	00	15	12	02	03	-01	-02	-03	23
44 Pouts and sulks	44	13	12	02	12	-01	-06	06	07	03	13	01	-22
67 Disobeys school rules	35	25	08	-06	18	34	01	04	-03	-01	-06	-04	30
70 Tells stories which did not happen	33	13	25	15	36	15	-02	00	02	08	09	-01	18
94 Disobeys parents	46	17	23	00	32	11	-03	-01	10	21	01	12	-02
P2 Immature—Inattentive													
30 Does not act his or her age	25	40	10	13	08	06	-05	03	20	-04	13	16	16
54 Fails to finish things he or she starts— short attention span	21	63	31	10	10	07	11	-05	02	08	07	-01	01
62 Difficulty in learning	10	61	03	14	03	08	07	-02	02	04	00	08	15
63 Dislikes going to school	13	31	-05	21	01	02	21	02	11	09	-09	13	20
65 Daydreams (in school)	06	56	12	13	08	01	03	03	06	00	02	-01	-05
79 Inattentive, easily distracted	21	69	27	09	10	05	09	-03	02	12	09	-11	-01
89 Easily bored by a repetitive activity	26	39	36	08	03	06	07	12	06	11	01	07	-10

Item														
92	Poorly aware of surroundings or time of day	20	*34*	19	08	07	19	-07	03	11	02	01	22	-10
96	Forgets to do important tasks, unreliable	*31*	*50*	*15*	*10*	*23*	*13*	*-07*	*-06*	*11*	*09*	*01*	*05*	*-03*
P3	**Hyperactive—Impulsive**													
52	Restless or overactive	24	17	*67*	03	03	09	23	04	06	00	-01	00	03
53	Excitable, impulsive	26	12	*67*	11	04	03	14	02	04	00	06	-01	01
80	Constantly fidgeting	17	*36*	*43*	01	18	11	19	00	07	00	10	-02	-06
82	Always climbing	13	11	*39*	01	22	-05	04	06	02	14	02	10	03
83	A very early riser	09	06	*33*	05	07	03	12	14	01	01	10	03	-06
85	Demands must be met immediately, gets frustrated	*36*	12	*40*	11	08	-08	09	15	07	25	15	20	-03
86	Gets over excited easily	16	12	*61*	14	08	-06	11	07	11	05	17	06	05
90	Acts as if driven by a motor	18	12	*60*	-03	04	13	09	14	07	05	-06	11	00
95	Always thirsty	07	13	*32*	-01	13	11	10	14	17	23	15	05	-05
P4	**Shy—Sensitive**													
8	Afraid of new situations	09	09	03	*54*	06	00	19	08	01	17	12	-01	-06
9	Afraid of people	01	02	02	*58*	05	-04	12	03	-01	21	08	02	06
36	Lets himself or herself get pushed around by other children	-09	24	09	*47*	08	-02	01	06	08	-02	13	00	-08
37	Unhappy	29	15	06	*40*	-01	13	05	03	29	-04	03	12	-01
42	Shy (making friends)	-03	03	-02	*67*	02	-05	04	09	-05	13	02	02	-06
43	Afraid they do not like him or her (making friends)	12	19	11	*61*	02	06	08	13	12	-04	09	00	01
44	Feelings easily hurt (making friends)	21	09	16	*48*	00	01	13	14	08	-02	26	-04	-15
45	Has no friends	20	13	05	*44*	-06	13	01	-01	16	-11	-08	14	09
64	Is afraid to go to school	-01	11	-03	*30*	-01	-03	17	06	06	02	01	15	22
P5	**Self-gratification—Hostility**													
59	Plays with own sex organs	06	09	10	04	*40*	-01	09	03	03	-03	12	04	06
60	Involved in sex play with others	11	00	00	-02	*37*	05	04	04	00	04	07	07	06

(continued)

Table 1. (Continued)

							Factor						
	I	II	III	IV	V	VI	VII	VIII	IX	X	XI	XII	XIII
68 Denies having done wrong	45	19	18	15	46	11	-07	-05	05	05	02	-04	01
69 Blames others for his or her mistakes	51	19	17	17	37	08	-05	03	07	11	06	-03	02
71 Stealing from parents	18	11	09	05	40	32	-02	-06	05	-08	-14	-07	02
87 Laces and zippers are always open	09	21	26	-05	33	06	01	-01	06	05	10	15	-02
P6 Antisocial													
72 Stealing at school	07	11	04	-01	22	60	-04	01	00	03	-03	03	04
73 Stealing from stores and other places	10	09	00	01	04	65	01	-01	-03	-05	01	-05	00
75 Gets into trouble with police	17	03	03	01	-09	74	02	-03	-03	01	-02	02	04
P7 Sleeping Difficulties													
4 Restless (sleep)	13	05	19	12	00	08	49	03	11	06	04	-06	-03
5 Nightmares	04	00	11	11	10	-04	52	01	15	05	00	07	04
6 Awakens at night	05	03	17	10	04	-01	53	-01	18	10	03	03	05
P8 Perfectionist—Compulsive													
76 Everything must be just so	08	-06	11	08	-03	-01	01	74	00	09	07	02	-03
77 Things must be done same way every time	10	00	09	13	09	-04	04	57	01	03	05	04	00
78 Sets goals too high	06	00	11	13	00	-02	05	61	09	-04	-03	06	04

P9 Psychosomatic Problems

21	Headaches	06	09	03	03	-06	07	17	08	37	-01	05	02	-08
22	Stomach aches	06	07	-04	11	00	-01	17	09	48	09	09	06	-03
23	Vomiting	08	01	02	02	01	-03	02	-02	42	06	02	05	00
24	Aches and pains	07	12	00	13	01	-04	22	08	42	02	07	01	-02
25	Loose bowels	02	-01	08	00	09	-01	05	-03	33	05	-04	-04	01

Items 22, 23, 24 bracketed: Complains although doctor can find nothing wrong

P10 Feeding Problems

1	Picky and finicky	12	02	06	14	00	-02	09	05	12	52	02	-03	-03
2	Will not eat enough	05	06	09	12	-06	00	10	05	13	49	02	-01	01

P11 Tearful—Dependent

10	Afraid of being alone	05	02	06	29	11	-01	32	08	04	19	30	03	08
31	Cries easily (childish or immature)	21	06	16	26	12	-03	06	01	16	-02	61	02	-03
32	Wants help doing things he or she should do alone	12	37	12	15	11	-01	11	02	11	22	32	07	22
33	Clings to parents or other adults	06	06	08	37	09	00	18	05	10	17	33	02	23
81	Cannot be left alone	12	12	24	18	14	18	18	05	05	16	26	20	15
88	Cries often and easily	21	10	28	23	11	-04	-03	01	15	01	58	08	-03

P12 Temperamental

55	Temper outbursts, explosive and unpredictable behaviour	49	09	33	06	03	01	08	02	08	11	10	36	-03
56	Throws himself or herself around	25	10	25	11	17	-07	12	02	02	-03	09	42	08
57	Throws and breaks things	24	11	30	09	15	-05	02	08	-03	06	02	44	04
91	Mood changes quickly and drastically	41	13	38	14	01	09	04	08	11	07	08	32	-03

(continued)

Table 1. (Continued)

							Factor						
	I	II	III	IV	V	VI	VII	VIII	IX	X	XI	XII	XIII
P13 "No Load" Items													
3 Overweight	09	05	-01	02	-09	03	05	-01	15	-10	04	00	05
7 Difficulties in falling asleep	08	02	11	15	-07	-02	27	08	12	-02	-04	-03	-12
11 Worries about illness and death	02	04	05	23	07	-02	23	17	16	-01	19	04	10
12 Gets stiff and rigid	09	01	09	09	15	01	18	-01	11	-04	02	10	-09
13 Twitches, jerks, etc.	01	09	09	09	11	03	13	07	00	-08	03	11	-13
14 Shakes	08	-02	07	10	16	20	15	-04	10	-09	08	12	-04
15 Stuttering	01	18	01	01	07	02	07	08	02	-14	09	13	09
16 Hard to understand (speech)	06	28	04	16	05	06	02	03	13	-11	05	15	11
17 Bed wetting	04	02	10	00	10	12	00	02	12	04	09	-03	00
18 Runs to toilet constantly	05	07	15	-05	10	02	05	10	27	08	13	-01	09
19 Soiling self	00	00	11	10	07	-04	-05	-08	22	16	-02	-07	04
20 Holds back bowel movements	06	03	17	10	02	-04	-03	-01	16	16	00	05	02
26 Sucks thumb	01	03	-03	05	09	00	03	01	01	02	09	02	-05
27 Bites or picks nails	06	12	03	05	-03	-02	13	04	01	04	09	-04	-14
28 Chews on clothes, blankets, etc.	04	12	09	05	18	04	20	03	00	-05	18	07	-10
29 Picks at things such as hair, clothing, etc.	09	09	09	03	19	-02	16	07	04	-09	12	07	-14
34 Baby talk	08	10	07	15	10	04	-10	00	20	08	13	07	21
35 Keeps anger to himself or herself	11	15	09	18	08	12	06	11	12	13	-02	05	-10
61 Too modest about his or her body	11	13	11	15	00	09	04	23	03	09	-01	-07	-03
66 Truancy	15	12	-02	00	08	03	-02	00	03	-05	00	02	27
74 Sets fires	11	12	10	00	21	09	02	-02	06	-02	-16	-05	07
84 Will run around between mouthfuls at meals	19	09	23	-01	16	01	02	08	06	29	12	19	-04
93 Still cannot fasten shoelaces	-05	07	08	02	16	02	-02	04	02	21	13	16	09

was added into a scale (P11). The thirteenth factor remained unrepresented by a scale, and 23 items remained unallocated. For these 23 items (with no factor loadings ≥.30), nonzero responses were counted to provide a score on the number of nonsyndromic items, P13. The reason for including this thirteenth measure was originally for completeness. It seemed odd to add scores from very diverse items such as firesetting and thumbsucking, so the number of non-zero items (out of 23) gives a score representing the breadth rather than severity of such difficulties. Subsequently it has been found (Glow & Glow, 1981, Glow et al., 1982) that this score (P13) is quite stable and has other properties that indicate that it may be measuring a variable of some developmental significance. The 12 factorially derived scales (P1–P12) were computed by taking the item scores (0–3, frequency–severity) into account.

Norms for the scales were then computed. Analysis of the effects of missing data showed that cases with incomplete data did not differ from those with complete data on the 13 main measures. (They differed on other aspects, e.g., incomplete records were less often filled in by both parents.) The N's vary slightly from scale to scale, since where scales had 25% or fewer items missing, the scale score was computed by averaging up from the score based on valid items.

Table 2 shows the normative data for boys, girls, and both sexes together.

A hierarchical multiple regression analysis was performed to determine the extent to which scale scores varied with area, school, family, child, and rater variables. The effects of the many variables examined were mostly nonsignificant or small. The greatest impact was of sex, boys being rated as more disordered on 7 of the 13 variables. Interestingly, there was no significant effect of sex on P3 (Hyperactive–Impulsive) despite much higher rates of referral of hyperactive boys. Age had significant impact on 7 of the 13 variables, and family intactness and surrogate variables for socioeconomic status also had significant impact on the majority of the scales. Even when all predictor variables were combined, the cumulative effects were small, never accounting for more than 7.5% of variance. There was no way of unconfounding rater from child variance in this study since, except for a few twin pairs, no rater contributed more than one rating and no child was doubly rated; thus, effects cannot be attributed to true differences in child behavior, but rather to reports of child behavior.

Method of Prevalence Estimation

The Trait Approach

In the area of child behavior disorder there is no external, objective criterion for determining the presence of disorder. The criterion chosen for trait prevalence determination was thus similar to that used in determination of mental retardation by means of an intelligence test. For this study, the criterion for

Table 2. Means and Standard Deviations of Adelaide Parent Rating Scales
P1–P13.

		Children		Boys		Girls	
	Scale	$\bar{X}$	S.D.	$\bar{X}$	S.D.	$\bar{X}$	S.D.
P1	Conduct Problem	3.931	4.384	4.45	4.79	3.46	3.99
P2	Immature—						
	Inattentive	3.844	4.173	4.56	3.74	3.13	3.74
P3	Hyperactive—						
	Impulsive	4.024	4.656	4.62	4.88	3.45	4.39
P4	Shy—sensitive	3.117	3.278	3.08	3.26	3.16	3.29
P5	Self-gratification—						
	Hostility	1.853	2.023	2.23	2.25	1.47	1.69
P6	Antisocial	0.044	0.329	0.07	0.45	0.02	0.16
P7	Sleeping						
	Difficulties	0.703	1.255	0.73	1.30	0.68	1.18
P8	Perfectionist—						
	Compulsive	0.891	1.513	0.88	1.49	0.91	1.55
P9	Psychosomatic						
	Problems	0.880	1.332	0.87	1.27	0.91	1.40
P10	Feeding Problems	0.981	1.300	0.95	1.28	1.01	1.32
P11	Tearful—						
	Dependent	2.395	2.851	2.31	2.73	2.50	2.98
P12	Temperamental	1.128	1.851	1.33	2.01	0.94	1.70
P13	Nonsyndromic						
	Problems	2.634	2.127	2.73	2.19	2.55	1.99
No. of Cases[1]		N = 1897–1916		N = 912–922		N = 893–902	

Note:
[1]N(s) vary because of incomplete data.

significant disorder was set at ≥ 2 SDs, while for severe disorder it was set at ≥ 3 SDs. Clearly this statistical approach ensures that the prevalences of different disorders in the same study will vary only as a function of the degree of departure from normality of the score distributions. It is thus of limited use in comparing disorders within a study. The trait approach is very useful for making comparisons of subject groups within a study (e.g., sex, age) or for comparing different samples.

The Categorical Approach

For the categorical approach, each case had to be assigned to one and only one category, the assumption being made that membership in one category precludes membership in another.

Along with the methodological advantage that each case is assigned to one and one only category comes the disadvantage that the precise order in which competing diagnoses are ruled out will have a profound effect on the distribution of cases. Additionally, the categorical approach makes the assumption that cases assigned to the same category are more like each other than they are like cases in other categories. Multivariate statistical methods such as cluster analysis potentially can be used to define naturally occurring classes of individuals that are indeed like each other. At present no complete empirical categorical system for child behavior disorder exists, and the assumption cannot be made that individuals given the same categorical diagnosis are identical.

The problem of assigning cases to categories is thus one of being informed by both clinical concepts and the underlying relationships in the data.

To explore these relationships, a further factor analysis of the 12 syndromic scales was performed. It should be remembered that although the principal factors extracted were orthogonal the scales were not necessarily so, since for each scale items have weightings only of 1 or 0. Two factors were extracted, corresponding to the dimensions of Conflict with the Environment and Conflict within the Self so often found in broadband studies of child behavior disorders (Achenbach & Edelbrock, 1978).

The factor solution is shown in Figure 1; Table 3 gives the Rotated Factor Loadings of the scales.

A clinician decides among competing child behavior disorder diagnoses by noting which of the competing disorders is predominant in the child's behavior. If none seems predominant, the clinician takes into account the consequences of the disorder. Troublesome behavior that represents a control problem (Antisocial behavior) may be of greater importance in this sense than other difficulties. Similarly, the difficulties in getting along with others manifested as conduct disorders without an antisocial aspect may be seen as of less significance than the child's state of inner turmoil, where both are present. Clearly there are likely to be differences in such judgments among institutions and countries. The above generalization thus probably reflects local practices to some degree.

Transformation of data from a set of 13 variables demands that some comparisons be made among them. The number of possible pairwise comparisons is very large. The first problem is thus to reduce this number of a manageable set. The second problem is to ensure that the comparisons are made in a predetermined order that is clinically meaningful. The third problem is that when comparing the severity of disorders within an individual, one needs a criterion for accepting that one disorder is predominant, since clearly each score on one of the relevant dimensions is subject to measurement error.

The solutions accepted for this study were as follows.

1. *A manageable set of comparisons.* The approach taken was modeled after analysis of variance (ANOVA). If an experiment contains k treatment levels, there are k-1 comparisons that do not utilize overlapping information, that

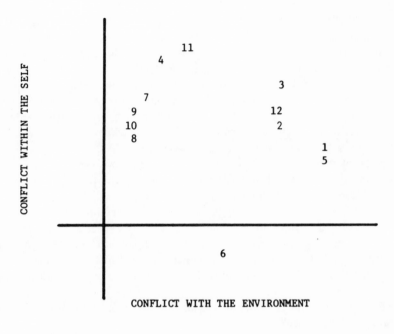

Key:

1 Conduct Problems
2 Immature—Inattentive
3 Hyperactive—Impulsive
4 Shy—Sensitive
5 Self-gratification—Hostility
6 Antisocial

7 Sleeping Difficulties
8 Perfectionist—Compulsive
9 Psychosomatic Symptoms
10 Feeding Problems
11 Tearful—Dependent
12 Temperamental

Figure 1. Results of the Higher Order Factor Analysis of Scales P1–P12.

is, k-1 independent hypotheses to be tested (Kirk, 1968). This corresponds to the degree of freedom among treatments in an ANOVA design. In this case, there are 13 independent variables (P1–P13), and thus up to 12 orthogonal comparisons can be made. The requirement that each comparison utilizes independent information ensures that the set is logically consistent. In practical terms this requirement can be met only if scales contributing to one side of any comparison are equally weighted.

2. *A clinically meaningful, predetermined order.* The order of comparisons decided upon for the 12 syndromic scales P1–P12 had five levels. The most general level of comparison determined for each case whether the child was predominantly Troublesome or predominantly Troubled. Scrutiny of Figure 1 shows that 6 of the 12 scales (P1, P2, P3, P5, P6, and P12) had relatively higher

loadings on the Conflict with the Environment factor, while six (P4, P7, P8, P9, P10, and P11) had greater loadings on the Conflict within the Self factor. At the second level, within the *Troublesome* set of cases, the comparison was made between the Antisocial dimension (P6) and the remainder of the *Troublesome* scales (called here Nondelinquent Troublesome Behavior). Both the factor results (Figure 1) and clinical lore justify the demarcation of antisocial children from those whose behavior problems are not of a delinquent nature.

With respect to the *Troubled* cases, the second level of comparison consisted of comparing those disorders where distress is clearly manifested (Tearful–Withdrawal, P4 and P11) from those where it is hidden or implied, called here Conversion–Displacement (P7, P8, P9, and P10).

At the third level, the Nondelinquent Troublesome cases were further categorized into Conduct disorders (P1 and P5) and Nonconduct overreaction disorders (P2, P3, and P12). This division is justified both by the results of the factor analysis and by the clear conceptual distinction between them. Conduct disorders have a strong interpersonal component, while the remainder have more to do with the child's habitual temperament, movement, and attention patterns.

With respect to Tearful–Withdrawn children, they were divided at this level of comparison into predominantly Tearful–Dependent (P11) or predominantly Shy–Sensitive (P4). Children in the Conversion–Displacement group were divided into those with predominantly Somatic disturbances (P7, P9, and P10) and those with predominantly Perfectionist–Compulsive tendencies (P8).

At the fourth level, Nondelinquent Conduct disordered children were divided into those with predominant disturbance on scale P1 (Conduct Problem) and those with predominant disturbances on scale P5 (Self-gratification–Hostility). Those with Nonconduct Overreactive problems were divided into those with predominant disturbance of Temperament (P12) and those with predominant

Table 3. Rotated Factor Matrix for the Adelaide Parent Rating Scales 1–12

		Factor I	*Factor II*	*Communality*
P1	Conduct Problem	.738	.297	.633
P2	Immature—Inattentive	.588	.390	.498
P3	Hyperactive—Impulsive	.555	.512	.570
P4	Shy—Sensitive	.165	.609	.399
P5	Self-gratification—Hostility	.718	.212	.560
P6	Antisocial	.362	−.061	.135
P7	Sleeping Difficulties	.133	.480	.248
P8	Perfectionist—Compulsive	.081	.310	.103
P9	Psychosomatic Problems	.082	.421	.184
P10	Feeding Problems	.054	.376	.144
P11	Tearful—Dependent	.296	.666	.532
P12	Temperamental	.567	.415	.494

Hyperactive–Inattentive disorders (P2 and P3). This decision was guided by the clinical concept of attention deficit disorder with and without hyperactivity, rather than the results of the factor analysis, the clinical entity being well established.

At the fourth level, children with predominant Somatic disturbances (P7, P9, and P10) were divided into those with Sleeping and Feeding disturbances (P7 and P10), called here Vegetative disturbance, and those with predominant Psychosomatic problems (P9).

At the fifth level, Hyperactive–Inattentive children were divided into predominantly Hyperactive–Impulsive (P3) or predominantly Immature–Inattentive (P2), and children with Vegetative disturbances were divided into those with predominant Feeding problems (P10) or Sleeping difficulties (P7).

As a subsequent step, for all cases not yet assigned, a comparison was made between the number of nonsyndromic problems (P13) and the combined syndromic disorders P1–P12.

The decision tree is shown in Figure 2.

3. *The criterion for predominance of one disorder over another.* To allow comparison among scales and combinations of scales, they had to be measured in the same units. Scales P1–P13 were standardized using the child norms in Table 2. No account was taken of sex. To allow comparisons of combinations of scales, scores from constituent scales were added (equally weighted) and the resulting compound scales were restandardized, again using empirical data. The means for these compound scales already were zero. The standard deviations were generally greater than would be expected if one added standardized, inde-

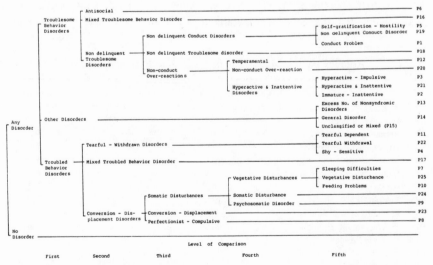

Figure 2. Decision Tree for Categorical Diagnosis of Predominant Disorder.

pendent, normal variates, since the scores were neither independent nor normal, most being very skewed.

Table 4 shows the computation rules for the compound scales.

The criterion for predominant disturbance was set at ≥1 SD in order to reduce the effect of slight variations in severity. While this reduces the effects of slight differences on the outcome for a particular comparison, it also results in many inconclusive comparisons, where two scales are within one standard deviation of each other.

It could be argued that in such a case—for example, if a case was high on both P15 (Troublesome) and P16 (Troubled) and not significantly higher (≥1 SD) on either—it should remain unassigned at that decision node, and be diagnosed as mixed disorder.

This would have the effect of increasing the number of cases given a mixed-disorders diagnosis. Instead, the decision was made to include such cases in all subsequent tests. This decision to include "unassigned ancestors" in later comparisons of the decision tree has profound effects on the outcome. The first and major effect is that cases will be assigned to much finer categories than would otherwise be the case. The second is that there will be a tendency for the diagnoses to reflect what could be called "local contrast effects." As an example, a case with similar, high scores on P16 and P17 (Troubled and Troublesome) might have generally high and even scores on the former (P4, P7 to P11) but much more variable scores on the latter, say, very high on P2 (Immature–Inattentive) and borderline high on P1, P3, P5, P6, and P12. Such a case would tend to be diagnosed Immature–Inattentive (P2) rather than Mixed disorder (P15). This decision was made in order to reflect clinical diagnostic thinking,

Table 4. Computation Rules for Compound Scales

Name of Compound Scale[1]	(No)	Contributing Basic Scales[2]
P14 General disorder	(13)	Scales P1–P13
P15 Mixed behavior disorder	(12)	Scales P1–P12
P16 Troublesome behavior	(6)	Scales P1–P3, P5, P6, P12
P17 Troubled behavior	(6)	Scales P4, P7–P11
P18 Nondelinquent Troublesome behavior	(5)	Scales P1–P3, P5, P12
P19 Nondelinquent Conduct disorder	(2)	Scales P1 and P5
P20 Nonconduct Over-reactive disorder	(3)	Scales P2, P3 and P12
P21 Hyperactive Inattention disorder	(2)	Scales P2 and P3
P22 Tearful withdrawal	(2)	Scales P4 and P11
P23 Conversion-Displacement	(4)	Scales P7–P10
P24 Somatic Disturbance	(3)	Scales P7, P9 and P10
P25 Vegetative disturbance	(2)	Scales P7 and P10

Notes:
[1] Restandardized
[2] Contributing scales were standardized and equally weighted

since a case with some predominant, relatively specific characteristic tends to be categorized accordingly, although the background of other problems can be recognized. The present system was designed to reflect a single diagnostic entity, and the aim was toward relative specificity, since finer categorizations can easily be collapsed into broader categories.

Diagnoses were made at two levels of severity. In order to determine significant disorder, the criterion was set at ≥ 2 SDs; to determine severe disorder it was set at ≥ 3 SDs. Otherwise the procedures remained the same for the two levels of severity.

Before the round of tests described above, cases with one and only one of the basic scales (P1–P13) above the severity criterion were given the appropriate diagnosis, as were cases with no disorder. At the end of the round of tests, some cases remained unassigned. Of these, some had no compound scale (P14–P25) above the severity criterion. These were given the diagnosis "unclassified" and scrutinized individually.

Those with only one compound score P15–P25 above the severity criterion were given the diagnosis corresponding to the uniquely disordered compound scale. Of those remaining, those with P14 above the criterion were diagnosed General disturbance. Those remaining undiagnosed and with more than one compound scale above the severity criterion were then tested to find a justifiable compound-disorder diagnosis, starting from the broadest categories and ending with finer ones. The order of the tests clearly has an effect on the outcome. It was a follows: Mixed disorder (P15), Troubled disorders (P17), Troublesome disorders (P16), Conversion–Displacement (P23), Tearful–Withdrawal (P22), Nondelinquent Troublesome disorders (P18), Somatic symptoms (P24), Nonconduct Over reaction (P20), Nondelinquent Conduct disorder (P19), Vegetative disturbance (P25), and Hyperactive–Inattentive disorder (P21). While this order is to

Table 5.   Brief Description of Unclassified Cases

Case 1. Significant problems of Self-gratification—hostility (P5) and Perfectionist—Compulsive (P8). Borderline on three other scales.

2. Severe problems of Temperament (P12) and Hyperactivity (P3) combined with superior Attention—Maturity (P2). Also high on P13 Nonsyndromic Problems and borderline on three other scales.

3. Severe antisocial problems (P6), significant Self-gratification—hostility (P5). Three other borderline problems.

4. Significant problems of Feeding (P10), Perfectionist-Compulsive (P8) and Tearful—dependent (P11). Borderline on seven other scales.

5. Significant problems of Self-gratification—hostility (P5) and Shy—sensitive (P4). Borderline on three other scales.

6. Significant problems of Temperament (P12), Immature—Inattentive (P2), Shy-sensitive (P4) and Feeding Problems (P10). Borderline on two other scales.

---

some degree arbitrary, it follows the rule that more general disorders are considered before more specific ones, and that Troubled disorders are considered before Troublesome ones (with the exception of Antisocial disorder which was eliminated from consideration in an earlier step).

The efficiency of this system was high. Only 6 cases of the 1831 with a complete set of scores on P1 to P13 remained undiagnosed with respect to significant disorder, while no case remained undiagnosed with respect to severe disorder.

Scale data (P1–P13) for the six undiagnosed cases were scrutinized to see whether any particular or meaningful patterns of behavior disturbance emerged. Each case is briefly summarized in Table 5. No recognizable pattern of child behavior disorder can be discerned in the set.

III. RESULTS

Prevalence Estimation

The prevalence of each of the 13 basic disorders is shown in Tables 6 and 7 for significant and severe disorder, respectively, using a trait approach. The ratio of

Table 6. Percent Prevalence of Basic Parent Perceived Child Disorders: Significant Disorder Using a Trait Approach

	Disorder	Boys %	Girls %	Children %	Ratio[1] Boys : Girls
P1	Conduct Problem	6.8	3.3	4.9	2.1 : 1***
P2	Immature—Inattentive	6.4	3.4	4.9	1.9 : 1**
P3	Hyperactive—Impulsive	6.8	4.5	5.5	1.6 : 1*
P4	Shy—Sensitive	5.2	5.3	5.4	1.9 : 1
P5	Self-gratification—Hostility	7.7	2.8	5.3	2.8 : 1***
P6	Antisocial	4.0	1.8	2.8	2.2 : 1**
P7	Sleeping Difficulties	4.0	3.7	4.0	1.1 : 1
P8	Perfectionist—Compulsive	7.8	6.9	7.3	1.1 : 1
P9	Psychosomatic Problems	3.9	5.7	4.7	0.7 : 1
P10	Feeding Problems	5.8	6.8	6.4	0.9 : 1
P11	Tearful—Dependent	4.2	5.3	4.8	0.8 : 1
P12	Temperamental	7.2	4.6	5.7	1.6 : 1*
P13	Excess number of non-syndromic behavior problems	6.2	4.9	6.9	1.3 : 1
	N	912–922	893–902	1897–1916	

Notes:
[1]Ratios are based on percentages because of differing Ns.
  *p < .05
 **p < .01
***p < .001
(χ^2 test for proportions).

Table 7. Percent Prevalence of Basic Parent Perceived Child Disorders:
Severe Disorder Using a Trait Approach

	Disorder	Boys %	Girls %	Children %	Ratio[1] Boys : Girls
P1	Conduct Problem	2.3	1.1	1.6	2.1 : 1
P2	Immature—Inattentive	1.9	1.3	1.6	1.5 : 1
P3	Hyperactive—Impulsive	3.1	1.9	2.4	1.6 : 1
P4	Shy—Sensitive	1.7	1.7	1.7	1.0 : 1
P5	Self-gratification—Hostility	2.8	0.8	1.8	3.5 : 1**
P6	Antisocial	0.4	0.2	0.3	2.0 : 1
P7	Sleeping Difficulties	2.5	1.2	2.1	2.1 : 1
P8	Perfectionist—Compulsive	1.8	2.5	2.1	0.7 : 1
P9	Psychosomatic Problems	1.6	3.0	2.3	0.5 : 1
P10	Feeding Problems	1.8	2.0	1.1	0.9 : 1
P11	Tearful—Dependent	1.3	3.1	2.2	0.4 : 1**
P12	Temperamental	3.6	2.0	2.7	1.8 : 1*
P13	Excess number of non-syndromic behavior problems	1.0	0.6	0.7	1.7 : 1
	N	912–922	893–902	1897–1916	

Notes:
[1]Ratios are based on percentages because of differing Ns.
  *p < .05
 **p < .01
***p < .001
(χ^2 test for proportions).

boys to girls is also shown. To reduce the complexity of the tables, values of χ^2 are not shown. Of course the χ^2 were computed from frequencies, although the ratios of boys to girls were computed from proportions because of differing N's.

Overall the percentage of children found to be significantly disordered ranged from 2.8% for Antisocial disorder to 7.3% for Perfectionist–Compulsive disorder. Since the same statistical criterion was used, this reflects the differences in distribution of scale scores. For severe disorder, the percentages of children detected were, of course, lower, ranging from .3% of children with severe Antisocial disorder to 2.4% of children found to be severely Hyperactive–Impulsive.

In several cases, boys were significantly more disordered than girls, as one would expect from clinical studies. Only in the case of severe Tearful–Dependent behavior were girls significantly more disordered than boys.

When the compound disorders, defined by the scales P14 to P25 (see Table 4) were considered, about 5% of the children were detected for each kind of significant disorder and about 2% of the children for severe disorders (see Tables 8 and 9). The preponderance of boys over girls was present, but not always statistically significant. No compound disorder was found to have a significantly greater percentage of girls than boys classified as disordered using the trait approach.

Many children were given multiple-trait diagnoses. Thus of those 31.6% of children categorized as having a basic disorder using the trait approach, the average child must have received just over two positive trait diagnoses, since the percentage of diagnosed cases summed to 68.6%.

Tables 10 and 11 show the diagnostic classification and percentage categorical prevalence of the various parent-perceived child disorders found in this study, for significant and severe disorder, respectively.

It can be seen (Table 10) that 31.6% of children were significantly disordered, with a larger proportion (18.7%) belonging to the Troubled disorders group than to the Troublesome disorders group (11.7%). Only a small proportion (1.2%) were in the remaining category. Of the children, 14.1% were found to be severely behavior disordered. Once again, more Troubled than Troublesome severely disordered children were found. There appears to be a weak tendency for boys to be reported as more Troublesome and girls as more Troubled.

Table 8. Percent Prevalence of Some Complex Parent Perceived Child Disorders: Significant Disorder Using a Trait Approach.

Disorder	Boys %	Girls %	Children %	Ratio[1] Boys : Girls
P14 General disorder	6.6	4.2	5.3	1.6 : 1*
P15 Mixed disorder	6.3	3.9	5.0	1.6 : 1*
P16 Mixed Troublesome behavior disorders	6.8	3.8	5.2	1.8 : 1**
P17 Mixed Troubled behavior disorders	4.5	4.2	4.4	1.1 : 1
P18 Nondelinquent Troublesome disorder	6.7	4.1	5.3	1.6 : 1*
P19 Nondelinquent Conduct disorder	6.7	3.1	4.8	2.2 : 1***
P20 Nonconduct Overreaction	6.3	4.0	5.1	1.6 : 1*
P21 Hyperactive-Inattention disorder	7.5	4.3	5.8	1.7 : 1**
P22 Tearful-Withdrawal	4.0	4.7	4.4	0.9 : 1
P23 Conversion-Displacement	4.5	4.5	4.5	1.0 : 1
P24 Somatic Disturbance	5.0	4.6	4.8	1.0 : 1
P25 Vegetative Disturbance	5.3	5.1	5.3	1.0 : 1
N	878–920	867–901	1830–1914	

Notes:
[1]Ratios are based on percentages because of differing Ns.
  *p < .05
  **p < .01
  ***p < .001
(χ^2 test for proportions).

Table 9.   Percent Prevalence of Some Complex Parent Perceived Child
Disorders: Severe Disorder Using a Trait Approach.

	Disorder	Boys %	Girls %	Children %	Ratio[1] Boys : Girls
P14	General disorder	1.8	1.6	1.6	1.1 : 1
P15	Mixed disorder	2.1	1.5	1.1	1.4 : 1
P16	Mixed Troublesome behavior disorders	2.5	1.6	2.0	1.6 : 1
P17	Mixed Troubled behavior disorder	2.0	1.8	1.9	1.1 : 1
P18	Nondelinquent Troublesome disorder	2.8	1.5	2.0	1.9 : 1
P19	Nondelinquent Conduct disorder	2.9	1.2	2.0	2.4 : 1*
P20	Nonconduct Overreaction	2.5	2.0	2.2	1.3 : 1
P21	Hyperactive-Inattention disorder	2.0	1.8	1.9	1.1 : 1
P22	Tearful-Withdrawal	1.3	2.2	1.7	0.6 : 1
P23	Conversion-Displacement	2.5	1.4	1.9	1.8 : 1
P24	Somatic Disturbance	2.2	1.6	1.9	1.4 : 1
P25	Vegetative Disturbance	2.2	1.2	1.8	1.8 : 1
	N	878–920	867–901	1830–1914	

Notes:
[1]Ratios are based on percentages because of differing Ns.
   *p < .05
(χ^2 test for proportions).

A problem with comparisons of prevalence of rare disorders is that very large numbers are required to demonstrate significant differences in proportions. Thus while it would not come as a surprise to find significantly more boys than girls classified as having predominantly Hyperactive or Inattentive disorders, only the combination of categories P2, P3, and P21 had a significant preponderance of boys. For each of the constituent categories the preponderance of boys was not significant.

The Effects of Age on Prevalence

The effect of age on parent ratings was assessed for both linear effects (using r) and curvilinear effects (ANOVA with eight age levels). There was no significant curvilinear effect of age for any of the 13 variables, but there were significant linear effects for several variables, with simple r and ANOVA giving slightly different results. For P1 (Conduct problem), P2 (Immature-Inattentive), and P9 (Psychosomatic problems), older children were rated as significantly more disordered by either method. For P3, P5, P7, P8, P11, and P13, younger children were rated as more disordered.

Despite the absence of curvilinear components in the age effects, the means

Table 10. Percent Prevalence of Predominant Parent Perceived Child Disorder: Significant Disorder Using a Categorical Approach and Various Degrees of Fineness of Classification

	Boys N = 876	Girls N = 867	Children N = 1831
First Level			
Troublesome disorders	16.2***	7.7	11.7
Troubled disorders	15.9	21.5**	18.7
Other disorders	1.8*	0.6	1.2
No disorder	66.1	70.2	68.4
(Any disorder)	(34.0)	(29.8)	(31.6)
Second Level			
6. Antisocial	3.1**	1.0	2.0
Nondelinquent Troublesome disorders	12.6***	6.6	9.4
16. Mixed Troublesome disorder	0.6	0.1	0.3
Tearful Withdrawn disorders	4.1	6.0	5.1
17. Mixed Troubled disorder	0.1	0.0	0.1
Conversion and Displacement disorders	11.7	15.4*	13.5
Other disorders	1.8*	0.6	1.2
No disorder	66.1	70.2	68.4
Third Level			
6. Antisocial	3.1**	1.0	2.0
Nondelinquent Conduct disorders	6.4***	2.7	4.5
Non-Conduct Over-reaction disorders	6.1**	3.7	4.8
18. Nondelinquent Troublesome disorder	0.1	0.2	0.2
16. Mixed Troublesome disorder	0.6	0.1	0.3
11. Tearful-Dependent	0.9	2.2*	1.5
22. Tearful Withdrawal	1.4	2.0	1.8
4. Shy-Sensitive	1.8	1.9	1.9
17. Mixed Troubled disorder	0.1	0.0	0.1
Somatic disturbances	7.9	10.0	8.9
8. Perfectionist-Compulsive	3.4	4.8	4.2
23. Conversion-Displacement	0.4	0.6	0.4
Other disorders	1.8*	0.6	1.2
No disorder	66.1	70.2	68.4
Fourth Level			
6. Antisocial	3.1**	1.0	2.0
1. Conduct Problem	2.1	1.5	1.7
19. Non-delinquent conduct disorder	1.7*	0.6	1.1
5. Self-gratification—Hostility	2.6***	0.6	1.8
12. Temperamental	1.3	0.9	1.0
Hyperactive-Inattention disorders	4.2*	2.3	3.2
20. Non-Conduct Over-reaction disorder	0.6	0.5	0.6
18. Nondelinquent troublesome disorder	0.1	0.2	0.2
16. Mixed Troublesome disorder	0.6	0.1	0.3
11. Tearful-Dependent	0.9	2.2*	1.5
4. Shy-Sensitive	1.8	1.9	1.9

(*continued*)

Table 10. (Continued)

		Boys N = 876	Girls N = 867	Children N = 1831
22.	Tearful Withdrawal	1.4	2.0	1.8
	Vegetative disturbances	5.1	7.6	5.8
9.	Psychosomatic Problems	2.1	3.1	2.6
24.	Somatic Disturbance	0.7	0.5	0.6
17.	Mixed Troubled Disorder	0.1	0.0	0.1
8.	Perfectionist-Compulsive	3.4	4.8	4.2
23.	Conversion-displacement	0.4	0.6	0.4
	Other disorders	1.8*	0.6	1.2
	No disorder	66.1	70.2	68.4

Fifth Level: Finest Categorisation

		Boys	Girls	Children
1.	Conduct Problem	2.1	1.5	1.7
2.	Immature-Inattentive	1.1	0.4	0.8
3.	Hyperactive-Impulsive	1.4	1.2	1.2
4.	Shy-Sensitive	1.8	1.9	1.9
5.	Self-gratification-Hostility	2.6***	0.6	1.8
6.	Antisocial	3.1**	1.0	2.0
7.	Sleeping difficulties	1.5	1.3	1.4
8.	Perfectionist Compulsive	3.4	4.8	4.2
9.	Psychosomatic Problems	2.1	3.1	2.6
10.	Feeding Problems	2.5	3.1	2.8
11.	Tearful-Dependent	0.9	2.1*	1.5
12.	Temperamental	1.2	0.9	1.0
13.	Excess No. of Non-syndromic Problems	1.3	0.5	0.8
14.	General disorder	0.0	0.0	0.0
15.	Mixed disorder	0.0	0.0	0.0
16.	Mixed Troublesome disorder	0.6	0.1	0.3
17.	Mixed Troubled disorder	0.1	0.0	0.1
18.	Nondelinquent troublesome disorder	0.1	0.2	0.2
19.	Nondelinquent Conduct disorder	1.7*	0.6	1.1
20.	Non-Conduct Over-reaction disorder	0.6	0.5	0.6
21.	Hyperactive Inattention disorder	1.7	0.8	1.2
22.	Tearful Withdrawal	1.4	2.0	1.8
23.	Conversion-Displacement	0.4	0.6	0.4
24.	Somatic disturbance	0.7	0.5	0.6
25.	Vegetative disturbance	1.1	2.1	1.6
	Unclassified	0.6	0.1	0.3
	No disorder	66.1	70.2	68.4

Notes: Disorders without prefix numbers refer to combined categories.

*, **, *** Sex with higher prevalence

   *p < .05

  **p < .01

***p < .001

(χ^2 test for proportions).

Table 11. Percent Prevalence of Parent Perceived Child Disorder: Severe Disorder Using a Categorical Approach and Various Degrees of Fineness of Classification

	Boys N = 876	Girls N = 867	Children N = 1831
First Level			
Troublesome disorders	7.2**	3.1	5.1
Troubled disorders	7.8	9.6	8.7
Other disorders	0.3	0.1	0.3
No disorder	85.2	87.2	85.9
(Any disorder)	(14.8)	(12.8)	(13.5)
Second Level			
6. Antisocial	0.7	0.1	0.4
Nondelinquent Troublesome disorders	6.1**	2.9	4.4
16. Mixed Troublesome disorder	0.5	0.1	0.3
Tearful Withdrawn disorders	1.8	3.7*	2.7
17. Mixed Troubled disorder	0.0	0.0	0.0
Conversion and Displacement disorders	5.9	5.9	6.0
Other disorders	0.3	0.1	0.3
No disorders	85.2	87.2	85.9
Third Level			
6. Antisocial	0.7	0.1	0.4
Nondelinquent Conduct disorders	2.5*	1.0	1.8
Non-Conduct Over-reaction disorders	3.4*	1.8	2.6
18. Nondelinquent Troublesome disorder	0.1	0.0	0.1
16. Mixed Troublesome disorder	0.5	0.1	0.3
11. Tearful-Dependent	0.5	1.6*	1.0
22. Tearful Withdrawal	0.7	1.0	0.9
4. Shy-Sensitive	0.7	1.0	0.9
17. Mixed Troubled disorder	0.0	0.0	0.0
Somatic disturbances	4.0	4.0	4.1
8. Perfectionist-Compulsive	1.6	1.6	1.6
23. Conversion-Displacement	0.3	0.2	0.3
Other disorders	0.3	0.1	0.3
No disorder	85.2	87.2	85.9
Fourth Level			
6. Antisocial	0.7	0.1	0.4
1. Conduct problem	1.0	0.5	0.7
19. Nondelinquent Conduct disorder	0.8	0.3	0.6
5. Self-gratification—Hostility	0.7	0.2	0.5
12. Temperamental	0.9	0.5	0.7
Hyperactive Inattention disorders	2.1	1.0	1.5
20. Non-Conduct Over-reaction disorder	0.5	0.3	0.4
18. Nondelinquent Troublesome disorder	0.1	0.0	0.1
16. Mixed Troublesome disorder	0.5	0.1	0.3
11. Tearful-Dependent	0.5	1.6*	1.0
4. Shy-Sensitive	0.7	1.0	0.9

(*continued*)

Table 11. (Continued)

	Boys N = 876	Girls N = 867	Children N = 1831
Fourth Level (continued)			
22. Tearful Withdrawal	0.7	1.0	0.9
Vegetative disturbances	3.0	2.1	2.6
9. Psychosomatic Problems	0.9	1.7	1.3
24. Somatic Disturbances	0.1	0.2	0.2
17. Mixed Troubled Disorder	0.0	0.0	0.0
8. Perfectionist-Compulsive	1.6	1.6	1.6
23. Conversion-Displacement	0.3	0.2	0.3
Other disorders	0.3	0.1	0.3
No disorders	85.2	87.2	85.9
Fifth Level			
1. Conduct Problem	1.0	0.5	0.7
2. Immature-Inattentive	1.0	0.7	0.9
3. Hyperactive-Impulsive	0.7	0.1	0.4
4. Shy-Sensitive	0.7	1.0	0.9
5. Self-gratification—Hostility	0.7	0.2	0.5
6. Antisocial	0.7	0.1	0.4
7. Sleeping difficulties	1.4	0.8	1.1
8. Perfectionist-Compulsive	1.6	1.6	1.6
9. Psychosomatic Problems	0.9	1.7	1.3
10. Feeding Problems	1.1	0.9	1.0
11. Tearful-Dependent	0.5	1.6*	1.0
12. Temperamental	0.9	0.5	0.7
13. Excess No. of Non-syndromic Problems	0.3	0.1	0.3
14. General disorder	0.0	0.0	0.0
15. Mixed disorder	0.0	0.0	0.0
16. Mixed Troublesome disorder	0.5	0.1	0.3
17. Mixed Troubled disorder	0.0	0.0	0.0
18. Nondelinquent Troublesome disorder	0.1	0.0	0.1
19. Nondelinquent Conduct disorder	0.8	0.3	0.6
20. Non-Conduct Over-reaction disorder	0.5	0.2	0.4
21. Hyperactive Inattention disorder	0.3	0.2	0.3
22. Tearful-Withdrawal	0.7	1.0	0.9
23. Conversion-Displacement	0.3	0.2	0.3
24. Somatic disturbance	0.1	0.2	0.2
25. Vegetative disturbance	0.5	0.3	0.5
Unclassified	0.0	0.0	0.0
No disorder	85.2	87.2	85.9

Notes: Disorders without prefix numbers refer to combined categories.
*, **; Sex with higher prevalence
 *p < .05
 **p < .01
(χ^2 test for proportions).

were plotted by age for each scale to see whether any discontinuities in means were discernible.

For some scales there appeared to be such a break at about 8 years.

The decision was thus made to divide children into younger and older and to re-examine the effects of age on prevalence.

It is interesting to note that the apparent break in the score distribution coincides with the cultural division between junior primary or infant schools in which relatively informal methods of education are used and the regular primary school where there is a more formal approach. Piaget (Inhelder & Piaget, 1958) places the transition from intuitive to concrete operational thought at the same age (7–8 years). Erikson (1964) referes to the "age of play" and the "age of industry" with the same age groups in mind. In this connection, it is notable that when year of schooling rather than age was used as a predictor variable, for 7 of the 13 scales the effect of immaturity was greater, all of these being scales where younger children showed higher rates of disorder. For 3 scales the opposite trend was found, with age showing greater impact than grade, and these were scales where older children were more disordered. These effects were never large but are consistently in the interpretable direction, since the least mature children are most likely to be held back in the infant grades despite the generally close relationship between age and grade in Adelaide schools.

For analysis of the effects of age on prevalence, children 8 years and above were considered older, while those up to and including $7^{11}/_{12}$ were considered younger.

Tables 12 and 13 show the trait prevalence by age for significant and severe basic disorders, respectively.

It can be seen that significantly more younger than older children were given trait diagnoses of Hyperactive–Impulsive, Self-gratification–Hostility, Perfectionist–Compulsive, Tearful–Dependent, Temperamental, and Excess Number of Nonsyndromic problems. In no case was there a significant tendency for more older than younger children to be given a trait diagnosis.

Comparison of Prevalence with Other Studies

The overall rates of significant parent-perceived child behavior disorders did not differ significantly from those previously found for teacher-perceived disorder (Glow, 1980, 1981; $\chi^2 = 3.10$, ns). For severe disorders, more disordered children were perceived by parents than teachers ($\chi^2 = 18.42$, df $= 1$, p $< .001$).

When the rates of overall child disturbance are compared with those found in other studies, the profound influence of study methodology on prevalence estimates must be kept in mind, and different findings should not be held to demonstrate true differences in the populations studied.

In 1942, Rogers estimated 33% of primary schoolchildren to be maladjusted,

Table 12.   Percent Prevalence of Basic Perceived Child Disorders:
Significant Disorder Using a Trait Approach,
Younger and Older Children Compared

Disorder		Younger %	Older %	All children %	Ratio[1] Younger : Older
P1	Conduct problem	4.3	5.5	4.9	1.5 : 1
P2	Immature—Inattentive	3.7	5.7	4.9	0.65 : 1
P3	Hyperactive—Impulsive	7.8	4.0	5.5	2.0 : 1***
P4	Shy-Sensitive	5.0	5.7	5.4	0.8 : 1
P5	Self-gratification—Hostility	6.6	4.0	5.3	1.7 : 1*
P6	Antisocial	2.5	3.6	2.8	0.8 : 1
P7	Sleeping difficulties	4.7	3.4	4.0	1.4 : 1
P8	Perfectionist—Compulsive	8.9	6.2	7.3	1.4 : 1*
P9	Psychosomatic problems	4.1	5.0	4.7	0.8 : 1
P10	Feeding problems	7.4	5.6	6.4	1.3 : 1
P11	Tearful dependent	6.2	3.7	4.8	1.7 : 1*
P12	Temperamental	7.0	4.7	5.7	1.5 : 1*
P13	Excess number of non-syndromic behavior problems	6.7	4.6	6.9	1.5 : 1*
N of cases		764–775	1027–1035	1897–1916	

Notes:
[1]Ratios are based on percentages because of differing Ns.
  *p < .05
***p < .001
(χ^2 test for proportions, df = 1)

including 12% severely maladjusted. This estimate was based on a weighted index including teacher ratings and school performance. Following Rogers's method, Mangus (1949) found 19% of children to be maladjusted but did not specify the degree of maladjustment. Ullman (1952) found 8% of ninth-grade children to be seriously maladjusted, using teacher ratings. The children would have been older than those in the present study.

Of the more recent studies, those of particular interest are the Isle of Wight study (Rutter, Tizard, & Whitmore, 1970) and the various studies using the Bristol Social Adjustment Guides described in Stott (1978).

In the Isle of Wight study, the whole cohort of 10- and 11-year-olds on that island were studied, first by means of teacher and parent questionnaires used as screening instruments. Face-to-face follow-up of parent nonrespondents ensured a high rate of participation, while school data were virtually complete. To check the validity of the screening instrument, various subsamples were selected for detailed study, including standardized psychiatric examination of the child, interview with the parent(s), interview with the teacher, and physical, educational, and psychological examination using standardized techniques. Children selected by a previously established cutoff criterion on the parent and teacher scales were subjected to the psychiatric examination and interview procedures.

When teacher ratings *or* parent ratings *or* psychiatric examination were used, about 6.7% of children were found to be psychiatrically disordered.

Although the three methods yielded similar estimates, they did not select the same children: About 44% of children selected by either the teacher or the parent screen were diagnosed, and one-fifth of the overall estimate were judged to have been missed by the double-screen procedure.

In a second study, using the teacher screens but a different psychiatric examination, the interview with the child was deleted since it had yielded little information additional to the interview with the parent in the previous study. Rutter, Cox, Tupling, Berger, and Yule (1975) found higher rates of psychiatric disorder on the Isle of Wight (12% of 10-year-olds). The same (second) method resulted in an estimate of 25.4% of 10-year-olds psychiatrically disturbed in an inner London borough which had high rates of social disadvantage. The second Isle of Wight estimate is not different from the estimate of parent-perceived severe disorder in the present study, although it is lower than the inner London borough

Table 13. Percent Prevalence of Basic Parent Perceived Child Disorders: Severe Disorder Using a Trait Approach: Younger and Older Children Compared

	Disorder	Younger %	Older %	All children %	Ratio[1] Younger : Older
P1	Conduct problem	1.2	1.1	1.6	2.1 : 1
P2	Immature—Inattentive	0.5	2.4	1.6	0.2 : 1
P3	Hyperactive—Impulsive	3.4	1.8	2.4	1.9 : 1*
P4	Shy-Sensitive	1.3	2.1	1.7	0.6 : 1
P5	Self-gratification—Hostility	2.3	1.5	1.8	1.5 : 1
P6	Antisocial	0.6	0.6	0.3	1.0 : 1
P7	Sleeping difficulties	2.2	1.7	2.1	1.3 : 1
P8	Perfectionist—Compulsive	3.2	1.3	2.1	2.5 : 1**
P9	Psychosomatic problems	1.9	2.4	2.3	0.8 : 1
P10	Feeding problems	2.2	1.6	1.1	1.4 : 1
P11	Tearful dependent	2.7	1.7	2.2	1.6 : 1
P12	Temperamental	3.5	2.2	2.7	1.6 : 1
P13	Excess number of non-syndromic behavior problems	0.9	0.6	0.7	1.5 : 1
N of cases		764–775	1027–1035	1897–1916	

Notes:
[1]Ratios are based on percentages because of differing Ns.
  *p < .05
 **p < .01
(χ^2 test for proportions, df = 1)

estimate. The latter is different from all of the Adelaide estimates. (All differences alluded to are significant by χ^2 tests for proportion, df = 1, p < .05.)

Using the Bristol Social Adjustment Guides, Stott, Marston, and Neill (1975) found 21.4% of a random sample of Liverpool children (7–8 years) to be unsettled and a further 11.3% to be maladjusted. No significance test could be used because the size of the sample was not stated, but these figures are similar to those found in Adelaide for significant and severe disorder, whether parent or teacher ratings are considered.

In a further study of 2491 children in the same age range as in the present study (5–14 years with relatively few 14-year-olds), Stott et al. (1975) found 26.8% of children to be unsettled and 9.5% to be maladjusted on the basis of teacher reports on the Bristol Social Adjustment Guides. The proportion at the more severe level was not significantly different from the present study, but the proportion of "unsettled" children detected in Stott and associates' (1975) Ontario study exceeded the proportion of significantly but not severely disordered children found in the present study (χ^2 = 348.20, p < .001, df = 1). Comparative overall prevalence rates for these studies are tabulated in Table 14.

All differences, apart from those bracketed, are significant (χ^2 tests for proportion). Thus the two Adelaide estimates (parent, teacher) of significant disorder were not different from each other, but they were significantly higher than Stott and associates' (1975) Ontario estimate of unsettled behavior, which was not significantly different from Rutter and co-workers' 1975 London estimate based on psychiatric examination but was higher than the London estimate based on teacher ratings.

It is clear that all of the estimates of unsettled or significant disorder were higher than those of psychiatric or severe disorder or maladjustment (except for the single case of London children judged by psychiatrists versus the Ontario estimate of unsettled children). There was no case of an estimate of prevalence of disorder of severe or "psychiatric" dimension in one study being higher than an estimate of a lower degree of severity in another study.

Additionally it can be seen that there may be a tendency for rates of disorder as judged by parents or psychiatrists (who rely greatly on parent report) to be somewhat higher than those made by teachers, expecially with respect to more severe disorders.

The closeness of the two Adelaide studies, which used the same statistical criteria for defining disorder (two and three standard deviations above the scale means) but had different data sources (teachers and parents) and different scales (7 in the case of the teacher instrument, 13 in the parent one, is remarkable and suggests the overwhelming importance of the severity criterion in determining overall prevalence rates. One might expect more children to be detected as disordered on the parent scale than on the teacher instrument since it has a greater bandwidth, detecting psychosomatic, vegetative, and habit disorders not covered in the teacher raing scale, but this was found only for severe disorder.

Table 14. Comparison of Prevalence of Child Behavior Disorder
in Various Studies

Study, place and data source	Criterion	N	Rate %	
Rutter et al., 1970				
Isle of Wight psychiatrist	psychiatric disorder	2199	6.8	
Glow				
Adelaide teacher	severe disorder	2475	9.3	
Stott et al., 1975				
Ontario teacher	maladjusted	2491	9.5	N.S.
Rutter et al., 1975	psychiatric disorder			
Isle of Wight teacher		1279	10.6	N.C.
Isle of Wight psychiatrist		1279	12.0	
Glow				
Adelaide parent	severe disorder	1831	13.5	
Rutter et al., 1975	psychiatric disorder			
London psychiatrist		1689	19.1	N.C.
London teacher		1689	25.4	
Stott et al., 1975				N.S.
Ontario teacher	unsettled	2491	26.3	
Glow	significant disorder			
Adelaide teacher		2475	29.2	N.S.
Adelaide parent		1831	31.6	

Notes:
N.S. = not significant
N.C. = not comparable (overlapping data)
All other differences are significant.

When particular disorders are compared with each other, the approach to diagnosis (trait or categorical) has a large impact on the prevalence rates, additional to the effects of severity criteria mentioned above.

In the parent study, the categorical approach resulted in more children being diagnosed in the Troubled (18.7%) than in the Troublesome (11.7%) major category, with very few children (1.2%) in the mixed or other residual grouping. Although the same tendency was present when the trait approach was used, it was not so marked, probably due to a greater overlap among diagnoses in the Troublesome than in the Troubled group. This tendency was also found in the teacher rating scale study (Glow, 1979, 1980), where 9.1% of children were found to have predominantly Troubled disorders. In the case of the teacher data, the algorithm used produced a larger group (6.2%) of mixed-disorder children.

Stott's Social Adjustment Guides have tended to produce the opposite effect, with a slight preponderance of children found maladjusted on the "Overact"

(Troublesome) than the "Underact" (Troubled) groupings, this trend being substantially due to differences among boys.

In the studies by Rutter and his colleagues (1970, 1975), about equal proportions of Neurotic and Conduct Disordered children (roughly corresponding to the Troubled and Troublesome groups here) were found, but Mixed Disorders formed a considerable proportion of the children given a diagnosis, and study of the characteristics of these Mixed-Disorder children suggested more similarity with the Conduct Disorder than with the Neurotic group. Rutter and Graham (1970) proceeded to combine these two groups for some subsequent analyses because of their similarity.

The present study appears to be relatively more sensitive to the Troubled child than to his Troublesome peers, unlike the Canadian (Stott et al., 1975), and British (Rutter et al., 1970, 1975) studies.

The Prevalence of Attention Deficit Disorders

Of particular interest are the estimates of Attention Deficit Disorder (ADD) in the various studies. For the present data, the best trait estimate is made by considering P21 (equally weighted P2 and P3), while the categorical approach could be approximated by adding together children classified as P2 (Immature–Inattentive), P3 (Hyperactive–Impulsive), and P21 (Hyperactive–Inattentive).

The various estimates are shown in Table 15. It can be seen first that in most estimates the proportion of ADD boys was significantly higher than the proportion of ADD girls. That boys are more often found to be Hyperactive–Inattentive comes as no surprise, since both clinical and research findings detect higher male than female rates.

When the trait approach is used, there is no difference between the overall ADD prevalence rates in the teacher and parent studies.

When the estimates using the categorical approach are compared (see Table 15), it can be seen that higher rates of predominantly ADD children were found in the parent than in the teacher study.

This no doubt arises from the fact that in the categorical approach to the teacher data (Glow, 1979, 1980), children with other disorders were excluded, while in the parent study the categorical diagnosis relied upon the notion of predominant, not exclusive, presence of ADD. When a second categorical, parent diagnostic classification was made, in which children above the 2-SD criterion on P2 (Immature–Inattentive), P3 (Hyperactive–Impulsive), or P21 (Hyperactive-Inattentive) were considered specifically ADD only if no other parent scale score was two standard deviations above the mean, the rate of disorder detected was lower, and not significantly different from the teacher-based exclusive estimates. More severely ADD children were detected by the exclusive, parent criterion than by the categorical (exclusive) teacher one.

The study by Rutter et al. (1970) on the prevalence of child psychiatric disorder on the Isle of Wight provides one point of comparison for the prevalence of ADD. In this study, Rutter et al. used a categorical, exclusive approach to diagnosis. The criterion for hyperkinetic reaction was "poorly organised and poorly regulated extreme overactivity, distractibility, short attention span and impulsiveness. . . . [It] was not secondary to any other psychiatric syndrome." The corrected prevalence was .11% for 10–11-year-old children.

A second relevant study is that of Miller, Palkes, and Stewart (1973), who had teachers select children who were overactive and distractible. The teachers were then interviewed about the selected children with respect to 26 other behavioral and achievement descriptors. Children were regarded as Hyperactive (ADD) if they were considered overactive and distractible and if 5 other of the 26 descriptors were also present. The study was of primary schoolchildren (approximately 5–12 years old). Miller et al. found 5.53% of the 847 attenders of a suburban St. Louis school sample to be ADD. Their approach exemplifies a trait one, using an *a priori* cutoff criterion which does not include "extreme" or "severe" in it.

Stott and associates' (1975) Ontario study used teacher ratings on the Bristol Social Adjustment Guides, a trait approach, and a nonsevere, empirically determined cutoff point. They found 9.35% of primary schoolchildren to be "Inconsequent". Using the same method but the stronger criterion of maladjusted, Davie, Butler, and Goldstein (1972) found 6.1% of British 7-year-olds to be above the maladjustment criterion on the Inconsequence Scale.

The relevance of the Inconsequence Scale to the clinical concept of ADD has not, as far as is known, been addressed directly, but the items appear to be very close to the behavioral descriptors used as criteria for the clinical syndrome.

In a more recent study, using a case-finding approach, Lambert, Sandoval, and Sassone (1978) located somewhat different groups of hyperative (ADD) children in the large (N = 5212) Californian school (kindergarten through grade 5) population studied, according to whether the hyperactive (ADD) children located were nominated by school personnel, parents (in response to a mail survey requesting participation in a study), or by physicians and clinics in the area. The case-finding approach has many limitations in the epidemiology of psychiatric disorders because of problems of referral, disclosure, and participation. The proportion of children detected as attending a physician and either recognized as or treated for ADD was 1.37%, within the range of estimates of severe disorder in the present study, significantly below the St. Louis estimate (Miller et al., 1973), and above the Isle of Wight estimate (Rutter et al., 1970). Lambert et al. applied a criterion which excluded medical conditions such as epilepsy but did not exclude other behavior problems such as conduct disorders. The criteria applied by the physicians before nominating the children are unknown. In these respects the study used a clinical, trait approach, but its results would have been affected by many extraneous factors such as local patterns of use of medical services, respondent self-selection, and individual physicians'

Table 15. Prevalence of Parent & Teacher Perceived Attention Deficit Disorder in Adelaide

	Parent[1]					Teacher					Comment
	Significant			Severe		Significant			Severe		
	N	n	%	n	%	N	n	%	n	%	
Approach											
TRAIT											
Boys	914	69	(7.5)	18	(2.0)	1281	118	(9.2)	34	(2.7)	Parent and Teacher
Girls	897	39	(4.3)	16	(1.8)	1191	32	(2.7)	7	(0.6)	estimates do not differ
Children	1904	110	(5.8)	36	(1.9)	2475	150	(6.1)	41	(1.7)	significantly.
Sex Diff.											
Boys > Girls		***		N.S.			***		***		
CATEGORICAL											

Predominant Disorder (following diagnostic algorithm in Fig. 2) Categories P21, P2 and P3 combined.

Boys	876	43	(4.9)	22	(2.5)					Significantly more ADD children than for Teacher exclusive categorical estimates
Girls	867	24	(2.8)	12	(1.4)					
Children	1831	70	(3.8)	35	(1.9)					
Sex Diff.		**		N.S.						
Boys > Girls										
Exclusive Disorder (all other disorders excluded)										
Boys	876	15	(1.7)	13	(1.5)	1281	29	(2.3)	8	(0.6)
Girls	867	4	(0.5)	5	(0.6)	1191	7	(0.6)	0	(0.0)
Children	1831	20	(1.1)	19	(1.0)	2475	36	(1.5)	8	(0.3)
Sex Diff.		**		**			***		***		Parent estimate of severe disorder is greater than corresponding Teacher estimate p < .01. Significant disorder N.S.
Boys > Girls		**					***				

Notes:
[1]The numbers for boys and girls in the parent study do not sum to the number of children because of missing data on sex.
**p < .01
***p < .001

209

perceptions of the nature of child psychiatric disorder. No control condition or procedure for assessment of the validity of the case nomination technique was used.

School personnel nominated more than twice as many ADD children as did physicians or parents. Since the number of children surveyed by the teachers was not stated, no statistical comparison can be made, but the estimate (4.78%) approached that of the St. Louis study (5.53%; Miller et al., 1973). Lambert et al. also had the teachers rate all of the children on a longer version of the Conners Abbreviated Symptom Questionnaire (Conners, 1976) and applied a criterion designed to classify those children previously detected consensually by all three case finders (physicians, parents, and school personnel). The cutoff score defined "about 10%" of their school population as hyperactive (ADD) but aparently missed two-thirds of the children previously located by one or two of the three case finders.

When taken together (Table 15 and 16), the results of these studies show that: (a) Different approaches to diagnosis result in vastly different prevalence rates, with trait approaches always yielding higher estimates than categorical approaches and the most exclusive categorical approaches yielding the lowest rates. (b) The severity criteria used have a profound effect on estimates made—inclusion of a requirement of "extreme" or "severe" disorder reduces the estimated prevalence. (c) Different observers tend to select similar proportions of children as disordered although the particular individuals selected are not the same, the degree of overlap being little different from chance when the methods are truly independent.

Attempts to draw conclusions about differential prevalence of child psychiatric disorders in different English-speaking countries by relying upon studies with different methodologies appear to be fatuous because of the influence of these

Table 16.   Some Estimates of the Prevalence of Attention Deficit Disorder

	N		%
Rutter et al., 1970	2199	'Hyperkinetic reaction'	0.11%[1]
Miller et al., 1975	849	'Hyperkinetic Impulse Disorder'	5.53%
Davie et al., 1972	—	'Inconsequent' (maladjusted)	6.1%
Stott et al., 1975	2491	'Inconsequent' (moderately adjusted)	9.35%
Lambert et al., 1978	5212	'Hyperactivity'	
		attenders of physicians,	1.37%
		nominated by school personnel	4.78%
		above cut-off on teacher ratings	"about 10%"

Note:
[1]Corrected for children judged on the basis of a validity check, to have been missed by the screening procedure.

methodological factors. When method is varied in a given study (the use of two cutoff criteria and two or three approaches to diagnosis) apparent cross-cultural differences are revealed as most likely due to such methodological factors. When like is compared with like [the Adelaide, significant trait estimates with Miller et al. (1973), and the Adelaide, severe, categorical, exclusive estimates with Rutter et al. (1970)], no significant differences are detected.

In a subsequent study in a single school using both teacher and parent ratings (Glow, 1981; Glow & Glow, 1980; Glow et al., 1982) the number of cases was not large enough for any sensible prevalence estimate to be made. However, when a very broad definition of ADD was used (Glow, 1981; above two standard deviations on any one of Teacher Scale T2 *or* P2 *or* P3), 40 Hyperactive–Inattentive children were selected. This was 15.6% of the sample. When children with other disorders were deleted, this fell to 23 (9%) of children significantly ADD, i.e., Hyperactive–Inattentive. When the stronger criterion of hyperactive inattentive behavior at school and at home was used, above two standard deviations on *both* T2 and either P2 or P3 only 3 cases (1%) were detected. None of these children were specifically or predominantly ADD, suggesting that pervasive problems of overactivity and inattention may often be accompanied by other behavior problems.

IV. DISCUSSION

Sex Effects on Prevalence

In the estimates of child behavior disorder in Adelaide, more boys than girls were found to be disordered both overall and in many specific categories. For parent-perceived Tearful–Dependent behavior disorder, both significant and severe, the proportion of girls detected rose above the proportion of boys, as it did for significant (but not severe) Troubled, and Conversion–Displacement disorders. sion–Displacement disorders.

The finding of more disorder in boys than girls is general, whether attendance at child guidance clinics or results of prevalence studies are considered. Most studies show a preponderance of behavior-disordered boys, at least until adolescence. For example, Stott (1978) found a preponderance of boys in four of the five categories defined by the Bristol Social Adjustment scales, whether in Canada (Stott et al., 1975) or in Britain (Davie et al., 1972). Only for Unforthcomingness in Ontario were significantly more girls than boys detected as Maladjusted. Similarily, Rutter's studies (Rutter et al., 1970, 1975) have found more disordered boys than girls both overall and in most categories. More neurotic girls than boys were found in the Isle of Wight (in the earlier 1970) study, but these findings were not replicated in the later study (Rutter et al., 1975), where more boys than girls were detected in all categories examined.

Among adults, women seek help for mental disorders with greater frequency than men, who have, however, much higher rates of psychopathic deviation detected by legal processes. Until there is clear evidence on this matter it is not safe to assume that there is a genuine shift in female mental health at adolescence. Rather, the index of suspicion that apparently higher rates of behavior disorder in boys than girls reflects methodological problems should remain high. It is likely, for example, that parents attend psychiatric facilities more readily when Troublesome behaviors are more salient. When Troubled behaviors are systematically studied, as in the APRS, there may be more likelihood of detecting behavior problems among girls. The development of standardized techniques for interviewing prepubertal children as to the extent of their troubled feelings and symptoms may resolve this question in the future.

Troubled vs. Troublesome Disorders

The present study, using parent data, found relatively more children with disorders broadly considered as indicating conflict within the self (Troubled) than with the environment (Troublesome). This differs from Stott's (1978) and Rutter's (1970) findings, where approximately similar prevalence of the two major types were found.

One reason for this is undoubtedly the wide scope of the items in the parent rating scale. The items cover a range of data not accessible to teacher studies. While it is true that Rutter and co-workers' (1970) study included a parent questionnaire covering some of these items and, in addition, the interview with parent and child should have allowed any neurotic disorders present to be detected, the clinical criteria used in the study were strict, and many problems judged by their clinicians as not severe enough to warrant clinical diagnosis may have been detectable if less stringent criteria were used. In the Adelaide parent study, the classification of parent-perceived behavior disorders, combined with the finding that sensitivity (APRS item 44) and crying (APRS item 31) were among those most frequently endorsed as being of most concern to the parent (Glow, 1979), suggest that the APRS detects a reservoir of parents' concern about their children's inner conflicts that is not tapped by some other approaches to detecting child behavior disorders.

Age and Prevalence

Overall the effects of age on prevalence were not striking, more younger than older children being found for 6 of the 13 trait diagnoses. Only in the case of P2 (Immature–Inattentive) and P3 (Hyperactive–Impulsive) were the data of theoretical interest, being compatible with the view that the same difficulty (ADD) is expressed at younger and older ages in different behaviors, Hyperactivity in younger children and Attention disorders in older children. A cross-sectional study such as the present one cannot provide strong evidence for such a thesis, which requires longitudinal study, although a longitudinal study over a single year (Glow et al., 1982) did not support such a thesis. Stott et al. (1975) have found some evidence of changing expression of Inconsequence, with items such as "Twists about in his seat" showing a falling incidence with age, and items such as "Never gets down to any solid work" showing a rising incidence with age. This would be compatible with transformation of hyperactivity into attention problems during development. In their analysis of the Fels Longitudinal Research Study data, Kagan and Moss (1962) discuss several examples of such genotypic continuity with phenotypic discontinuity. Weiss, Minde, Werry, Douglas, and Nemeth (1971) reported a similar finding, in that hyperactive patients were found, 5 years later, to have diminished hyperactivity but prominent attention disorders.

The findings of the present study are consistent with this view of the changing expression of an ADD trait with age and suggest that longitudinal study, over the period from early elementary school to adolescence, could resolve this intriguing hypothesis.

V. CONCLUSIONS

The results of the prevalence estimation procedures show that realistic prevalence estimates can be made on the basis of the APRS. The part that the approach to diagnosis (trait, categorical) and the severity criteria play in both clinical diagnosis and epidemiological studies is highlighted.

The similarities of the prevalence estimates from various studies suggest the following generalization: Different data sources will yield broadly similar prevalence rates, as long as diagnostic decision processes and severity criteria are similar.

The apparently greater prevalence of ADD in the United States than in Britain can thus be assumed for the present to result from the different views of the syndrome. In the United States the broader definition applies, with the consequence that more children are detected.

In both the clinical and research literature on child psychopathology, the assumptions underlying the choice of subject selection techniques are often unrecognized. Studies of treatment, for example, assume the similarity of groups of individuals given the same treatment, whereas studies of the correlates of a disorder fit more readily into a multivariate framework, compatible with a trait view of behavior disorder.

Exploration of a possible approach to the translation of multivariate information into discrete categories of behavior disorder suggests that this can yield interpretable results, at least when applied to the problem of prevalence estimation.

Whether this interpretability will be maintained when clinical diagnosis and APRS categorization are compared is presently being studied. It has been demonstrated that the overlap between different data sources (parents, teachers, child peers, and the children themselves) is highly dependent on the extent of the similarities in the context in which the behavior occurs (Glow & Glow, 1980), suggesting that most of the common child behavior disorders behave like middle-level traits with some, rather than complete, context generality. This is expected to place limits on the amount of overlap when different data sources (clinician, parent) are used, even though it appears that clinicians rely heavily upon parent report when making child diagnoses.

The question of whether broadband or narroband syndromes are likely to prove most useful has not been resolved in the area of child psychopathology. At present, several degrees of fineness of categorization seem appropriate for different purposes, and only the broadest division, into Troublesome and Troubled (or Conduct and Neurotic, etc.) is practically universally recognized.

Since the clinical concept of ADD appears to be well established, it seems likely that at least some degree of finer categorization than the two broadest will come to dominate the field. The diagnostic algorithm presented in this chapter allows for various degrees of fineness of categorization to be used, depending upon the issue to be addressed.

Agreement about subject selection and diagnostic issues should promote the cumulativeness of findings in the area of child behavior disorder. At present there is disagreement, but its extent and nature are rarely examined, and it consists largely of differing methodological assumptions about the nature (trait vs. syndrome, exclusive vs. nonexclusive, significant vs. severely incapacitating) of disorder. In this study, differing methodological assumptions were systematically applied to the same data, and the apparently huge differences in the results of previous prevalence studies were rendered meaningful.

The extent to which these kinds of methodological assumptions can be articulated will necessarily impact on the rate at which the field of systematic child psychopathology progresses.

REFERENCES

Achenbach, T. M., & Edelbrock, C. S. The classification of child psychopathology: A review and analysis of empirical efforts. *Psychological Bulletin*, 1978, *85*, 1275–1301.
American Psychiatric Association. *Diagnostic and statistical manual of mental disorders* (3rd ed.). Washington D.C.: American Psychiatric Association, 1980.
Barkley, B. A. Predicting the response of hyperkinetic children to stimulant drugs: A review. *Journal of Abnormal Child Psychology*. 1976, *4*, 327–348.
Cattell, R. B. *Factor analysis*. New York: Harper, 1965.
Comrey, A. L. *A first course in factor analysis*. New York: Academic Press, 1973.
Conners, C. K. A teacher rating scale for use in drug studies with children. *American Journal of Psychiatry*, 1969, *126*, 152–156.
Conners, C. K. Symptom patterns in hyperkinetic, neurotic and normal children. *Child Development*, 1970, *41*, 667–682.
Conners, C. K. Independent pediatric scales. In W. Guy (Ed.), *ECDEU* (Early Clinical Drug

Evaluation Unit) *Assessment Manual for Psychopharmacology, 1976.* U.S. Department of Health, Education and Welfare, N.I.M.H., 5600 Fisher Lane, Rockville, Maryland.

Davie, R., Butler, N. R., & Goldstein, N. *From birth to seven: Second report of the national child development study.* London: Longman and the National Children's Bureau, 1972.

Erikson, E. H. *Childhood and society.* New York: W. W. Norton & Co., 1964.

Glow, P. H., & Glow, R. A. Hyperkinetic impulse disorder: A developmental defect of motivation. *Genetic Psychology Monographs,* 1979, *100,* 159–231.

Glow, R. A. *The measurement of teacher and parent perceived hyperkinetic impulse disorder.* Doctoral dissertation, The University of Adelaide, 1979.

Glow, R. A. A validation of Conners TQ and a cross-cultural comparison of prevalence of hyperactivity in children in. In G. D. Burrows and J. S. Werry (Eds.), *Advances in human psychopharmacology,* Vol. 1. Greenwich, Conn.: JAI Press, 1980, pp. 303–320.

Glow, R. A. Cross-validity and normative data on the Conners' Parent and Teacher Rating Scales. In K. D. Gadow & J. Loney (Eds.), *The psychological aspects of drug treatment for hyperactivity.* Boulder, Colo.: A.A.A.S. and Westview Press, 1981, pp. 107–150.

Glow, R. A., & Glow, P. H. Peer and self rating: Children's perception of behavior relevant to hyperkinetic impulse disorder. *Journal of Abnormal child Psychology,* 1980, *8*(4), 471–490.

Glow, R. A., & Glow, P. H. *Non syndromic behaviour problems in children.* Geigy Psychiatric Symposium on Behavioural Medicine, Vol. 9, 143–153, Melbourne, 1981.

Glow, R. A., Glow, P. H., & Rump, E. E. The stability of child behavior disorders: A one year test-retest study of Adelaide versions of Conners Teachers and Parent Rating Scales. *Journal of Abnormal Child Psychology,* 1982, *10,* 33–60.

Inhelder, B., & Piaget, J. *The growth of logical thinking from childhood to adolescence* (Translated by A. Parsons and S. Milgram). New York: Basic Books, 1958.

Kagan, J., & Moss, J. A. *Birth to maturity.* New York: Wiley, 1962.

Lambert, N. M., Sandoval, J., & Sassone, D. Prevalence of hyperactivity in elementary school-children as a function of social system deficiencies. *American Journal of Orthopsychiatry,* 1978, *48,* 446–463.

Kirk, R. E. *Experimental design: Procedures for the behavioral sciences.* Wadsworth: Brook/Cole, 1968.

Mangus, A. R. *Mental health of rural children in Ohio.* OHIO: Research Bulletin No. 682, Wooster Agricultural Research Station. 1949.

Miller, R. G., Palkes, H. S., & Stewart, M. A. Hyperactive children in suburban elementary schools. *Child Psychiatry and Human Development,* 1973, *4,* 121–127.

Rogers, C. R. Mental health findings in three elementary schools. *Educational Research Bulletin,* 1942, *21,* 69–79. (Ohio State University Research Bureau.)

Rosnow, R. L., & Rosenthal, R. The volunteer subject revisited. *Australian Journal of Psychology,* 1976, *28,* 97–108.

Rutter, M., Cox, A., Tupling, C., Berger, M., & Yule, W. Attainment and adjustment in two geographical areas. 1 - The prevalence of psychiatric disorder. *British Journal of Psychiatry,* 1975, *126,* 493–509.

Rutter, M., & Graham, P. Epidemiology of psychiatric disorder. In Rutter, M., Tizard, J., & Whitmore, K. (Eds.), *Education, health and behaviour.* London, Longman, 1970.

Rutter, M., Tizard, J., & Whitmore, K. (Eds.). *Education health and behaviour.* London, Longman, 1970.

Sroufe, L. A. Drug treatment of children with behavior problems. In *Review of Child Development Research, 4.* Chicago: University of Chicago Press, 1975, pp. 347–407.

Stott, D. H. Epidemiological indicators of the origins of behavior disturbance as measured by the British Social Adjustment Guides. *Genetic Psychology Monographs,* 1978, *97,* 127–159.

Stott, D. H., Marston, N. K., & Neill, S. J. *Taxonomy of behaviour disturbance.* London: Hodder and Stoughton, 1975.

Ullman, C. A. *Identification of maladjusted school children.* Public Health Monographs No. 7, U.S. Federal Security Agency, Public Health Service, Washington D.C., 1952.

Weiss, G., Minde, K., Werry, J. S., Douglas, V. I., & Nemeth, E. Studies on the hyperactive child: A five-year follow-up. *Archives of General Psychiatry,* 1971, *24,* 409–414.

MEASURING THE NATURAL HISTORY OF DELINQUENCY AND CRIME

David P. Farrington

ABSTRACT

The Cambridge Study in Delinquent Development is a prospective longitudinal survey of a sample of 411 males, who are predominantly white, urban, working class, and of British origin. Data collection began in 1961/2, when most of the boys were 8 years old, and ended in 1980. The boys were interviewed and tested at intervals of 2–3 years from age 8 to 24, their parents were interviewed every year from when the boy was 8 until when he was 14–15, and their teachers filled in questionnaires about them every 2 years from when the boy was 8 until he was 14. In addition, conviction records were obtained for the boys from age 10 to 25, for their parents, and for their siblings.

This chapter shows how self-reported and official delinquency vary with age. For most offenses, both peaked within a year or two of the seventeenth birthday. Self-reports suggest that many more offenses were committed than appear in official records, but the two methods were in reasonable agreement in identifying the proportion of the sample who committed offenses.

There was some continuity of troublesome, delinquent, deviant, and criminal

Advances in the Behavioral Measurement of Children, Volume 1, pages 217–263.
Copyright © 1984 by JAI Press Inc.
All rights of reproduction in any form reserved.
ISBN: 0-89232-282-9

behavior from childhood to adulthood. The best predictors of convictions and self-reported delinquency at any age were convictions and self-reported delinquency at an earlier age. The best predictor of convictions at the earliest age (10–13) was troublesome behavior at 8–10, as rated by peers and teachers. Apart from behavioral measures, other independent predictors of troublesome, delinquent, and criminal behavior were as follows: (a) economic deprivation, as seen in low family income, poor housing, and low social class; (b) family criminality, as seen in convicted parents and delinquent siblings; (c) parental mishandling, as seen in poor supervision and parental child-rearing behavior; and (d) school failure, as seen in low vocabulary, low IQ, and truancy.

This chapter discusses lessons which can be learned from this research about method, measurement, and analysis. The advantages of the prospective longitudinal method are outlined, as are the advantages of multiple measures, using records, interviews, ratings, tests and questionnaires, physical indices, and observed behavior. The difficulties of analyzing a large, complex longitudinal dataset including primarily categorical variables are discussed. This research aimed to have one empirical variable measuring each theoretical construct, and it used partial correlations and loglinear/logit analytic methods to establish which variables were independent predictors of the measures of crime and delinquency.

I. INTRODUCTION

This chapter is concerned with investigating the natural history of delinquency and crime, or the incidence and prevalence of delinquent and criminal behavior at different ages. It is also concerned with measuring factors which influence the course of development of this behavior. Key issues of definition, measurement, design, analysis, and theory arise in this investigation.

II. SOME PROBLEMS OF CRIMINOLOGICAL RESEARCH

Definition

Many different acts are prohibited by the criminal law in different countries and at different times. Delinquency and crime are heterogeneous concepts, covering behavior as apparently diverse as theft, vandalism, violence against the person, drug use, and various kinds of heterosexual and homosexual indecency. There is usually an important distinction between more and less serious offenses. For example, minor motoring offenses are not usually included in the category of delinquency. Acts prohibited at the present time may not have been prohibited 20 years ago, and vice versa. For example, homosexual behavior between consenting adult males in private was legalized in England by the Sexual Offenses Act 1967. Similarly, acts prohibited in England may not be prohibited in certain parts of North America, and vice versa.

A particular problem arises over the term "delinquency." In North America, delinquency has been a very wide-ranging term traditionally, including not only acts such as theft which are also prohibited for adults but also "status offenses" such as drinking alcohol and violating curfew. In England, the juvenile court has had both civil and criminal jurisdiction since its inception, and the term delinquency usually refers only to acts such as theft which are dealt with under its criminal jurisdiction. Behavior dealt with under its civil jurisdiction, such as truancy and being beyond parental control, is not usually considered delinquent. The recent moves in North America to eliminate status offenses from the category of delinquency (e.g., National Council on Crime and Delinquency, 1975) may result in more comparability between Great Britain and North America in this category.

In spite of the heterogeneity, instability, and relativity of the concepts of crime and delinquency, most research has been designed to investigate these concepts rather than more specific ones (such as theft). In practice, most socially disapproved acts tend to be associated, in the sense that people who commit one kind of deviant act relatively frequently also tend to commit others relatively frequently. For example, West and Farrington (1977) reported that there was little evidence of specialization in offending, since most youths convicted of aggressive crimes, damaging property, or drug use had also been convicted of dishonesty. Similarly, convicted youths tended to drink more, to gamble more, to commit more motoring offenses, to have had sexual intercourse with more girls, and to have more unstable job records.

The extent to which different kinds of behavior are associated is an important empirical question which will be discussed later. It may be that some kinds of delinquent behavior are more closely associated with some kinds of nondelinquent behavior than with other kinds of delinquent behavior. For example, taking and driving away vehicles may be more closely associated with taking risks and seeking excitement in nondelinquent activities than with receiving stolen property. When youths were asked why they committed different kinds of delinquent acts, they usually ascribed taking vehicles to seeking excitement or enjoyment, and ascribed receiving stolen property to rational or economic motives (West & Farrington, 1977). Nevertheless, it seems reasonable to argue that "there exists a single syndrome made up of a broad variety of antisocial behaviors arising in childhood and continuing into adulthood" (Robins & Ratcliff, 1980, p. 248), and to propose theories to explain the development of a single underlying theoretical variable termed "delinquency" or "criminality."

The above discussion emphasizes legal definitions, which usually rely on the concept of intent. For example, the major law defining theft in England (the Theft Act 1968) states that a person is guilty of theft if he or she dishonestly appropriates property belonging to another person with the intention of permanently depriving the other person of it. One problem with this kind of definition is to establish intent. The legal procedures and rules governing this often seem unsatisfactory to the social scientist, who knows that there may be considerable discrepancy between words and deeds (e.g., see Deutscher, 1973) and that people may not have much insight into the mental events underlying their behavior (Nisbett & Wilson, 1977).

Another problem with legal definitions is that the boundary between what is legal and what is illegal may be poorly defined and variable. There is often continuity between legal and illegal behavior, as when school bullying gradually escalates into criminal violence. Conversely, legal categories are so wide that they may include acts which are behaviorally quite different. For example, "robberies" may range from armed bank robberies carried out by gangs of masked men to thefts of small amounts of money perpetrated by one schoolchild on another.

From the viewpoint of social science research, it might be better to move toward behavioral definitions of crime and delinquency, and associated observational measures. However, little of this kind of research has yet been carried out (for a recent example, see Graham, 1981; several studies are reviewed in Farrington, 1979a). The work described in this chapter is primarily based on legal definitions of crime and delinquency.

Measurement

In conformity with the widespread use of legal definitions, the major method of measuring crime and delinquency is to use official records collected by the police and other criminal justice agencies. These records have many well-known defects (e.g., see Farrington, 1979b). For example, acts appearing in official records form a biased and underrepresentative sample of all delinquent or criminal acts committed, records are kept for the benefit of agency personnel rather than researchers, and they are often kept inefficiently and unsystematically. There are many reasons why delinquent acts fail to appear in an official record, such as failure to define the act as delinquent, failure to report the act to the police, failure to record the act by the police, and failure to apprehend any offender. The major problem is that official records of crime reflect the behavior both of offenders and of official agencies, and it is difficult to disentangle these.

The most important alternative methods of measuring crime involve self-report and victim surveys, in which respondents are asked to say if they have committed specified acts, or if they have been the victims of specified acts, within a specified period. Victim surveys are of only limited use in providing information about offenders, partly because some crimes have no identifiable victim (e.g., drug use) and partly because victims usually do not know the identity of offenders. However, where there is some contact between the victim and the offender, as with personal crimes such as rape and robbery, some information about offenders can be derived from victim surveys.

Hindelang (1981) analyzed information collected in the U.S. National Crime Survey, in which more than 130,000 people in 65,000 households were interviewed in a given 6-month period. Victims of crimes were asked to report the sex, race, and age group of the offender, if possible. Hindelang used this information to estimate rates of offending for different groups in the population. For example, for all personal crimes (rape, robbery, assault, and theft from the person), he calculated that there were 85 crimes per year committed by every 100 black males aged 18–20. These crimes peaked at age 18–20, and the rates were higher for blacks and males than for whites and females, respectively. One problem with this method is that it is impossible to estimate the number of offenders who were involved in the estimated number of offenses.

The use of victim reports of offenders is a very recent development. The most popular method of obtaining information about offenders in the last 20 years has been by means of self-report surveys. Indeed, it would be no exaggeration to say that, especially in the United States, the major theoretical and empirical advances in juvenile delinquency in this period have all used this method. Self-reports of offending have rarely been obtained from adults, although Tittle (1980) interviewed random samples of adults in the United States, primarily to investigate deterrence.

The key question arising in self-reported delinquency surveys is validity. To what extent are people able and willing to give accurate reports of their delinquent behavior, and to what extent are they prone to exaggerate, conceal, or forget? The major method of establishing validity has been to compare self-reports with official records (e.g., see Farrington, 1973; Hindelang, Hirschi, & Weis, 1981). Generally, juveniles who have been arrested or convicted have a high likelihood of admitting the offenses involved. For example, West and Farrington (1977) found that only 6% of convicted youths denied being convicted, and only 2% of unconvicted youths claimed to have been convicted. Furthermore, among unconvicted youths, large numbers of admitted offenses predicted future convictions. All these results suggest that self-reports of delinquency are reasonably valid, and that official records and self-reports can be viewed as alternative measures of an underlying theoretical delinquency variable, no doubt subject to different biases.

In England, according to official records, juvenile delinquency has increased dramatically in the last 20 years or so. However, this increase may reflect changes in official processing rather than in juvenile misbehavior. During this period, there has been an increasing tendency for the police to "divert" juveniles from the court by issuing official cautions. According to Farrington and Bennett (1981), this has led to an increased willingness to arrest juveniles and, consequently, to an increased likelihood of juveniles appearing in official records. Whether there has been any change in juvenile delinquent behavior is unknown.

This issue could be resolved more easily if changes in official records of juvenile offending could have been compared with changes in self-reports of offending. In the United States, Gold and Reimer (1975) interviewed national samples of juveniles in 1967 and 1972. During this period, the number of juveniles arrested in the United States increased by 30% for males and by 74% for females (Giallombardo, 1980). However, in the national surveys, self-reported delinquency of males fell by 11%, and that of females increased by only 19% over the same period. These figures suggest that the increase in recorded juvenile crime might have been caused largely by the increased likelihood of a juvenile offender being arrested.

To conclude, it is desirable to measure crime and delinquency using both official records and self-reports. This chapter provides information about offending at different ages derived from both sources.

Design

Most research on crime and delinquency is essentially correlational in design. For example, consider the study by Johnson (1979). This was an attempt to investigate the relationship between juvenile delinquency and a number of theoretically derived factors, such as attachment to parents, school success, the father's occupation, delinquent associates, delinquent values, and the perceived risk of apprehension. Johnson arranged for over 700 Seattle high school students aged 15–16 to complete a questionnaire including self-reported delinquency items and questions designed to measure the above factors. All the information was collected within one school period of 50–60 min.

One of the major problems with this kind of research concerns causal order. For example, if high self-reported delinquency is correlated with low perceived risk of apprehension, does this mean that thinking there is a low probability of being caught makes juveniles more likely to commit delinquent acts? Or does it mean that the more delinquent acts juveniles commit, the more they realize how low the probability is of being caught? Or does it mean that the kinds of juveniles who commit many delinquent acts also give low estimates of the probability of being caught, without there being any causal relationship between these two factors? These kinds of questions can be asked for many of the above factors.

The best method of establishing causal order is to carry out a randomized experiment, but these are difficult to arrange in criminology (for a review, see Farrington, 1983). There are ethical and practical difficulties in systematically investigating the effects of independent variables on the dependent variable of delinquent behavior, although this design has methodological advantages. The second best method of establishing causal order is to carry out a longitudinal survey, especially if this can be analyzed as a quasi-experiment (see Cook & Campbell, 1979). In a longitudinal survey, it is possible to establish if one factor precedes another, which helps in trying to establish causal order. For example, Farrington (1977) could demonstrate that convictions preceded an increase in self-reported delinquency, and Farrington (1978) could show that newly emerging parental disharmony at age 14 preceded newly emerging aggressive behavior at age 16–18.

A second problem of much research on crime and delinquency centers on its retrospective nature. The memories of respondents who are attempting to provide information about past events may be faulty or biased. For example, consider a mother of a 15-year-old convicted male who is attempting to answer questions about how she brought him up. The methods of child rearing she used before the conviction are likely to be of most relevance to the investigator who is interested in explaining delinquency, since those used afterward may have been affected by the conviction. However, the problem is that the mother's memory of child-rearing methods used before the conviction may be affected by it. Many people search for explanations of delinquency, and the mother may feel that her child-rearing methods must have been unsatisfactory because her son became a convicted delinquent.

The best way of avoiding problems of retrospective bias is to carry out a longitudinal survey and collect information contemporaneously, or as soon after events as possible, before outcomes of interest (such as convictions) are known. More research is needed to establish to precise nature and extent of retrospective bias in criminological investigations.

Other problems of bias arise in research such as Johnson's (1979), derived from a single source on a single occasion. If self-reports of high offending are related to self-reports of low attachment to parents, is this because of a social desirability response bias? In other words, these results could be produced artifactually according to each person's willingness to admit unfavorable things about himself or herself on that particular occasion. Assuming that each measured variable reflects both a theoretical variable and bias due to the method of measurement, the best way of establishing a relationship between two theoretical variables is to measure them in different ways. For example, if self-reports of offending were related to parent reports of attachment and teacher reports of school success, it might be concluded that offending was related to attachment to parents and school success. If self-reports of the three variables were related, it could always be argued that the relationships were produced artifactually by common self-report biases.

Another problem of much research on crime and delinquency is that it usually involves a limited number of measured variables. In attempting to demonstrate that a certain factor has an influence on delinquent behavior, it is desirable to hold constant all other factors. This can be achieved statistically in nonexperimental research, for example by using some kind of partial correlation analysis, but only if all other relevant factors are measured. In doubtful cases, researchers should err on the side of inclusion rather than exclusion. Theoretically guided research can be undesirable if it leads the investigator to exclude important factors. The unwillingness of many American sociologists to believe in the importance of individual differences has led them to exlcude possibly important factors, such as IQ, from their studies (see Hirschi & Hindelang, 1977).

Another problem, especially with older research on crime and delinquency (e.g., Glueck & Glueck, 1950), is the use of extreme groups of incarcerated delinquents and nonincarcerated nondelinquents. Because of the use of extreme groups, this design is likely to overestimate differences between convicted and unconvicted people. Also, of course, any differences between such groups may relate to or be caused by incarceration rather than reflect delinquency. The measurement of delinquency as a dichotomous variable confuses types of behavior with types of people and fosters a false view of delinquency as a dichotomous phenomenon, that "the delinquents" can be contrasted with "the vast majority of law-abiding people." Self-report research and common sense suggest that delinquency is a continuous variable, and that people vary in the frequency and seriousness of offending rather than in whether or not they offend.

The problem then becomes to measure the frequency and seriousness of offending and to establish how it varies with key factors such as age, sex, and race. The research described in this chapter throws no light on the issues of sex and race, but it does provide information about changes in offending with age (and in relation to other variables). As a prospective longitudinal survey, it overcomes the design problems discussed in this section.

Analysis

Many criminological researchers, especially in England, are openly hostile to systematic empirical research, preferring unsystematic participant observation and other essentially hypothesis-generating methods (e.g., Parker & Giller, 1981). Their reports tend to be journalistic in style, and the major evidence quoted in support of their conclusions consists of statements by juveniles and (perhaps rather surprisingly) official records. A major problem with these studies is the small number of people on which they are based. Parker (1974) hung around with about 30 boys, and Gill (1977) knew about 25. This raises the issue of how far the results can be generalized. Subjectivity is another problem, since it is possible to support almost any argument by judicious choice of quotations. Verbatim statements by juveniles can be illuminating, but they need to be coupled with quantitative information so that the reader can assess how typical the statements are. Similarly, the reader needs to know how the researcher elicited the statements, to avoid the charge that the researcher was implicitly or explicitly encouraging the respondents to say what he or she wanted to hear (e.g., see Martin, 1979).

Even where criminological researchers use systematic empirical methods, they often do not progress very far (if at all) beyond the presentation of simple two-way relationships. For example, Hindelang (1973), undoubtedly one of the better researchers, presented the relationships between self-reported delinquency and such factors as parental attachment, school ability, delinquent friends, and respect for the police. However, he did not investigate whether a relationship with one factor held independently of others.

Even where researchers attempt multivariate analyses, they usually use parametric methods such as multiple linear regression and factor analysis (see, e.g., Wiatrowski, Griswold, & Roberts, 1981). Almost invariably, criminological data violate the underlying statistical assumptions of these techniques, such as that variables are measured on interval scales and are normally distributed. It is sometimes argued (e.g., Johnson, 1979, p. 98) that such violations do not invalidate the conclusions, since some statistical techniques give reliable results (e.g., reasonably accurate p values) with some violations. In general, however, researchers cannot be sure that their data, with their particular violations, will not produce misleading results with these techniques.

Instead of using techniques which are, strictly speaking, inapplicable to criminological data, it would surely be better to use methods which are applicable. In particular, the loglinear method is designed for the multivariate analysis of categorical data, and therefore should be used in criminological research. It is used in this chapter. It is based on a multivariate contingency table, assuming that the logarithm of the frequency in each cell in some additive function of the main effects of and interactions between the variables concerned. For example, in studying the interrelationship between three variables A, B, and C, the most general equation (the full model) is of the following kind:

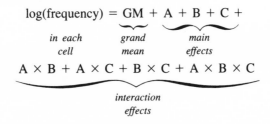

(where A indicates a term in the equation representing the main effect of A, etc.) The purpose of loglinear analysis is to establish which of the terms on the right-hand side of the equation (parameters typically estimated by maximum likelihood techniques) are needed to fit the observed frequencies. For example, assuming that all three variables are independent, the equation takes the following form:

$$\log(\text{frequency}) = GM + A + B + C$$

The estimated frequencies derived from this equation can then be compared with the observed frequencies (using the log likelihood ratio statistic, G^2, distributed asymptotically as χ^2) to establish the goodness of fit of the model to the data. If the estimated and observed frequencies are significantly different, interaction terms are then added to the equation. For example, if the data are fitted by an equation including an A × C term, this shows that A and C are not independent (i.e., that they are significantly related). A proper mathematical exposition of this technique cannot be attempted here; the reader is referred to Fienberg (1980).

Theory

Measurement and theory are interrelated, of course. Ideally, a theory should specify which theoretical constructs are important and how they are related. In testing the theory, it is then necessary to measure empirical variables which are operational definitions of the theoretical constructs. If two empirical variables are not related, this may mean either that the theoretical constructs are not related or that the operational definitions are inadequate. One problem with theories of delinquency and crime is that the theoretical constructs are not discrete events in general, but continuing states. This is true not only of delinquency but also of constructs such as having delinquent friends, being attached to parents, and being successful in school. It might be best to specify how the state of delinquency is produced by other states in one part of a theory, and to specify how the state of delinquency (or delinquency potential) is transformed into delinquent behavior in a second part. The first part of the theory might specify historical influences on development, while the second part might concentrate on immediate situational influences.

It is often desirable to specify causal relationships between the theoretical constructs. In the social sciences, probabilistic causes are more plausible than deterministic ones. Thus, it might be stated that if theoretical construct A occurs, theoretical construct B will follow with a certain probability. The implicit time dimension in causal relationships is often neglected. It is desirable to specify that B will follow A within a certain time period, or to specify a distribution of probabilities over time. If a theory could be specified mathematically as a series of equations relating independent and dependent variables, the concept of cause might become unnecessary, but criminological theories are a long way from this stage.

Many criminological theories are so poorly specified as to be almost untestable. Many theorists are hostile to the idea of empirical testing. For example, one of the most influential theories in the last 20 years has been labeling theory, popularized by Becker (1963) and Lemert (1972). Once empirical researchers attempted to test this theory, its protagonists (e.g., Becker, 1974) denied that it was a testable theory. As Hirschi (1980) pointed out:

> Although the assertions of labelling theorists often appear to have the form X causes Y, more careful inspection of their assertions reveals that either X or Y or both X and Y are unspecified. The reason the labelling theorist does not specify X and Y is clear: If X and Y were specified, the labelling theorist would be making assertions about the relations between concepts, he or she would be making testable theoretical predictions, and that would be positivism, something no respectable labelling theorist would be caught dead committing. (p. 298)

Theories proposed by empirical researchers are also difficult to test, because they are so complex. For example, the model proposed by Clarke (1977) suggests that delinquent acts depend on: (a) heredity (e.g., low IQ), (b) early environment and upbringing (e.g., broken home), (c) criminal personality (e.g., impulsive), (d) socioeconomic and demographic status (e.g., young, black, unskilled male), (e) current living circumstances (e.g., inner city residence), (f) crises and events (e.g., loss of job), (g) the situation (e.g., poorly lit streets), and (h) the person (e.g., cognitive processes and motivational states). The most carefully specified theory of delinquency is that of Trasler (1962), whose presentation should serve as an example to others.

In the United States, another influential theory in the past decade has been the control theory of Hirschi (1969). This suggests that people commit delinquent acts when they do not have a strong bond to society. The bond has four elements: attachment, commitment, involvement, and belief. *Attachment* refers to internalization of norms, or being concerned about the wishes and expectations of others (e.g., parents). *Commitment* refers to obeying the law because of fear of the consequences of not obeying it (the loss of the investment is conventional behavior). *Involvement* refers to involvement in conventional activities. *Belief* refers to the belief that delinquency is wrong. This theory predicts that delinquency will be related to a large number of empirical variables which are thought to measure these theoretical concepts, such as supervision by parents, affectional identification with parents, liking for school, delinquent friends (attachment) smoking, drinking, dating (commitment), homework, having nothing to do (involvement), and respect for police and the law (belief).

The Hirschi theory seems somewhat analogous to a multiple regression equation, with one dependent variable and a large number of independent ones. Later elaborations of this theory often involve path diagrams in which variables can act as both causes and effects. For example, in one of the diagrams of Johnson (1979, p. 140), parental unconcern for the child produces school failure, which in turn produces delinquent associates, which in turn produces delinquent behavior. It is very difficult to test this kind of theory in cross-sectional research. Longitudinal research is needed to demonstrate the time ordering implied in the different parts of the diagram. The problem in using path analysis is that many different path diagrams can be consistent with the results of cross-sectional research, and choosing among them is often a subjective process.

My own view is that it is a little premature to propose complex theories of delinquency before basic facts have been established. The present chapter presents information about how delinquency varies with age and about the predictors of delinquency at different ages. The choice of variables to measure was determined theoretically, but not by only one theory. An attempt was made to measure factors which were alleged to be important in the production of delinquency in many different theories. The variables which independently predicted delinquency at each age were determined objectively, and this knowledge should be the starting point in devising a theory of delinquency.

III. THE CAMBRIDGE STUDY IN DELINQUENT
DEVELOPMENT

Design

The present analyses use data from the Cambridge Study in Delinquent Development, which is a prospective longitudinal survey of 411 males. Data collection
began in 1961/2, when most of the boys were 8 years old, and ended in 1980,
when the youngest person was aged 25 years 6 months. The major results of the
survey can be found in four books (West, 1969, 1982; West & Farrington, 1973,
1977), and a concise summary is also available (Farrington & West, 1981).

At the time they were first contacted in 1961/2, the boys were all living in a
working-class area of London, England. The vast majority of the sample was
chosen by taking *all* the boys aged 8–9 who were on the registers of six state
primary schools which were within a 1-mile radius of a research office which had
been established. There were other schools in this area, including a Roman
Catholic school, but these were the ones which were approached and which
agreed to cooperate. In addition to 399 boys from these six schools, 12 boys from
a local school for the educationally subnormal were included in the sample, in an
attempt to make it more representative of the population of boys living in the
area.

The boys were almost all white Caucasian in appearance. Only 12, most of
whom had at least one parent of West Indian origin, were black. The vast
majority (371) were being brought up by parents who had themselves been reared
in the United Kingdom or the Republic of Ireland. On the basis of their fathers'
occupations, 93.7% could be described as working class (categories III, IV, or V
on the Registrar General's scale), in comparison with the national figure of
78.3% at that time. This was, therefore, overwhelmingly a white, urban, working-class sample of British origin.

The boys were interviewed and tested in their schools when they were aged
about 8, 10, and 14, by male or female psychologists. They were interviewed in
the research office at about 16, 18, 21, and 24, by young male social science
graduates. Up to and including age 18, the aim was to interview the whole
sample on each occasion, and it was always possible to trace and interview a high
proportion. At age 18, for example, 389 of the original 411 (94.6%) were
interviewed. Of the 22 youths missing at this age, one had died, one could not be
traced, 6 were abroad, 10 refused to be interviewed, and in the other 4 cases the
parent refused on behalf of the youth.

At age 21, the aim was to interview only the convicted delinquents and a
similarly sized, randomly chosen sample of unconvicted youths. At this age, 218
of the target group of 241 were interviewed (90.5%). At age 24, the aim was to
interview four subgroups of youths: persisting recidivists (those with two or more
convictions up to age 19 and at least one more in the next 5 years), temporary

recidivists (those with two or more convictions up to age 19 and no more in the next 5 years), unconvicted youths from seriously deprived backgrounds (from large families, in poor housing, with convicted parents, and with families supported by state welfare), and a random sample of unconvicted youths. At this age, only 85 of the target group of 113 (75.2%) were successfully interviewed, primarily because so many of these youths had left home and were difficult to trace.

At most ages, most boys were interviewed between 5 and 11 months after their birthdays. For the interview at 14, for example, 211 of the 406 seen were aged between 14 years 7 months and 14 years 11 months, while 97 were younger and 98 older. The median age at interview was 14 years 9 months. For the interview at 18 the median age was 18 years 7 months, and for the interview at 21 it was 21 years 5 months. There was most variability in age for the interview at 24, where the median age was 24 years 11 months. Of the 85 youths interviewed, 11, 34, 23, and 17 were aged 23, 24, 25, and 26, respectively.

In addition to interviews and tests with the boys, interviews with their parents were carried out by female social workers who visited their homes. These took place about once a year from when the boy was about 8 until when he was aged 14–15 and was in his last year of compulsory schooling. The primary informant was the mother, although the father was also seen in the majority of cases. Most of the parents were cooperative. At the time of the final interview, when the boy was 14–15, information was obtained from the parents of 399 boys (97.1%). The boys' teachers also filled in questionnaires about their behavior in school, when the boys were aged about 8, 10, 12, and 14. Again, the teachers were very cooperative, and at least 94% of questionnaires were completed at each age.

It was also possible to make repeated searches in the central Criminal Record Office in London to try to locate findings of guilt sustained by the boys, by their parents, by their brothers and sisters, and (in recent years) by their wives. These searches continued until March 1980, when the youngest sample member was aged 25 years 6 months. The criminal records of the boys who have not died or emigrated are believed to be complete from the tenth birthday (the minimum age of criminal responsibility in England and Wales) to the twenty-fifth birthday.

The Cambridge Study in Delinquent Development has a unique combination of features:

a. It is a prospective longitudinal survey over a period of nearly 20 years.
b. The focus of interest in on crime and delinquency.
c. Many variables were measured before any of the youths were officially convicted, to avoid the problem of retrospective bias.
d. The study involved frequent personal contacts with a group of boys and their parents, so records were supplemented by interview, test, and questionnaire data.
e. A fairly representative sample of urban working-class youths was fol-

lowed up, rather than extreme groups of (predicted or identified) delinquents and nondelinquents, so that all degrees of delinquency were
present.

f. The officially delinquent minority became gradually differentiated from
their nondelinquent peers, avoiding the problem of selection of control
groups.

g. Both official and self-report measures of delinquency were used.

h. At least up to age 21, there was a very low attrition rate.

i. Many variables from different sources were measured, making it possible
to test many hypotheses about delinquency, to investigate the relative
importance of variables, and to study the importance of some variables
while controlling for others.

The sample was limited to males from a working-class urban area because of
the prior expectation of a high prevalence of convictions (about a quarter) among
them. The sample size was set at about 400 because this was considered large
enough for statistical comparisons between convicted and unconvicted boys but
small enough to interview each boy and his family and build up intensive case
histories. Nationally representative samples of many thousands (e.g.,
Wadsworth, 1979) provide excellent bases for generalizations and statistical
analyses, but with such numbers it is difficult to collect anything other than
easily available objective information.

Ethical problems of privacy, confidentiality, and informed consent arose in
this project, as in many others. Current ethical guidelines adopted by American
federal agencies would make it very difficult nowadays to carry through a study
of this kind successfully. When this research began more than 20 years ago,
ethical requirements were less stringent. Nevertheless, many difficulties had to
be overcome.

The initial contacts with the boys and their parents depended upon the cooperation of the education department and the schools. At first, the education department made a ruling that group tests could be given if teachers were agreeable, but
that any individual testing of children could not be done without the written
consent of parents given on a prescribed form. The education department allowed the researchers to have names and addresses of the boys, but would not
allow them to call on the parents to ask for cooperation. Instead, an official
letter, partly composed by the education department and signed by headmasters,
was sent to the parents with a request that they sign and post an enclosed form
signifying their consent to be visited by one of the research team. Predictably, in
the area where standards of literacy were not high, the response was poor (about
60%). A great amount of time and effort had to be spent before the study social
workers could contact all the parents, using calls by cooperative parents on their
less cooperative neighbors and using local welfare agencies to secure
introductions.

The basic problem seems to be that, from the point of view of crime and delinquency, the most interesting and important people are the most uncooperative and most elusive. In our research, the boys from the most uncooperative families were significantly more likely to be convicted than the remainder, and the convicted boys tended to be more uncooperative themselves to the research. If uncooperative people are excluded from research (e.g., by the requirements of informed consent), false conclusions may be drawn about the phenomena of crime and delinquency.

The researchers were not required to obtain permission from the parents or from the boys before searching for them in the Criminal Record Office. We were very fortunate in that one researcher was allowed to visit this Office and was supplied with files for direct inspection. It is unlikely that this facility would be given to a new project nowadays. The parents and boys were told that the research was concerned with child upbringing and development, and that the intention was to follow up all boys in certain classes in certain schools. They were not told explicitly about the interest in crime and delinquency, although of course questions were asked about these topics, and they were not told that the research was being carried out by the Cambridge Institute of Criminology. These disclosures might have decreased cooperation by the most criminal families.

The boys and their families were given repeated guarantees of absolute confidentiality, and we have taken stringent precautions to preserve their anonymity and to make sure that no individual could be harmed by the leakage of personal information. Even when the researchers were told about serious, undetected criminal offenses, or about intentions to commit such offences, this information never left our office. Our guiding principle throughout has been that no person should suffer any negative consequences as a result of participating in our research.

Diener and Crandall (1978) pointed out that one approach frequently used in evaluating whether a project was ethical was to consider whether its likely benefits (usually consisting of, or consequent upon, advancement of knowledge) outweighted its likely costs (e.g., in terms of deception, invasion of privacy, or harm caused by subjects). It is, of course, difficult to assess the benefits and costs of research. The costs of crime—of murder, rape, robbery, incarceration in degrading conditions, etc.—are all too obvious. Research which increases our knowledge about crime and delinquency may (if government agencies take any notice of it) eventually help to decrease crime and the social reaction to it. In my estimation, the benefits of the present research are likely to outweigh its relatively small ethical costs.

Measurement

Information was obtained in this research from records, interviews, ratings, tests and questionnaires, physical measures, and observed behavior. Further details about these measures can be obtained in West and Farrington (1973, 1977).

As mentioned above, information about convictions was obtained from searches in the Criminal Record Office. In order to obtain identifying particulars which would enable these searches to be carried out, the full name and date of birth of each family member, including the mother's maiden name, was sought during interviews. These data were checked against, and frequently supplemented by, information from medical and social service records and from birth and marriage certificates obtained from the General Register Office in London. Repeated searches were necessary, because convictions were sometimes located in one search but not in another. When offenders are known to have died, their names are deleted from the Criminal Record Office, and there is also a tendency to "weed out" records of minor offenses after a number of years.

Convictions were only counted if they were for offenses normally recorded in the Criminal Record Office, which are more or less synonymous with "serious" or "criminal" offenses. For example, no convictions for traffic offenses were included, nor convictions for offenses regarded as minor (e.g., public drunkenness or common assault). The most common offenses included were thefts, burglaries, and unauthorized takings of motor vehicles. In a few cases where information from the boy or elsewhere did not agree with that in the Criminal Record Office, the discrepancies were resolved by reference to local police or court records. Since the information in the records was supplemented by extensive interviews and other inquiries, it is unlikely that any convicted boy in the sample escaped identification.

Most information in this research was derived from interviews. The boys' parents provided details about such things as family income, family size (also checked against school records), the social class of the family breadwinner, their degree of supervision of the boy, and their child-rearing behavior (which was a composite variable reflecting attitude, discipline, and parental agreement). The boys provided details about their job histories and leisure habits, such as spending time hanging about, drinking, and sexual activity. The interviews with the boys at age 18 and later ages were fully tape recorded and transcribed, making verbatim quotations possible.

Ratings were obtained from the boys' teachers about their troublesome and aggressive behavior in school, about their truancy, and about their school attainments. Ratings were also obtained from the boys' peers when they were in their primary schools, about such things as their troublesomeness, daring, dishonesty, and popularity.

Many psychological tests and self-report questionnaires were given, not only to the boys but also to their parents. These have the dual advantages of comparatively objective scoring and ease of administration. Nonverbal IQ was measured using the Progressive Matrices test; vocabulary, using Mill Hill synonyms; and personality, by the New Junior Maudsley Inventory (at ages 10 and 14) and the Eysenck Personality Inventory (at age 16). Psychomotor clumsiness was measured using three tests, the Porteus Mazes, the Spiral Maze, and the Tapping test. Self-report questionnaires were used not only to measure the commission of delinquent and violent acts, but also to measure attitudes (e.g., to the police) and the delinquent behavior of a boy's friends. The questionnaires filled in by the parents provided information about their health and about their child-rearing attitudes.

The major physical measures were of the boys' heights and weights at different ages, although other measures were also taken (e.g., of grip strength, using a dynamometer, at age 10, and of pulse rate, using a pulsimeter, at age 18). Ratings of physical appearance were made by the interviewers, regarding such things as racial characteristics, wearing glasses, tattoos, nail biting, and hair length. Finally, a small number of behavioral measures were taken, by systematically giving the youths opportunities to smoke and to gamble part of their interview fee.

A great deal of effort was expended in investigating and maximizing the reliability and validity of the various measures. Problems arose especially with the ratings derived from the earliest interviews conducted with the families by the psychiatric social workers. In order that the psychiatric social workers might work in the way they were accustomed, and elicit the maximum cooperation, they were given a list of topics to be covered but were allowed to conduct unstructured interviews. They took a few written notes during the interviews, but they mainly relied on dictating into a tape recorder afterwards. A good deal of this information proved to be too subjective and too much influenced by halo effects to be of use for research purposes. West (1969, pp. 124–134) has described some difficulties in deriving relatively objective measures from it.

The later interviews were more structured. For example, the interview with the youths at age 18 was entirely structured, with the exception of the questions about delinquency, violence, and sexual experiences. It was thought that these sensitive topics should be approached in an unstructured fashion. Also, as already mentioned, the whole interview was tape recorded, and this facilitated consistent and relatively objective coding decisions. The major test of validity involved a comparison between what the youths said about their convictions and information available in official records. As already mentioned, only 6% of convicted youths denied being convicted, and only 2% of unconvicted youths claimed to have been convicted. Reliability was studied in a number of ways, including comparing different accounts of the same incident by different youths, responses given at age 18 with those given by the same youth at age 16, and responses in one part of the interview with those in another. Differences between interviewers were also investigated. None of these checks suggested that the interview information was unreliable or invalid.

The low attrition rates in this study were achieved at the cost of a great deal of interviewer effort and time. The interviewers would go to great lengths to track down a youth's address, using a variety of methods. Some were traced through the local housing department; some were located by probation officers; some were provided by neighbors, relatives, or present occupants of old addresses; some were derived from criminal records, marriage certificates, or telephone directories; and letters were forwarded to some youths by the Department of Health and Social Security, the Post Office, or by employers. The interviewers would make repeated calls at an address in an attempt to find someone in, and would go back to try to secure an interview even if a youth refused on the first occasion.

It is not possible to establish the effects on the boys or their families of being followed up over a long period. In retrospect, a control group of other (older and younger) boys from the original six schools should have been selected and followed up in records but never contacted personally. However, this was not done. The occasional intrusions of the researchers into their lives probably had little effect on the boys and their families. In general, the researchers did not do anything to change the lives of the families, although on occasions the social workers could not refrain from advising troubled parents where to go for help with their financial, housing, or health problems.

Analysis

In terms of statistically significant relationships, this study suffered from an embarrassment of riches. The majority of measured variables significantly differentiated between convicted and unconvicted youths. On any particular factor, it was almost invariably the category which, on commonsense grounds, would be defined as the most adverse which included the highest percentage of convicted youths. For example, more delinquents were drawn from the poorest families, those with low IQs, and those whose parents exercised poor supervision over them. The problem was to reduce the very large number of measured variables (over 4000 in the whole dataset) to a more manageable number.

Certain principles were adopted to guide the reduction procedure. In particular, the aim was to have each empirical variable measuring only one theoretical concept, as far as possible. This was achieved by identifying clusters of variables which were related empirically and theoretically, and then either choosing one variable as the best representative of this cluster or combining a number of the variables in the cluster into a single composite variable.

As an example, the psychiatric social workers' ratings of maternal attitude, maternal discipline, paternal attitude, paternal discipline, marital disharmony, and parental inconsistency, were all closely related. Parents tended to be seen as bad in many respects, or good in many respects, but rarely bad in some respects and good in others. It is probable that the psychiatric social workers had found difficulty in rating one aspect of parental behavior independently of another, and this is one manifestation of the halo effect mentioned above. In view of these relationships, it was decided to combine all the variables into one global rating called parental behavior. The rules of combination were very simple, both in this example and in others. Each boy was given 1, 2, or 3 points on each variable, and his scores were simply added over all the variables. The features contributing to the rating of poor parental behavior were parents with cruel, passive, or neglecting attitudes, very strict, harsh, or erratic discipline, and parents who were in conflict with each other.

There were other reasons for combining variables. For example, the nonverbal IQ scores at ages 8 and 10 were combined (by averaging), on the grounds that the combined score would have less variability than either individual score. Measures of the same theoretical concept obtained from different sources were combined in the expectation that the biases present in the sources might cancel out to some extent. For example, the measures of troublesomeness obtained from teachers and peers were combined, as were the measures of daring obtained from parents and peers.

Another way in which the number of variables in the analysis was reduced was by eliminating those which were very subjective or not well defined. For example, the rating of mothers' past health was eliminated because it depended on mothers' recollections and admissions of past events. The rating of present health of mothers, which in some cases was supplemented by hospital records, varied markedly with socioeconomic status, as expected, with the lower status mothers having poorer health. However, poor past health was not related to socioeconomic status, suggesting that the lower status families were underreporting. The rating of sibling disturbance was eliminated because there were marked differences between the psychiatric social workers in the proportion of boys said to have disturbed siblings, and these differences could only be explained by interviewer bias. The rating of unstable personality of mothers, which was intended to identify behavior-disordered individuals who did not necessarily have anxiety symptoms, was eliminated because it was not defined very explicitly. In choosing between variables, those which were more objectively measured were preferred.

For the purpose of the present analysis, each variable was dichotomized into the "worst" quarter and the remaining three-quarters, wherever possible. There were various reasons for this. First, in order to compare variables, it was desirable that each should be measured equally sensitively (or insensitively). Second, in order to carry out loglinear analyses, it was desirable to have as few categories as possible for each variable. Third, the one-quarter/three-quarters split had been used from the beginning of this study, because of the prior expectation that about one-quarter of the sample would be convicted, and the desirability of equating the proportion of those identified who were convicted and the proportion of those convicted who were identified. In addition, variables on which less than 350 boys were known (out of the 411) were eliminated. On most variables included, the number of missing cases was 5% or less, and there were no missing cases on many variables measured at age 8–10.

The variables included in the present analysis are listed in the Appendix.

IV. CHANGES IN OFFENDING WITH AGE

Convictions at Each Age

Table 1 shows the number of youths first convicted for offenses committed at each age, the number of different youths convicted at each age, and the number of convictions at each age. The ages shown in this table are those at which offenses were committed rather than at the times of the convictions. There was sometimes a substantial delay between commission and conviction, especially in the case of the more serious offenses, where a youth might spend a year or more awaiting trial at the Crown Court. For example, perhaps the most serious criminal in the sample was a youth who carried out two robberies using guns, stealing more than $65,000. Both of these were committed when he was 24 years old, but he was not convicted for them until more than a year later, when he had passed his 25th birthday.

In this sample, the peak age for the number of different youths convicted (47) and for the number of convictions (63) was 17. By age 22, these figures had

Table 1. Prevalence and Incidence of Convictions at Each Age

Age	Number of First Convictions*	Number of Different Boys Convicted	Number of Convictions
10	6(1.5)	6	7
11	6(3.0)	8	10
12	8(5.0)	12	14
13	15(8.7)	21	27
14	19(13.5)	34	44
15	17(17.7)	33	43
16	13(20.9)	32	47
17	19(25.7)	47	63
18	8(27.7)	41	50
19	8(29.7)	38	47
20	9(31.9)	29	41
21	2(32.4)	18	20
22	2(32.9)	24	33
23	2(33.4)	11	11
24	2(33.9)	13	18
Total	136		475

Note:
*Cumulative percentage prevalence in parentheses, based on N = 401.

fallen by half, to 24 youths convicted and 33 convictions. By age 24, the figures were only about a quarter of their peak values, at 13 youths and 18 convictions. The peak period of official delinquency for this sample was from 14 to 20, with over 40 convictions (10 per 100 youths) at each age.

Table 1 also shows the cumulative percentage prevalence of convictions, which reached 33.9% by the 25th birthday. In calculating this, 10 unconvicted youths who had emigrated before age 25 were eliminated, since they were not at risk of a known conviction for the whole period. Of the convicted youths, 5 died and one emigrated before age 25, and all 16 dead or emigrant youths are eliminated in some subsequent analyses (e.g., concerning convictions between the 21st and 25th birthday, since none were at risk of this for the whole period). The information about death and emigration is complete only up to age 22. The information about juvenile convictions (i.e. those before age 17) is complete for all 411 youths, since inquiries were made abroad in regard to the 6 youths who had spent at least a year of their juvenile period outside England and Wales.

The number of youths convicted for the first time declined dramatically after the 21st birthday. The period from the 10th to the 25th birthday spans four legal categories in England: children (10th to just before 14th birthday), young persons (14th to just before 17th birthday), young adults (17th to just before 21st birthday), and older adults (21st birthday onward). Children and young persons together are legally juveniles. It can be seen that 35 boys were first convicted as children, 49 as young persons, 44 as young adults, and only 8 as older adults.

Overall, 35 boys were convicted as children, 74 as young persons, 95 as young adults, and 46 as older adults. These categories overlap, of course. For example, 25 of the 35 convicted as children were among the 74 convicted as young persons. Over one-fifth of the boys (84) were convicted as juveniles, and over one-quarter (110) as adults. There was a close relationship between juvenile and adult convictions. Of the 13 boys with 4 or more juvenile convictions, 10 also had 4 or more adult convictions. Conversely, 83.6% of those with no juvenile convictions also had no adult convictions (265 out of 317). Over 70% of those convicted as juveniles were also convicted as adults (55 out of 78, excluding the 16 youths who died or emigrated before age 25).

Twenty-three youths had 6 or more convictions. They amassed a total of 230 convictions, or almost exactly half (49.1%) of the total number of 468 convictions of the sample at risk in this analysis. This demonstration that about 6% of the sample accounted for 49% of the convictions is very similar to the results obtained by Wolfgang, Figlio, and Sellin (1972) in their follow-up of nearly 10,000 Philadelphia boys. They found that 6% of the boys (the "chronic offenders") were responsible for 52% of the arrests. Characteristics of the chronic offenders in the present sample are investigated later in this chapter.

The youths who began their conviction careers at the earliest ages (10–12) tended to become the most persistent offenders. The average number of convictions was 7.17 for those first convicted at 10–12, 3.94 for those first convicted at

13–15, 2.32 for those first convicted at 16–18, and 1.40 for those first convicted at 19–24. This decline was probably not an artifact of the cutoff point of this analysis at the 25th birthday. As Table 1 shows, convictions declined considerably after the 21st birthday. The negative relationship between age at first conviction and total number of convictions (or length of official criminal career) would almost certainly hold if the analysis was extended to the 30th or 40th birthday. Of the 23 chronic offenders, 11 were first convicted at 10–12, and the other 12 at 13–15.

Offenses Leading to Convictions

Table 2 shows changes in the percentages of youths convicted of specified offenses at different ages, as well as changes with age in the number of offenses leading to conviction. The ages are inclusive, and the age ranges are consecutive, so that, for example, age 10–13 means from the 10th until just before the 14th birthday. As before, only offenses normally recorded in the Criminal Record

Table 2. Offenses Leading to Convictions at Different Ages

	Ages (N = 411)			
	10–13	14–16	17–20	21–24
Percentage of Youths Convicted of:				
Assault	0.5	0.5	3.7	2.5
Damage	0.5	1.2	3.7	1.0
Burglary	1.9	6.1	6.2	2.8
Taking Vehicles	1.0	7.1	7.5	2.3
Stealing from Vehicles	1.9	2.2	2.7	1.0
Shoplifting	1.5	2.7	1.5	1.3
Stealing from Machines	1.0	0.5	0.5	0.3
Drug Use	0.0	0.0	1.5	1.5
Any of Above	6.3	13.4	17.4	7.8
Any Offense	8.5	18.0	23.6	11.6
Number of Offenses per 100 Youths Per Year of:				
Assault	0.1	0.2	1.0	0.6
Damage	0.1	0.4	1.0	0.3
Burglary	0.7	3.6	2.8	0.8
Taking Vehicles	0.3	2.8	3.0	0.9
Stealing from Vehicles	0.7	0.8	0.7	0.3
Shoplifting	0.5	1.2	0.6	0.6
Stealing from Machines	0.2	0.5	0.3	0.1
Any of Above	2.7	9.6	9.4	3.6
Any Offense	4.3	15.1	18.8	7.8

Office are included in this table. This means, for example, that assaults had to be quite serious (causing actual or grievous bodily harm) to be included, since common assault is not normally recorded. Only offenses leading to convictions are included in this table, not offenses "taken into consideration." Only 39 of the 475 convictions (8.2%) involved offenses taken into consideration, which were usually of the same kind as those leading to the conviction.

The youths were convicted of 683 offenses on their 475 occasions of conviction, showing that a youth was usually convicted of only one offense on each occasion. The types of offenses shown in Table 2 are chosen for comparability with those for which self-reports are available at different ages. However, the seven types shown in the bottom half of the table accounted for the majority of offenses leading to conviction. There were 115 burglaries, 103 offenses of unauthorized taking of motor vehicles, 42 thefts from shops, 37 thefts from vehicles, 30 assaults, 28 offenses of damaging property, and 16 thefts from automatic machines such as telephone boxes, cigarette machines, and parking meters—a total of 371 offenses.

Of the remaining 312, 108 were miscellaneous thefts, and 56 were offenses of "suspicious behavior" (e.g., going equipped to steal), which were often included as ancillary charges when a youth was convicted of burglary, taking vehicles, or stealing from vehicles. There were 36 offenses of handling or receiving stolen property, 32 of fraud or forgery, 22 of drug use, 21 of disorderly conduct (e.g., breach of the peace or threatening behavior), 20 of possessing an offensive weapon, 11 of robbery, 5 of sex offense, and 1 of arson. Self-report data are available about some of these other offenses (e.g., receiving stolen goods, stealing from employers, defrauding the government, possessing an offensive weapon), but only at one or two ages. In the case of drug use, self-report data are available about the proportion of youths who have taken drugs but not about the number of occasions. It was thought more important to try to classify the youths as "regular" or "occasional" users than to try to obtain accurate estimates of drug consumption.

Table 2 shows that the peak incidence of most offenses leading to convictions was either at 14–16, or 17–20. For taking vehicles, 7.1% of the youths were convicted between 14 and 16, and 7.5% between 17 and 20. There were 2.8 offenses per 100 youths per year between 14 and 16, and 3.0 between 17 and 20. For burglary, 6.1% of the youths were convicted between 14 and 16, and 6.2% between 17 and 20. There were 3.6 offenses per 100 youths per year between 14 and 16, and 2.8 between 17 and 20.

Shoplifting, stealing from vehicles, and stealing from automatic machines were offenses which tended to be most frequent at relatively early ages. The peak incidence of stealing from machines was at 10–13 (1.0% of the youths convicted), and for shoplifting it was 14–16 (2.7%). The rate of stealing from vehicles was fairly constant from 10–20, at about .7 or .8 offenses per 100 youths per year. On the other hand, assault, damaging property, and drug use tended to peak at relatively later ages. The clear peak for assault and damage was at 17–20, with 3.7% of youths convicted and 1.0 offenses per 100 youths per year. Drug use was equally common at 17–20 and 21–24.

In most cases, the peak rate of committing offenses not shown in Table 2 was at 17–20. For example, miscellaneous theft reached a peak of 3.0 offenses per 100 youths per year between 17 and 20; handling or receiving stolen goods reached a peak of 1.0; possessing an offensive weapon, .7; and robbery, .4. An exception to this general trend was fraud or forgery. There were no offenses of this kind between 10 and 13, .4 per 100 youths per year at 14–16, .7 at 17–20, and .9 at 21–24. It may be that fraud or forgery has yet to reach its peak in this sample.

Self-Reported Offending

Table 3 shows changes in the percentages of youths admitting specified offenses at different ages, as well as changes with age in the number of offenses admitted. The age ranges shown in this table are not inclusive or consecutive. During the interview at age 14, the youths were asked to admit offenses which they had ever committed up to that time, and to say whether they had committed each once or twice, sometimes, or frequently (see Farrington, 1973). Therefore, precise information about frequency is not available at this age. It can be assumed that most acts admitted would have been committed after the tenth birthday. At age 18, the youths were asked to admit the number of offenses they had committed in the previous 3 years (see West & Farrington, 1977), while at ages 21 and 24 they were asked to admit the number of offenses committed in the previous 2 years (see Knight, Osborn, & West, 1977; Osborn & West, 1980). On the basis of the median ages at interview (supra), the self-reported delinquency information is available for the period up to 14 years 9 months, from 15 years 7 months to 18 years 7 months, from 19 years 5 months to 21 years 5 months, and from 22 years 11 months to 24 years 11 months.

With one exception, the questions asked at ages 18, 21, and 24 were exactly the same. The exception was that the burglary question at ages 21 and 24 specified "Breaking and entering and then stealing money or things worth 5 pounds or more," whereas at age 18 it merely specified "Breaking and entering and then stealing." The questions asked at age 14 were less comparable. For example, the incidence of burglary is calculated from the responses to four questions, "Breaking into a big store, garage, warehouse, pavilion, etc.," "Breaking into a small shop (private tradesman) whether or not anything was stolen," "Planning well in advance to get into a house, flat, etc. and steal valuables (and carrying the plan through)," and "Getting into a house, flat, etc. and stealing things (Don't count cases where stealing results from planning well in advance)." A youth was counted as admitting burglary at age 14 if he admitted any of the above four acts.

Table 3. Self-Reported Offenses at Different Ages

	Ages (adjusted to N = 387)			
	10–14	15–18	19–21	22–24
Percentage of Youths Admitting:				
Fighting	23.8	62.3	39.5	30.3
Damage	11.9	21.2	3.6	3.6
Burglary	13.2	10.9	4.5	2.6
Taking Vehicles	7.5	15.2	6.4	1.8
Stealing from Vehicles	9.3	13.4	4.1	2.4
Shoplifting	39.3	15.5	6.7	4.2
Stealing from Machines	14.7	19.1	2.4	2.4
Drug Use	0.3	31.5	20.4	18.2
Motoring Convictions	—	16.3	17.0	12.4
Number of Offenses per 100 Youths per Year of:				
Fighting	—	272.5	71.2	42.5
Damage	—	53.7	12.8	12.8
Burglary	—	29.5	11.5	3.5
Taking Vehicles	—	36.3	47.5	1.2
Stealing from Vehicles	—	39.4	14.5	24.2
Shoplifting	—	113.2	65.4	26.2
Stealing from Machines	—	48.1	2.7	4.8
Any of Above	—	592.6	225.6	115.1
Motoring Convictions	—	10.1	10.9	8.0

Note:
— = Not available

Burglary is a rather extreme case because there was no other instance where admissions at 14 were based on four questions. Admissions at 18, 21, and 24 were based on only one question. There was only one other case at age 14 where admissions were based on more than one question. The admissions for shoplifting at 14 were derived from "Stealing things from big stores, supermarkets, multiple shops (while shop open)" and "Stealing things from small shops or private tradesmen (shop open)." The corresponding item at later ages specified "Shoplifting from shops, market stalls, stores, supermarkets, etc." Other items were more comparable at all ages. For example, "Stealing goods or money from slot machines, juke boxes, telephones, etc." at age 14 became "Stealing from slot machines, such as gas or electricity meters, parking meters, phone boxes, cigarette machines" at ages 18, 21, and 24. The procedure was the same at all four ages, since the acts were presented to the youths on cards as part of a face-to-face interview.

The admission rates shown in Table 3 are estimated for the sample of 387 youths (94.2% of the total) who were interviewed both at 14 and at 18. The admission rates for these 387 at 14 were very close to those for all 406 (98.8%) interviewed at 14, and it was concluded that working with a sample of 387 rather than 411 introduced a negligible error (less than 1%). Convicted youths (and self-reported delinquency admissions) were overrepresented in the samples interviewed at 21 and 24, so it was necessary to adjust the admissions to what might have been expected from the whole sample. This was done very simply and will be explained in the case of burglary, although the principles are the same in all cases.

Of the 387 youths interviewed at 14 and 18, 13.2% admitted burglary at 14 and 10.9% at 18. Only 217 youths were interviewed both at 18 and at 21. Of these, 16.6% admitted burglary at 18 and 6.9% at 21. The proportionate reduction in burglary between 18 and 21 for this sample was .584 (since 6.9 divided by 16.6 is .416). This reduction was then applied to the original figure of 10.9% of 387 to produce an estimated admission rate at 21 of 4.5% (10.9 × .416 = 4.5). Only 60 youths were interviewed both at 21 and 24. Of these, 11.7% admitted burglary at 21 and 6.7% at 24. The proportionate reduction in burglary for this sample, then, was .427. When this figure was applied to the previous estimate of 4.5% at age 21, it produced an estimate of 2.6% at age 24.

The estimated number of offenses per year was calculated in the same way. The 387 youths interviewed at 14 and 18 admitted a total of 342 burglaries (in the previous 3 years) at 18, or 29.5 per 100 youths per year. The 217 youths interviewed at 18 and 21 admitted 317 burglaries at age 18 and 82 at age 21, a proportionate reduction of .741. Applying this to the total of 342 burglaries for the whole sample of 387 produced an estimated number of burglaries at age 21 of 89, or (in view of the 2-year admission period) 11.5 per 100 youths per year. The 60 youths interviewed at 21 and 24 admitted 49 burglaries at age 21 and 15 at age 24, a proportionate reduction of .794. Applying this to the previous estimate of 11.5 burglaries per 100 youths per year produced an estimate of 3.5 at age 24 (see Table 3).

This estimation method is simple and rough. The estimate at age 24 is likely to be the most inaccurate, since it is based on only 60 youths. On the other hand, the youths left in the sample at ages 21 and 24 tended to be those admitting the most acts. Therefore, the reduction estimate is likely to be adequate as a measure of the future law-violating behavior of the most delinquent youths at age 18. It will only give an inaccurate estimate for the whole sample if substantial numbers of the less delinquent youths at 18 were increasing their law-violating behavior at 21 or 24 or, at least, not decreasing it to the same extent as the more delinquent youths. This seems very unlikely. for example, considering the 217 youths interviewed at ages 18 and 21, 181 admitted no burglaries at age 18. Of these, 173 (95.6%) also admitted no burglaries at age 21, 5 (2.8%) admitted one burglary at age 21, and only 3 (1.7%) admitted more than one burglary at age 21.

In general, there was a highly significant relationship between admissions at one age and admissions at the next.

Table 3 shows that the incidence of most offenses peaked between ages 15 and 18. During this period 62.3% were involved in fights, 21.2% damaged property, 15.2% took vehicles, 13.4% stole from vehicles, 19.1% stole from machines, and 31.5% used drugs. However, burglary and shoplifting were more common before age 14 than between 15 and 18. The burglary result may be affected by the noncomparability of the measurements at ages 14 and 18 (supra). The four acts were admitted by between 4.0 and 6.4% of the youths, although 13.2% admitted at least one. Both shoplifting acts at age 14 were admitted by a higher proportion of the youths than admitted the corresponding act at age 18, so it is reasonable to conclude that the peak age for shoplifting is before 14. After age 18, the incidence of all acts declined, although it is interesting to note that the rate of motoring convictions per 100 youths per year stayed fairly constant from 15 to 24.

It might be thought that the declining incidence between ages 18 and 21 shown in the top half of Table 3 is affected by the recall period (3 years at 18 and 2 years of 21). However, when the analyses were repeated for youths who admitted at least one offense per year (as opposed to at least one offense) the results were virtually unchanged. For the 217 youths interviewed at ages 18 and 21, the average percentage admitting each of the first seven offenses listed in Table 3 was 30.0% at age 18 and 12.4% at age 21, a proportionate reduction of .587. The average percentage admitting these offenses at least once a year was 18.3% at age 18 and 7.5% at age 21, a very similar proportionate reduction of .601.

Comparing Tables 2 and 3, the most startling difference between official and self-reported offending is in the rate of offending. The seven offenses specified in the bottom half of the tables were committed at a rate of nearly 10 per 100 youths per year between ages 14 and 20, according to official records of convictions. According to self-reports, they were committed at a rate of nearly 600 per 100 youths per year from 15 to 18, and at 225 per 100 youths per year from 19 to 21.

Of course, there are problems of comparability between official and self-reported offending. The least comparable offense was assault. In the official records it referred to relatively serious assaults, but the self-reports referred to fights, most commonly occurring in bars or streets. How many of these fights could have led to a charge of serious criminal assault is uncertain. What is certain is that only a tiny fraction of assaultive behavior involving working-class youths ever leads to a conviction for assault.

The least discrepancy between official records and self-reports concerned the most serious offense, burglary. This was admitted by 10.9% between 15 and 18 and 4.5% between 19 and 21. These figures are not out of line with the 6.1% convicted of burglary between 14 and 16 and the 6.2% convicted between 17 and 20. The rate per 100 youths per year was more out of line, being 11.5–29.5

according to self-reports and 2.8–3.6 according to convictions. It was true with some other offenses that, while rates of commission were much higher according to self-reports than according to official records, the incidence of commission (the proportion of the sample committing) was less discrepant. For example, 7.1% were convicted of taking vehicles at 14–16 and 7.5% at 17–20; 15.2% admitted taking vehicles at 15–18 and 6.4% at 19–21.

Tables 2 and 3 agree in showing that, for most offenses, the peak age of incidence was within a year or two of the 17th birthday. This was true for taking vehicles, stealing from vehicles, damaging property, assault, and drug use, although assault and drug use did not decline with age as quickly as the other offenses. The peak age for shoplifting and for stealing from machines was earlier than 17. The peak age for burglary was less certain. According to official records, it was around 17, but according to self-reports it was earlier.

V. PREDICTING CRIME AND DELINQUENCY

Convictions at 10–24

The Appendix shows the relationship between all the variables included in this analysis and convictions between the 10th and 25th birthdays (based on N = 401, as in Table 1). For example, 48.9% of 92 boys whose family income was rated low at age 8 were convicted, in comparison with 29.4% of the remainder, a statistically significant difference (χ^2 = 11.13, 1 df, p < .001). Only variables measured up to and including age 10 (i.e., the first 27 listed in the Appendix) are strictly predictive here. The main purpose of this table is to display all the variables and to summarize their relationship to being convicted between ages 10 and 24 inclusive. It can be seen that the majority of variables produced significant relationships (54 out of 74, far in excess of the chance expectation of 5%).

It was common for the "worst" category of a variable to include a majority who were convicted youths. The most significant relationship was between convictions and the measure of "antisocial tendency" at age 18. This was the only variable whose definition overlapped with that of any other. Generally, the convicted youths were leading more deviant life-styles than the remainder, and the aim of the antisocial tendency index was to measure the extent of this deviant life-style, excluding the kinds of deviance which usually led to convictions (i.e., property offenses such as thefts and burglaries). Therefore, antisociality reflects deviant behavior which is rarely, or in some cases never, dealt with by the police and courts. The antisocial tendency score was based on 11 factors which were interrelated (heavy gambling, heavy smoking, driving after drinking, use of prohibited drugs, sexual promiscuity, unstable job record, spending time hanging about, involvement in antisocial groups, most aggressive in behavior, anti-establishment attitudes, and tattoos). The youths scoring 4 or more were identified as the most antisocial at age 18.

In the Appendix, the categories at any given age are not necessarily comparable to those at any other age. For example, the fact that fewer youths had housing classed as "poor" at 14 than at 8–10 does not necessarily mean that their housing had improved during this period. As mentioned earlier, more details about the categories can be obtained in West and Farrington (1973, 1977).

The Chronic Offenders

An analysis was carried out to investigate which factors, out of all those measured at 8–10, significantly predicted, out of all convicted youths, who would become the chronic offenders. The comparison was between the 23 youths with six or more convictions and the remaining 109 convicted youths at risk up to the 25th birthday. Table 4 shows the only variables which discriminated significantly between these groups. It can be seen that, in comparison with other convicted youths, the chronics tended to come from low-income families, to be rated troublesome in their primary schools, to have low IQ and attainment, to be clumsy on psychomotor tests, to have convicted older siblings, and to come from Roman Catholic families (which often indicated Irish immigrants).

Juvenile Convictions

The major point of the analyses described in the remainder of this chapter was to establish which variables predicted each of a number of measures of delinquency and crime independently of other variables. The major results of these

Table 4. Predicting Chronic Offenders

Variable at Age	% of 23 Chronics	% of Remaining 109 Convicted	Corrected χ^2	$p<$
Low Family Income 8	65.2	27.5	10.39	.005
Troublesome 8–10	69.6	33.0	9.14	.005
Junior Attainment 10	66.7	30.4	8.38	.005
Psychomotor Clumsiness 8–10	56.5	27.5	6.01	.025
Low IQ 8–10	60.9	31.2	6.00	.025
Convicted Sibling 10	39.1	14.7	5.89	.025
Catholic Family 8	56.3	26.6	4.33	.05

Notes: Not knowns excluded from each table.
χ^2 corrected for continuity.

analyses are shown in Table 5. Except in the case of troublesomeness, only independent variables prior in time to each dependent measure were included in each analysis, so each is genuinely predictive. Thus, family income at age 8 was investigated as a predictor of self-reported delinquency at age 14, but family income at age 14 was not. Dependent measures at one age were included as independent variables in the analysis of a later dependent measure. Thus, convictions at 10–13 were investigated as predictors of self-reported delinquency at 14.

The method will be explained in connection with the prediction of juvenile convictions. This is not shown in Table 5, which displays the prediction of convictions at 10–13 and 14–16 separately. However, the prediction of juvenile convictions has been a major aim of this project in the past (West & Farrington, 1973). Previously, matching techniques were used, but nowadays (as mentioned earlier) the most defensible method of multivariate analysis of categorical data is the loglinear modeling technique (Fienberg, 1980).

Since loglinear analysis is based on a multidimensional contingency table, it cannot be used to investigate many variables at a time, given the present sample size. With all variables dichotomous and a sample size of about 400, the maximum number of variables which can safely be included in a loglinear analysis is six (five independent and one dependent), totaling 64 cells and an average cell size of about six. It would not be safe to carry out a loglinear analysis with an average cell size of less than five. If the variables had not all been dichotomized, fewer variables could have been included in the loglinear analysis.

Actually, a logit analysis was used rather than the loglinear method since, where there is a clear dichotomous dependent variable, the two techniques give exactly the same results. Repeating the three-variable example mentioned earlier, and taking C as the dichotomous dependent variable, the logit analysis is based on the following kind of equation:

$$\log\frac{(\text{frequency } C_1)}{(\text{frequency } C_2)} = \text{constant} + \underbrace{A + B}_{\substack{\text{Main effects} \\ \text{of A and B} \\ \text{on C}}} + \underbrace{A \times B}_{\substack{\text{ABC} \\ \text{interaction}}}$$

where frequency C_1 means frequency in category 1 of variable C (for each value of A and B). If an A $\times$ C term is necessary to fit the data in the loglinear analysis, an A term will be necessary to fit the data in the logit analysis. The great advantage of the logit analysis is that it takes far less computer time (about 2 sec on the Cambridge IBM 370/165 using the GLIM program package, as opposed to over 40 sec for the comparable loglinear analysis).

Since each investigation of the prediction of crime or deviance had to include many more than five independent variables, it was decided to use partial correlations to identify a small number of variables which were independently important, and then to carry out a logit analysis with these. With dichotomous vari-

Table 5. Relationships with Crime and Deviance at Different Ages

Dependent Measure	Independent Variables	φ	Partial φ	Corrected χ²	G²
Troublesomeness 8–10 (92)	Psychomotor clumsiness 8–10 (104)	.251	.162	24.60	3.43
	Poor Supervision 8 (74)	.268	.161	25.90	6.81
	Convicted Parent 10 (104)	.211	.123	17.16	7.56
	Low Vocabulary 10 (124)	.222	.120	18.64	8.05
	Low Income 8 (93)	.254	.100	25.01	3.86
Convictions 10–13 (35)	Troublesomeness 8–10 (92)	.296	.216	33.57	11.77
	Uncooperative Family 8 (43)	.209	.189	15.59	2.86
	Poor Housing 8–10 (151)	.183	.141	12.49	6.63
	Poor Parental Behavior 8 (96)	.194	.117	13.29	3.88
	Low IQ 8–10 (103)	.186	.113	12.67	5.76
	Catholic Family 8 (73)	.157	.111	7.19	4.31
Self-Reported Delinquency 14 (108)	Convictions 10–13 (35)	.281	.256	29.63	21.50
	Daring 8–10 (121)	.231	.190	20.35	13.54
	Convicted Parent 10 (104)	.190	.162	13.70	9.70
Convictions 14–16 (74)	Convictions 10–13 (35)	.424	.393	70.06	20.86
	Daring 8–10 (121)	.307	.236	36.76	25.99
	Convicted Parent 10 (104)	.237	.181	21.70	13.02
	Dishonest 10 (88)	.239	.142	18.75	6.30
	Convicted Sibling 10 (46)	.195	.116	14.09	3.47
Convictions 17–20 (95)	Convictions 14–16 (74)	.443	.296	76.07	28.21
	Delinquent Friends 14 (101)	.319	.165	38.79	9.10
	Low Social Class 14 (58)	.157	.138	8.18	8.83
	Truancy 12–14 (73)	.330	.136	41.88	12.78
	Convicted Parent 10 (104)	.273	.131	28.53	5.63
	Aggressive 12–14 (134)	.275	.125	29.12	2.72
	Convicted Sibling 10 (46)	.248	.117	22.95	3.85

(*continued*)

Table 5. (Continued)

Dependent Measure	Independent Variables	φ	Partial φ	Corrected χ²	G²
Self-Reported Delin-quency 18 (97)	Convictions 14–16 (74)	.353	.259	46.29	20.51
	Self-Reported Delin-quency 14 (108)	.277	.140	28.34	5.29
	Aggressive 12–14 (134)	.232	.126	19.86	4.64
	Neurotic Extraversion 16 (118)	.152	.115	8.20	4.48
Antisocial Tendency 18 (110)	Convictions 14–16 (74)	.436	.252	71.36	17.44
	Self-Reported Delin-quency 14 (108)	.401	.240	60.37	18.33
	Aggressive 12–14 (134)	.305	.158	34.85	6.02
	Convicted Parent 10 (104)	.289	.139	31.09	8.60
	Truancy 12–14 (73)	.330	.129	40.47	7.22
	Large Family Size 10 (99)	.237	.123	20.62	7.96
Convictions 21–24 (46)	Convictions 17–20 (95)	.379	.202	53.91	15.13
	Convictions 14–16 (74)	.378	.199	53.36	9.58
	Unstable Job Record 18 (92)	.275	.139	26.57	5.60
	Low Family Income 14 (79)	.161	.123	7.64	6.54
	Anti-Establishment Atti-tude 18 (98)	.228	.113	18.01	2.99
	Hostile to Police 14 (90)	.254	.112	23.38	3.96

Notes:

Number in parentheses = number in extreme category (e.g. 92 most troublesome)

φ correlation and χ² (corrected for continuity) derived from the 2 × 2 table relating each independent and dependent measure.

Partial φ controls for all other variables listed.

For the first 5 independent variables listed in each section, G² controls for the other 4. For the sixth or seventh, G² controls for the first 4 independent variables.

φ = partial φ = .100 corresponds approximately to p = .05.

χ² = G² = 3.84 corresponds to p = .05.

ables the partial correlation method is less defensible statistically, but it seemed unlikely that it would produce misleading results. Zero-order (φ) correlations derived from 2 × 2 tables are simply related to χ² without the correction for continuity ($\chi^2 = \phi^2/N$), and first-order partial φ correlations produce results almost identical to those obtained in comparable logit analyses (Farrington, Biron, & LeBlanc, 1982).

Concentrating on juvenile convictions, the first step was to investigate which of 27 variables measured at 8–10 (see the Appendix) predicted these convictions significantly. The criterion used to select variables was whether the ϕ correlation was .100 or greater, since this value of ϕ almost always corresponded to a significant χ^2 value (corrected for continuity). It should perhaps be pointed out that ϕ^2 should not be interpreted as the percentage of the variance explained. The maximum value of ϕ^2 depends on the marginal frequencies of the 2×2 table, and may be considerably less than 1. For example, in the table relating troublesomeness (marginals 92 and 319) to convictions at 10–13 (marginals 35 and 376), the maximum value of ϕ^2, if all convicted boys were troublesome, is .323 (319×35 divided by 376×92). The actual value of ϕ in this case was about half the maximum (.296 as opposed to .568).

Of the 27 variables investigated in the first stage of the analysis, 19 significantly predicted juvenile convictions, that is, all except social class of the family at 8–10, job of the mother at 8–10, nervous mother and father at 10, neurotic extraversion at 10, weight at 8–10, popularity at 8–10, and nervousness at 8. The best predictor was troublesomeness at 8–10. Nearly half (41, or 44.6%) of the 92 troublesome boys were convicted as juveniles, in comparison with 13.5% of the remaining 319 ($\chi^2 = 40.54$, 1 df, $p < .001$, $\phi = .321$).

The next stage of the analysis was to investigate first-order partials, to see if each variable predicted juvenile convictions independently of each other variable. The criterion for the retention in the analysis at each stage was a partial ϕ of .100 or greater. All partials were calculated, but when the number of variables in the analysis was greater than about 10 it was not always feasible to scrutinize them all. (For example, the analysis of convictions at 17–20 began with 36 significant variables, and 12 were still in the analysis when fourth-order partials were calculated; any 4 from 12 produces 495 unique combinations of 4 variables, and 8 partial correlations calculated in each case.) The technique used was to investigate partials controlling for variables with the highest zero-order correlations.

In the case of juvenile convictions, psychomotor clumsiness, parental supervision, Catholic family, and height were not related independently of troublesomeness. Junior attainment and IQ were not related to juvenile convictions independently of vocabulary. Family size and family income were not related independently of the job record of the father, and housing was not related independently of convicted parents. The advantage of this successive partialing technique is that it is possible to explain why each variable with a significant zero-order relationship was dropped from the analysis.

Second-order partials were then calculated for 10 variables. Convicted siblings and vocabulary were not related to juvenile convictions independently of troublesomeness and the job record of the father, and separations were not related independently of troublesomeness and convicted parents. Third-order partials were calculated for seven variables, showing that parental behavior was not related to juvenile convictions independently of troublesomeness, dishonesty, and convicted parents taken together. Succeeding partial correlation analyses showed that troublesomeness, daring, dishonesty, convicted parents, job record of the father, and uncooperative family significantly predicted juvenile convictions independently of each other (singly and in combination; the fifth-order partials were .152, .162, .155, .135, .114, and 134, respectively).

The final stage was to carry out a logit analysis. The main aim of this was to investigate if each independent variable had a main effect on each dependent variable over and above the main effects of all other independent variables. Thus, the contributions of all other independent variables were investigated first, and then the additional contribution of the independent variable under investigation. (The G^2 log likelihood ratio test statistic can be used to study whether the addition of a term to the equation significantly improves the fit of the model to the data.) If G^2 was statistically significant, this showed that the independent variable under investigation had to be in the equation (i.e., had a significant main effect on the dependent variable). If the data could not be fitted by the model containing only main effects, it was then necessary to study interactions.

As mentioned above, a maximum of five independent variables can be investigated in these logit analyses. When more than five survived the partial correlation analyses (as in the case of juvenile convictions), more than one logit analysis was carried out. The first logit analysis investigated the separate contributions of the five independent variables with the highest partial correlations. Each other logit analysis investigated the separate contribution of each other independent variable over and above the four with the highest partial correlations. In the case of juvenile convictions, the first logit analysis investigated the separate contributions of troublesomeness, daring, dishonesty, convicted parents, and uncooperative family. The second logit analysis investigated the contribution of the job record of the father over and above the first four of these variables.

The results of the logit analyses for juvenile convictions were more complex than those for the other dependent measures shown in Table 5 because of interaction effects. For the other dependent measures, the model containing main effects only was not significantly different from the data. However, this was not true for juvenile convictions.

The results of the logit analyses for juvenile convictions showed that troublesomeness, daring, dishonesty, and convicted parents were independently predictive (The G^2 values were 4.65, 14.07, 7.63, and 10.71, respectively, 1 df; a value of 3.84 corresponds to $p = .05$.) An uncooperative family and the job record of the father, which had significantly predicted juvenile convictions in the partial correlation analyses, were not significantly predictive according to the logit analyses ($G^2 = 3.48$ and 2.75, respectively, 1 df). In the case of an uncooperative family, this was almost certainly because the logit analysis only included boys known on all variables. Boys whose parents were rated as uncooperative toward the social workers tended to be rated as not known and hence to be excluded from the logit analysis. This problem was avoided in the partial correlation analysis by using pairwise deletion of cases in calculating zero-order correlations.

Unfortunately, the model containing main effects only was significantly different from the data, showing that it was necessary to include interaction effects. Furthermore, the model containing all two-way interaction effects was significantly different from the data, showing the necessity to consider three-way interaction effects. The most important interaction effects were (a) between criminal parents and dishonesty, and (b) between criminal parents, daring, and troublesomeness. ($G^2 = 11.84$, 1 df, p < .001 in the former case, after allowing for all other two-way interactions; $G^2 = 13.60$, 1 df, p < .001 in the latter case, after allowing for all other three-way interactions.) The model containing main effects and the above two interaction effects fitted the data ($G^2 = 24.20$, df = 17, n.s.).

Therefore, juvenile convictions were independently predicted by troublesomeness, daring, dishonesty, convicted parents, and the above two interaction effects. In regard to the interaction between convicted parents and dishonesty, it was clear that the conviction rate was highest for those who were both dishonest and had convicted parents (67.7% convicted out of 21). In regard to the interaction between convicted parents, daring, and troublesomeness, the conviction rate was about the same for all those with at least two of the three adverse factors (57.1% of 28 daring and troublesome; 54.5% of 11 troublesome and with convicted parents; 53.8% of 13 daring and with convicted parents; and 52.9% of 17 daring, troublesome, and with convicted parents). Overall, 55.1% of 69 boys with at least two of these three factors were convicted as juveniles, in comparison with 7.0% of 186 boys with none of them, and 17.3% of 98 with one.

With categorical data commonly obtained in the social sciences, there is no ideal way of handling a large multivariate problem. The methods used here—partial ϕ correlations and loglinear analyses—both have advantages and disadvantages, but they are probably the best available. The results from both methods are presented in Table 5. When both indicate that a variable makes an independent contribution to a measure of crime or deviance, it is reasonable to accept this conclusion. When a variable is identified by only one method, its contribution is less certain. Only variables identified by both methods will be discussed below.

Other Measures of Crime and Delinquency

Table 5 investigates the extent to which behavior during any given age range depends on that during a previous age range. It summarizes the prediction of convictions at ages 10–13, 14–16, 17–20, and 21–24, and the prediction of self-reported delinquency at ages 14 and 18. It also shows the prediction of troublesomeness, which was the best predictor of juvenile convictions, and of antisocial tendency, which was the factor most significantly related to all convictions. It might be argued that the understanding of why boys get convicted would be helped by an understanding of why they behave badly at 8–10 and of why they adopt a deviant life-style at 18.

Table 5 shows that the boys who were rated troublesome at age 8–10 tended to be those from low-income families, those having poorly supervising, convicted parents, and those having a low vocabulary. Troublesomeness was the most significant determinant of whether a boy was convicted at age 10–13. However, in addition to troublesomeness, these convictions were predicted by poor housing, poor parental behavior, low IQ, and coming from a Catholic family. The absence of any of the predictors of troublesomeness from this list suggests that they may have had their effect in producing troublesomeness at 8–10, and that they may not have any effect on convictions over and above their effect on troublesomeness.

Self-reported delinquency at age 14 and convictions at age 14–16 were predicted best by convictions at age 10–13. However, being rated as daring, having convicted parents, and being rated at dishonest (for convictions at 14–16 only) all had additional independent effects. Convictions at 17–20, self-reported delinquency at 18, and being antisocial at 18 were all predicted best by convictions at 14–16. However, whereas self-reported delinquency at age 14 added to the prediction in the cases of self-reported delinquency at age 18 and antisociality, it was a boy's reported delinquency of his friends at age 14 which added to the prediction of convictions at age 17–20. (Self-reported delinquency and reported delinquency of friends were highly correlated, no doubt because most delinquent acts were committed with friends.) Teachers' ratings of aggressiveness, convicted parents, and truancy were other factors which appeared more than once in predicting these three measures. In contrast, low social class and having a delinquent sibling predicted only convictions at 17–20, neurotic extraversion predicted only self-reported delinquency at 18, and large family size predicted only antisociality.

Finally, adult criminal convictions at 21–24 were predicted best by convictions at 17–20 and by convictions at 14–16. However, if the boy himself had an unstable job record at age 18, if he came from a low-income family at age 14, and if he had a hostile attitude to the police at age 14, all of these made additional contributions to his likelihood of sustaining adult criminal convictions.

VI. CONCLUSIONS

Implications for Criminological Knowledge and Theory

This research shows that the peak age for most offenses is within a year or two of the 17th birthday, although shoplifting and stealing from machines seem to peak earlier, and fraud later. To my knowledge, these are the first published data showing variations in both official and self-reported delinquency with age, although similar data are now being collected in the United States (see Elliott &

Ageton, 1980). The fact that self-reported and official delinquency tend to peak at about the same age suggests that there is a real peak in law-violating behavior around the age of 17.

The most obvious explanations for this peak age center on peer group influence, life-style, and opportunity. Around age 17, working-class youths have left the influence of their families, spend time hanging around the streets with their male friends, and have not yet "settled down" with a female. The more delinquent youths at age 17 tended to have relatively well paid, dead-end jobs, and could afford to go out drinking with their friends most nights. However, they could not afford to satisfy their desire for excitement in socially approved ways. One youth at age 24 said that he gave up stealing cars once he got his own car. At age 21, the youths are less under the influence of their peers, more under the influence of a female and a family life once again, and able to satisfy at least some of their desires in socially approved ways.

This research also suggests that the causes of adult criminal convictions can be traced back to childhood. The best predictors of convictions at age 21–24 were convictions at 17–20 and convictions at 14–16; the best predictors of convictions at 17–20 were convictions at 14–16; the best predictors of convictions at 14–16 were convictions at 10–13 and daring behavior at 8–10; and the best predictor of convictions at 10–13 was troublesome behavior at 8–10. The same is true of other measures of deviance. The best predictors of self-reported delinquency at 18 and antisocial tendency at 18 were convictions at 14–16 and self-reported delinquency at 14, and the best predictors of self-reported delinquency at 14 were convictions at 10–13 and daring behavior at 8–10. As with aggression (Olweus, 1979), the continuity of troublesome, delinquent, deviant, and criminal behavior from childhood to adulthood seems striking.

It might be argued that convictions at one age predict convictions at a later age because of continuity in police and court bias rather than continuity in behavior. However, it is interesting that the two self-reported delinquency measures (at ages 14 and 18) were best predicted by earlier convictions, and the same was true of antisocial tendency. As argued earlier, it might be expected that convictions and self-reports would be subject to different biases, and that similar results obtained with the two measures might reflect offending behavior rather than bias. The continuity between convictions and self-reports supports the hypothesis that there is continuity in behavior rather than in biasing factors.

Against this, it could be argued that convictions predict self-reports because convicted youths are more likely to admit delinquent acts than unconvicted youths. Continuity in delinquent behavior is best demonstrated by the prediction of convictions by self-reports, which did happen but was not shown in Table 5. Nearly half of those high on self-reported delinquency at age 14 (42.9%) were convicted at 17–20, in comparison with only 16.7% of the remainder ($\chi^2 = 28.03$, 1 df, $p < .001$, $\phi = .271$). However, self-reported delinquency at age 14 was dropped from the analysis of convictions at 17–20 because it did not predict independently of reported delinquency of friends at 14 and convictions at 14–16. Similarly, self-reported delinquency at ages 14 and 18 significantly predicted convictions at 21–24, but neither prediction held independently of antisociality and earlier convictions. In turn, antisociality at age 18, which had been expected to be one of the most important predictors of convictions at 21–24, did not predict independently of earlier convictions and an unstable job record at 18.

Of course, if self-reported delinquency, convictions, reported delinquency of friends, and antisociality are all measures of the same underlying theoretical construct (delinquent tendency?), it is not surprising that they do not predict independently. Perhaps the best evidence in favor of the argument that there is continuity in deviant behavior rather than in biasing factors is the earlier demonstration that self-reported delinquency predicts convictions *among unconvicted youths* (Farrington, 1973). Taking into account other evidence about the validity of self-reported delinquency measures (supra), the most plausible conclusion is that the continuity of troublesome, delinquent, deviant, and criminal behavior from childhood to adulthood is real rather than artifactual.

Over and above the continuity in behavior, some factors had persistent effects. In particular, convicted parents contributed to troublesomeness, self-reported delinquency at age 14, convictions at 14–16 and 17–20, and antisocial tendency at 18. Low family income at age 8 contributed to troublesomeness at 8–10, and low family income at 14 contributed to convictions at 21–24. The boy's own unstable job record at age 18 contributed to his convictions at 21–24, just as his father's unstable job record was related to his troublesomeness at 8–10 (although not independently of low family income).

The kinds of youths who were convicted or who admitted large numbers of delinquent acts were identified as troublesome, daring, dishonest, and aggressive by their teachers, peers, and parents from an early age. Perhaps the best place to start in attempting to explain the development of delinquent and criminal behavior is with troublesomeness at 8–10, which was clearly one step on the road toward an adult criminal career. Troublesomeness was predicted by poor parental supervision, convicted parents, low vocabulary, and low income. These four factors, or others closely related to them, appear elsewhere in Table 5.

There seem to be at least four major explanatory factors:

1. Economic deprivation, as seen in low family income, poor housing, and low social class
2. Family criminality, as seen in convicted parents and delinquent siblings
3. Parental mishandling, as seen in poor supervision and poor parental child-rearing behavior
4. School failure, as seen in low vocabulary, low IQ, and truancy

Most other variables in Table 5 seem to be measures of deviance rather than of an explanatory factor (e.g., daring, dishonesty, delinquent friends, aggressiveness, and hostile attitudes to the police).

The above results are not surprising to practitioners in the criminal and juvenile justice systems. They are consistent with conclusions reached in other projects in Great Britain and North America. For example, in a study with 10–11-year-old boys in England, Wilson (1980) identified three factors which were related to delinquency: poor parental supervision, convicted parents, and "social handicap," which included low social class, large family size, parental neglect, and truancy. In an impressive American longitudinal survey, McCord (1979) found that criminal behavior was predicted by maternal affection, parental conflict, paternal deviance (alcoholism or convictions), parental supervision, and parental aggressiveness (especially in disciplining children).

Implications for Method and Measurement

It is hoped that this research shows the usefulness of the longitudinal method in studying the natural history of a phenomenon, its course of development, its incidence and prevalence at different ages, its peak age, and continuities and discontinuities between earlier and later ages. Future work on this and similar projects should make more effort to investigate the effects of specific events on the course of development, since this is one of the unique uses of longitudinal research. While randomized experiments are especially useful in answering causal questions and developing causal models, nonexperimental longitudinal research can also demonstrate quite persuasively the effects of events on the course of development. This is especially true if the subjects of the research are interviewed at regular, frequent intervals (e.g., every year).

This project was able to investigate the prospective prediction of crime and delinquency, avoiding retrospective bias. It is desirable to study the importance of retrospective bias in more detail, in order to know in what circumstances a prospective design is essential. Future work on this and similar projects could throw some light on this question by comparing later reports on (for example) child-rearing methods with earlier contemporaneous reports.

Any single project has limitations, of course. The present results are based on one cohort of white, English, working-class, urban males born about 1953. How far they might apply to other cohorts, to blacks, to Americans, to middle-class people, to rural areas, or to females, etc., is uncertain. In general, it is best to combine a longitudinal survey with overlapping cross-sectional surveys, to try to disentangle changes with age from changes in the time period. For example, when these youths were growing up there were a number of changes in legislation which affected conviction records. One of the effects of the Theft Act 1968 was to change the distribution of offenses between burglary and theft. Before the Theft Act, it was necessary to prove that a person had "broken in" to secure a conviction for breaking and entering. After this Act, it was merely necessary to prove that a person had "entered as a trespasser" to secure a conviction for burglary. This had the effect of classifying offenses as burglaries which would previously have been classified as thefts. Also, of course, there were changes in social habits while these youths were growing up. The enormous increase in reported drug use from age 14 to 18 could be related to the period (approximately 1967–71) rather than to the increase in age.

An advantage of longitudinal research which should not be forgotten is its ability to establish reliability and validity. When subjects are being seen repeatedly, it is hard for them to present a false picture of themselves to researchers without being detected. Also, there are advantages in repeated searches of records. In this project, it was common to locate a criminal record at one time but not at another. This was caused partly by a deliberate agency policy to destroy certain kinds of records after certain periods of time, but is also reflected inconsistent information given by the subjects (e.g., the use of aliases), inconsistency in reporting by police and courts, the concurrent use of records by other agencies, and human errors and inefficiency in record keeping and searching. Estimates of the prevalence of convictions based on only one search of records are likely to be too low.

A major problem in longitudinal surveys is attrition, or loss of subjects for a variety of reasons, including death, emigration, unknown addresses, and refusals. The present project was successful in reducing attrition to a low figure (only 55% over the first 10 years). This success could have been achieved more easily if we had had more cooperation from government agencies in providing addresses. It was greatly to our advantage that we tried to interview each youth at regular intervals. For example, at age 18, more than three-quarters of the youths were still living at the same address as at age 16. The remainder were traced by inquiring at old addresses, or with the help of the local housing department, probation officers, relatives, employers, the post office, marriage certificates, and telephone inquiries. Discovering addresses and making contact with the youths cost a great deal of time and money.

It would be desirable in a future longitudinal project to attempt to estimate testing effects, or the effect of being interviewed at regular intervals. This could be achieved either by having a control group who were followed up in records but never interviewed, or by testing only a subsample of the total sample on each occasion. The absence of either of these fa features in the present project means that we cannot be sure that our sample were unaffected by our occasional intrusions in their lives.

Moving on to measurement problems, it might have been better if the present project had been more theoretically guided from the start. If there had been more explicit statements about which theoretical constructs were being measured by which empirical variables, and about expected causal relationships between theoretical constructs, it might have been easier to analyze the data collected. On the other hand, in some cases the derivation of empirical variables which each measured one theoretical construct could only be done in the light of empirical relationships between variables. Also, as explained earlier, there are advantages in casting the net wide and trying to measure every theoretical construct alleged by past researchers to be important, for example, in stablishing if certain variables predict delinquency independently of others. Researchers who are guided by only one theory are in danger of failing to notice relationships between theoretical constructs not included in that theory.

Information was obtained in this research from records, interviews, ratings, tests and questionnaires, physical measures, and observed behavior. Multiple methods of measurement are desirable for validation purposes and in order to avoid the argument that results might reflect measurement biases or errors rather than theoretical constructs. Also, if composite variables are derived by combining measures from different sources or at different ages, such variables are likely to contain less bias or error than the constituent measures, because of canceling out. It is desirable to have comparable measures at different ages, but this is sometimes difficult to achieve, because questions which are applicable at one age may not be applicable at another.

There are particular benefits in measuring both official and self-reported delinquency, collecting information from records and from interviews. As pointed out earlier, if only convictions had been measured, it could have been argued that the observed continuity did not lie in behavior but in official processing. Also, research based only on criminal records would miss the fact that offending is only one element of a socially deviant life-style. Another advantage of having both records and interviews is that in some cases records were only found because of special searches instituted as a result of interview information. The quality of both was improved by having both.

This research shows the relationship between many variables and crime and delinquency measures. Four factors (economic deprivation, family criminality, parental mishandling, and school failure) seemed to be particularly important and should be measured in any delinquency project.

In general, the information from interviews, records, and ratings proved the most useful. The psychological test data and physical measures were either unrelated to delinquency or did not add significantly to data collected by other methods. In the exceptional cases where this was not true (e.g., the importance of tattoos), interviews were needed to help in understanding the meaning of the results. Very few attempts to use direct observation of behavior were made in this research. Because this method is likely to be subject to less bias than more indirect methods, it course, the direct observation of delinquent behavior is not easy to arrange.

In this research, special problems of reliability and validity arose in the earliest unstructured interviews with parents carried out by the social workers. These problems were overcome in later interviews by having more structured, fully tape-recorded interviews carried out by young social science graduates who were carefully monitored. More methodological research on interviews is desirable, for example, of the kind carried out by Cannell, Oksenberg, and Converse (1979).

The later interviews were rpreceded by more pilot work than the earlier ones. In the beginning, the researchers were under great pressure to collect data quickly, and the then Director of the Institute of Criminology was unwilling to lengthen an already lengthy project by extensive pilot work. However, in a longitudinal survey, the earliest measurements are particularly valuable, making initial pilot work even more important than in cross-sectional surveys. Another problem dating back to the start of the project centers on sampling. From the point of view of generalization, it would have been better if the population from which the sample was drawn had been specified more carefully.

The analysis of a large, complex longitudinal dataset including primarily categorical variables raises many difficulties, as explained above. The present survey is unusual in the frequency of data collection and in the large number of variables from different sources. The analytic methods used (partial correlations and loglinear/logit methods) are by no means ideal. Social scientists will be grateful when statisticians devise better methods for the multivariate analysis of categorical data.

An alternative strategy is to try to convert the data into a form suitable for standard parametric techniques such as multiple linear regression and path analysis. This would involve trying to measure theoretical constructs on normally distributed interval scales. How far the present data could be converted into this form is unclear, although it is hoped that this will be attempted at some stage. One problem is that many of the categorical variables seem very rough (e.g., ratings of child-rearing methods), so the conversion process might produce scales with a spurious impression of exactness and sensitivity. There might be advantages if a future project could plan from the start to measure all theoretical constructs on interval scales, although how far the resulting selection of measures might exclude or distort key constructs is unknown.

It would be desirable with these data, as in other nonexperimental research, to carry out more explicitly quasi-experimental analyses following Cook and Campbell (1979). In other words, the effect of one variable on another could be investigated, expecially suing change scores, and then a series of plausible alternative explanations of the observed effects could be systematically studied. These alternative explanations would center on such topics as history, maturation, testing, instrumentation, mortality, regression, selection, and causal order (e.g., see Farrington, 1977).

To summarize, this chapter has aimed to present some basic information about the natural history of delinquent and criminal behavior and about variables related to it. Any theory of the development of delinquency needs to take account of and explain these results. In the interests of cumulative knowledge, it has also discussed lessons which can be learned about method, measurement, and analysis.

APPENDIX:
SUMMARY OF ALL RELATIONSHIPS WITH CONVICTIONS
AT AGE 10–24

Variable at age	'Worst' group Description	N (%C)	Remainder N(%C)	Corrected χ^2	p<
Family Income 8	Low	92(48.9)	309(29.4)	11.13	.001
Housing of Family 8–10	Poor	149(45.0)	252(27.4)	12.15	.001
Social Class of Family 8–10	Low	79(39.2)	322(32.6)	0.97	N.S.
Job Record of Father 8–10	Erratic	47(53.2)	323(30.3)	8.65	.005
Job of Mother 8–10	Full-time	110(28.2)	273(34.8)	1.27	N.S.
Family Size 10	Large	97(51.5)	304(28.3)	16.72	.001
Convicted Parent 10	Convicted	103(55.3)	298(26.5)	27.11	.001
Convicted Sibling 10	Convicted	45(57.8)	356(30.9)	11.71	.001
Parental Behavior 8	Poor	91(47.3)	295(28.5)	10.27	.005
Separation from Parent 10	Separated	90(51.1)	311(28.9)	14.34	.001
Parental Supervision 8	Poor	70(52.9)	303(28.4)	14.32	.001
Catholic Family 8	Catholic	71(50.7)	272(28.3)	11.79	.001
Nervous Mother 10	Nervous	122(41.8)	255(28.6)	5.91	.025
Nervous Father 10	Nervous	78(37.2)	281(32.4)	0.43	N.S.
Uncooperative Family 8	Uncooperative	43(51.2)	358(31.8)	5.56	.025
IQ 8–10	Low	102(48.0)	299(29.1)	11.35	.001
Psychomotor Clumsiness 8–10	High	102(44.1)	299(30.4)	5.76	.025
Vocabulary 10	Low	122(45.1)	271(28.4)	9.74	.005
Junior Attainment 10	Low	90(51.1)	287(28.2)	15.06	.001
Neurotic Extraversion 10	High	112(33.9)	275(33.1)	0.00	N.S.
Height 8–10	Low	71(43.7)	328(31.7)	3.21	N.S.
Weight 8–10	Low	73(38.4)	327(33.0)	0.54	N.S.
Troublesomeness 8–10	High	89(61.8)	312(26.0)	38.10	.001
Daring 8–10	High	120(53.3)	278(25.9)	26.84	.001
Dishonesty 10	High	87(49.4)	259(27.8)	12.77	.001
Popularity 8–10	Low	123(39.8)	263(30.0)	3.20	N.S.
Nervousness 8	High	91(24.2)	288(36.1)	3.92	.05
Family Income 14	Low	79(38.0)	265(30.9)	1.07	N.S.
Housing of Family 14	Poor	45(44.4)	351(31.6)	2.41	N.S.
Social Class of Family 14	Low	58(43.1)	311(32.5)	2.01	N.S.

(continued)

APPENDIX   (*Continued*)

Variable at age	'Worst' group Description	N (%C)	Remainder N(%C)	Corrected χ^2	p<
Job of Mother 14	Full-time	100(32.0)	284(33.1)	0.01	N.S.
Family Size 14	Large	83(50.6)	313(29.1)	12.68	.001
Parental Attitude 14	Cruel, Passive, Neglecting	87(40.2)	290(30.7)	2.34	N.S.
Broken Home 15	Broken	48(54.2)	353(31.2)	8.98	.005
IQ 14	Low	117(47.0)	281(28.1)	12.37	.001
Vocabulary 14	Low	91(47.3)	308(29.5)	9.10	.005
Neurotic Extraversion 14	High	90(34.4)	309(33.3)	0.00	N.S.
Height 14	Low	97(37.1)	300(32.3)	0.55	N.S.
Weight 14	Low	97(33.0)	279(33.3)	0.00	N.S.
Aggressiveness 12–14	High	131(54.2)	270(24.1)	34.38	.001
Truancy 12–14	High	73(63.0)	328(27.4)	32.15	.001
Nervousness 14	High	106(37.7)	272(32.4)	0.76	N.S.
Hostile to Police 14	High	88(54.5)	310(27.7)	20.87	.001
Self-Reported Delinquency 14	High	105(60.0)	293(24.2)	42.69	.001
Delinquent Friends 14	High	98(59.2)	300(25.3)	36.40	.001
School Leaving Age 15	Early	162(45.1)	239(26.4)	14.24	.001
Neurotic Extraversion 16	High	115(45.2)	276(29.7)	7.99	.005
Pulse Rate 18	Low	97(39.2)	285(32.3)	1.24	N.S.
Height 18	Low	108(36.1)	276(33.0)	0.22	N.S.
Weight 18	Low	91(30.8)	293(34.8)	0.34	N.S.
Gambling 18	Heavy	86(54.7)	297(27.9)	20.04	.001
Smoking 18	Heavy	103(48.5)	281(28.5)	12.68	.001
Drinking 18	Heavy	77(48.1)	307(30.3)	7.89	.005
Drug Use 18	Used	121(49.6)	263(26.6)	18.52	.001
Motoring Convictions 18	Convicted	62(58.1)	322(29.2)	18.09	.001
Driving after Drinking 18	Involved	83(53.0)	300(28.7)	16.12	.001
Fights after Drinking 18	Involved	124(50.0)	260(26.2)	20.27	.001
Sexually Active 18	High	163(51.5)	218(20.6)	38.38	.001
Antisocial Groups 18	Involved	80(57.5)	304(27.6)	23.92	.001
Job Record 18	Unstable	92(59.8)	291(25.4)	35.41	.001
Job Status 18	Low	54(64.8)	324(28.7)	25.36	.001
Relation with Parents 18	Poor	86(46.5)	298(30.2)	7.22	.01
Uncooperative 18	Uncooperative	64(45.3)	313(30.0)	4.97	.05

(*continued*)

APPENDIX (*Continued*)

Variable at age	'Worst' group Description	N (%C)	Remainder N(%C)	Corrected χ^2	p<
Money Saved 18	None	142(46.5)	234(25.6)	16.30	.001
Pro-Aggression Attitude 18	High	97(45.4)	287(30.0)	7.00	.01
Anti-Foreigners Attitude 18	High	78(42.3)	306(31.7)	2.67	N.S.
Pro-Drugs Attitude 18	High	117(41.9)	267(30.3)	4.34	.05
Anti-Establishment Attitude 18	High	96(51.0)	288(28.1)	15.88	.001
Tattooed 18	Tattooed	35(68.6)	349(30.4)	19.06	.001
Hospitalized for Injury 18	Hospitalized	137(42.3)	247(29.1)	6.27	.025
Spends Time Hanging About 18	Hangs About	61(57.4)	323(29.4)	16.69	.001
Antisocial Tendency 18	High	109(71.6)	275(18.9)	94.29	.001
Self-Reported Violence 18	High	79(69.6)	305(24.6)	54.82	.001
Self-Reported Delinquency 18	High	97(66.0)	287(23.0)	57.91	.001

Notes:
%C = % Convicted between ages 10 and 24 inclusive
Not knowns excluded from each table
χ^2 corrected for continuity

ACKNOWLEDGMENT

The analyses on which this paper is based were comleted while the author was a Visiting Fellow at the National Institute of Justice, Washington D.C.

REFERENCES

Becker, H. S. *Outsiders*. New York: Free Press, 1963.

Becker, H. S. Labelling theory reconsidered. In P. Roch & M. McIntosh (Eds.), *Deviance and social control*. London: Tavistock, 1974.

Cannell, C. F., Oksenberg, L. & Converse, J. M. *Experiments in interviewing techniques*. Ann Arbor: University of Michigan Institute for Social Research, 1979.

Clarke, R. V. G. Psychology and crime. *Bulletin of the British Psychological Society*, 1977, *30*, 280–283.

Cook, T. D., & Campbell, D. T. *Quasi-experimentation*. Chicago: Rand McNally, 1979.

Diener, E. & Crandall, R. *Ethics in social and behavioral research*. Chicago: University of Chicago Press, 1978.

Deutscher, I. *What we say/What we do*. Glenview: Scott Foresman, 1973.

Elliott, D. S., & Ageton, S. S. Reconciling race and class differences in self-reported and official estimates of delinquency. *American Sociological Review*, 1980, *45*, 95–110.

Farrington, D. P. Self-reports of deviant behavior: Predictive and stable? *Journal of Criminal Law and Criminology*, 1973, *64*, 99–110.

Farrington, D. P. The effects of public labelling. *British Journal of Criminology*, 1977, *17*, 112–125.

Farrington, D. P. The family backgrounds of aggressive youths. In L. Hersov, M. Berger & D. Shaffer (Eds.), *Aggression and antisocial behavior in childhood and adolescence*. Oxford: Pergamon, 1978.

Farrington, D. P. Experiments on deviance with special reference to dishonesty, In L. Berkowitz (Ed.), *A vances in experimental social psychology*, vol. 12. New York: Academic Press, 1979. (a)

Farrington, D. P. Longitudinal research on crime and delinquency. In N. Morris & M. Tonry (Eds.), *Crime and justice*, vol. 1. Chicago: University of Chicago Press, 1979. (b)

Farrington, D. P. Randomized experiments on crime and justice. In N. Morris & M. Tonry (Eds.), *Crime and justice*, vol. 4. Chicago: University of Chicago Press, 1982.

Farrington, D. P., & Bennett, T. Police cautioning of juveniles in London. *British Journal of Criminology*, 1981, *21*, 123–135.

Farrington, D. P., Biron, L., & LeBlanc, M. Personality and delinquency in London and Montreal. In J. Gunn & D. P. Farrington (Eds.), *Abnormal offenders, delinquency and the criminal justice system*. Chichester: Wiley, 1982.

Farrington, D. P., & West, D. J. The Cambridge study in delinquent development. In S. A. Mednick & A. E. Baert (Eds.), *Prospective longitudinal research*. Oxford: Oxford University Press, 1981.

Fienberg, S. E. *The analysis of cross-classified categorical data* (2nd ed.). Cambridge: MIT Press, 1980.

Giallombardo, R. Female delinquency. In D. Schicor & D. H. Kelly (Eds.), *Critical issues in juvenile delinquency*. Lexington: Heath, 1980.

Gill, O. *Luke street*. London: Macmillan, 1977.

Glueck, S., & Glueck, E. T. *Unraveling juvenile delinquency*. Cambridge: Harvard University Press, 1950.

Gold, M., & Reimer, D. J. Changing patterns of delinquent behavior among Americans 13 through 16 years old: 1967–72. *Crime and Delinquency Literature*, 1975, *7*, 483–517.

Graham, F. Probability of detection and institutional vandalism. *British Journal of Criminology*, 1981, *21*, 361–365.

Hindelang, M. J. Causes of delinquency: A partial replication and extension. *Social Problems*, 1973, *20*, 471–487.

Hindelang, M. J. Variations in sex-race-age-specific incidence rates of offending. *American Sociological Review*, 1981, *46*, 461–474.

Hindelang, M. J., Hirschi, T., & Weis, J. G. *Measuring delinquency*. Beverly Hills: Sage, 1981.

Hirschi, T. *Causes of delinquency*. Berkeley: University of California Press, 1969.

Hirschi, T. Labelling theory and juvenile delinquency: An assessment of the evidence. In W. R. Gove (Ed.), *The labelling of deviance* (2nd ed.). Beverly Hills: Sage, 1980.

Hirschi, T., & Hindelang, M. J. Intelligence and delinquency: A revisionist review. *American Sociological Review*, 1977, *42*, 571–587.

Johnson, R. E. *Juvenile delinquency and its origins*. Cambridge: Cambridge University Press, 1979.

Knight, B. J., Osborn, S. G., & West, D. J. Early marriage and criminal tendency in males. *British Journal of Criminology*, 1977, *17*, 348–360.

Lemert, E. M. *Human deviance, social problems, and social control* (2nd ed.) Englewood Cliffs: Prentice-Hall, 1972.

Martin, F. M. Letter to the editor. *Howard Journal*, 1979, *18*, 64.

McCord, J. Some child-rearing antecednets of criminal behavior in adult men. *Journal of Personality and Social Psychology,* 1979, *37,* 1477–1486.

National Council on Crime and Delinquency. Jurisdiction over status offenses should be removed from the juvenile court: A policy statement. *Crime and Delinquency,* 1975, *21,* 97–99.

Nisbett, R. E., & Wilson, T. D. Telling more than we can know: Verbal reports on mental processes. *Psychological Review,* 1977, *84,* 231–259.

Olweus, D. Stability of aggressive reaction patterns in males: A review. *Psychological Bulletin,* 1979, *86,* 852–875.

Osborn, S. G., & West, D. J. Do young delinquents really inform? *Journal of Adolescence,* 1980, *3,* 99–114.

Parker, H. J. *View from the boys.* Newton Abbot: David & Charles, 1974.

Parker, H. & Giller, H. More and less the same: British delinquency research since the sixties. *British Journal of Criminology,* 1981, *21,* 230–245.

Robins, L. N., & Ratcliff, K. S. Childhood conduct disorders and later arrest. In L. N. Robins, P. J. Clayton, & J. K. Wing (Eds.), *The social consequences of psychiatric illness.* New York: Brunner/Mazel, 1980.

Tittle, C. R. *Sanctions and social deviance.* New York: Praeger, 1980.

Trasler, G. B. *The explanation of criminality.* London: Routledge & Kegan Paul, 1962.

Wadsworth, M. *Roots of delinquency.* London: Martin Robertson, 1979.

West, D. J. *Present conduct and future delinquency.* London: Heinemann, 1969.

West, D. J. *Delinquency: Its roots, careers and prospects.* London: Heinemann, 1982.

West, D. J., & Farrington, D. P. *Who becomes delinquent?* London: Heinemann, 1973.

West, D. J., & Farrington, D. P. *The delinquent way of life.* London: Heinemann, 1977.

Wiatrowski, M. D., Griswold, D. B., & Roberts, M. K. Social control theory and delinquency. *American Sociological Review,* 1981, *46,* 525–541.

Wilson, H. Parental supervision: A neglected aspect of delinquency. *British Journal of Criminology,* 1980, *20,* 203–235.

Wolfgang, M. E., Figlio, R. M., & Sellin, T. *Delinquency in a birth cohort.* Chicago: University of Chicago Press, 1972.

AUTHOR INDEX

265

SUBJECT INDEX

Research Annuals in the
BEHAVIORAL SCIENCES

Advances in Behavioral Medicine
Series Editors: Edward S. Katkin, *State University of New York at Buffalo*
and Stephen B. Manuck, *University of Pittsburgh School of Medicine*

Advances in Descriptive Psychology
Series Editors: Keith E. Davis, *University of South Carolina* and
Thomas O. Mitchell, *Southern Illinois University*

Advances in Development and Behavioral Pediatrics
Series Editors: Mark Wolraich and Donald K. Routh, *University of Iowa*

Advances in Early Education and Day Care
Series Editor: Sally Kilmer, *Bowling Green State University*

Advances in Family Intervention, Assessment and Theory
Series Editor: John P. Vincent, *University of Houston*

Advances in Human Psychopharmacology
Series Editors: Graham D. Burrows, *University of Melbourne* and
John S. Werry, University of Auckland

Advances in Law and Child Development
Series Editor: Robert L. Sprague, *University of Illinois*
Associate Editor: Kenneth M. Slaw, *University of Illinois*

Advances in Learning and Behavioral Disabilities
Series Editors: Kenneth Gadow and Irv Bialer, *State University of New York-Stony Brook*

Advances in Mental Retardation and Developmental Disabilities
Series Editors: Stephen E. Breuning, *Western Psychiatric Institute and Clinic, University
of Pittsburgh School of Medicine,* Johnny L. Matson, *Northern Illinois University* and
Rowland P. Barrett, *Western Psychiatric Institute and Clinic, University
of Pittsburgh School of Medicine*

Advances in Motivation and Achievement
Series Editor: Martin L. Maehr, *University of Illinois*

Advances in Psychophysiology
Series Editors: Patrick K. Ackles, J.P. Richard Jennings, *Western Psychiatric Institute and Clinic,
University of Pittsburgh School of Medicine* and Michael G.H. Coles, University of Illinois

Advances in Reading/Language Research
Series Editor: Barbara Hutson, *Virginia Polytechnic Institute and State University*

Advances in Special Education
Series Editor: Barbara K. Keogh, *University of California-Los Angeles*

Advances in Substance Abuse: Behavioral and Biological Research
Series Editor: Nancy K. Mello, *Harvard Medical School-McLean Hospital*

Advances in the Behavioral Measurement of Children
Series Editor: Roslyn A. Glow, *University of Adelaide*

Annals of Child Development
Series Editor: Grover J. Whitehurst, *State University of New York-Stony Brook*

Annual Review of Health Education and Promotion
Series Editor: William B. Ward, *University of South Carolina*

Biocultural Perspectives on Nutrition and Human Functioning
Series Editor: Dorothy J. Cattle, *University of California, Berkeley*

Perspectives in Personality: Theory, Measurement and Interpersonal Dynamics
Series Editors: Robert Hogan and Warren H. Jones, *University of Tulsa*

Research in Community and Mental Health
Series Editor: Roberta G. Simmons, *University of Minnesota*

Research in Organization Behavior
Series Editors: Barry M. Staw, *University of California-Berkeley* and L. L. Cummings, *Northwestern
University*

Please inquire for our complete catalog

**JAI PRESS INC., 36 Sherwood Place, P.O. Box 1678
Greenwich, Connecticut 06836**
Telephone: 203-661-7602   Cable Address: JAIPUBL